Baseball's Last Golden Age, 1946–1960

To Kathy

Baseball's Last Golden Age, 1946–1960

The National Pastime in a Time of Glory and Change

by J. RONALD OAKLEY

McFarland & Company, Inc., Publishers
Jefferson, North Carolina, and London

Cover: Joe DiMaggio is greeted at the plate after hitting a home run in
the 1949 World Series against the Brooklyn Dodgers. Courtesy National
Baseball Library and Archive, Cooperstown, N.Y.

British Library Cataloguing-in-Publication data are available

Library of Congress Cataloguing-in-Publication Data

Oakley, J. Ronald.
    Baseball's last golden age, 1946–1960 : the national pastime in a
time of glory and change / by J. Ronald Oakley.
        p.   cm.
    Includes bibliographical references (p.   ) and index. ∞
    ISBN 0-89950-851-0 (sewn softcover : 50# alk. paper)
    1. Baseball—United States—History—20th century.   I. Title.
GV863.A1024   1994
796.357′0973—dc20   93-40432
                                                              CIP

Manufactured in the United States of America

McFarland & Company, Inc., Publishers
  Box 611, Jefferson, North Carolina 28640

Contents

Acknowledgments

A book of this nature could not have been written without the direct and indirect help of many individuals. Besides the obvious ones — the hundreds of authors and editors who over the past half century produced the written materials I have drawn upon in my research — I am indebted to the many librarians, especially those at the University of North Carolina at Chapel Hill and the University of North Carolina at Greensboro, who assisted me in locating materials. During the week I spent at the National Baseball Library in Cooperstown, New York, Patricia Kelly and several other staff members were generous with their time, helping me find valuable research materials. Brenda J. Farmer, a library technician at my own institution, Davidson County Community College, was helpful in obtaining hard-to-find books through the interlibrary loan system. Tony Garitta read parts of the manuscript and offered many helpful suggestions, Peggy Bumgardner and Marsha Hondros served as my computer gurus, and Sharon Koontz rendered invaluable secretarial assistance.

Finally, I am indebted to my wife, Kathy, who shares my love of baseball, helped me locate and photocopy materials scattered in libraries from North Carolina to New York, read and criticized various drafts of the manuscript, and encouraged me every step of the way.

Preface

"Baseball is everybody's game, still the American pastime," Roger Angell, one of baseball's most respected reporters, wrote in 1954. "Baseball preoccupies us, fascinates us, excites us, charms us, lulls us, bores us, and otherwise takes up more of our time and attention from late winter to early autumn than all our other sports put together. . . . More than a sport, baseball is an environment, a condition of our warm weather existence."[1]

Baseball's Last Golden Age, 1946–1960 is a narrative history of the major league game during that nostalgic decade and a half when baseball, as Angell so passionately believed, was still the unchallenged king of American sports. It begins with an introductory account of the national pastime during World War II, then looks at the game as it entered the postwar period, when it was still played outdoors on real grass, mostly in the daytime, by the same 16 clubs that had played it since 1903 and, except for the Yankees and Indians, in parks built before World War I. The rest of the book chronicles the history of each pennant race and World Series, relives the great games and great moments, depicts the outstanding teams and players, and provides an ongoing analysis of the changes and problems affecting the game between the end of World War II and 1960.

This was the time of some of baseball's greatest pennant races, including the most celebrated of them all, the Dodgers-Giants battle of 1951 that ended with Bobby Thomson's "shot heard 'round the world." It was the time of some of the most exciting World Series, including several "Subway Series" in New York. It was the time of some of the game's most legendary moments, from Enos Slaughter's mad dash from first to home in the seventh game of the 1946 World Series to Bill Mazeroski's dramatic home run that clinched the 1960 fall classic. It was the time of some of the game's best teams, from the 1946 Cardinals to the 1960 Pirates, and the Dodgers and Yankees in almost all the years in between. It was the time of Hall of Famers like Joe DiMaggio, Ted Williams, Stan Musial, Bob Feller, Willie Mays, and Mickey Mantle, and of men like Bobby Thomson and Don Larsen, who never made it to Cooperstown but are more famous than many of those who did. Finally, it was the time of brave pioneers like Jackie Robinson, colorful managers like Leo Durocher and Casey Stengel, and innovative owners like Branch Rickey and Bill Veeck.

Besides being an era of colorful personalities and dramatic events, this was a revolutionary period in the history of the national pastime. Within a few short years, black players were taking their rightful place in the formerly all-white major and minor leagues, television was bringing the game into the living rooms of fans across the country, night contests were becoming as popular as day games, and teams were beginning to travel by air rather than by rail. The game on the field was being altered by an ever-increasing emphasis on the home run, the rise of the specialized relief pitcher, an increase in strikeouts and walks, and a decline in batting averages and stolen bases. Baseball players themselves were changing, becoming better educated, more businesslike, and more vocal, demanding pension plans, bargaining rights, and a greater voice in how the owners ran the game.

The postwar game also was troubled. Individual players, Congress, and the U.S. Supreme Court were beginning to challenge the monopoly the owners had held over their players and markets for over a half century. The integration of white professional baseball was bringing the demise of the old Negro leagues, while the televising of major league games in minor league markets was contributing to the death of many minor league teams and leagues and threatening to dry up the source of major league talent. Television, competition from other sports and amusements, and declining neighborhoods around old ballparks were bringing falling attendance and revenues, precipitating the first franchise shifts in 50 years. Five clubs would move within five years, beginning with the Braves' transfer from Boston to Milwaukee in 1953 and ending with the Dodgers' and Giants' flights to California in 1958, helping to make what had once been a regional pastime truly a national one. By 1960, the last golden age had ended and baseball faced a period of even greater upheaval, with football and other diversions competing for the sports fan's interest and entertainment dollars.

This narrative of a magnificent period in baseball history is written for the serious baseball fan who loves the game for its complexity, drama, colorful players, rich store of humorous anecdotes, and detailed documentation. It is designed for the fan who believes, as baseball historian Lawrence Ritter has written, "that the strongest thing in baseball has going for it today is its yesterdays."[2] It is hoped that it will evoke pleasant memories and provide new insights for fans who grew up during this period, and create new memories and a better understanding of the game for younger fans who have no personal recollection of the era.

Baseball's Last Golden Age includes references (placed at the end of the text) and an extensive bibliography. Scholars of the game will find the notes and bibliography helpful in their own work, but the general reader can ignore them and read the book for the dramatic narrative history it is intended to be.

1. War's End

On June 21, 1945, after spending the past four years in an army uniform, Hank Greenberg walked into Briggs Stadium to resume his baseball career with the Detroit Tigers. He was the first major league star to return to civilian life, and Detroit manager Steve O'Neill was happy to see him. "We need some long hits," he told reporters, "and Hank is the boy who will deliver them!"[1]

Before he went off to war in the Far East, Greenberg had been one of baseball's biggest names. After joining the Tigers in 1933, he won or tied for the American League home run crown three times, captured the RBI title three times, and won the MVP Award twice. Perhaps his best year was 1938, when he hit .315, drove in 146 runs, and hit 58 homers, just two shy of Babe Ruth's record set in 1927. But the big outfielder had been away from baseball for so long that many wondered if he could ever play competitively again. Sportswriters searched their memories and record books and reported that no one had ever returned to successful major league play after such a long hiatus. Just a few days before Greenberg rejoined the team, Arthur Daley of the *New York Times* had written that while younger players returning from service would regain their edge quickly, the older ones were "going to find out that in baseball a man is 'old' at 34."[2] But the Tigers were in the midst of a pennant fight, and after 10 days of intense training, O'Neill announced that his 34-year-old slugger would be in the lineup when the Philadelphia Athletics came to town on July 1.

When the big day arrived, over 47,000 fans crowded into Briggs Stadium to see the return of their favorite Tiger. His last plate appearances in the majors had been on May 6, 1941, when he said farewell to the game with career home runs number 248 and 249. Now, over four years later, he was back in the batter's box, with his body aching from unaccustomed exercise and his hands blistered from intensive batting practice. In his first four trips to the plate, he went hitless, and it appeared that perhaps he had been away from the game too long. But then in the eighth inning, with the bases empty, he tagged left-hander Charley Gassaway for a 375-foot homer to left field. The Tigers went on to win, 9–5, tightening their grip on first place.

Greenberg's dramatic homecoming meant more than just an added chance for the Tigers to win the pennant. Along with the return of other major league regulars who had spent the last few years in military service rather than on the big league diamonds, his appearance in the lineup was a sign that World War II was nearly over. Germany and Italy had been crushed, Hitler and Mussolini were dead, and the Japanese were nearly finished. It was only a matter of time until the boys who had won the war would be marching home, and millions of Americans could resume their lives out from under the shadows of war. For baseball fans, Greenberg's appearance in the lineup also signaled the return of real major league baseball and the end of the pale imitation of the past three years. The lame, the old, and the young who had filled the major league slots during the war years would soon give way to Greenberg and most of the game's other top names — such as Ted Williams, Joe DiMaggio, Stan Musial, and Bob Feller — who had been away in service.

Like almost everything else in American life, baseball at both the minor and major league levels had been dramatically affected by the war. By the beginning of 1945, approximately 5,400 of the 5,800 professional baseball players at the time of Pearl Harbor had traded their baseball woolens for military uniforms. Many of them spent much of their military career playing baseball for one of the many outstanding teams fielded by the various branches of the armed forces, which used the teams to entertain the troops and raise money for service charities. Some of the service teams boasted more major league stars than some of the 16 clubs back home. While his service team was on Guam, former White Sox pitcher Ted Lyons pitched against a powerful army club led by Joe DiMaggio. "I left the country to get rid of DiMaggio," Lyons joked, "and here he is."[3]

But many major and minor league players spent their military years on the battlefield, and it cost some of them dearly. Nearly 50 were killed, including two, Harry O'Neill and Elmer Gedeon, who had played briefly in the majors before the war. War wounds, age, and rusty skills prevented many from regaining their baseball jobs, while some of those who were fortunate enough to return to the diamond did so after losing several prime years in their career. But most did not resent the time given to military service in a time of national emergency. "I thought what I did was right," Feller said. "I may have lost a chance to break a helluva lot of records, because it cost me a few years, but it was worth it." Pitcher Hugh Mulcahy, who had suffered through so many losing games with the dismal Phillies, also went off to war willingly, reportedly with the words, "At last I'm on a winning team."[4]

The military's demands for young manpower — some 15 million men served in the war — caused severe problems in many areas of American life, and baseball was no exception. Although all 16 major league clubs survived and played their full schedules every year, 32 minor league teams suspended play for the duration of the war. Both the majors and the minors resorted to using men who could have never played professional ball if the war had not taken away so many established players. As the war progressed, major league owners pressed into service more and more 4-F's, baby-faced teenagers, graying veterans past the retirement age, and Cubans, Mexicans, and other players from south of the border. In February of 1943, the St. Louis Cardinals even resorted to placing an advertisement in the *Sporting News* announcing that the club had openings on several of its farm clubs for experienced professional players and imploring prospective applicants to "Write Today." The *New York Times* said that this was "probably without precedent in the history of baseball," but Cardinal president Sam Breadon had a good explanation: "These are unusual times," he said.[5]

Many of the players who escaped military service had been exempted because they had families or parents to support or suffered from minor medical problems, such as allergies, bad feet, trick knees, or heart murmurs. Rookie pitcher Charley Schanz, who won 13 games for the Phillies in 1944, was classified 4-F because his eyesight was so bad that he had to wear glasses even while he was shaving. Leo Durocher, the volatile Dodger player-manager, was rejected because an examination showed that he had a punctured eardrum suffered in a 1933 beaning, an ailment gleefully headlined in the *New York Daily News* as "LEO HAS HOLE IN HEAD."[6]

But the desperate major league owners employed others with more serious disabilities. Outfielder Dick Sipek, the first deaf player in the majors since William "Dummy" Hoy retired in 1902, appeared in 82 games for the Reds in 1945, mostly as a pinch hitter, and managed to collect 38 hits and compile a .244 batting average. Bert Shepard, who had lost one leg when his plane was shot down by the Germans in 1944, returned to the states with an artificial limb, signed on as a pitcher and coach with the Washington Senators, and made one relief appearance, giving up three hits and one run in five innings. Pete Gray, a one-armed outfielder, appeared in 77 games with the Browns in 1945, hitting .218, stroking six doubles and two triples, and stealing five bases. Although he had his troubles at the plate and in the field, the fans loved him. "To the fans," *Newsweek* said, "Pete Gray is more than a one-armed player in the majors. To them, he seems the symbol of the disabled serviceman."[7]

Other spots on the diamond were filled by youngsters of high school age. The youngest was Joe Nuxhall, who at 15 years, 10 months, and 11 days was the youngest player ever to appear in a major league game. He made his debut in June of 1944, when the Cincinnati Reds sent him in to relieve in the ninth inning when they were on the short end of a 13–0 game with the Cardinals. He was so nervous that as he came out of the dugout to walk to the mound, he tripped and fell flat on his face. He managed to get two men out, but in the process he yielded five runs, five walks, two singles, and a wild pitch before departing the game with a 67.50 ERA. He was quickly dispatched to the minors for seasoning, not to return to the big time until 1952.

Another youngster rushed into the majors too soon was 16-year-old Tommy "Buckshot" Brown, inserted into the lineup by the Dodgers in 1944 when shortstop Bobby Bragan was drafted. Brown hit .211 in 103 games spread over the 1944 and 1945 seasons. Not long after he turned 17, hitting against Pittsburgh's Preacher Roe, he became the youngest player to hit a major league home run. Then he, too, was sent down to the minors for more experience, and did not make it back to the Dodgers until 1947. He would later say that "some players, the war helped. They got to play. It hurt me 'cause I wasn't ready."[8]

At the other extreme were older players prolonging their careers or coming out of retirement to bask in the limelight one last time. Among them were Joe Cronin, Lloyd and Paul Waner, Louis "Bobo" Newsom, John "Pepper" Martin, Floyd "Babe" Herman, and Jimmie Foxx. Hired first by the Cubs and then by the Phillies, the 38-year-old Foxx, who had 527 home runs to his credit when he first retired in 1942, even tried his hand at pitching, appearing in 22⅔ innings and compiling a 1–0 record and a very respectable 1.59 ERA. Old "Double X" also added seven homers to his total. And then of course some rosters included mediocre players who in peacetime would have never been given a shot at the majors, such as Danny Gardella of the New York Giants and Irv Hall of the Philadelphia Athletics.

The increasing use of subpar players naturally led to a declining quality of play as the war years progressed. From 1942 through 1945, major leaguers committed a total of 9,474 errors, an average of around 1,500 more each year than in the immediate prewar years. The level of play dropped so low that even the normally hapless St. Louis Browns, carrying eighteen 4-F's players on their squad, were able to capture the pennant in 1944. This was the first flag in the club's 44-year history. Brownie fans were heartbroken when their favorites lost the World Series to the Cardinals in six games in the first fall classic played in a single ball park since the Giants and Yankees squared off in the Polo Grounds in 1922.

Wartime play was made even worse by the occasional use of inferior baseballs, caused by wartime shortages in wool, leather, and natural rubber. The wartime baseball was not only dead—some players estimated that its carry was reduced by 25 percent—but it was sometimes knocked lopsided. The dead ball, along with the absence of most of the game's best players, helped to account for the drop in homers during the war.

The war naturally exerted severe financial pressures on club owners and players alike. After reaching a high of 9.8 million in 1940, major league attendance steadily declined, dropping to a low of 7.5 million in 1943 before rebounding to 8.8 million in 1944 and a record 10.8 million in 1945. Falling attendance brought declining revenues, causing several teams to lose money during the war and forcing one, the Philadelphia Phillies, to go on the selling block, where it was purchased by Bob Carpenter in 1943. Like workers in other jobs, players were subjected to wage freezes imposed by the Federal govenment in 1943, when the average player salary stood at around $6,400. Even before the freeze, some owners had used the war as an excuse to keep a lid on salary increases. When pitcher John "Dutch" Leonard asked Washington owner Clark Griffith for a raise in 1942 after winning 18 games the previous season, Griffith turned him down, arguing that "in these war times, with conditions as they are, anybody ought to welcome the same salary as he received last year."[9]

Many owners worried that major league play might be suspended altogether because of the manpower drain or by a decree of the Federal government, leaving them with empty ballparks and declining bank accounts. In 1943, these concerns led Chicago Cubs owner Philip K. Wrigley to establish the All-American Girls Professional Baseball League (AAGPBL), hoping it would serve as a substitute for major and minor league ball if the war shut them down. With advice and support from Branch Rickey and several other major league officials, Wrigley put $250,000 of his own money into the league, which began play in 1943 with teams in four Midwestern towns—Rockford, Illinois; Racine and Kenosha, Wisconsin; and South Bend, Indiana. Playing a fast game that was a cross between baseball and softball, the clubs drew 176,000 fans for the season, but in 1944, confident that the war was winding down and that major league baseball would not be suspended, Wrigley sold the league to Chicago advertising executive Arthur Meyerhoff and devoted his time to the Cubs. The AAGPBL would continue into the postwar years and enjoy considerable success before succumbing to financial troubles in 1954.

Sensitive to the charges that young men were cavorting on baseball diamonds while millions of others were fighting on foreign soil or working in defense plants, professional baseball tried to show that it was doing its part for the war effort. Although the "Star Spangled Banner" had been played before some games prior to the war, the major leagues began the practice of playing it before every contest in 1942. Major and minor league clubs promoted drives to sell war bonds and to collect blood, iron, rubber, aluminum, paper, cardboard, and other materials desperately needed by the military. Servicemen in uniform were often given free passes, balls hit into the stands were thrown back onto the field to be donated to service teams overseas, and many games resembled giant patriotic celebrations. Pregame ceremonies often honored veterans and medal winners, tanks and other military vehicles paraded around the field, military bands marched and ran up the colors, and former players like Babe Ruth and entertainers like Frank Sinatra and Bing Crosby made pregame speeches promoting patriotism and the buying of war bonds. All-star teams featuring Ruth, Walter Johnson, and other old stars played benefit games to raise money for the Red Cross, the USO, and army and navy relief agencies. Minor and major league teams played hundreds of exhibition games to raise money for these same organizations.

With many war industries running three shifts, clubs tried to accommodate the fans by providing more night games and even some late morning ones. In an attempt to cut down on travel so as to reserve the rails for the transportation of military men and materials, teams scheduled more doubleheaders, five-game series, and even six-game series. From 1943 until the end of the war they abandoned the warm climates of Florida and California for spring training, instead conducting training camps as close to home as possible. Saying that "I do not propose to have athletes lolling about on the sands in some semitropical climate," the baseball commissioner, Judge Kenesaw Mountain Landis, ordered all the clubs except the Browns and Cardinals to train east of the Mississippi River and north of the Potomac and Ohio rivers. The two St. Louis clubs were given the option of training in their home park.[10] With the Giants and Yankees training in New Jersey and the Dodgers at Bear Mountain Inn on the Hudson River near West Point, it was not surprising that some players found themselves limbering up during spring training by hurling snowballs at one another rather than by throwing or hitting baseballs.

While helping to boost morale at home and fighting for its own survival, major league baseball did not forget its fans and former players who were fighting on foreign soil. Major league teams and all-star squads went on off-season tours to entertain the troops, films of the World Series were shipped to military bases, and the Armed Forces Radio Service broadcast World Series games and some regular games to troops all across the world over its 166 outlets. Home on a brief leave in January of 1945, Bob Feller told reporters that "on our ship we heard the World Series by short wave when we were a lot of miles from home. You can't imagine the thrill it gave us."[11]

Some of these broadcasts were monitored in the Pacific by the Japanese, who were avid fans of the American game. Enos "Country" Slaughter later recalled that when he was stationed on Saipan, Japanese soldiers hiding in the hills would even risk their lives to "sneak out and watch us play ball. We could see them sitting up there watching the game. When it was over they'd fade back into their caves."[12] At Guadalcanal, one American soldier said that one of the first things one Japanese he had taken prisoner asked was, "Who won the World Series?"[13]

The winter months preceding baseball's last wartime season, 1945, were clouded with uncertainty. Germany's desperate counterattack at the

Battle of the Bulge in December and Japan's surprising tenacity in the Pacific raised the specter of an even more prolonged conflict and further demands on manpower. With the Kentucky Derby, Indianapolis 500, and other sporting events being cancelled, there were some who felt that the 4-F's who were playing baseball were healthy enough to fight or work in defense plants and that perhaps all spectator sports should suspend play for the duration of the war. James F. Byrnes, head of the Office of War Mobilization, expressed the views of many when he said that a young man could be bothered by a trick knee, "but if it doesn't get tricky on a football field, the chances are it won't get tricky at Verdun or in Belgium."[14]

But President Franklin Roosevelt and other government officials refused to yield to pressures to cancel the baseball season, and in the first few months of 1945 the war began to wind down. Russian troops entered Germany from the East, and British and American troops came in from the West, putting a fatal squeeze on the Third Reich. The Japanese were also near collapse, though their fanatical defense of their homeland was temporarily stalling the inevitable conclusion of the war in the Pacific. But at least the major league clubs began spring training in their northern camps with the reasonable assurance that the 1945 season would be played in its entirety. The only casualty of the schedule would be the All-Star Game, which was scrapped after Germany's surrender in May ensured that America's railroads would soon be jammed with veterans returning home from the European theater. This was a far cry from World War I, when the last month of the 1918 season was cancelled.

The opening of the season was overshadowed by the nationwide mourning over the death of President Roosevelt, who died in Warm Springs, Georgia, on April 12, just a little over a month after he began his fourth term. Two days later, as his body lay in state in Washington, all the major league parks were closed in tribute to the man who had led the country through the dark days of the depression and war and had been one of baseball's most valuable supporters. Before the war placed such heavy demands on his time, he had thrown out the first ball at eight season's openers in Griffith Stadium, and in 1942, when major league officials were wondering if professional baseball would have to suspend play for the duration of the war, he had written Commissioner Landis a letter praising baseball as a morale booster and valuable diversion during times of sacrifice and struggle. As long as players were given no special treatment by the draft, he said, "I honestly feel that it would be best for the country to keep baseball going."[15] Widely referred to as the "green light" for the continuation of the national pastime, Roosevelt's letter and subsequent defense of baseball helped it survive the attacks of some reporters and politicians who called for the cessation of professional baseball until the end of the war. This support from a strong and popular president led the *Sporting News* to eulogize him as "Baseball's Savior" and to claim that he "deserves a niche at Cooperstown."[16]

The 1945 season was played under a new baseball commissioner. Judge Landis, who had ruled baseball with an iron hand for nearly 25 years, disciplining players and owners alike and helping to restore confidence in the game after the Black Sox Scandal of 1919, had died of coronary thrombosis in November of 1944. The owners had moved slowly in choosing his successor, but finally, on April 24, after arguing behind closed doors for nearly five hours, they settled on Albert B. "Happy" Chandler, a former college athlete and folksy Kentucky politician who resigned his Senate seat to take the commissioner's post. The new job brought with it a seven-year contract calling for $50,000 a year, five times his annual salary in the Senate and far more than the salary of all but a few of the top stars of the game he was now to oversee.

The 46-year-old politician was chosen because he had been one of baseball's most vocal defenders during the war and because the owners thought he would be content to be a figurehead while they ran the game from behind the scenes. But when he was asked if he expected to have the same authority Landis had enjoyed, Chandler replied, "It never occurred to me that it would be anything less. I can't go in there standing in the shadow of Judge Landis and not have authority to do a good job."[17] Obviously, his tenure as commissioner was destined to be a difficult one.

In this last wartime season, the majors continued to lose players to the military. Hardest hit were the St. Louis Cardinals, who had won three pennants and two World Series during the war years but now had to do without the services of Stan Musial, Max Lanier, Walker Cooper, Danny Litwhiler, and Freddy Schmidt. The windup of the war also brought discharges for some players in time for them to join their teams in mid-season. Still, by season's end, only 9 percent of the major league players in the military had been released in time to rejoin their old clubs. Some did, while others, like Joe DiMaggio, decided it was too late to get into playing shape and delayed their return until 1946.

Besides Greenberg, the most famous of the returning stars was Bob Feller, who rejoined the Cleveland Indians in August. Although the plane bringing him to Cleveland did not land at the airport until 2:20 in the morning, it was met by a crowd of reporters, and when club officials announced that he would be the starting pitcher against the Detroit Tigers on the night of August 24, so many fans called seeking tickets that the overloaded switchboard broke down for the first time in its history. A luncheon held in his honor in the Hotel Carter drew over a thousand people, with many others turned away for lack of space.

Over 46,000 fans jammed the stands to welcome the 26-year-old pitcher back to the big leagues. After being honored in pregame ceremonies with speeches and gifts, including a new jeep for his Iowa farm, Feller strode to the mound for his first major league appearance in almost four years. He quickly showed that he still had the fastball that had earned him the nickname of "Rapid Robert" and allowed him to lead the American League in wins and strikeouts in the three years preceding his induction into the navy after the 1941 season. Although he was naturally not in top form, he still struck out 12 and allowed only four hits en route to a 4–2 victory over the Tigers' ace left-hander, Hal Newhouser. His 5–3 record over the last month of the season could not prevent the Indians from finishing in fifth place, but his presence offered hope for future seasons.

In spite of the return of Feller and a few other stars, the 1945 season turned out to be as dismal as those of the other war years. In an early spring game against the Yankees, Red Sox first baseman George "Catfish" Metkovich set a new record by making three errors in one inning, while in another spring game, the Pittsburgh Pirates played so poorly in dropping a doubleheader that the fans threw cushions and pop bottles at the players and poured onto the field as an angry mob. In June the last-place Phillies, who had 11 players 35 years old or older and were heading toward 108 losses for the year, dropped 16 games in a row before finally beating the Braves 5–4 in 15 innings, thanks to eight Braves' errors. Then in August, Washington pitcher Joe "Fire" Cleary came in to relieve starter Sandy Ullrich in the fourth with the Senators trailing the Red Sox by a 6–2 score. Cleary managed to strike out the opposing pitcher, Dave "Boo" Ferriss, but he faced eight other players without getting a single out. He left the game with the bases loaded, Washington trailing 14–2, and the major league record for the highest career ERA, an incredible 189.00. It was his first, and last, major league game.

Throughout the season, the game was marred by a record or near-record number of dropped fly balls, booted grounders, collisions between confused outfielders, dropped third strikes, missed batting signals, errant throws, and all the other mental and physical errors it was possible for players to make at bat and in the field. Right fielder Buddy Lewis, who had returned to the Senators after three years in the service, moaned that the baseball he came back to "was so inferior that it was almost like playing sandlot ball."[18]

Although the overall quality of play was low in 1945, the fans were treated to two exciting pennant races. In the National League, the Cardinals began the year looking for their fourth consecutive pennant. But manager Billy Southworth's club was severely crippled by the loss of several key players to the military and by an ankle injury that benched shortstop Marty Marion for several crucial contests. The Cardinals still managed to be serious contenders for the entire season, and in head-to-head confrontations with their main rivals, Charlie Grimm's Chicago Cubs, they took 16 of

22 games. But the Cubs—led by right-handed pitcher Hank Wyse (22–10), center fielder Andy Pafko (.298 and 110 RBIs), and first baseman Phil Cavarretta, the National League MVP and batting champion (.355)—padded their won-lost record at the expense of second division clubs and swept a record 20 doubleheaders. The Cubs clinched the pennant on September 29, the next-to-the-last day of the season, by taking the first game of a doubleheader from the Pirates, 4–3. The Cards finished second, three games out.

The American League race was even more dramatic. The Tigers were seeking revenge for the 1944 season, when they lost the final game of the season to the last place Senators, allowing the Browns to capture the only pennant in their history. Led by the strong arms of Newhouser (25 wins and his second consecutive MVP Award) and Dizzy Trout (18–15), and by the hitting of first baseman Rudy York and right fielder Roy Cullenbine, the Tigers made a strong early season showing and were then given a big lift by Greenberg's return. After such a long layoff, Greenberg naturally suffered from a variety of aches and pains, but he became the leader and inspiration of the team. In the half season that was left, he hit .311, slammed 13 home runs, and knocked in 60 runs.

The American League race went right down to the wire. Several teams made a strong bid for the flag, but eventually it turned out to be a battle between the Tigers and the Senators, whose roster included one 20-game winner (knuckleballer Roger Wolff), three other starting knuckleball pitchers, one .300 hitter (Buddy Lewis), three Cubans, one Venezuelan, and one Italian. They had no home run punch, hitting only 27 all season and managing only one of those in Griffith Stadium, an inside-the-park fluke by Joe Kuhel, who hit only two homers all year. As late as June 12, manager Ossie Bluege's unusual collection of ballplayers was buried in seventh place. They then began a slow climb up the standings, thanks to good pitching and the hitting of Lewis, who returned from service in time to compile a .333 batting average in 69 games. By the middle of July they had pulled to within 4½ games of the league-leading Tigers, and they continued to press them the rest of the year.

The outcome of the race would not be decided until September 30, the last day of the campaign. The Senators had already ended their season with an 87–67 record, placing them one game behind the Tigers, who were in St. Louis for a doubleheader with the Browns. The Tigers needed just one victory to clinch the pennant. If they lost both games, they would play the Senators in a playoff to determine the league winner.

At game time it was raining and the temperature was a cool 57 degrees, helping to hold the attendance to only 5,582. The rain finally let up and the groundskeepers pronounced the field ready for play. The Browns started their screwball artist, Nels Potter, while the Tigers went with Virgil Trucks, who had been discharged from the navy just three days before and had not pitched a major league game in two years. Potter went the entire game, but Trucks ran out of steam in the sixth and had to be relieved by Newhouser. In a tight, see-saw battle marred by a muddy field and intermittent rain, the Browns carried a 3–2 lead into the ninth. In the top of the inning, with one out and two Tigers on base, the Browns decided to walk center fielder Roger "Doc" Cramer to set up the double play, even though Greenberg was the next hitter.

The strategy backfired. In the fading light, Greenberg took Potter's first pitch, a screwball, for a called ball. The second pitch was also a screwball, but Greenberg slammed it down the left field line toward the bleachers. Umpire Cal Hubbard ran down the line, hesitated momentarily, and then gave the fair sign, evoking a loud chorus of boos from the home crowd as Greenberg ran out his grand slam and was welcomed at the plate by the entire Tiger club. His dramatic blast gave the Tigers a 6–3 lead, and in the bottom of the ninth, reliever Al Benton shut out the Browns to preserve Newhouser's 25th victory and give Detroit the flag. Few players or fans cared that the second and now meaningless game of the doubleheader was rained out. Detroit had won the pennant with an 88–65 record, a .575 won-lost percentage that was the worst in baseball history for a pennant winner.

The Tigers had their revenge. The Senators, who had helped to deny them the pennant in 1944, wound up in second place, 1½ games out, and the defending champion Browns came in third, six games behind. Joe McCarthy's Yankees, who had taken three pennants and two world titles during the war years, found themselves in an unaccustomed fourth place. The Yankees' second baseman, George "Snuffy" Stirnweiss, did have one consolation—he won the American League batting championship with a .30854430 average, edging Tony Cuccinello of the White Sox by just .00008659. No other batting race in major league history had ever been decided by such a narrow margin. Stirnweiss's average was the lowest of any batting champion since 1906.

The last World Series of the war years opened in Detroit on Wednesday, October 3. The Cubs, who had won seven of the nine World Series they had played in, were slight favorites over the Tigers, who had one world championship to show for six trips to the fall classic. Although some war veterans had straggled back to both clubs before the end of the season, both were still largely staffed by mediocre wartime players. When someone asked Chicago sportswriter Warren Brown his predictions on the Series, he considered the question for a moment, then replied, "Really, I can't conceive of either team winning a single game!"[19] New York reporter Frank Graham described the Series as "the fat men against the tall men at the annual office picnic."[20]

As expected, the forty-second World Series was characterized by inept play — missed signals, defensive errors, boneheaded baserunning, and other embarrassing imitations of the real game. The Tiger outfielders allowed seven balls that should have been caught to drop in between them for singles or extra-base hits. In the seventh inning of the sixth game, pinch hitter Charles Hostetler, a 42-year-old former semipro player, was trying to score from second to give the Tigers the lead and possibly the game and the Series, but as he rounded third he tripped over the bag, fell, and was easily tagged out. The Cubs went on to win 8–7, in 12 innings, forcing the Tigers to seven games before Newhouser gave them the Series with a 9–3 win. For the world champions, Greenberg hit .304 with two homers and seven RBIs, Cramer hit .379 with four RBIs, Newhouser took two games, and Trout and Trucks won one game each. The Cubs' Phil Cavarretta led all hitters with a .423 average.

Although it has often been called the worst World Series ever played, the seven games brought in 333,057 paying customers and $1,492,454 in ticket revenues, both new records. In the third game, a sellout in Detroit, wartime altruism still prevailed as 716 ticketholders responded to newspaper appeals and gave up their seats to wounded veterans from a Battle Creek hospital.

The wartime baseball era was history. In had been an unusual period in the history of the game, an era that defied comparisons with the other years in the history of the sport. As Red Barber said, "It's like apples and oranges, you can't compare it. It was just a matter of playing anyone who was breathing." Besides, he added, "Nobody asked too much. It was interesting and it gave people something to do."[21]

Even before the 1945 season ended, the fans were looking ahead to better times. In August, shortly after atomic bombs dropped over Hiroshima and Nagasaki brought World War II to an abrupt end, reporter Dan Daniel could not contain his enthusiasm. He wrote in the *Sporting News* that "back to the parks of the major leagues will come the heroes of the game — Ted Williams, Enos Slaughter, Joe DiMaggio, Spud Chandler, Johnny Beazley, Charlie Keller, Johnny Mize, Babe Young, Pee Wee Reese, Pete Reiser, Terry Moore — oh, the list seems endless. How have we got along without them? . . . It seems incredible. But major league baseball soon will be back in the major leagues."[22]

It would be, but like the rest of the war-weary nation, it would never be the same again.

2. The National Pastime

In the fall of 1945, the great war was over and most of the 15 million men who had fought it were on their way home. The war had cost the nation 407,316 deaths, 670,846 wounded, and $625 billion, but it had put millions of people to work and cured the depression almost overnight. For most Americans, the future looked brighter than it had in many years.

Many felt it was time to enjoy the good life, to forget about the horrors of the depression and the war, to forget about shortages, rationing, separated families, and calls for personal sacrifice for the war effort. It was time to return to life as it had existed before Pearl Harbor — without the depression, of course — to the lifestyle and values of small town America, where the father worked, the mother stayed at home with the children, the children obeyed their parents, neighbors talked over the backyard fence, families stayed in the living room at night and read, played games, or listened to the radio, and young women remained chaste until marriage even if young males did not always use such restraint. In short, it was time to return to the uncomplicated world depicted by Norman Rockwell on the covers of the *Saturday Evening Post*. Of course, this world had not truly existed before the war. The very fact that Rockwell chose to romanticize this way of life indicated that it was rapidly becoming a thing of the past. But most Americans preferred to remember the myth about prewar America, not the reality.

The reality was that the war had radically altered the nation's course in foreign and domestic affairs. A second-rate military power when the conflict began, the United States had joined with Great Britain, Russia, and other nations to defeat Germany, Japan, Italy, and the rest of the Axis powers. As the fascist nations were defeated and Britain and France ended the war exhausted and unable to regain their former positions as world powers, the United States and the Soviet Union emerged as the world's greatest powers. The sole possessor of the most destructive weapon in history, the atomic bomb, the United States was now the world's most powerful nation and President Harry Truman was educating Americans to the fact that power brought responsibilities that could not be evaded.

Peace was turning out to be elusive. The alliance of Great Britain, Russia, and the United States had been a fragile one held together by a common foe—Hitler—and as soon as Germany collapsed the alliance began to unravel. Fearing future invasions from the West and hoping to profit from the war, the USSR was already breaking its wartime treaties and promises as it attempted to set up satellite states in Eastern Europe, taking advantage of the power vacuum created by the collapse of Nazi Germany. The hot war of World War II was rapidly becoming the Cold War of the postwar period. Soon, Americans would be called upon to make still more sacrifices in the name of freedom and democracy.

The nation of 140 million people had undergone rapid domestic changes. Having served as the "arsenal of democracy" for four years, it was now an industrial and technological giant, the richest nation in the world. The war had accelerated industrialization, automation, the concentration of industry, and the development of electronics. It had fed urbanization, as millions flocked to the cities to work in the war plants. It had uprooted millions of people, sending young men off to fight, putting women into factory jobs and other work formerly reserved for men, and sending blacks to war industries in the North and into battle all across the world. For women and blacks, the war brought increased opportunities, broadened horizons, and a new sense of dignity and worth that would in the postwar years bring demands for an end to the sexism and racism that had helped to keep both in a subservient role for so long.

The war had also brought an educational revolution. Some 8 million GIs would return from the war to use their veteran's benefits to acquire college educations and to buy new houses at low interest rates, sparking a rise in marriages and the inevitable climb in the birth rate. Over 3.4 million children would be born in 1946, a half million more than in 1945. Though not realized at the time, America was in the inaugural year of the baby boom that would produce 76.4 million children by 1964, revolutionizing the country in the process.

The nation was prosperous, but it was not without economic problems as it tried to convert to a peacetime economy and absorb millions of returning veterans into the labor force. Prices were rising and there were shortages of red meat, razor blades, clothing, golf balls, automobiles, nylons, and other consumer items. Eager automobile buyers bribed car salesmen to put their names high on the waiting list for new automobiles and agreed to pay more than the sticker price if they could just get one. Veterans with liberal GI loans were competing with other eager homebuyers to buy houses in a nation suffering from a severe housing crunch. Nearly 4.6 million workers from the automotive, steel, coal, and railroad industries went on strike after the war, and President Truman even threatened to draft railroad workers into the army and force them to run the railways during the spring railroad strike.

In this changing, complicated world, baseball was still the national pastime. To many of its fans it seemed to be one of the few stable institutions in a world being riddled with change. It was one of the most shared of all experiences. Few Americans had grown up without playing it, or its close cousin, softball, if only for a few years in grade school. Millions of boys and young men played it in various youth leagues, church and industrial leagues, high schools and colleges, and in pickup games wherever an empty field or lot could be found. Major and minor league games were carried on the radio, and stories of the game dominated the sports pages. It was a frequent topic of conversation between friends and even strangers on buses, trains, or in offices and other workplaces. At World Series time, schools transmitted radio broadcasts of games over the intercom, and in homes, offices, and workplaces all across the land fans did not dare venture too far from their radios.

Baseball was intricately bound up with the seasons. Every spring baseball was reborn. Winter was over, school would soon let out, and young boys and men would be playing baseball in short sleeves. Little boys and young men dreamed of making the major leagues, older men thought back to their youth and to the time when they played the game and had not yet acquired so many of the cares of adult life. As summer arrived, the baseball season was in full swing and the pennant races became serious, with more and more riding on each play and game. By the first week of September both the summer and the season were on the wane. School began, and time soon ran out for all but two teams, who would meet in the first week of October to decide who would be the world champions.

With the last out of the World Series, the baseball season, and summer itself, were over. It was now time for football and basketball to fill the void between the end of the last baseball season and the beginning of the new one. But in the fall and winter baseball was still in the news. It was hot stove league time, time for postmortems on the previous season and speculations on the one still to come. There were trades and rumors of trades. Contracts were extended or withheld, sometimes with pay hikes and sometimes with cuts. There was a lot of suspense—how much would Joe DiMaggio make next year, or Stan Musial, or Ted Williams? Could a star pitcher come back after a bout with a sore arm or an operation on his shoulder? Could an aging outfielder return for one more good season before hanging up his spikes? Fans talked with one another and searched the pages of the *Sporting News*, *Baseball Digest*, and the newspapers for clues to these and other questions and for stories about their favorite teams and players.

Then—would it ever come?—February arrived and the players gathered in Florida and the Southwest for spring training, a practice that began back in 1886 when Cap Anson took his Chicago White Stockings to Hot Springs, Arkansas, to tone their muscles and hone their skills for the coming season. Spring training provided the occasion for more speculation. Were there future stars in the fresh crop of rookie hopefuls that showed up every year hoping to stick with a professional team? Could the aging veterans get into shape and hold their jobs and places in the limelight for just one more year? Soon the exhibition season began, and the teams began to make their way northward, playing intersquad games or each other in small towns, giving many fans the only chance in their lifetimes to see a major league game.

Finally, the second week of April came around. It was still cool or even cold in most major league cities, but when the President of the United States threw out the first ball in Washington's Griffith Stadium, the major league season was under way. Warm weather, then summer, could not be far away. Baseball was called the summer game, and it was, but in an age when it had so few competitors for attention the summer game lasted all year long.

Baseball helped satisfy the American people's love of nostalgia. The nation had long ago outgrown its rural, pastoral nature and become a complex, urban society with worldwide responsibilities, problems, and commitments. But baseball was a link with a more pastoral, leisurely time, or at least it looked that way through the misty eyes of nostalgia. It was still played outdoors on a dirt and grass surface, primarily in the daytime, by men who chewed tobacco, fought with one another and with the umpires, and did anything legal, and sometimes illegal, to win. The uniforms still looked much like they did in the late 1920s, when the Yankees began the practice of putting the players' numbers on the back of their shirts. Teams in both leagues still wore white at home and gray on the road, and the range of colors used for trim, lettering, stockings, and caps was still rather narrow — red, orange, maroon, black, and navy. Made of flannel, the uniforms were loose-fitting, baggy, heavy, and hot.

Most players used bats made in an old brick factory in Louisville, Kentucky, by the Hillerich and Bradsby Company, which had been turning out Louisville Sluggers for major league players and for many other players across the country since the 1880s. The game was played with a ball which had changed very little in official circumference (from 9 to 9¼ inches) and weight (from 5 to 5¼ ounces) since 1872, although after 1920 its yarn was wound much tighter to make it livelier. Gloves had changed more than bats or balls over the years, becoming larger and better padded.

The game was played by rules that had changed very little over the past half century and in the same 10 cities it had been played in since 1903, making it easy to keep up with the cities, leagues, teams, and players. There were three teams in New York, two in Boston, Chicago, Philadelphia, and St. Louis, and one team in Cincinnati, Detroit, Cleveland, Pittsburgh, and Washington. The limitation of train travel had kept the baseball universe confined to this narrow northeastern and midwestern section of the nation, with St. Louis having the only teams west of the Mississippi. There were two leagues with eight teams each, and there were 25 players on each team for a total of 400. The regular season was 154 games long, with each team playing each of the other teams in the league 22 times, half the time at home and half on the road. The games were played in old parks built to fit the configurations of the neighborhood, and most had short fences, especially down the foul lines. Seated close enough to the field to hear the chatter of the players, managers, and umpires, the fans felt a part of the game.

At a time when the individual seemed to be losing power and significance, baseball still extolled the exploits of individuals. In no other team sport did the individual play such a dominant role. Much of the action was centered around the battle between the pitcher and the hitter, and the catcher or fielders against the baserunners. Played on a large outdoor area with few participants on the field at one time, the heroics and failures of the individual stood out starkly. While copious statistics were kept on team performance, the ones most remembered were those of individuals—home runs, batting averages, fielding averages, games won and lost, strikeouts, stolen bases, and the like.

Baseball was the most documented game in the world, as it had been since the nineteenth century, when newspapers first began to carry box scores and accounts of games and the *Sporting News* (founded as a baseball newspaper in 1876) and other sports newspapers and magazines began to appear. Baseball had a vast store of funny stories, quips, insults, and anecdotes that rabid baseball fans carried around in their heads along with hundreds of statistics: Babe Ruth's season's high of 60 home runs in 1927 and 714 lifetime, Ty Cobb's record 96 stolen bases in 1915, Ted Williams's .406 average in 1941, Joe DiMaggio's 56-game hitting streak of that same year, Lou Gehrig's 2,130 consecutive games, Cy Young's 511 victories. Each time a player came to bat or a pitcher went to the mound, he and the fans knew that he was competing not just against the opposing team but against those of yesteryear. No other sport could match this constant link with the past, this vast storehouse of memories that made each game just one small incident in the long and rich history of the game.

Baseball took on many characteristics of a civic religion. The nation's capital had its team, the Washington Senators ("first in war, first in peace, and last in the American League," according to the club's detractors), and almost every year since William Howard Taft began the practice back in 1910, the president of the United States had traveled to Griffith Stadium to inaugurate the new season by throwing out the first ball. No other sport received such an official blessing from such high quarters. Baseball followed the cycle of the seasons, like religious fertility rites. It had its gods— Babe Ruth, Lou Gehrig, Cy Young, Christy Mathewson, and so many others—who were worshiped while they played and then enshrined in the pantheon of baseball gods in the Hall of Fame in Cooperstown after they had retired.

Like the ancient Greek city-states, the major league cities were the focus of intense rivalries and loyalties, and each year the cities and the teams and the players were part of a Greek tragedy, replete with heroes and scapegoats, winners and losers, reward and punishment, individual and team glory. When the World Series was over, the winning city held a parade to honor the conquering heroes and delirious fans danced in the streets, while in the city of the loser, players and fans sulked and began planning for revenge next year. Many Americans would have agreed with umpire Bill Klem, who once said, "Baseball is more than a game to me. It's a religion."[1]

Ironically, the major league game that was so popular with so many fans was never seen by most of them. With the 10 major league cities concentrated in one region of the nation, most fans had to be content to follow the games through newsreels at the movie theaters, their daily newspapers, the *Sporting News* (commonly called the Baseball Bible), and baseball magazines like *Baseball Digest, Baseball Magazine,* and mass circulation general interest magazines like *Time, Newsweek, Look, Life, Collier's,* and the *Saturday Evening Post,* or on radio.

At the end of the war the home games of most teams were broadcast live over local stations, but broadcasts of away games were still "recreated" accounts of the actual contests. It was too expensive to send broadcast crews to distant cities, so announcers would recreate games from Western Union telegraph reports, using special effects to imitate the noise of the crowd and the bat meeting the ball. In 1946, the Yankees became the first club to carry every game live. Whether live or recreated, radio broadcasts helped to promote major league baseball and create loyalty to teams. In the late 1940s and early 1950s, announcers such as Mel Allen of the New York Yankees, Red Barber of the Brooklyn Dodgers, Curt Gowdy of the Boston Red Sox, Bob Prince of the Pittsburgh Pirates, and Harry Caray of the St. Louis Cardinals built up a large following of fans.

For most fans, a visit to Yankee Stadium, Ebbets Field, or some other cherished battleground was out of the question. The remoteness of the major league game seemed to heighten the reverence with which it and its players were held—heroes often seem greater when they are never seen by those who idolize them. Millions of fans made heroes out of Joe DiMaggio, Ted Williams, Stan Musial, and dozens of other players they had never seen in person. Not until the coming of television would most fans actually get to see their heroes in action.

With most major league teams so far away, most fans who wanted to see live baseball had to rely on high school and college games, factory leagues, semipro teams, and the American Legion and Little League teams. For professional baseball, they had to be content watching minor league teams, whose history went back as far as organized baseball itself. On the eve of World War II, there were 43 minor leagues across the country, but during the war the number dropped to a low of 10 and still stood at only 12 in 1945. With the end of the war, minor league baseball exploded across the country, taking advantage of prosperity and a nationwide desire to live it up after the sacrifices of the war years. It seemed that every town with a population of 10,000 or more had to have its own team. The peak year came in 1949, when there were 464 teams organized into 59 leagues, ranging from class AAA to D, and attendance reached almost 42 million.

Life was hard for most minor league players. With only 400 available jobs on major league rosters and close to 9,000 minor league players, the likelihood of ever making it to the big time was slim. Even on many of the teams in the higher classifications, minor league ball meant low pay, poorly-lit and rocky playing fields, shabby clubhouses, long rides on run-down buses, fleabag hotels and boardinghouses, greasy meals at cheap restaurants and hamburger stands, inadequate equipment and coaching, and a constant battle with heat and fatigue. But in spite of these hardships, thousands of players pursued the dream of one day playing in Yankee Stadium, Ebbets Field, Fenway Park, or even with the lowly Browns or Senators.

At war's end there were still other professional leagues that played far away from the white majors and minors These were the professional black leagues that had sprung up after blacks were excluded from the white majors and minors in the late nineteenth century. As late as the 1880s, close to 20 blacks had played on the professional clubs that arose after the Civil War. Among the most famous of them were the Walker brothers, Moses Fleetwood and William Welday, who played for Toledo in the American Association in the mid–1880s. But the latter part of the century saw the hardening of race relations and the rise of Jim Crow laws in the South, establishing the segregation of blacks and whites in public schools, public transportation, housing, hotels, and almost all other areas of life. It was perhaps inevitable that this southern approach to race relations would migrate across the Mason-Dixon line to the major league clubs, which had large numbers of southern white players on their rosters. From the mid–1890s on, the national pastime was the white pastime, at least in the major and minor leagues. Owners occasionally used Native Americans and light-skinned Cubans and other players from south of the border, but no African Americans. As players and owners often cynically remarked, a good dark-skinned player was not really black if his native tongue was Spanish.

In 1945 it seemed that the segregation of professional baseball would continue. Baseball was a tradition-bound sport, slow to change, and for many whites the fact that there were no blacks in major league ball was good enough reason not to recruit any. Many whites simply did not think about the absence of blacks in baseball because here, as in so many other parts of American life, they were largely invisible. When owners, players, managers, and others connected with organized ball were asked why there were no blacks in the game, they gave the same litany of reasons they had recited for decades: there were none good enough to play major league ball, white players from the South would walk off the field rather than play on the same team with blacks, it might cause a riot in the stands if blacks and whites played together and got into a rhubarb on the field, the presence of blacks would divide the team or drive away white fans, and it just would not work out for whites and blacks to work together, travel together, eat together, and sleep in the same hotels—in short, live with one another in close quarters for seven months out of the year. This problem would be even worse during spring training when the teams were in the deep South getting ready for the regular season. Many white owners also made a handsome profit from renting their parks to the Negro league teams when their own club was out of town, and if the integration of the majors killed the Negro leagues, as many thought it would, the white owners would lose this source of income.

There was another reason, too. One major league owner once told Mrs. Effa Manley, the general manager of the black Newark Eagles, "I would like to sign Negro players, but you know how fans idolize ballplayers. Many of our fans are white women. It might cause unpleasantness if these women became 'attached' to a Negro home run hitter."[2] Thus in baseball, as in the public schools and other areas of social relations, the specter of interracial mixing was raised to prevent blacks from taking their rightful place.

One of the greatest obstacles to the end of segregation in baseball was the denial that official segregation actually existed. Both Commissioner Landis and the rest of the baseball establishment had long insisted that the absence of black players was due to the fact that there just were not any good enough to make major league teams. In 1933, National League President John A. Heydler said, "I do not recall one instance where baseball has allowed either race, creed or color to enter into its selection of players,"[3] and in 1942, Commissioner Landis, a diehard foe of integration, claimed that "there is no rule, formal or informal, or any understanding—written, subterranean, or sub-anything—against the hiring of Negro players by the teams of organized ball."[4]

When blacks were shut out of white organized ball in the late nineteenth century, they began to form teams and leagues of their own. The heyday of the Negro leagues was the period from the end of World War I to the integration of the white major leagues in the late 1940s. There were two "major" Negro leagues, the Negro American League and the Negro National League, obvious imitations of the white majors. It was difficult to tell how good they really were. They did not keep good records, they played irregular schedules, they often performed in shabby rented parks, and the competition was uneven, ranging from contests with one another to games against black minor league teams, black college teams, white major league and all-star teams, and South American clubs.

Most contemporary experts felt that player-for-player and club-for-club, the black majors were no match for the white major leagues. However, when the top Negro league teams played against white major league teams and all-star teams in exhibition games, the Negro clubs beat their white competition nearly 60 percent of the time. This was so embarrassing to organized baseball that Commissioner Landis once issued an order prohibiting white major league clubs from wearing their regular uniforms in these games and requiring the promoters to bill the games as "all-star" exhibition games.

Although the Negro league teams did not have the depth of the white major league clubs, they had many individual stars who could have played with the white clubs if they had been given a chance. Perhaps the most prominent of these were pitcher Leroy "Satchel" Paige, who would eventually get his chance to play in the white majors, and catcher Josh Gibson, who never did.

Many felt that Gibson was the greatest of all the Negro league hitters. Thirty-three years old in 1945, he had spent 15 years in the Negro leagues, first with the Pittsburgh Cardinals and then with the Homestead Grays, for whom he played in 1945. A powerful 6 feet 2 inch, 215-pound catcher known for both his defensive and offensive abilities, the Black Bambino led his league in batting average four times and home runs nine times. Some records credit him with 89 home runs in one year, 75 in another, and over 100 more career homers than Babe Ruth. Roy Campanella, who had played against Gibson as well as Hank Aaron, Willie Mays, Mickey Mantle, and other great major league sluggers in the late 1940s and 1950s, once said, "Josh Gibson was the greatest home run hitter I have ever seen."[5] Hall of Fame pitcher Walter Johnson said that Gibson "is a catcher that any big-league club would like to buy for $200,000.... Too bad that Gibson is a colored fellow."[6] And Dizzy Dean, who pitched against Gibson in off-season exhibition games, once told him: "Josh, I wish you and Satchel played with me on the Cardinals. The pennant would be clinched by the Fourth of July. We could fish until the series."[7]

In 1945, Gibson hit .393 and won the Negro National League batting crown. Roy Campanella came in fourth at .365. But as *Newsweek* wrote that year, "When Negroes are finally given the opportunity to try out for the majors, it may be too late for Gibson."[8]

Among the many other Negro league players who could have played in the white majors if they had only been given a chance were the great first baseman Buck Leonard, third baseman Ray Dandridge, and outfielder James "Cool Papa" Bell, who was so fast, according to Satchel Paige, that he once "drilled one right through my legs and was hit in the back by his own ground ball when he slid into second."[9] Solid evidence of the strength of the Negro leagues is also given by just a partial list of Negro league veterans who made it to the white majors after Robinson opened the door in 1947: Campanella, Monte Irvin, Hank Aaron, Willie Mays, Elston Howard, Joe Black, Larry Doby, and Don Newcombe.

As World War II came to an end, several forces were operating to break down the racial barriers in baseball and other areas of American life. Large numbers of black soldiers had fought well in the war, and they came home with new pride in themselves and a renewed determination not to submit to Jim Crow laws and other manifestations of racism. As one black veteran said, "I spent four years in the Army to free a bunch of Frenchmen and Dutchmen, and I'm hanged if I'm going to let the Alabama version of the Germans kick me around."[10] The war against Nazi racism, and all the publicity surrounding the Holocaust, made it harder for Americans to justify the continuation of racism and segregation at home. During the war and immediate postwar years, the federal government issued executive orders or passed laws prohibiting segregation on military bases and discrimination in hiring. Many states also passed laws prohibiting discrimination in hiring.

The war had brought other changes, too. The mass migration of southern blacks to northern cities that had started before World War I was accelerated, as blacks left the rural South seeking jobs in northern war industries and the freedoms and rights that were denied them in the South. The migration created racial tensions that sometimes led to riots, as in Detroit in 1943, but it also increased the size of the new black middle class that was gaining political consciousness and would fight the civil rights battles of the postwar period. In addition, the migration was creating millions of potential black baseball fans who would be more likely to come out to the major league parks if they could see black players on the field. This lesson was not lost on some of the white owners. In May of 1944, the St. Louis Cardinals and St. Louis Browns, the last two clubs having segregated seating, integrated the seating at Sportsman's Park.

There was also pressure from the press and from the political arena. As the war progressed, many black and white newspapers and magazines campaigned for an end to segregation in baseball, and in the last year of the war calls for the end of discrimination in baseball became more strident. One congressman urged the Interstate Commerce Commission to hold hearings on discriminatory hiring practices in organized baseball, and another introduced a bill in the House of Representatives in April of 1945 providing for an end to racial discrimination in baseball, but it never got out of committee. The American Communist Party took up the issue, attacking baseball's color ban in the *Daily Worker*, collecting petitions calling for an end to discrimination, and organizing protests.

The last wartime baseball season also saw the establishment in New York of a pressure group called the "End to Jim Crow Baseball Committee," and a "Committee of Ten," appointed by Mayor Fiorello LaGuardia, to study racial discrimination in organized baseball. The chairman of the "Committee of Ten" was Branch Rickey, and it was no surprise that it recommended the end of segregation in the national game as soon as possible. Unknown to the rest of the committee, Rickey was already planning to break the color ban by integrating his own team, the Brooklyn Dodgers.

The death of Judge Landis and appointment of Happy Chandler helped to pave the way for the integration of the national game. Shortly after he took office, Chandler told sportswriter Ric Roberts of the black *Pittsburgh Courier*, "I'm for the Four Freedoms. . . . If a black boy can make it in Okinawa and Guadalcanal, hell, he can make it in baseball. . . . I don't believe in barring Negroes from baseball just because they are Negroes."[11] This was no promise to actively promote the integration of the game, but it certainly indicated a more positive attitude than Landis had ever exhibited.

Black athletes in other sports helped to pave the way for the integration of the majors. One was Jesse Owens, who gained the respect and admiration of many Americans for his victories over Hitler's Nazi "supermen" during the 1936 Olympics held in Berlin and was still a popular figure in the United States in the postwar era. Another was boxer Joe Louis, the heavyweight champion of the world from 1937 until 1949. White and black Americans alike admired the Brown Bomber's boxing skills. When the nation entered the war, he joined the army, participated in War Bond rallies, and fought several exhibition matches for military relief societies that were trying to raise money for the families of men killed in the war. The army proudly promoted him as an example of America's racial tolerance and wartime unity in the face of Nazi militarism and racism.

At the end of the war, then, the time was ripe for the integration of the all-white national pastime. What was needed was a club owner with the courage and skills to be a successful pioneer, and a black player with the ability to play as well — or better than — most white major leaguers and the fortitude to withstand the tremendous pressures — even dangers — he would face as he tried to break into the game against the wishes of most of the white owners, players, and fans. That owner was Branch Rickey, and the player was Jackie Robinson.

Rickey was one of the most innovative and influential men in baseball history. A native of Ohio, he had a baccalaureate degree from Ohio Wesleyan University, a law degree from the University of Michigan, and extensive athletic experience. He had worked his way through college playing professional baseball and football, coached baseball at three colleges, toiled as a major league catcher for nearly four years, worked as a scout for the St. Louis Browns, had a 10-year career as a manager of the Browns and Cardinals and a 17-year career as vice president and business manager for the Cardinals. At the end of 1942, he came to the Dodgers as president and general manager, and in 1944 he joined with Walter O'Malley and John L. Smith (president of Charles Pfizer Chemical Corporation) to buy 75 percent of the club's stock.

During his 24 years (1919–1942) with the Cardinals, Rickey gained a reputation as one of the shrewdest minds in the baseball business. A workaholic who poured his boundless energy into the study and practice of baseball, he was always thinking of new ways to develop talent, win ball games, and capture pennants. He introduced "ladies' days" to St. Louis, put numbers on the backs of his players' uniforms, and most importantly, began the farm system. In 1919 he began to buy up minor league teams all across the country and to use them as a training ground to develop players for the Cardinals or to sell at a handsome profit to other clubs. Other club owners and newspaper critics called the farm players "Rickey's chain gang," but they had to admire the results. While he was in St. Louis the Cardinals, who had not won a pennant since they helped form the league in 1876, won six, and the players he had developed there won three more after he moved on to Brooklyn.

When Rickey came to the Dodgers he soon transformed the franchise into a dynasty that would dominate the National League for years to come. To maximize profits and keep the players hungry for World Series money, Rickey paid meager salaries, leading his players and the press to call him "El Cheapo." He sold or traded some of the city's favorites to begin a youth movement designed to bring future pennants, and developed the Dodger farm system into one of the best in the majors. During the war years, when most major league teams cut back on their scouting and signing of young players on the theory that they would soon be working for Uncle Sam, Rickey sent scouts all across the country to snap up the available young talent. With little competition from other clubs, who would later have to shell out huge sums to untested "bonus babies," he signed Carl Furillo, Carl Erskine, Edwin "Duke" Snider, Clem Labine, Gil Hodges, and many others. And at the end of the war he bought an abandoned naval station at Vero Beach, Florida, and turned it into an elaborate training and tryout camp for his present and future players.

The 64-year-old Rickey who ran the Dodgers in 1945 was not the typical baseball executive. Owlish, well-educated, and articulate, he read Greek tragedies and other literary works with titles most baseball men would not even recognize, much less read. He was a devout Christian, a teetotaler, rarely cursed or said anything stronger than "Judas Priest," and would not attend baseball games on Sunday, partly out of piety and partly out of a promise he had made to his mother when he was a child. A familiar figure with his glasses, hat, cigar, and rumpled suits, Rickey had a disheveled appearance that once prompted his wife to remark, "Mr. Rickey is not, and never has been, one of the ten best-groomed men in America."[12] He was, indeed, an unusual man, and his influence on the game, some experts think, was second only to that of Alexander Cartwright and Babe Ruth.

Rickey had not been with the Dodgers long before he decided that his search for talent would extend to black players. He had long felt that the ban on black players was morally wrong, but it was not until the war began to revolutionize the role of blacks in America that he felt that the integration of the majors would be accepted by the players and the fans. Besides being the right thing, the hiring of blacks would bring talent to the Dodgers, help build them into a position of dominance in the National League, and bring black fans into the stands. The integration of baseball, then, would not only be the moral and humanitarian thing to do, it would also be good baseball and good business.

Rickey moved cautiously, knowing that if he moved too fast, alienated too many people, and chose the wrong player, his attack on segregation would be set back for years. As he would later write, "This shocking move would require . . . some Booker T. Washington compromises with surface inequality for the sake of expediency."[13] Perhaps no one else in baseball could have pulled it off so successfully.

He began his efforts in 1943. After getting the support of the club's board of directors, who promised to keep the plan secret, Rickey spent thousands of dollars sending scouts all over the country and the Caribbean looking for black talent, particularly for that one special player who would have all the right qualifications for being the pioneer in the integration of the majors. In May of 1945, still keeping his plans to integrate the Dodgers a secret from all except his family and a few close associates, he announced that he was forming a new baseball team, the Brooklyn Brown Dodgers, to play in the newly formed six-team all-black league, the U.S. League. Rickey apparently planned to use the Brown Dodgers to camouflage his scouting of black players for the Dodgers and also as a legitimate black team that could play in Ebbets Field while the Dodgers were on the road, bringing extra dollars into the treasury.

As the summer months of 1945 passed, the search for the pioneer player narrowed. From the names submitted by his scouts, Rickey rejected several because they did not have the right combination of offensive and defensive skills, some because they were too young or too old, others because they lacked intelligence or education, and still others because they did not have the personal traits that would enable them to withstand the pressures and abuses they would be subjected to on and off the field. Finally, he settled on Jackie Roosevelt Robinson, a shortstop for the black Kansas City Monarchs. On August 28, 1945, as the pennant races went into their last stages, scout Clyde Sukeforth brought Robinson to Rickey's Brooklyn office to endure a personal grilling by Rickey himself.

Robinson had been born in Cairo, Georgia, but when he was only a few months old his mother, abandoned by Jackie's sharecropper father, had moved to Pasadena, California. There she worked as a domestic to raise her five children. A natural athlete, Jackie starred in football, baseball, basketball, and track in high school, Pasadena Junior College, and UCLA. After family financial difficulties forced him to quit UCLA in his senior year to help support the family, he served as an assistant athletic director at a National Youth Administration camp and played professional football with a barnstorming team, the Los Angeles Bulldogs.

In 1942 Robinson was drafted into the army, where he rose to the rank of second lieutenant while facing and protesting racism at every turn. In 1944, while he was at Ft. Hood, Texas, he was arrested and court-martialed for insubordination when he disobeyed an army bus driver's order to "get to the back of the bus where the colored people belong" and then got into a heated argument with the bus driver and a military policeman. He was acquitted of all charges of insubordination, and in November of 1944 was honorably discharged.[14] He served as a coach at the Samuel Houston College for Negroes in Austin, Texas, for one semester before joining the Kansas City Monarchs, a member of the Negro American League. He played shortstop, hit .340, and starred on the base paths and on defense.

From what his scouts had told him, Rickey felt that Robinson had the requisite physical tools to play in the major leagues, and he also had other qualities he was looking for. He was a church-goer, a non-smoker, a teetotaler, and was engaged to an educated young woman. He was intelligent, well-educated, articulate, and poised. He had played with whites in college and had proved in the army that he could be a leader among men. He was also fiercely competitive, proud, courageous, and quick to take offense at racial slurs, discrimination, and other indignities. Rickey knew all these things, but what he did not know was Robinson's temperament. Faced with the greatest pressure and abuses any athlete had ever been subjected to, how would he react? This was the question Rickey hoped to have answered in his session with Robinson.

As Robinson sat in a leather chair across from Rickey's desk, Rickey stunned him by telling him, "You are not a candidate for the Brooklyn Brown Dodgers. You were brought here to play for the Brooklyn organization, to start out, if you can make it, playing for our top farm club, the Montreal Royals . . . . Later on — also if you can make it — you'll have a chance with the Brooklyn Dodgers." Rickey went on to emphasize that it would take more than good hitting, baserunning, fielding, and other skills that showed up in the box score. In this pioneering venture, good ballplaying would not, in itself, be enough. It would take courage, drive, guts, tolerance, and almost superhuman self-control. He would be the target of beanballs, raised spikes on the base paths, curses and racial slurs from opposing players and fans, and other physical and verbal assaults. When these occurred, Rickey asked, "What would you do?"[15]

"Mr. Rickey," Robinson asked, "Do you want a ball player who's afraid to fight back?" Rickey roared, "I want a ball player with guts enough not to fight back! You've got to do this job with base hits and stolen bases and fielding ground balls, Jackie. Nothing else!"[16]

Rickey continued his role as the Devil's advocate, posing as a prejudiced sportswriter, an opposing player bowling into Robinson at second base spoiling for a fight, a racist hotel-keeper denying him a room, a railroad ticket-seller making racist comments. As he talked, Rickey often stuck his face right in front of Robinson's and called him "nigger," "dirty black bastard," "coon," and the whole range of pejorative phrases that had always brought the blood rushing to Robinson's head. He even swung at Robinson's face, missing it by only a few inches. Robinson would later write that Rickey's "acting was so convincing that I found myself chain-gripping my fingers behind my back."[17] After he swung at Robinson, Rickey glared at him and bellowed, "What do you do?" Robinson looked at him, his lips trembling, and then he answered, "Mr. Rickey, I've got two cheeks—is that it?"[18]

Rickey had the answer he wanted. The interview continued, with more role playing and with more admonitions about how much courage it would take to make this experiment work. He emphasized that in the beginning almost everyone would be against them—the opposing players, the umpires, the fans, the press, perhaps even his own teammates. Rickey impressed upon him, "You will symbolize a crucial cause. One incident, just one incident, can set it back twenty years."[19] If he lost his composure and fought back, it would lend ammunition to the racists who claimed that black players were hot-tempered and dangerous and should not be allowed to play on the same field with whites. Robinson thought about it for a few minutes, then replied, "Mr. Rickey, if you want to take this gamble, I will promise you there will be no incident." Sukeforth, the lone witness to this historic meeting, would later say that when Robinson said this, "I thought the old man was going to kiss him." Astonished at the whole scene he witnessed that day, Sukeforth later said, "Oh, they were a pair, those two! I tell you, the air in that office was electric."[20]

Near the end of the interview, Rickey looked into Robinson's eyes and said, "You will have to promise me that for your first three years in baseball, you will turn your other cheek. I know that you are naturally combative.

But for three years . . . you will have to do it the only way it can be done. Three years. Can you do it?" Robinson looked at him and said, "Mr. Rickey, I've got to do it."[21] At the close of the three-hour interview, Robinson accepted a $3,500 bonus and a salary of $600 a month to play for the Royals. He was told to keep the offer a secret from everyone except his mother and fiancée until Rickey felt that it was time to sign a formal contract and announce it to the press.

Rickey waited until after the 1945 World Series to spring his surprise on the rest of the world. On October 23, 1945, the top officials of the Montreal Royals and Branch Rickey, Jr., (Branch, Sr., remained back in Brooklyn) held a press conference in Montreal and announced that the Dodgers had signed Robinson to play for the Royals in 1946. Robinson spoke briefly before the 25 reporters assembled there, describing himself as "just a guinea pig in this noble experiment. . . . If I can make good here . . . then it will be a new deal in baseball for men of my race. I'm truly grateful for the chance thus offered. It could be that I'll be subjected to many snubs, the target of some abuse, especially from the fans in hostile quarters, but I'm ready to take the chance."[22] Even Robinson could not have been aware of how many snubs, how much abuse, and how much fan hostility, he was to experience in the years to come.

The news stunned the nation. Some newspapers, including several black-owned ones, labeled the signing a publicity stunt, an attempt to defuse the efforts of pressure groups to force the hiring of black players. All across the South, newspapers and fans lambasted the signing as northern meddling in race relations and a serious threat to the national pastime and the southern way of life. *Atlanta Journal* sports editor Ed Danforth expressed surprise that a Negro league star would even want to play in the white majors and claimed, "The only menace to peace between the races is the carpetbagger white press and agitators in the Negro press who capitalize on racial issues." But there were dissenters from the orthodox southern point of view, such as Smith Barrier of the *Greensboro* (North Carolina) *Daily News,* who said, "I don't see anything wrong with the signing of Jackie Robinson."[23]

The *Sporting News* was unhappy with Robinson's signing, referring to it as "this perplexing problem." Always a staunch supporter of baseball tradition, the paper expressed the opinion that Robinson "is reported to possess baseball abilities which, were he white, would make him eligible for a trial with, let us say, the Brooklyn Dodgers' Class B farm at Newport News, if he were six years younger." It predicted, "Robinson conceivably will discover that as a 26-year-old shortstop just off the sandlots, the waters of competition in the International League will flood far over his head."[24]

Baseball men reacted in various ways. Clark Griffith, president of the

Washington Senators, expressed concern that the integration of the majors would destroy the Negro leagues, but William Benswanger, president of the Pirates, held that "it is the business of the Brooklyn and Montreal clubs." Several white major leaguers claimed that they did not care if blacks played in the major leagues as long as it was not on their team, while others said that they flatly opposed playing with them or against them.[25]

While most white newspapers relegated the news of Robinson's signing to the sports pages, the black press headlined it on the front page. This was big news for black America, a foot in the door of a major white institution, a victory for black Americans everywhere. Although the black press lauded the signing, it warned that much difficulty lay ahead for the young player. Black columnist Ludlow Werner wrote in the *New York Age:* "I'm happy over the event, but I'm sorry for Jackie. . . . To 15,000,000 Negroes he will symbolize not only their prowess in baseball, but their ability to rise to an opportunity. . . . And Lord help him with his fellow Negroes if he should fail them."[26]

Most black players publicly applauded Robinson's signing. They were proud that someone of their race was being given a chance and they did not want to criticize him and give ammunition to the whites who were already attacking him. Besides, if he made it, perhaps they could make it, too. But many felt that he was not the best choice. Buck Leonard later claimed, "We had a whole lot better ballplayers than Jackie, but Jackie was chosen 'cause he had played with white boys" in college.[27] Cool Papa Bell would later say, "Most of the black ballplayers thought that Monte Irvin should have been the first black in the major leagues. Monte was our best young ballplayer at the time."[28]

There were others who felt that Josh Gibson or Satchel Paige should have been given the first shot at the majors, in spite of their ages. Of course Gibson and Paige both resented being passed over. Paige praised Robinson publicly at the time he signed his contract with Montreal, but he later said that Robinson's signing "hurt me deep down" and that "it was still me that ought to have been first."[29]

One of the most perceptive reactions to Robinson's signing came not from the press, the major leagues, the Negro leagues, or a sociologist or some other expert on baseball or race relations. It came from Louis Odoms, a retired black Pullman porter who worked as a janitor at the *New York Herald Tribune.* When Al Laney of the *Tribune* asked him about Robinson, Odoms replied, "They got the right boy. . . . I see him plenty of times. He gonna make it. And when he do, . . . the stars ain't gonna fall. . . . Then after he make it, all the colored boys good enough gonna make it." But Odoms warned, "This boy Robinson got to take it. I hate to think what he got to take. He gonna take a good lickin', that what he gonna take. . . . The fans and the players, too. They'll give it to him to see if he can take it. And he got to take it. . . . . He got to take it for all the colored boys gonna come after him. If he do take it they won't have to."[30]

But Robinson still had to prove himself at Montreal and break through the wall of prejudice and tradition that surrounded white professional baseball. The next two years would be among the most difficult ones of his life.

3. The Return of the Major Leagues (1946)

Although World War II was rapidly receding, the changes left in its wake were becoming clear in 1946. The first session of the United Nations, the latest attempt to prevent future wars, opened in London in January, with Norway's Trygve Lie as the first Secretary-General. But the rift between the Allies was widening, and by March Winston Churchill was touring the United States and warning that an "iron curtain" had descended across Eastern Europe as Stalin attempted to isolate the liberated nations from the West and install Communist governments that would be puppets of the Soviet Union. In July, the United States conducted atomic bomb tests on Bikini Island in the Pacific, and with the Axis powers defeated it was becoming obvious that the next bombs would be aimed elsewhere, perhaps at the Soviet Union. Meanwhile, a full scale civil war broke out in China, Korea was "temporarily" divided into provisional governments in the North and South, the Nuremberg War Trials sentenced 12 Nazis to death by hanging, and war crime trials began in the Far East that would eventually result in the execution of over 700 Japanese.

At home, the Republicans won both houses of Congress for the first time in 18 years. Sixty-nine veterans were elected to the two houses, including John F. Kennedy, Richard M. Nixon, Lyndon B. Johnson, and Joseph McCarthy. Most wage and price controls were lifted, strikes hit the coal, steel, and railroad industries, two race riots occurred in the North, six blacks were lynched in the South, and Jackie Robinson played his first season in white professional baseball at Montreal.

After the hard times and sacrifices of the war years, the nation was looking for good times. While some preferred to stay home with "Jack Benny," "Bob Hope," "Fibber McGee and Molly," and other radio favorites, or with new books like Daphne Du Maurier's *The King's General* or Carson McCullers's *The Member of the Wedding*, others flocked to theaters, nightclubs, ballparks, race tracks, gymnasiums, arenas, and other entertainment sites. Broadway was packing them in with Eugene O'Neill's *The Iceman Cometh*, Cole Porter's *Around the World in 80 Days*, and Irving Berlin's *Annie Get Your Gun*, which contained three of the year's most

31

popular songs — "They Say It's Wonderful," "I Got the Sun in the Morning," and "Doin' What Comes Naturally." The movie theaters were still dominated by the grade B Hollywood productions of the war years, when people would go see almost anything as a diversion from work and the war, but a few quality films appeared, including the *The Best Years of Our Lives, The Postman Always Rings Twice,* and *The Razor's Edge.*

Spectator sports boomed in 1946 as athletes returned from the war and the government eased travel restrictions. On New Year's Day, over 93,000 fans jammed the Rose Bowl to see Alabama defeat Southern California 34–14 in the nation's premier bowl game. King Ranch's "Assault" joined the rare group of triple crown winners by winning the Kentucky Derby, Preakness Stakes, and Belmont Stakes. Jack Kramer captured the U.S. Lawn Tennis Association men's singles championship, George Robson won the Indianapolis 500, Ben Hogan won five major golf tournaments and pocketed $42,566, and Patty Berg took the USGA Women's Open. The Chicago Bears defeated the New York Giants 24–14 for the National Football League championship, while in the upstart rival league, the All-American Football Conference, the Cleveland Browns defeated the New York Yanks 14–9.

In the finals of college basketball's premier postseason playoffs, the National Invitational Tournament, Kentucky beat Rhode Island 46–45. In the less prestigious NCAA tournament, Oklahoma A & M took the title with a 43–40 win over North Carolina. Professional basketball, still struggling to establish a strong league and attract paying customers, formed a new 11-member National Basketball League. In professional boxing, aging heavyweight Joe Louis knocked out Billy Conn in the eighth round in the first heavyweight title fight ever televised. Since only about 6,000 sets were produced that year, as many people probably saw the fight in the arena as viewed it on New York's WNBT television station.

With the war over, organized baseball began the year in a confident mood. In February the major league teams abandoned the training camps of the North for the more familiar warm weather training sites in Florida and the Southwest. The camps were flooded with an overabundance of players, and there was so much talent around that the majors did not have to count on marginal wartime players or players with reputations as "troublemakers." When Giants' outfielder Danny Gardella, widely regarded as a clown and practical joker, got into a dispute with manager Mel Ott over his salary, the dining room dress code, and other club rules, no tears were shed by club officials when Gardella left the club in a huff and took his bat and glove to the Mexican League. "The time has passed when we have to worry about players like that," Ott told reporters.[1]

Although the returning servicemen dominated baseball in 1946, there were some rookies who were getting plenty of attention. One was Ralph

Kiner, who had played two years of minor league ball before going off to war as a navy pilot in the Pacific. In the spring of 1946 he was a hitting sensation, and the *Sporting News* was touting him as the number one rookie of 1946. Pirate manager Frankie Frisch was also high on his young prospect. "He's got it," he told reporters. "I've seen some pretty fair Buc outfielders during the seven years I've managed at Pittsburgh — such as Vince DiMaggio and the Waners. But Kiner looks like he's going to be the best we've had."[2] Kiner hit 23 home runs in 1946, the first of seven consecutive years in which he would capture or share the National League home run crown.

During spring training baseball owners and managers had to be concerned with far more than talent. According to the G.I. Bill of Rights, employers were required to give veterans their old jobs back for at least a year unless they were unqualified for the job or other unusual circumstances made it impossible to rehire them. Attempting to satisfy their moral and legal obligations, the team owners collectively decided that the returning war veterans would be provided 15 days' pay at or above their last salary level and would be given a trial period of 30 days during spring training or 15 days during the regular season. When the trial period had ended and the players' performance evaluated, they would either be kept on the major league roster, put on waivers, sent to the minors if no other club claimed them, or given their unconditional release.

While many veterans worked their way back onto the roster or into the starting lineup, others came home from the war too old or fat to regain their playing form or were simply beaten out by young rookies. Most of the veterans who did not survive the spring cuts went quietly, but others, such as first baseman Tony Lupien of the Philadelphia Phillies and outfielder Bruce Campbell of the Washington Senators, took their grievances into federal courts. Most of the legal disputes were settled out of court, with the players agreeing to accept minor league jobs if the parent major league club paid them the difference between their major and minor league salary for one year. In all, about 300 returning servicemen made the rosters of the 16 major league clubs in 1946, when each club was temporarily allowed to carry 5 more than the usual 25-man limit.

When the 1945 season was drawing to a close, Red Sox outfielder Catfish Metkovich said to his teammates, "Well, boys, better take a good look around you, because most of us won't be here next year."[3] As he predicted, the return of the veterans meant an end to the careers of most of the underage, overage, mediocre, and lame players who had taken the field during the war years. Some were quickly traded, sent down to the minors, or simply given their unconditional release. Tony Cuccinello, who had been edged out of the batting crown by Snuffy Stirnweiss in 1945, was released simply because the White Sox felt that at 38 he was too old. His 37-year-old teammate, LeRoy Schalk, who had led the team in RBIs in

1945, was also released. By opening day Pete Gray, Jimmie Foxx, Chuck Hostetler, and most of the other fill-ins were also missing from the rosters. In the 1946 season, only 32 of the 128 starting players (not counting pitchers) of 1945 were still in the starting lineup.

On April 16, President Harry Truman journeyed to Griffith Stadium to throw out the first ball of the new season. Players on both teams lined up in front of the president's box for the presidential pitch, and as the *Sporting News* reported, "The President reared back and let the ball fly. The first peacetime baseball in five years was on!"[4] The players scrambled for the ball, and Boston rookie Andy Gilbert finally came up with it. Some wags claimed of Truman that "it's the first time in months that he's found anybody in Washington to play ball with him."[5] The president seemed to enjoy himself. Sitting with his wife, daughter, and several top government officials, he chatted, joked, and downed soda pop and peanuts as he watched the Red Sox ruin the Senators' opener with a 6–3 victory. Ted Williams showed that the three-year layoff had not harmed his batting skills by hitting a 440-foot home run into the center field bleachers.

Opening day ceremonies were also held in other ballparks around the league, and in several of them, as in Washington, it was a day for veterans to shine—Bob Feller pitched a shutout, Hank Greenberg and Joe DiMaggio hit homers. The real players were back, and so was major league baseball. But there were signs of major coming changes. In Jersey City, New Jersey, 25,000 fans jammed Roosevelt Stadium to see Jackie Robinson take the field with the Montreal Royals. Playing second base, he made one error in six chances. After grounding out in his first time at bat, he reeled off four straight hits, including a home run, and stole four bases as the Royals drubbed the Jerseys 14–1. Six months after Rickey had startled the nation with the announcement of Robinson's signing, the great experiment in the desegregation of professional baseball had begun.

Other signs of coming change appeared even before the season began, when the major leagues were faced with two major threats to the club owners' monopolistic control over their talent. One came from the Mexican League, which tried to raid the talent of the major leagues. The other came from a Boston lawyer, Robert Murphy, who attempted to form a players' union.

Both were challenges to the "reserve clause," which had been developed by professional baseball club owners before the passage of the federal antitrust laws in the 1890s and the fair labor practice laws of the twentieth century. Radically different from other business contracts, the contracts signed by professional baseball players contained a reserve clause that severely limited their freedom to market their services. Once he signed his first contract, a player was owned by the club, could not be offered a contract by another club, and was bound not just for the duration of the contract but between contracts as well. He could not break the contract, but the club could. It could trade him to another team, send him back down to the minors, or simply release him with 10 days notice. If he could not come to terms with the club that owned his contract, then he would have to leave baseball and seek some other line of work. The reserve clause could doom a major-league caliber player to spend several years—perhaps his entire career—in the minors if the parent club had so many good players ahead of him that it did not need him, yet refused to trade him or allow him to sign with another club that would put him on its major league roster.

The owners claimed that the reserve clause was the only way to prevent inflated salaries, develop the club loyalties of players and fans, and keep a competitive balance among clubs by preventing the wealthier ones from buying up all the good players. But the players had not always seen it that way, and over the years had occasionally tried to fight back against the system by attempting to engage in collective bargaining. Player unions were formed in 1885, 1900, and 1912, and unsuccessful union efforts were also made in the 1920s and 1930s. But the owners survived these weak challenges to their monopolistic practices, just as they survived the threat of rival leagues like the Federal League, which folded in 1915 after a brief attempt to raid the two established leagues of their talent and form a third league.

The monopolistic practices of the owners were upheld by the Supreme Court in several landmark decisions, particularly a 1922 case arising out of the disputes between the majors and the Federal League. In the *Federal Baseball Club of Baltimore v. National League of Professional Baseball Clubs,* the Court ruled that baseball was a "game" and not a business. Hence it was exempt from the Sherman Act and other antitrust laws, which Congress had intended to apply only to business or commerce crossing state lines.[6] Handed down at a time when baseball was trying to recover from the Black Sox scandal, this decision protected the reserve clause and other special baseball laws and regulations and gave baseball a preferential treatment that was denied to other forms of entertainment, including other spectator sports. This special treatment would continue into the postwar period, when it began to come under attack from many sources.

The first challenge came when the Mexican League, led by its president, Jorge Pasquel, and his four brothers, conducted the first raid on major league talent since the days of the old Federal League. Rumored to control a family fortune of $60 million, the Pasquels came north in the winter of 1945–1946 and openly declared war on major league owners, dangling huge bonuses and long-term contracts before major league players. Most turned them down, but some put their names on the dotted line, packed their gear, and headed for Mexico. The chief victims of the Mexican raids were the New York Giants (eight players, including outfielder Danny Gardella and pitcher Sal Maglie), the St. Louis Cardinals (second baseman Lou Klein and pitchers Max Lanier and Freddie Martin), and the Brooklyn Dodgers (catcher Mickey Owen and outfielder Luis Olmo). Several other clubs lost a handful of players. Perhaps the biggest star among the "Mexican jumping beans," as the press called them, was St. Louis Browns' shortstop Vern Stephens.

But the major leagues' biggest names did not succumb to the tempting offers. Bob Feller, Ted Williams, Stan Musial, Terry Moore, Enos Slaughter, Hank Greenberg, Joe DiMaggio, Pete Reiser, and the Dodgers' most famous minor leaguer, Jackie Robinson, all turned down large contracts, some of them in the six-figure range, far more (in some cases 10 times more) than their owners were paying. Feller and Williams were reportedly offered $500,000, and Greenberg $360,000, for three years. Pasquel even treated Babe Ruth, still the biggest name in baseball, to a two-week vacation in Mexico, trying to recruit him to become the league president, but he did not take the job.

Faced with these attempts to steal their talent, the major league owners responded with indignation, condemnation, and an occasional offer to raise (slightly) the salaries of the players being courted. Commissioner Happy Chandler took a hard line, announcing in March that the players who were under major league contract and signed with the Pasquels would have until opening day, April 16, to return to their clubs. If they did not return by then, they would be suspended from playing major league ball for five years.

April 16 came, and only a few players, notably Vern Stephens, heeded Chandler's warning and returned to their old clubs. After playing just two games with Veracruz, Stephens was so fed up with the parks, the fans, the low caliber of play, and the cold postgame showers that he forfeited his $25,000 contract and returned to the St. Louis Browns, telling reporters, "I decided that while Mexico might be good for the song writers, it was not good for ball players like Vern Stephens."[7] But most of the other players were not intimidated by Chandler's ultimatum. Gardella, still angry at his manager, claimed "I'm just as happy as Ott and probably less confused." Pitcher Alex Carrasquel said, "I have no regrets—who would, leaving the White Sox?"[8]But some had second thoughts only to discover that they had waited too long. Mickey Owen returned to the States in August, asked Chandler for a reinstatement, and was turned down. In all, 18 players were affected by Chandler's ban.

In spite of all the brave talk, most major leaguers who headed south found out that the only good thing about playing in Mexico was the money. They soon tired of the high altitude, the food, the long bus rides between cities, the dirty hotels, the antiquated locker rooms, the rocky and poorly-lit playing fields, the rowdy fans (some of whom showed up at the games with firecrackers and even firearms), the broken contracts and broken promises, the low caliber of play, the feeling of being a foreigner in a Spanish-speaking culture, and the realization that playing on a Mexican club was even worse than being back in the minors. At Tampico, a railroad track went right through the outfield. Max Lanier later recalled, "They'd actually open the gates on both sides of the outfield to let the trains go through."[9] One American reporter who saw the train tracks at the field quipped that he expected one day to see a bulletin saying, "Game called end of 8th. Slow freight."[10]

The Mexican League raids worked to the detriment of all the parties concerned. Most of the jumpers regretted the decision yet found themselves blocked from playing ball in the States until Chandler lifted the ban in 1949. By then, many of them found that their places on their former club's roster had been taken by younger or better players. Some of the major league clubs were hurt, too, for they had lost the services of some of their starting players. Even the Pasquels suffered. They lost much of the advance money they had paid to the players who returned to the States, and so few stars jumped to the Mexican League that it was unable to attract enough fans — and pesos — to swell the Pasquels' bank accounts. After losing a small fortune in his baseball ventures, Jorge Pasquel abandoned baseball in 1948 to concentrate on more profitable business and political ventures. By 1955, the animosities generated by the raids had dissipated enough to allow the Mexican League to join the American minor league circuit as a Class AA league.

As the baseball establishment struggled to deal with the Mexican League challenge in 1946, it was also attempting to fight off the fourth serious attempt to unionize ballplayers since the late nineteenth century. This time the union bid was led by Robert Murphy, a 35-year-old Harvard graduate, Boston lawyer, and former examiner for the National Labor Relations Board. On April 16, opening day in the majors, he formed the American Baseball Guild. Among its demands were an end to the reserve clause, the establishment of a $7,500 minimum annual salary, pay for spring training, and the initiation of a policy giving players 50 percent of their purchase price when they were sold from one team to another. These proposals got a sympathetic ear from many players, and several chapters of his guild were formed.

The owners immediately lashed out against the guild. Clark Griffith, the owner of the Washington Senators, told *Newsweek*, "Such a move would destroy the reserve clause. It would wreck baseball; knock it flat on its face."[11] But Murphy continued his efforts. In June he tried to convince the Pittsburgh Pirates to strike on the grounds that the club owners were engaging in unfair labor practices. On the night of June 7, while the fans sat in the stands waiting for the game to begin, the players met in the clubhouse and engaged in a heated debate over the proposed strike. Just when it seemed that the game would be called off, pitcher Rip Sewell told his teammates, "I'm going out to the mound and I hope eight others follow me." The strike effort failed by three votes.[12]

The stinging defeat did not deter Murphy. He next went to Washington to present his case to the National Labor Relations Board. When the board dismissed it he went to the Pennsylvania Labor Relations Board, which ordered another election to be held among the Pirate players to decide if they wanted Murphy's guild to serve as their bargaining agent. By the time the election was held in a Pittsburgh hotel on the morning of August 21, the baseball owners had met and promised concessions to their players. Not surprisingly, the final vote was 15 to 3 against the guild, with the rest of the team abstaining. Clearly anti-union sentiment, Murphy's status as an outsider, and the concessions the owners had made in July hurt his cause. In the months after the August defeat, he continued his efforts to unionize the players, but in 1947 he quietly dropped his cause and went on to other interests. Bitter about the failure of his union, Murphy told reporters, "The players have been offered an apple, but they could have had an orchard."[13]

The Mexican raids and Murphy's union efforts helped to pressure the baseball owners into making some concessions to the players. In a series of meetings held in the summer, the club owners, commissioner, and league presidents agreed to give the players a greater voice in the operation of the game by allowing them to have two kinds of player representatives. The commissioner was authorized to appoint one player from each team to meet with his team owners to discuss grievances and problems concerning that team, and the players in each league would also choose a representative from the league to sit as non-voting members on the Executive Council, the ruling body of the major leagues.

Organized in 1921 to run baseball after the Black Sox scandal, the Executive Council was composed of the commissioner, the presidents of both leagues, one club owner from each league, and, beginning in 1946, one non-voting player representative from each league. The owners also agreed to provide a minimum salary of $5,000, to increase players' meal money, to give players $25 a week for expenses (beyond room, board, and travel) during spring training, to pay the salaries and medical expenses of players injured on the job, and to establish a pension system. A key goal of almost all the players, the pension system, set up in February of 1947, established a $50 to $100 monthly pension, depending on age and service, to players, coaches, and trainers 50 years old or older with at least five years of service. The pension was paid primarily from radio receipts from the World Series and All-Star games and from modest player contributions.

The first player representatives elected to represent the leagues were Dixie Walker of the Dodgers and Johnny Murphy of the Yankees. From then through the mid–1950s, the players made many requests on salaries, contracts, or conditions through their club or league representatives. Some of the minor requests were quickly granted, such as the placement of water coolers in the dugout or the installation of a green blanket on the outfield fence to give hitters a better background to hit against. Others, such as fewer night games and doubleheaders and modifications of the reserve clause, got a hearing but no real action. The owners had a company union and they intended to keep it that way.

If these problems were not bad enough, major league baseball also had to contend with a nationwide railroad strike, along with government restrictions on "non-essential" air travel, early in the new season. Before the strike ended on May 25, teams had to resort to special charter planes, buses, and taxis to get from city to city and to the ballparks inside the cities. The Cleveland Indians once rode a bus for over 16 hours to get from Cleveland to St. Louis. On another occasion Bobby Adams and Bob Usher of the Cincinnati Reds rode from Buffalo to Cincinnati in a baggage truck carrying the team's equipment and hand luggage.

The railroad strike helped to speed up decisions by some clubs to make more use of airlines to transport their players and equipment. One of the leaders in this was Larry MacPhail, who had joined with Dan Topping and Del Webb in January of 1945 to buy the New York Yankees from the Ruppert estate and Ed Barrow. MacPhail had already established a reputation in the minors and as general manager of the Reds and Dodgers as an innovative promoter and executive. The new Yankee president would be credited in his long career with instigating the first major league night game (1935), the first televised game, the first regularly scheduled radio broadcast of all home and road games, the first "old timer's game," and the first season ticket plan.

When he came to the Yankees, he added lights, established a stadium club for holders of season's box seat tickets, and built a ladies' lounge, a new clubhouse, and a new press box. In a May 1946 game with the Red Sox he gave away 500 boxes of nylon stockings and put on a pregame fashion show with young women walking on the field with the latest fashions. He shocked some conservative baseball people with his newspaper advertisements promoting ticket sales, such as an early season advertisement asking, "Can Washington's famous 'knuckleball' pitchers stop what experts call the sluggingest team in the league? Or will DiMaggio, Keller, and Co. make mincemeat of the Senator's pitching staff? Come out to the ball game and see."[14]

In 1941, while he was still with the Dodgers, MacPhail's team had made a few trips by plane, and now he was ready for a more ambitious air travel plan. He announced in May that his Yankees would fly some 13,000 miles in 1946 in their own C-54 plane. The first flight occurred on May 13.

The trip from New York to St. Louis took 4 hours and 35 minutes, as opposed to a normal 25 hours by rail.

Other clubs followed the Yankees example, and as they did several had some rather harrowing experiences. On May 15, in their maiden flight of the season, the Red Sox had a terrible trip from Chicago to St. Louis. Their C-14 took off during a heavy downpour, had a bumpy ride the entire way, then had to circle the St. Louis airport three times before the rear wheel would descend so the plane could land. When it finally touched down, Catfish Metkovich said, "I've flown plenty, but this is my finale. I'll tell you I was scared more than I've ever been in my life before. From now on, I'm a railroad man."[15] When the team left St. Louis for Detroit, several reporters and players took a train rather than going back by air. However, Metkovich got over his earlier fears and flew after all.

The ever-innovative MacPhail would also continue to press for more night baseball. In this game so rich with history and tradition, some players, owners, and baseball purists opposed night baseball. In 1940, nearly 10 years after night ball was introduced in the minor leagues and five years after MacPhail brought it to the majors at Cincinnati, the two leagues played only 70 night games. But during the war more and more clubs added lights and scheduled additional night games to accommodate wartime workers. At the end of the war, most owners finally realized that in the affluent postwar period the American public had more money than ever to spend on entertainment, but because of changes in the work force they would have to seek this entertainment at night, and if baseball wanted to compete with other amusements it had better offer its product when the public wanted it.

In May of 1946 MacPhail brought night baseball to Yankee Stadium, and other teams quickly followed suit. The Boston Braves added lights in 1946, the Red Sox in 1947, and the Detroit Tigers in 1948, leaving the stubborn Chicago Cubs as the only club without lights. From then on, the number of night games in both leagues would grow steadily.

In the spring of 1946 baseball boomed at all levels. The nation was prosperous, people wanted to enjoy themselves after the hardships and sacrifices of the depression and war years, and the big stars were back. Huge crowds turned out for the spring exhibition games, and in the first six days of the season, in spite of cool weather in some major league cities, over a million fans watched major league baseball. By the end of June, they had attracted close to 7 million, nearly twice the number for the comparable period the year before. By season's end the total figure was 18.5 million, a 71 percent increase over 1945. Baseball was also prospering at all minor league levels, where the number of leagues had jumped from 12 in 1945 to 42 in 1946. Baseball was not alone in the sports boom, for there was also a big surge in other warm weather sports—horse racing, golf, tennis, yachting, and fishing.

There were several sideshows in 1946—the Mexican League raids, Murphy's union, the integration experiment going on in Canada—but on the field it was a return to exciting, high quality baseball. In the American League race most experts predicted a battle between the Yankees and the Red Sox, one of the oldest and hottest rivalries in baseball, with the Yankees taking the flag and the Red Sox coming out second best, just as they had in 1938, 1939, 1941, and 1942. The Yankees were a good team made even better by the return of Bill Dickey, Phil Rizzuto, Charlie Keller, Joe Gordon, and most of all, Joe DiMaggio, who in the late thirties had assumed Ruth's mantle as the biggest star in baseball. But Joe Cronin's Red Sox, welcoming back 17 servicemen, were stronger, too. Ted Williams was back, ready to resume his hitting wars with the Yankee Clipper. Dom DiMaggio (the Yankee star's less famous brother), Johnny Pesky, Bobby Doerr, Cecil "Tex" Hughson, and Mickey Harris were also back in Boston uniforms.

It was never much of a race. Thanks to the powerful bats of Williams (.342), Pesky (.335), and DiMaggio (.316), and the strong arms of Boo Ferriss (25–6), Hughson (20–11), Harris (17–9), and Joe Dobson (13–7), the Sox took 41 of their first 51 games, 61 of 77 home games, and strung together two major winning streaks, one of 15 games and another of 12. After building a 10-game lead at the All-Star break, they coasted to the finish line, beating the Cleveland Indians 1–10 on September 13 to clinch their first flag in 28 years.

The Red Sox hitting star in 1946 was left fielder Ted Williams, who returned to baseball after spending three years in service flying bombing missions and serving as a flight instructor. Before he left for war he had managed a four-year batting average of .356, won the Triple Crown in 1942, and hit .406 in 1941, becoming the first player (and so far the last) to hit .400 since Bill Terry in 1930. He had also gained a reputation as a brash, cocky, immature player prone to temper tantrums and arguments with fans and the press. He was known for having the major's best pair of "rabbit ears"— ballplayers' lingo for players who listened to the taunts and catcalls of the fans and became upset at what they said. He was always candid and outspoken, and sometimes abrasive and tactless as well. He had a running battle with the press, and he was often booed by the "Fenway Faithful," to whom he often showed his contempt in actions and words. He refused to acknowledge the fans' cheers by tipping his cap, once saying, "Never, never will I tip my cap to those damned New England buzzards."[16] Over the years he showed his feelings in other ways, such as giving the fans the finger or spitting toward them or the press box.

The 1946 Williams was as confident as ever. Early in the season he told reporters, "I think I am the greatest hitter in the world. I may not be—but I think I am."[17] Williams was a great hitter, perhaps second only to Babe Ruth in his ability to hit for power and average. A left-handed pull-hitter who swung from an open stance, he was tall and thin (6 feet 3 inches, and 185 pounds), with long arms and legs, powerful wrists, exceptional eyesight, good reflexes, and excellent timing. He looked like a natural hitter who expended little effort, but in actuality he had been a diligent student of hitting since his early days on the sandlots of San Diego. He practiced his swing during batting practice, when he was standing in his position in left field, in his hotel room, and on the train. When he met great hitters such as Ruth, Cobb, Speaker, Hornsby and others, he grilled them for tips about hitting, and he was always studying the movements of opposing pitchers and hitters.

He seldom swung at a pitch even slightly out of the strike zone. The umpires respected his keen eyesight so much that they rarely charged him with a called third strike. Some fans and writers condemned him for refusing to swing at balls outside the strike zone, claiming that he too often settled for a walk when there were men on base that he could have driven in by hitting a ball that was just barely outside the strike zone. But he won the RBI crown four times in his career and was usually among the league leaders in the other years.

Williams was often criticized for lackadaisical fielding. He was a competent defensive player, but he never concentrated on fielding like he did his hitting, which he felt was his main job. "They'll never get me out of the game running into a wall after a fly ball," he said in 1946. "I'll make a damned good try, but you can bet your life I won't get killed. They don't pay off on fielding."[18]

In the first half of the 1946 season he stayed around the .400 mark much of the time, and at the All-Star Game he put on an incredible hitting exhibition. Before 35,000 fans in Fenway Park, he went four-for-four (two homers and two singles), walked once, and drove in five runs to lead the American League in a 12–0 rout of the National. His second homer came in the eighth with two outs and two men on base and Pittsburgh pitcher Rip Sewell on the mound. Sewell was known for his "blooper" or "eephus" pitch, a pitch thrown with such great backspin that it headed for the plate in a high arc and then slowly dropped down into the strike zone, upsetting the hitters' timing, causing them to swing far too soon and look foolish in the process. Sewell decided to try one on Williams, but Williams was waiting for it. He stepped forward, swung, and sent the ball rocketing into the right field bullpen, 400 feet away. As he circled the bases he could not hold back his laughter, and after the game he was still laughing as reporters gathered around his locker.

Cleveland manager Lou Boudreau decided that something had to be done to stop Williams and the Red Sox, who were running away from the rest of the American League. Five days after the All-Star game, Boudreau unveiled a new defensive strategy against Williams that came to be called the "Boudreau shift." The entire infield, the right fielder, and center fielder shifted to the right of second base, leaving only the left fielder to cover the entire left side of the diamond. When he first encountered the shift, a surprised Williams grounded out to the right side of the infield. In his next two at bats he walked. The Red Sox still won, 6–4, and Williams quipped after the game, "I'll have to turn around and hit 'em righthanded."[19]

Williams stubbornly refused to alter his stance and batting stroke to try to foul up the Boudreau shift, which was soon adopted by other American League clubs. A natural power and pull-hitter, he rarely tried to foul up the shift by bunting down the third base line or trying to punch the ball to the opposite field. He believed that swinging at balls outside the strike zone or trying to hit to the opposite field would upset his carefully nurtured batting stroke. His stubbornness may have cost him a few hits and a few points, and in fact he did go into a slump in August. But he still managed to hit .342, second only to the Senators' Mickey Vernon (.353), and he drilled 38 homers, scored 142, drove in 123, and drew a league-leading 156 bases on balls. Ironically, when the Red Sox clinched the pennant on September 13 by beating the Cleveland Indians 1–0, Williams provided the game-winning run by hitting an inside-the-park homer over the left fielder's head.

Detroit finished in second place, 12 games out, in spite of Hank Greenberg's league-leading 44 homers and 127 RBIs. The Yankees, suffering from injuries to DiMaggio (who finished the year with a subpar .290 average), mediocre performances by most of the other players, and the trauma of going through three managers (Joe McCarthy, Bill Dickey, and Johnny Neun), finished third, 17 games behind.

The league pitching stars were Hal Newhouser of the Detroit Tigers and Bob Feller of the Cleveland Indians. Newhouser fashioned a 26–9 record, tying Feller for the most wins and leading the league in ERA with 1.94. Feller also pitched the second no-hitter of his career and finished with 348 strikeouts, breaking the old record of 343 set by Rube Waddell back in 1904. Although he had lost four years to the war, most hitters felt that he had lost little, if anything, off his fastball, which was clocked at 98.6 miles per hour in one test performed in August by a special army machine.

The National League race was far more dramatic than the American League cakewalk. Most experts had predicted that the Cardinals, who had dominated the league during the war years, would make a mockery of the race. But it did not happen. Early in the year the pennant chase turned into a two-team race between the Cardinals and the other team built by Branch Rickey, the Brooklyn Dodgers. The defending champions, the Chicago Cubs, bowed out early because of injuries to several key players and the superior play of the two front runners.

The Dodgers were managed by Leo Durocher, who predicted early in the season that his team would be in the thick of the race and that "after this year, Brooklyn will win five of the next ten pennants."[20] The Dodgers were led by veteran outfielders Fred "Dixie" Walker (.319 and 116 RBIs) and Pete Reiser (.277), one of the best double-play combinations in either league in second baseman Eddie Stanky (.273) and shortstop Pee Wee Reese (.284), the offensive (.284) and defensive play of rookie center fielder Carl Furillo, and the pitching of veteran Kirby Higbe (17–8), rookie Joe Hatten (14–11), and sophomore Vic Lombardi (13–10).

The Cardinals had a new manager, Eddie Dyer, who took over when Billy Southworth departed to manage the Boston Braves. Stan Musial, Enos Slaughter, Howie Pollet, and other veteran Redbirds were home from the war, but the Cardinals were hit harder than any other team by defections to the Mexican League. Slaughter hit .300 and led the league in RBIs with 130, and third baseman Whitey Kurowski contributed a .301 average and 89 RBIs. Pollet led the league in wins (21) and ERA (2.10), while Harry Brecheen and Murry Dickson contributed 15 wins each.

But the leader of the club was Stan Musial. If Ted Williams was the best hitter in the American League and perhaps in all of baseball between 1946 and 1960, Musial was the best hitter in the National League in that same period. A native of Donora, Pennsylvania, a mill town about 25 miles east of Pittsburgh, Musial was a promising minor league pitcher and outfielder until a shoulder injury suffered near the end of the 1940 season left him with a dead pitching arm. Leaving the mound behind, he blossomed as an outfielder and hitter. In September of 1941 he was brought up to the Cardinals from Rochester in the International League to show what he could do. What the 20-year-old outfielder did was hit .426 in 12 games and guarantee that he would go to spring training with the Cardinals in 1942.

In 1942 Musial carved out a place in the starting lineup as a full-time outfielder, hitting .315, stroking 10 homers, and driving in 72 runs. In his first three seasons (1942–1944) the Cardinals won three pennants and two world championships. He spent 1945 in the navy, and in 1946 he rejoined a Cardinal club badly in need of his bat and glove. Besides hitting 16 homers and driving in 103 runs, he led the league in batting average (.365), doubles (50), triples (20), slugging percentage (.587), and runs (124).

This performance reestablished Musial as the premier hitter in the league and one of the best all-around players in the game. Early in his career admiring fans had dubbed him "Stan the Man," and the name stuck. At 6 feet, 175 pounds, he was a superb athlete, a good fielder and baserunner as well as a good hitter. In the first part of his career he was used primarily as a right fielder, but he also played center field, left field, and first base when needed. In the latter years of his career he would play primarily at first base and become one of the best glove men in the league at that spot.

But what he did best was hit, and he did it from a bizarre, corkscrew stance. A left-hander, he stood in a crouch, with his feet planted barely 12 inches apart, his knees slightly bent, the bat held high over his head and almost 25 inches from his body, and his right shoulder facing the mound, while he peered over his shoulder at the pitcher. White Sox pitcher Ted Lyons once said that Musial's stance reminded him of "a kid peeking around the corner to see if the cops were coming." In Musial's' rookie year, one reporter took one look at him and said, "With that crazy stance, he'll never last."[21] In spite of his unorthodox stance, his keen eyesight, quick reflexes, and powerful wrists made him an excellent hitter with the ability to hit the ball where it was pitched. He could hit to all fields, bunt, pull the ball for a homer, hit behind the runner, punch the ball through holes in the infield and outfield. He had great power, hitting 30 or more home runs six times in his career to go along with a high average.

Musial had few, if any, weaknesses at the plate. When managers were going over the opposing lineups with their pitchers, discussing the hitters' weaknesses, they usually simply skipped over Musial. Pitchers joked that they tried to get Musial out by giving him four wide ones and then trying to pick him off first base. Dodger ace Carl Erskine once quipped, "I've had pretty good success with Stan. By throwing him my best pitch and backing up third."[22]

Musial's personality was far different from that of the competitor he was so often compared to in the other league, Ted Williams. Friendly, cheerful, and easygoing, Musial was liked by teammates, opponents, umpires, fans, and the press. One of his teammates in the fifties, Ken Boyer, once said, "The man who doesn't like Stan Musial hasn't been born yet,"[23] and sportswriter Jimmy Cannon once described him as "the small boy's dream of what a ballplayer should be."[24] In 1963, when Musial closed out his career with two hits in his last two times at bat, Commissioner Ford Frick would call him "baseball's perfect warrior ... baseball's perfect knight."[25] This phrase would also be inscribed on a statue of Musial erected outside St. Louis' Busch Stadium.

Musial's Cardinals engaged in a see-saw battle with the Dodgers for the pennant. The Cardinals took over first place early in the season, but after several key Cardinal players defected to Mexico on May 23, the Dodgers captured the lead and held it for most of June, July, and August. On August 28 the Cardinals regained the top spot and stayed there until September 27, when the two teams deadlocked. When the 154-game season ended two days later, both contenders had a 96–58 record, setting the stage for the first pennant playoff in major league history.

Although the Cardinals had beaten the Dodgers in 14 out of 22 meetings during the regular season, many experts felt that the Redbirds were slumping and that the Dodgers would take the playoffs. The Dodgers won the coin toss by league President Ford Frick, and Durocher gambled, electing to play the first game in St. Louis so that the Dodgers could play the second and third (if necessary) in Ebbets Field. But his strategy failed. The Cardinals took the first game, 4–2, behind the pitching of Howie Pollet. They then held on to win the second, 8–4, when reliever Harry Brecheen struck out Stanky and pinch hitter Howie Schultz with the bases loaded in the ninth. The Cardinals had their fourth pennant in five years and a ticket to the World Series, while Dodger players and fans ended a disappointing season with the cry, "Wait until next year," a phrase first popularized by the *Brooklyn Eagle* after the heartbreaking loss to the Yankees in the 1941 Series. It would not be the last time the lament would be heard.

On October 6 the Red Sox and Cardinals met in Sportsman's Park for the opening game in the first real World Series since the war disrupted the national pastime. On the basis of their waltz to the American League flag, the Red Sox were widely favored over the Cardinals, who were riddled with injuries and had to win a playoff just to get into the classic. The Red Sox had a perfect record in five previous World Series, including the very first one in 1903 when they beat the Pirates. But they had not played in one since 1918, when they had a good-hitting young pitcher named Babe Ruth. The Cardinals had played in eight Series and won five of them.

It was a dramatic battle. The Red Sox won games one, three, and five, while the Cardinals took two, four, and six. After the sixth game, Boston pitcher Tex Hughson said, "It's our time to win the next one. . . . One game in this Series is a winning streak."[26] On October 15 they met in St. Louis for the deciding game. The hero for this game would be 30-year-old Enos "Country" Slaughter, a North Carolina native known for his hustle and fearless win-at-any-price style of play. He was still hurting from an injury he suffered in the fourth inning of the fifth game, when he had been hit on the elbow by pitcher Joe Dobson. He had stayed in the game, stolen a base, and gotten another hit, but the elbow swelled up and caused so much pain that he finally went to manager Eddie Dyer and, for the first time in his career, asked to be taken out of the game.

When X-rays revealed a blood clot, doctors advised Slaughter to hang up his spikes for the year or face the possibility of a career-ending arm problem. But Slaughter refused, telling Dyer that "it's my arm and I want to play even if the damn thing falls off."[27] His arm was treated with cold packs, and he took the field for game six. Although he could hardly lift his arm, he hit a single and drove in a run as the Cards took the game 4–1 to even up the Series at three games apiece.

The seventh game followed the see-saw pattern of the others. The Red Sox scored a run in the first, but the Cardinals tied it up in the second, then scored two in the fifth to take a 3–1 lead. The Sox then came back in the top of the eighth to knot the score at 3–3. This set the stage for the heroics of Slaughter, the Cardinal leadoff man in the bottom of the eighth against reliever Bob Klinger. Slaughter singled, and the home crowd began cheering for a rally. But when third baseman Whitey Kurowski popped out to the pitcher and catcher Del Rice flied out to Williams in left, it looked as if Slaughter might die on first.

The next hitter was left fielder Harry Walker, the brother of Brooklyn's famed Dixie. Dyer gave the run-and-hit signal, and as soon as Klinger went into his windup Slaughter took off for second. Walker hit a line drive over shortstop into left-center field for what looked like a long single that, at the most, would advance Slaughter to third.

But when center fielder Leon Culberson momentarily fumbled the ball, Slaughter rounded second and headed for third, where the coach, Mike Gonzalez, was signaling for him to hold up. Slaughter ignored his shouting coach, rounded third at full speed, and raced for home. Culberson fielded the ball and threw it to shortstop Johnny Pesky, who had run out on the outfield grass to take the cutoff throw. Pesky had seen Gonzalez give Slaughter the hold sign, and when he received the ball from Culberson he hesitated a moment—looking toward second, where Walker had wound up—before he realized that Slaughter had not stopped at third. He had to hurry his throw to home plate. The throw was off-line and catcher Roy Partee had to come 10 feet down the line to field it. Slaughter slid across the plate, giving the Cardinals a 4–3 lead.

In the top of the ninth, Brecheen gave up two singles but managed to hold on to the lead and give the Cardinals the game and the Series. Looking back over the incredible pennant race and World Series, Dyer said, "We never lost a game we had to win."[28] While St. Louis celebrated, the Red Sox began the agonizing, 25-hour train trip back to Boston.

Brecheen won three of the Cardinals' games, allowing only one earned run in 20 innings, and Walker hit .412 and drove in six runs. But the real standout was Slaughter. He hit .320, clubbed one home run, drove in two runs, and scored five. His mad dash for home could have turned him into the goat of the Series had it failed, but it was a gamble that paid off, immortalizing him in the pantheon of World Series heroes. The goat's horns were unfairly placed on the head of Pesky, who was destined to be remembered for the slight hesitation that allowed Slaughter to score. Forty years later, Pesky would say, "Even to this day, some people look at me like I'm a piece of shit."[29]

Ted Williams and Stan Musial had disappointing performances in the Series. The National League MVP hit just .222, scored three runs, and drove in four. Williams had five hits, all singles, and wound up with a .200 average, one RBI, two runs, and five strikeouts. Although Williams would play through 1960 and Musial through 1963, neither would ever get a chance to play in a World Series again. The Cardinals would not return to the Series until 1964; the Red Sox would not make it back until 1967.

Meanwhile, in faraway Montreal, another World Series also concluded in October. This was the Little World Series, the annual contest between the pennant winners in the International League and the American Association for the championship of the minor leagues. The hero of this series was Jackie Robinson, modern baseball's pioneer in the integration of the national pastime.

Just two weeks before he reported for spring training, Robinson married his college sweetheart, Rachel Isum, but this happy event in his life would be followed by several months of almost unbearable tension and conflict. His manager in Montreal was Clay Hopper, a Mississippi native who would have preferred that Branch Rickey try out his great experiment with some other manager in some other town. Robinson was tried out at first and second base and finally installed at second, where he would be a frequent target of sliding baserunners. Throughout the league, opposing players and fans taunted and cursed him, fans booed and shouted racial slurs, pitchers threw at his head, and runners tried to upend him on the base paths. In one game opposing players held up a black cat and yelled, "Hey Robinson. Here's one of your relatives." By August the physical and emotional pressure brought him close to a nervous breakdown, but he toughed it out, and he kept his promises to Rickey. One rival manager said, "We have tried everything against him. We have thrown at him, knocked him down, called him names, but we can't get a rise out of him."[30]

Robinson answered the insults, jeers, curses, and other indignities by leading the league in hitting (.349), driving in 66 runs, stealing 40 bases, tying for the lead in runs (131), and topping all second basemen in fielding. To the delight of team owners around the league, he also drew huge crowds everywhere he went, with over a million fans coming through the gates in Montreal alone. His inspired and inspiring play paced the Royals to the pennant with a huge 18½ game bulge over the runner-up, and in the Little World Series with the Louisville Colonels of the American Association, his bat, glove, and baserunning helped the Royals take the minor league championship four games to two.

In spite of his objections to being part of Rickey's grand plan to integrate the majors, Hopper had treated Robinson fairly. At the end of the year he went into Rickey's office to tell his boss that if Robinson could not make it with the Dodgers in 1947 he would be glad to have him back at Montreal. He also said, "Mr. Rickey, you don't have to worry about that boy. He's the greatest competitor I ever saw, and what's more, he's a gentleman."[31]

Robinson had passed all the tests. Now he had several months to think about what lay in store for him in the spring of 1947.

4. Ty Cobb in Technicolor (1947)

Before the new year was a month old, Josh Gibson, one of the greatest baseball players of all time, died. His call to the majors had never come. Branch Rickey and other major league executives thought that the talented catcher and powerful slugger was too old and had heard the rumors of the steady deterioration of his physical and emotional health. In January of 1943 doctors at Pittsburgh's St. Francis Hospital had diagnosed a brain tumor and recommended surgery. Gibson had refused, fearing it would leave him nothing more than a vegetable. Although he played through the 1946 season, he suffered from headaches, blackouts, alcoholism, mental instability, and several other ailments. To make matters worse, Jackie Robinson and Roy Campanella had gotten the call to join the Dodger organization, leaving him bitter and frustrated at being passed over.

Gibson died on January 20, not long after his 35th birthday, at his mother's home in Pittsburgh. He was buried in a grave provided by the county in Pittsburgh's Allegheny Cemetery. No plaque or gravestone was placed on his grave, just an oval metal marker bearing the plot number. His old friend and teammate, Ted Page, lamented, "People say Josh Gibson died of a brain hemorrhage. I say he died of a broken heart."[1] Less than three months later, Jackie Robinson took the field as the first baseman of the Brooklyn Dodgers.

Robinson went to spring training still unaware of whether he would spend the year with the Dodgers or with the Royals. To avoid the problems the Florida Jim Crow laws would inevitably bring, Branch Rickey switched the Dodger training camp from Florida to Cuba and scheduled several exhibition games in Panama. Robinson was listed on the Montreal roster, but Rickey booked 11 games between the Dodgers and the Royals so he would have a chance to prove himself in the tryouts. Instead of forcing Robinson on the team, Rickey was hoping that he would play so well that the Dodger players, recognizing a meal ticket when they saw one, would ask that he be added to the club. Robinson responded to the challenge by hitting .519 in exhibition games against major league teams.

But as spring train progressed, serious troubles surfaced when Dixie Walker, Bobby Bragan, and several other southern players circulated a petition saying that they would not play if Robinson were brought up to the club. Only a few players signed the petition, but several others agreed with it. Word of the petition reached Dodger officials after pitcher Kirby Higbe, with his tongue loosened by too many beers in a Panama bar, spilled the news to Harold Parrott, the Dodger road secretary. Parrott immediately called Rickey and Leo "the Lip" Durocher, the Dodger manager.

Durocher had already heard rumors of the petition, and when he received the news from Parrott he called a late night meeting of the entire Dodger ball club and proceeded to squelch the rebellion. Dressed in pajamas and a yellow bathrobe, "He looked," Parrott later recalled, "like a fighter about to enter the ring." Confronting the alleged ringleaders face-to-face and ranting and raving in his inimitable style, Durocher read them the riot act. "I don't care if the guy is yellow or black, or if he has stripes like a fuckin' zebra," he screamed. "I'm the manager of this team, and I say he plays. What's more, I say he can make us all rich. And if any of you can't use the money, I'll see that you're traded."[2] Rickey flew down the next day, called the dissidents in for one-on-one conferences, and gave them the same clear message.

Already doomed by its inability to recruit Pee Wee Reese, Pete Reiser, and several other players, the rebellion died without ever really getting off the ground. On April 10, Rickey released a statement announcing, "The Brooklyn Dodgers today purchased the contract of Jackie Roosevelt Robinson from the Montreal Royals. He will report immediately."[3]

Momentous as this announcement was, it had to share space in the sports pages with another astounding news item. Just one day earlier, Commissioner Happy Chandler had suspended Durocher for the entire season. Such drastic action did not come as a surprise to some baseball insiders, for Durocher was one of the most colorful and controversial personalities in major league baseball, and in the past couple of years he had been even more colorful and controversial than usual.

Durocher had starred as a shortstop for the Yankees, Reds, and Cardinals, but he was best known as a member of the scrappy "Gas House Gang" that had led the Cardinals to the 1934 pennant and a World Series victory over the Detroit Tigers. After playing five years for the Cardinals, the fiery shortstop was traded to the Dodgers in 1938, where he became the captain and player-manager. He led the Dodgers to the pennant in 1941 and to second-place finishes in 1942 and 1946.

Durocher was a crafty manager skilled at winning individual ball games but inclined to fall short in the difficult strategy of planning for an entire season. He played hunches, took gambles, and did the unpredictable, often calling for bunts, squeeze plays, and base thefts when they were least expected. The Lip also had a reputation as a mouthy, scrappy, quarrelsome player and manager and as an expert in bench-jockeying and other psychological tactics aimed at unnerving opponents. He was famous for his verbal and physical fights with players and fans and for frequent battles with umpires. Few players or managers were ejected or fined as often as Durocher for arguing—often profanely—with the men in blue.

Durocher never tried to court the image of being a nice guy. In 1946, after announcer Red Barber had told him that he ought to be a nice guy once in a while, Durocher snapped, "Who wants to be a nice guy? Look over there at the Giant bench. Where would you find a nicer guy than Mel Ott? And where is he? In eighth place."[4] This remark was quickly turned into "nice guys finish last" and regarded as Durocher's credo, along with the Machiavellian corollary, "It doesn't matter how you win, just so you win." Durocher liked to jest that "I'd trip my mother. I'll help her up, brush her off, tell her I'm sorry. But mother don't make it to third."[5] When Durocher later wrote his autobiography with Ed Linn, it was appropriately titled, *Nice Guys Finish Last.*

Away from the park, Durocher was a wealthy man who enjoyed the good life. He had a luxurious terrace apartment on New York's East 64th Street, which he shared with his third wife, young movie star Laraine Day, whom he had married in January of 1947 after she obtained a Mexican divorce that had received frequent front-page newspaper coverage. He was often seen in the company of movie stars, gamblers, and other high livers, a lifestyle supported by his annual salary of $60,000, the highest of any manager in the majors. Along with his fondness for fashionable clothes, people, and parties, he had a love of the race track, racy sports cars, golf and billiards. Now in 1947, he would have plenty of time to pursue all these interests, for on April 9 Chandler suspended him from baseball for the entire 1947 season.

Chandler's suspension of Durocher just six days before the beginning of the season was the result of a complicated public and private feud involving Durocher and top officials of the Dodgers and Yankees. During the offseason, Chandler had talked with Durocher and warned him about his behavior on and off the field, especially about his alleged association with big-time gamblers. Meanwhile, over the winter Yankee owner Larry MacPhail had raided the Dodgers' coaching staff to hire Chuck Dressen and John Corriden, both of whom had worked for MacPhail when he ran the Dodgers before Rickey took over. In March, during an exhibition game in Havana between the Dodgers and Yankees, both Rickey and Durocher claimed that MacPhail had entertained gamblers in his box at the ballpark. Durocher protested to reporters, "If I even said hello to those guys, I'd be called up before Chandler and probably barred." Rickey agreed, contending that "apparently there are rules for Durocher and other rules for the rest of baseball."[6] MacPhail vehemently denied any association with gamblers in Havana or anywhere else and filed complaints against Rickey and Durocher with the commissioner's office. Harold Parrott was involved, too, for it was no secret that the ex-sportswriter was the ghost for Durocher's column in the *Brooklyn Eagle,* "Durocher Says," which frequently questioned the character and actions of the Yankee executives.

Chandler examined the tangled mess, studying the charges and countercharges and interviewing the major participants. On April 9, he announced his decision from his Cincinnati office. It was a bombshell. Condemning the actions of all the involved parties "as detrimental to baseball," he fined the Yankee and Dodger organizations $2,000 each, fined Parrott $500, and suspended Dressen for 30 days. But the most severe punishment was meted out to the Dodger manager. "Durocher has not measured up to the standards expected or required of managers of our baseball teams," Chandler said. "As a result of the accumulation of unpleasant incidents . . . Durocher is hereby suspended from participating in professional baseball for the 1947 season." It was, the *New York Times* said, "the most drastic action ever taken against a major league baseball pilot," ranking in severity behind only the lifetime suspensions of the members of the 1919 White Sox team involved in the World Series scandals and Chandler's own five-year suspension of the Mexican jumpers.[7]

Although Chandler's suspension statement did not provide the details of the "accumulation of unpleasant incidents detrimental to baseball" Durocher was guilty of, it was widely believed they included his frequent outbursts on the field, his association with gamblers and other unsavory characters, his highly publicized fight with a fan under the stands at Ebbets Field in 1945, and the publicity surrounding his courtship and marriage of Laraine Day. Coming after these events, Durocher's instigation of a public feud about the gamblers in MacPhail's box at the game in Havana seemed to be the last straw.

Dodger scout Clyde Sukeforth temporarily filled in for Durocher, but three days into the season Rickey replaced him with Burt Shotton, another Dodger scout and longtime friend. Shotton had played for the St. Louis Browns, managed the Philadelphia Phillies, and served as Rickey's Sunday manager when Rickey was managing the Browns and Cardinals and would not take the field on the Sabbath. Shotton was an old-fashioned pilot who, like Connie Mack of the Athletics, wore street clothes instead of a uniform on the field, directed the team from the bench rather than from the third base coach's box, and rarely emerged from the dugout.

The events surrounding Robinson and Durocher in 1947 kept the Dodgers in the sports headlines for most of the season. On April 15, baseball history was made in Ebbets Field when Jackie Robinson took the field in the opening day game against the Boston Braves. Since Dodger officials thought his arm was too weak for third base and Eddie Stanky and Pee Wee Reese were firmly anchored at second and short, the 28-year-old rookie was installed at first base, a position he had rarely played and was rapidly trying to learn. It was a cold, cloudy day, and only 26,623 fans came through the turnstiles to watch the first black man to play in the majors in close to 60 years. Although Robinson went 0-for-3 at the plate, he reached base on a throwing error and scored one run as the Dodgers won 5–3. At the end of the game, he told a reporter, "Give me five years of this and that will be enough. If I can make enough money to build my own little place and give my boy a good education, everything will be all right. I realize I have a great opportunity, and I believe I can make it."[8]

In the second game with the Braves, Robinson got his first major league hit, a bunt single off of Glenn Elliott. The Dodgers next played against the New York Giants at the Polo Grounds, and in his third major league game, Robinson drilled his first major league home run off Dave Koslo. The next afternoon, 52,000 fans came to the Polo Grounds to watch him go 3-for-4 in a losing effort against the Giants. Facing the enormous double pressure of having to prove that as a rookie and as a black man he could play major league ball, Robinson seemed to be passing the test.

Robinson had the most difficult rookie season of any player in the history of the game. The obstacles seemed almost insurmountable. Most of the team owners did not want him in major league ball; in fact, Rickey and Chandler would later claim that in a secret meeting in 1946, the owners of the other clubs had voted unanimously to oppose the integration of white professional baseball. Their claim has been the subject of much controversy, but most owners made no secret of their opposition to Rickey's experiment. It was also clear that many opposing players, fans, and even some of Robinson's own teammates, did not want him in the big leagues. To make matters worse, Rickey paid him the minimum rookie salary of $5,000, and prohibited him from endorsing commercial products, though this rule was relaxed later in the year. Rickey also forbade him to argue with umpires or other players, answer racial slurs, appear at dinners and other special occasions held in his honor by the black community, or go nightclubbing. The latter was no problem for Robinson, a devoted husband and father who told reporters late in the season, "You know, colored people do not really like music or dancing better than white people . . . White people just think they do."[9]

Robinson encountered racial slurs and discrimination in hotels and restaurants in cities all around the league. On his first visit to Philadelphia he was refused a room at the Benjamin Franklin Hotel where the Dodgers usually booked rooms when they were in town. Though angered, Robinson did not press the issue and stayed elsewhere. From then on, when the Dodgers came to Philadelphia the whole team stayed at the Warwick, which would accommodate him. In St. Louis the Chase Hotel would not accept Robinson, so he stayed at the Adams Hotel, a black hotel that had no air conditioning to help guests endure the sultry summer nights. In

Cincinnati, Robinson was allowed to stay in the Netherlands-Plaza Hotel with the rest of the team, but he had to eat his meals in his room. The hotel manager thought it would upset the rest of the guests if they saw a Negro doing anything in the dining room besides serving guests or cleaning tables.

But it was on the field that Robinson faced the greatest indignities. It was hard enough to have to learn to play a new position and hit major league pitching, but on top of that he had to endure obscene racial slurs and taunts from the stands, bench-jockeying from opposing dugouts that went far beneath even the normally low standards of major league ball, bean balls, and "accidental" spikings. Robinson received abuse from all around the league, but the worst came from the Philadelphia Phillies and the St. Louis Cardinals.

In April, when the Phillies made their first trip to Brooklyn for a three-game series, manager Ben Chapman ordered his players to bombard Robinson with the worst they had to offer: "Hey, coon, do you always smell so bad?" "Hey, nigger, why don't you go back to the cotton field where you belong." "They're waiting for you in the jungles, black boy!" "Hey, snowflake, which one of those white boys' wives are you shacking up with tonight?" "We don't want you here, nigger," and practically every other racial slur that had circulated in the nation since the days of slavery.[10]

This continued for three days, and Robinson would later write that this vicious harassment "brought me nearer to cracking up than I ever had been." As the heckling continued, he later recalled, "I thought what a glorious, cleansing thing it would be to let go. . . . I could throw down my bat, stride over to that Phillies dugout, grab one of those white sons of bitches and smash his teeth in with my despised black fist. Then I could walk away from it all." But he quickly recovered control of himself and remembered his promise to his boss. "Mr. Rickey had come to a crossroads and made a lonely decision," he later wrote. "I was at a crossroads. I would make mine. I would stay."[11]

The abuse that Robinson suffered in the first Philadelphia series helped rally Robinson's teammates behind him. Dixie Walker, a friend of Chapman's and one of the leaders in the petition against Robinson just weeks before, warned his fellow Alabaman to stop the abuse. By the third game, Eddie Stanky, another Alabaman, was shouting at the Phillies, "Listen you yellow-bellied cowards, why don't you yell at somebody who can answer back?"[12]

Chapman claimed that he and his ballplayers were only subjecting Robinson to the same time-honored treatment accorded all rookies, but the Phillies had received so much negative publicity that Commissioner Chandler and Carpenter finally ordered Chapman to tone down the needling and to make peace with Robinson. Dodger and Philly officials arranged for Robinson and Chapman to come together and strike a friendly pose for the photographers. Robinson agreed out of deference to Rickey, and Chapman complied because his job was on the line. When the two posed for the photograph, an incredulous Dixie Walker said to Harold Parrott, "I swear, I never thought I'd see ol' Ben eat shit like that."[13]

The bench-jockeying continued, and although the verbal abuse was moderated the Phillies' dugout came up with something even more vicious than words. Pointing their bats at Robinson, they swung them in an arc and made "rat-a-tat" noises, as if they were brandishing machine guns, an obvious reference to the newspaper revelations that Robinson and his family had received death threats. Between 1947 and 1953, Robinson would receive 10 death threats, some promising to kill him on the field. After one of these in Cincinnati in 1952, the Dodgers provided him with armed body guards until they left town.

More problems for the young rookie surfaced in a column appearing in the *New York Herald Tribune* on May 9. Written by sports editor Stanley Woodward, the story claimed that several of the Cardinal players had planned a strike to protest Robinson's presence in the lineup when the Cardinals arrived in Brooklyn for a series beginning on May 6. According to Woodward, the players hoped that the strike would spread to other clubs and produce a general strike throughout the National League, eventually forcing Rickey to abandon his attempt to integrate major league baseball. Woodward claimed that Cardinals' owner Sam Breadon and National League President Ford Frick heard about the strike and confronted the St. Louis players. As Woodward reported it, Frick gave them a ringing speech, telling them, "If you do this you will be suspended from the league. . . . The National League will go down the line with Robinson whatever the consequence. You will find that if you go through with your intention that you have been guilty of madness."[14]

The Cardinal officials and players all denied Woodward's story, and it has been the subject of controversy ever since. While many baseball historians have accepted his version of the events, many others have believed that he had little or no hard evidence and that if he had any he greatly exaggerated much of what he had. There apparently was talk among some of the Cardinals of not wanting to play against Robinson, rumors of a strike did circulate, Frick and Breadon did discuss the rumors, and Frick did instruct Breadon to tell the Cardinal players that the National League office would stand behind Robinson and suspend any player who refused to take the field against him. But apparently Frick never talked to the Cardinal players directly, the strike had few supporters, and if there were any plans for a strike they were ended by Breadon's relay of Frick's warning. By the time Woodward's story appeared, the Dodger-Cardinal series was over and no signs of a strike had materialized.

During these early season tribulations, Robinson's play suffered. At the time of the alleged Cardinal strike, his batting average was a puny .250, thanks to a long slump which at one point saw him go 0-for-20 at the plate. But he gradually regained his concentration. In the middle of June he went on a 21-consecutive-game hitting streak that raised his average to well above .300, grabbed the league lead in stolen bases, and led the Dodgers into first place. Not only had he broken baseball's color line, he was becoming the spark plug of the team.

As the season progressed, Robinson was joined in the majors by four other black players. The first, and the one who received the most attention, was Larry Doby, an infielder with the Newark Eagles of the Negro National League when he was signed by Cleveland Indians' owner Bill Veeck on July 5. The 22-year-old Doby would experience many of the same problems Robinson was facing. Veeck would later say that after he signed Doby he received around 20,000 letters, "most of them in violent and sometimes obscene protest."[15] Doby received threats on his life, was shunned by many of his teammates, and was the target of racial epithets from fans and opposing players, with the bench jockeys yelling such things as, "You're not supposed to be in this league. You're supposed to be in that bush league with that other nigger."[16]

Doby was not able to crack the regular lineup in 1947. He appeared in just 29 games, mostly as a pinch hitter, and managed only a .156 average. A utility infielder when he broke in with Cleveland, he would break into the starting lineup in 1948 and spend most of his outstanding 13-year career in the outfield for the Indians and White Sox.

The other black players to make it to the majors in Robinson's rookie year were infielder Hank Thompson and outfielder Willard Brown of the Browns and pitcher Dan Bankhead of the Dodgers. None of the three aroused as much attention as Robinson or Doby or stayed long in the majors. Thompson and Brown were released after about a month, and although Bankhead became the first National League hurler to hit a home run in his first at bat in the major leagues, he pitched poorly. The Dodgers sent him back to the minors at the end of the season and did not recall him until 1950.

The appearance of four other black players did not shift the spotlight off of Robinson. As the season entered the hot summer months he was exhibiting more and more of the skills and intense competitiveness that would make him one of the most feared players in the game over the next decade. Robinson, Durocher once said, "didn't just come to play, he came to beat you. He came to stuff the goddamn bat right up your ass."[17] At 5 feet 11 inches and 195 pounds, he was powerfully built, but he was not a power hitter, although he could—and did—hit home runs. He was a contact hitter, a line-drive hitter, a great clutch hitter, and one of the best two-strike hitters ever to play the game. He was a skillful bunter, whether trying to advance the runner or to scratch out a bunt single when the infield was playing too far back. Absolutely fearless at the plate, he dug in, and if brushed back or knocked down he got back up determined to hit the next pitch, and often did.

When he got on base, he, not the hitter, became the center of attention. With his distinctive pigeon-toed run, he was a demon on the base paths — fast, hard to throw out, difficult to pick off, maddeningly elusive in a rundown situation. With his long leads, fake breaks, and taunts of the pitcher, he was a thorn in the side of the defense, a constant distraction who could cause the pitcher to throw the ball away trying to pick him off base or lose his concentration and serve the hitter a fat fastball or hanging curve. He was unpredictable, even reckless, on the bases, stretching singles into doubles and doubles into triples, tagging up and advancing to the next base on short flies to the outfield, stealing when the "book" said that you should not, and perfecting that most dramatic of all baserunning moves, the steal of home. In the age of the long ball, Robinson brought the art of baserunning and base-stealing back into the game. Long before his premier season was over, he was being called an "Ebony Ty Cobb."

Robinson quickly became the best gate draw in baseball since Babe Ruth. In every National League park, black and white fans alike jammed the stands, coming at first out of curiosity but returning because he was so exciting to watch. Black fans filled trains and chartered buses to travel to see their idol play, especially when the Dodgers were in Cincinnati and St. Louis, the league's southernmost cities. His play was eagerly followed in the newspapers, on radio, in newsreels, and eventually on that new media marvel, television. A popular record by the Buddy Johnson Orchestra with Ella Johnson on vocal, "Did you Ever See Jackie Robinson Hit That Ball," appeared in 1947, to be followed in 1950 by a movie, *The Jackie Robinson Story,* with Robinson playing the lead role. Wherever he appeared in public, he attracted stares, whispers, well-wishers, and autograph-seekers. During his first month with the team he received over 5,000 invitations to appear at various functions, and he received so much mail that the club had to hire a secretary to handle it.

Robinson was emerging as the hero of the nation's black minority, becoming even better known and loved than the aging Joe Louis. He became the universal favorite player of black fans, and the Dodgers their favorite team. Even blacks who did not normally follow baseball began to listen to the Dodger games on radio. One elderly black woman who caught Red Barber's broadcasts of Dodger games was indignant when she heard that Robinson had stolen a base. "I knew they would accuse that boy of something wrong, of stealing, just 'cause he's colored," she said. "But I know Jackie's a fine boy and wouldn't steal anything."[18]

It was not just blacks who followed Robinson's play and idolized him. Many whites, including the Southerners who caught the games on Barber's broadcasts, came to admire him for his baseball skills, his courage, and his tremendous poise and self-control under terrible pressure. This was difficult for many whites, especially those who had learned racial prejudice at their mother's knee, and Robinson's appearance and demeanor made it even harder for them. He was not light-skinned like Joe Louis and some other black athletes and entertainers who had found acceptance in the white world, nor was he an obsequious Uncle Tom. While he kept his anger under control in 1947, it was obvious to all who saw him that he was a proud, aggressive, and confident black athlete.

As the 1947 season unfolded, dramatic changes occurred in the attitudes of the other Dodger players toward Robinson. Spring training began with a petition against Robinson and with demands to be traded if he were added to the team. But Pee Wee Reese, Ralph Branca, and several other players befriended him from the very beginning, and as the Phillies and other teams unmercifuly berated the player who could not fight back, some Dodgers began to come to his defense while others came to tolerate him because he was helping the team win the pennant, which could put extra money in their pockets in October. By the middle of the summer, Robinson had few closes friends on the team, but he had been accepted by most of his teammates and the novelty of playing with a black man had worn off.

Led by their rookie first baseman, the Dodgers pulled away from the Cardinals, mounting a 13-game winning streak in the latter part of July to increase their lead to 10 games. But the Cardinals, refusing to fold, rallied and cut the lead to five before the Dodgers came to town in mid–September for a three-game series. Robinson hit .461 as the Dodgers took two of the three games to halt the Cardinals' drive.

As the series in St. Louis concluded, the *Sporting News* chose Robinson as the first recipient of its new Rookie of the Year Award. In announcing the honor, which in its first two years would be awarded to only one player but would be expanded in 1949 to one from each league, the newspaper that had initially opposed Robinson's signing wrote that the choice was not influenced by race, the obstacles he had to overcome, or his role as a trailblazer or as part of a "sociological experiment." Instead, "He was rated and examined solely as a freshman player in the big leagues — on the basis of his hitting, his running, his defensive play, his team value." Based on these criteria, the paper said, "Robinson had it all, and compared to the many other fine first-year men that 1947 produced, he was spectacularly successful."[19]

The Dodgers clinched the pennant on September 22, and the next day, "Jackie Robinson Day" was held at Ebbets Field. During the ceremonies, Robinson's mother, Mallie, stood proudly near home plate while her famous son was being honored. Gifts had come in from Robinson's admirers from all across the country, including a Cadillac, a television, and a gold watch.

The keys to the new car were presented by another famous Robinson, Bill "Bojangles" Robinson, the popular dancer, who told the crowd, "I'm sixty-nine years old and I never thought I would live to see the day when I would stand face to face with Ty Cobb in Technicolor."[20]

Robinson finished the season with impressive statistics for any rookie, especially one who played under such tremendous pressure. Appearing in 151 games, all at first base, he hit .297 and stroked 12 home runs, 31 doubles, and 5 triples. Batting in the second spot for most of the year, he struck out only 36 times, drew 74 walks, scored 125 runs (second highest in the league), knocked in 48 runs, and led the league in stolen bases with 29.

Long before the season ended, he had been accepted as a baseball player, as Rickey had planned. Black players had long insisted that all they wanted from major league baseball was the chance to show that they could play. Rickey gave Robinson the chance, and his success opened the door for hundreds of others. Willie Mays would later say, "Every time I look at my pocketbook I see Jackie Robinson."[21]

The Dodgers had avenged the 1946 playoff loss to the Cardinals by bouncing back to capture the flag by five games. While Robinson was the spark plug of the club, Pete Reiser and Dixie Walker hit over .300, sophomore outfielder Carl Furillo hit .295, and shortstop Pee Wee Reese and second baseman Eddie Stanky continued to star at bat and in the middle of the infield. The pitching staff also came through, with young Ralph Branca leading the way with a 21–12 record. Joe Hatten won 17 games and Vic Lombardi 12, and veteran reliever Hugh Casey won 10.

A sad note in the midst of the Dodger successes were the injuries sustained by popular outfielder Pete Reiser, nicknamed "Pistol" because of his love of western movies. Once characterized by Rickey as "the greatest natural talent I have ever seen,"[22] Reiser came up to the majors with the Dodgers in 1940. In 1941, his first full season, he won the league batting crown with a .343 average and was touted as a sure Hall of Famer. He was a talented fielder and left-handed hitter, and a very intense player—too intense. Relentless pursuit of ground and fly balls on defense and of extra base hits and stolen bases (he stole home a record seven times in 1946) on offense brought him two broken ankles, a broken right arm, a dislocated shoulder, two beanings, torn cartilage in his left knee, torn muscles in his left leg, and several concussions. He crashed into outfield walls (they were unpadded back then) several times while chasing long fly balls. A collision with a cement outfield wall in 1942 left him with a fractured skull and a severe concussion. In 1947 another encounter with a wall in Ebbets Field sent him to the hospital with paralyzed legs. Remarkably, he recovered, returned to the team, and helped lead them to the pennant, then broke his ankle in the World Series.

Reiser was never the same after the 1947 season. His long list of injuries had turned him into a shadow of the player he had once been. In 1948 he appeared in only 64 games with the Dodgers, mostly as a pinch hitter, and he was traded to the Braves at the end of the season. "I was only twenty-nine when traded," he later said, "but the fun and pure joy of it were gone."[23] From Boston, he went to Pittsburgh and then to Cleveland, where he finished his career in 1952. His reckless, even foolish, style of play had ruined a promising career. His teammate, Cookie Lavagetto, said, "Pete had one failing—he never knew where the hell the walls were."[24]

A good year at the plate by Musial (.312) and Kurowski (.310) could not prevent the Cardinals from finishing in second place. Billy Southworth's Braves finished third, eight games out, behind the great pitching of Warren Spahn and Johnny Sain, both of whom had 21 wins. Third baseman Bob Elliott won the MVP Award, hitting .317 with 22 homers 113 RBIs. With Johnny Mize leading the way with 51, the fourth-place Giants set a record of 221 home runs. Although the Giants had the league's big bats, their pitching faltered in the second half of the season.

The National League batting champion was Harry Walker (.363), who had been traded from the Cardinals to the Phillies early in the season. The Phillies tied the Pirates for last place. Attempting to draw in the fans and improve their record, the Pirates had acquired aging Hank Greenberg from the Tigers, paid him $80,000, and shortened Forbes Field's left field fence from 360 to 330 feet by constructing an enclosed bullpen which was quickly dubbed "Greenberg's Gardens." But the old slugger's best years were behind him. He hit only 25 homers, 19 below his 1946 production, and his batting average tailed off to .249. He retired at the end of the season, and soon joined Bill Veeck in the front office at Cleveland. Kiner, in just his second season, hit 51 homers, but still had to share the home run crown with Johnny Mize. After Greenberg left, his gardens became "Kiner's Korner."

The American League race lacked the drama or the controversy of the National League one. The Red Sox added lights at Fenway Park and hoped to repeat as pennant winners, but arm troubles on the pitching staff contributed to a disappointing season that saw the Sox drop to third place, 14 games behind the front-running Yankees and 2 behind the second-place Tigers. Ted Williams, who had won the Triple Crown in 1942, became the first American Leaguer to win the award twice, taking it with a .343 average, 32 homers, and 114 RBIs. In spite of obviously superior offensive numbers, he lost the MVP award to his New York rival, Joe DiMaggio, because one vindictive Boston writer refused to put Williams's name anywhere in the top 10 on his ballot.

Under new manager Bucky Harris, the Yankees ran away with the flag, taking over first place on June 19 and fattening their lead with a 19-game winning streak, tying a league record set by Chicago in 1906. As usual, Joe

DiMaggio spearheaded his team's pennant drive with clutch defensive play and a .315 average, 20 home runs, and 97 RBIs, while Allie Reynolds, acquired in a trade that sent Joe Gordon to the Indians, led all Yankee pitchers with 19 wins. One of the bright spots for the Yankees in 1947 was the play of rookie catcher Yogi Berra, who in 87 games hit .280 with 11 homers and 54 RBIs, while trying to learn the art of catching from his very patient instructor, Bill Dickey.

The worst team in 1947 — worse even than the Senators or Pirates — was the St. Louis Browns, who won only 59 games and finished 38 games off the pace. As the Browns struggled on the field, their famous radio announcer, former Cardinal pitching star Jay Hanna "Dizzy" Dean, filled the air time with his cornpone humor, fractured English, and frequent criticisms of the players on the field, especially the pitchers, saying such things as "I swear, I could beat nine out of ten of the guys that calls themselves pitchers nowadays," or "Gosh, folks, I haven't pitched baseball since 1941, but I feel sure I could go out there today and do better than a lot of those throwers who are drawing big salaries as major league pitchers." After several fans called or wrote the Browns asking that they "let Diz make good his boast,"[25] the Browns decided to put him in uniform. What could they lose? Attendance during the year had dropped as low as 315 on one occasion, and Dean would probably draw a large crowd.

So on September 17, they signed him to a contract for $1 for the rest of the year. He worked out briefly with the team, and on September 28, the last day of the season, took the mound against the White Sox before a crowd of 15,916. He proved to be more than a windbag, pitching four shutout innings, facing 14 men, and allowing three hits and a walk. In his one plate appearance he hit a single, but he pulled a leg muscle when he slid (or as he would say, "slud,") into second and had to be taken out of the game. At the end of the game, he bragged that he could still pitch in the majors "but I don't intend to try it. I have a contract as a radio announcer and I'm going to stick to that job."[26]

The drama of the 1947 season was reflected in the attendance figures, which rose to nearly 20 million. Riding the crest of the postwar sports boom, the minor leagues jumped to 52 leagues and 388 clubs, with attendance rising by nearly 8 million to an all-time high of 40.6 million. All in all, with minor and major league attendance combined standing at 60.6 million, it had been a great year for organized baseball. And the World Series was yet to come.

As the Series approached, both the Dodgers and the Yankees were swamped with more ticket orders than they could fill, but some disappointed ticket-seekers could console themselves with the knowledge that they could still catch the game on television, if they could gain access to that

new invention. In 1947, for the first time in history, the Series would be on
television, carried by NBC, which paid $65,000 for the rights to televise all
seven games. The televised games were sponsored by Gillette and the Ford
Motor Company.

Television was still in its infancy, but it was growing rapidly. Only
6,000 sets were manufactured in 1946, but in 1947 the number jumped to
179,000 and regularly scheduled programming began. Still, very few households had sets, and for sporting events, which were very popular television
fare, many fans had to go into bars or restaurants to follow their favorite
teams. By June of 1947 nearly 3,000 bars in New York City were equipped
with sets to receive programs over the city's three channels. Bar and grill
owners reported that business had increased from 30 to 60 percent since
the installation of the sets.

The historic first telecast of a World Series game came in the opener
at Yankee Stadium on September 30, when NBC beamed the contest to four
eastern cities—New York, Philadelphia, Washington, and Schenectady—
containing a total of only about 150,000 sets. It was estimated by RCA that
nearly 4 million viewers flocked to bars, hotel ballrooms, and friends' homes
to watch the game. Although poor picture quality and occasional total
blackouts were common and there were no close-up shots, instant replays,
or other special effects that fans would become accustomed to in later years,
they loved it. The Series helped to promote the sale of thousands of television sets in the coming months, and it effectively launched the long and
prosperous marriage of television and major league baseball.

Playing before huge crowds in Yankee Stadium—a record 73,365 for
the first game and 69,865 for the second—the Yankees took easy 5–3 and
10–3 victories in the first two games. The teams then moved to Ebbets
Field, where the Dodgers ended Yankee dreams of a sweep by scoring six
runs in the second inning and going on to a 9–8 victory, in spite of a home
run by DiMaggio and a pinch-hit home run, the first in World Series history,
by Yogi Berra.

The fourth game of the Series provided the forum for one of the most
dramatic plays in series history. The Dodgers started Harry Taylor (10–5),
while the Yankees went with Floyd "Bill" Bevens, who had managed only
a 7–13 record for the season. But in this game Bevens flirted with baseball
immortality. Although he walked 10 men—a new Series record—he held
the Dodgers hitless through 8⅔ innings, and with a 2–1 lead, he was just
one out away from his first World Series victory and the first World Series
no-hitter in history. His last obstacle was Harry "Cookie" Lavagetto, a weak-
hitting (.261 in just 41 games) utility infielder who came to the plate with
Eddie Miksis on first and Al Gionfriddo on second. Lavagetto swung on
Bevens's first pitch and missed. Bevens threw his second pitch, and
Lavagetto, a right-handed hitter, hit the ball off the right field wall for a

double, bringing both runners home. With one pitch Bevens lost the game and his no-hitter while the Dodgers picked up a 3–2 victory and squared the series at 2–2.

Bevens stood on the mound in a daze as the runs scored and Lavagetto was mobbed and carried off the field by his happy teammates. Later in the Dodger clubhouse, Pee Wee Reese deadpanned to a reporter, "You know, I was sorry for that guy—Bevens. It just broke my heart right square in two when I saw those two runs crossing the plate. I just couldn't stand it." And then he began laughing and yelling with the rest of his teammates.[27]

It was a tough loss for Bevens and a lucky break for Lavagetto, who had not had a single hit to right field all year and would have only this one hit in seven plate appearances for the Series. Dodger reliever Hugh Casey, who had come into the game in the ninth and thrown just one pitch to retire the Yankees, was credited with the victory, becoming the first pitcher in World Series history to win a game with just one pitch. The Dodgers became the first team to win a World Series game with just one hit. As the *Philadelphia Bulletin* wrote on October 4, "It could only happen in Brooklyn."

In the fifth game the Dodgers could not solve the pitching of Frank "Spec" Shea and went into the last of the ninth trailing 2–1. Lavagetto was sent in to pinch hit with the tying run on base, but this time he could not repeat the heroics of the day before. He struck out, and the Yankees won the game. Afterwards, Shea said, "That three-and-two ball . . . was a belt-high fast one. He never saw it. Revenge is sweet."[28]

The teams went back to Yankee Stadium for the last two games. Game six was played before 74,065, another record crowd, and like the fans in game four they saw one of the all-time great moments in Series history. In the bottom of the sixth with the Dodgers leading 8–5, Shotton sent Al Gionfriddo into left field as a defensive replacement. Gionfriddo was an obscure player who had played in only 228 games since breaking in with the Pirates in 1944 and had a career average of .266. For the 1947 season, he had played in only 38 games and compiled a puny .175 batting average.

The Yankees rallied in the sixth, putting men on first and second with two men out. This brought DiMaggio to the plate with the tying run. The Yankee Clipper swung on Joe Hatten's first pitch and sent a long drive to left center field, over Gionfriddo's head. But at the crack of the bat he turned and raced back toward the visitors' bullpen, caught up with the ball, and leaned over and snagged it as it went over the swinging gate to the bullpen, right at the 415-foot marker. The momentum of his long run caused him to nearly tumble over the gate. But he held on to the ball, robbing DiMaggio of a home run. DiMaggio, who had rounded first and was heading for second, slowed and kicked the dirt in frustration, one of the rare displays of emotion he ever showed on the diamond. The fans gave Gionfriddo a five-minute ovation for the seemingly impossible catch. The *New York Times* called it "a breathtaking catch" that "stunned the proud Bombers and jarred even the usually imperturbable DiMaggio."[29] Gionfriddo's catch kept the Yankees from tying the score and possibly going ahead and eliminating the Dodgers, who held on to win 8–6 and force a seventh game.

In the seventh game the Dodgers took an early 2–1 lead, but then used five pitchers trying to stop the Yankee bats. The Bombers won, 5–2, to wrap up still another world championship. The Dodgers came away empty-handed for the fourth time, once again forcing their fans to cry, "Wait until next year." A disappointed Burt Shotton consoled himself with the belief that "we'll beat the Yankees during the next ten years a whale of a lot more times than they'll beat us."[30]

The seven games drew 389,763 fans, while millions more watched on television. It was a Series to remember, one of the greatest since the classic began in 1903. It had been a see-saw affair, with many dramatic moments capped by Lavagetto's double and Gionfriddo's catch, the appearance of the first black player (Robinson, who hit .259, drove in three runs, scored three, and stole two bases in a losing cause), the first pinch-hit home run, and the first televised game.

Ironically, three of the major participants in the series never played another major league game. Bevens injured his arm while pitching the near no-hitter and spent the next four years in the minors trying to pitch his way back into the big leagues. He never made it. Lavagetto and Gionfriddo, marginal big league players at best, were both sent down to the minors in 1948 and never worked their way back up. But in spite of their careers before and after the 1947 World Series, they had won a place in baseball history that they and the fans would never forget. In 1985, Gionfriddo, who had opened a restaurant in Santa Barbara, California, after his baseball career was over, told reporter George Vecsey that his catch was "not a bad way to go out. . . . I've got an enlargement of the photo in my living room. I see Joe once in a while, and we put our arms around each other and say, 'Those were great days.'"[31]

They certainly were.

5. The King, the Hustler, and the Satchel Man (1948)

Opening day, 1948. The interminable wait between the last World Series game and the onset of a new baseball season was finally over, and it looked as if major league baseball was in for a banner season. A record 331,000 fans came out for games around both leagues, with the biggest crowd — 73,000 — showing up in Cleveland, where owner Bill Veeck provided a pregame show featuring Spike Jones' Band, a comic musical group. Cleveland ace Bob Feller pitched a two-hit shutout over the St. Louis Browns, getting the Indians off to a six-game winning streak, their best in years. Detroit did not get off to its best start in years, but its rookie first baseman, George Vico, had what must have been the greatest moment of his short (two years) career. In his first time at bat in the major leagues, he hit the first pitch for a home run.

But as the season opened the biggest baseball story of the year was unfolding off the diamond, not on it. Babe Ruth, the first sports superstar, was dying. This tragedy overshadowed the game on the field for the first four months of the season. Ruth had not played a regular major league baseball game since the spring of 1935, when he called it quits after 28 games and six homers with the Boston Braves. But he had never been out of the public eye, and as the years passed the stories of his baseball feats and activities off the diamond had been told and retold, and often embellished, adding to his stature as baseball's most legendary and heroic figure.

Beginning his career with the Red Sox as a pitcher in 1914, Ruth fashioned an 89–46 record, one of the best won-loss records in either league, over the next six years. Even while toiling as a Red Sox pitcher he had shown that he could hit, and playing part-time in the outfield he hit 11 homers in 1918 and 29 in 1919. When he demanded a salary of $20,000 for the 1920 season, the Red Sox sold him to the Yankees for $100,000, a high price in that era but surely the best bargain in the history of professional sports. The Yankees took him off the pitcher's mound and made him a full-time outfielder, and he responded by hitting 54 home runs in 1920. He now replaced Ty Cobb as the most exciting player and biggest gate draw in baseball.

Ruth helped to save and transform the national pastime. Mired in the Black Sox scandal of 1919 that first came to light in 1920, baseball seemed in danger of losing its integrity and popularity until his home run dramatics caused fans to forget about the scandals and worship the new hero of the bat. Ruth also changed the nature of the game. Until he came along, baseball was a low-scoring scientific game, a game of precision and balance that emphasized the hit-and-run, steal, sacrifice, pitching, defense, and Wee Willie Keeler's admonition to "hit 'em where they ain't." Ruth changed the game to one that emphasized putting men on base and letting the big sluggers drive them in with the long ball. As sportswriter Arthur "Bugs" Baer wrote in the 1920s, "Willie Keeler hit em' where they ain't. Babe Ruth hits 'em where they're never going to be."[1]

The other club owners, seeing how Ruth was drawing fans all around the league, began to acquire heavy hitters and emphasize the long ball, too, and the baseball itself was livened up. But nobody could keep up with Ruth. From 1918, when he was still a pitcher playing part-time in the outfield, until 1934, his last full season, he averaged 40 homers a year. Between 1926 and 1931 he averaged just over 50 home runs a year. For decades his single season record of 60 homers and lifetime record of 714 were considered two of baseball's unassailable records, and all future sluggers would be compared with him and would feel the pressure to equal some of his feats. But Ruth remained the "King," "the Sultan of Swat," "the Colossus of Clout."

When he retired, he left behind an impressive record. In spite of the abuse he inflicted upon his body with food, drink, and late hours, he had played nearly 22 full seasons and in nearly 90 percent of his teams' games after he left the mound for the outfield. He would be most remembered for his home run records, but he left behind many other impressive statistics as well, including a .342 batting average and all-time highs of 2,056 bases on balls and a .690 slugging average. In 10 World Series, he set records that would last, in some cases, for decades: 41 games, 15 home runs, 37 runs, and 33 RBIs. Then there was his pitching record: 94 wins, 46 losses, a .671 winning percentage, a 2.28 ERA, a 3–0 World Series mark, and a record 29 consecutive scoreless innings in World Series play that would stand until Whitey Ford broke it in 1961. In 1936 he became a charter member of the Baseball Hall of Fame in Cooperstown, New York, along with Ty Cobb, Honus Wagner, Walter Johnson, and Christy Mathewson.

Part of Ruth's popularity with the fans was due to his own colorful personality. Reared in an orphanage in Baltimore, he grew up to become the most famous athlete in the world and a Bunyanesque personality, idolized for his exploits on and off the field. Teammate Joe Dugan once said of Ruth that "all the lies about him are true,"[2] and another teammate, Joe Sewell, claimed that "there never was such a personality on a ball field. Talking about him can never do him justice. You had to be there, you had to see for yourself."[3] Ruth was a flamboyant figure and a man of legendary appetites who led a life of hedonism: he loved food, alcohol, cigars, women, automobiles, parties, gambling, practical jokes, and all-night carousing. But he was also warm and friendly, and he loved children, often staying for hours after a game to sign autographs and frequently visiting children in orphanages and hospitals.

Ruth's home run feats and colorful personality made him the most popular of all American heroes, more popular even than movie stars like Rudolph Valentino or pioneers like Charles Lindbergh, and helped make baseball the preeminent sport in America. Although boxing, football, golf, and other spectator sports enjoyed a rise in popularity in the 1920s and 1930s, none could match the popularity of baseball. The game enjoyed a great attendance boom, in large part due to the exploits of Ruth and his imitators. Ruth's baseball feats also brought him a great deal of money, far more than any athlete of his time: $925,000 in regular salary and another half million from World Series games, exhibition games, barnstorming, and commercial promotions.

Ruth drew millions of fans into American League parks and enriched their owners, especially the Yankees, who were able to build a new $2 million stadium and to acquire and pay many of the best players in baseball for years to come, winning more pennants and more World Series than any other team. After acquiring Ruth in 1920, the Yankees won 33 pennants and 22 World Series. For the Red Sox, the sale of Ruth would turn out to be one of the worst blunders in the history of sports franchises. When Red Sox owner Harry Frazee announced on January 5, 1920, that he had sold Ruth to the Yankees, he told reporters "with this money we can now go into the market and buy other players and have a stronger and better team in all respects than we would have had if Ruth had remained with us."[4] But it did not turn out that way. The Red Sox, who won three pennants and three World Series while Ruth was with them, have won only four pennants and no World Series since 1919.

When Ruth retired in 1935, he had hoped to go directly into managing at the major league level. But the call never came, primarily because it was widely believed in baseball circles that the man who had such a difficult time managing and disciplining himself could not manage and discipline others. In 1938, Larry MacPhail of the Brooklyn Dodgers hired him as a baseball coach, but this was primarily designed to draw fans into Ebbets Field to watch the Babe take batting practice and to get his autograph. This was the only baseball job he had in retirement, and it lasted for only one season. But thanks to the earnings of his playing years, he was able to lead a comfortable retirement, spending his time golfing, hunting, bowling, vacationing in Florida, listening to his favorite radio shows, and going to an occasional baseball game.

During the war years Ruth kept in the public eye. He appeared as himself in the movie, *Pride of the Yankees* (1942), about Lou Gehrig. He also promoted war bond sales and performed charity work for the Red Cross and other agencies. He had become such an American icon that Japanese soldiers, when facing American troops at close range on remote Pacific islands, would scream the ultimate insult, "To hell with Babe Ruth," along with other, more vulgar blasphemies that could not be printed in the newspapers and magazines of the day. When Ruth heard of this practice, he replied, "I hope that every Jap who mentions my name gets shot—and to hell with all Japs anyway."[5]

At the end of the war, Ruth was still looking for the chance to manage and also considered taking up the Pasquel brothers' offer to become the president of the Mexican League. But he began to have headaches and facial pains, and in January of 1947 surgeons at the French Hospital in New York operated on the left side of his neck, where they found a malignancy wrapped around his carotid artery. They removed most of the cancer and treated the rest with radiation, but in the process the artery was damaged and several nerves had to be cut, including some affecting his larynx.

On February 15, 1947, after a stay of 82 days, he was discharged from the hospital, but the cancer continued to spread, and in January of 1948 he was back in the hospital for more treatment. He was soon discharged, but his condition was rapidly deteriorating. How little time he had left would be painfully evident when he made a public appearance in Yankee Stadium on Sunday, June 13, for "Silver Anniversary Day."

Almost 50,000 fans attended the celebration of the twenty-fifty anniversary of the opening of the "House that Ruth Built." Among the celebrities gathered were Mrs. Lou Gehrig, several players from the 1923 Yankee team, and New York mayor Bill O'Dwyer, who threw out the first ball, the same one Governor Al Smith had used to inaugurate the first game played there back in 1923. The old-timers were introduced, wreaths were placed on the memorials to Lou Gehrig, Miller Huggins, and Jacob Ruppert in center field, and Ruth's uniform and famous number "3" were both retired by American League president Will Harridge.

Clearly excited about the events of the day, Ruth came to the stadium early enough to spend some time in the locker room with his old friends from the 1923 team. Accompanied by his male nurse, Frank Dulaney, he bantered with his old teammates, posed for pictures, signed autographs, and, with Dulaney's help, pulled on his uniform for the last time. It was a cool and damp day, so he slipped an overcoat over his shoulders and waited in the dugout until it was time for him to be introduced. He then took off his coat and began the slow walk to home plate, using his bat to steady himself, while the crowd and the players from both dugouts stood and cheered.

Then, as Arthur Daley wrote in the *New York Times*, "There was a reverent hush when the Bambino, no longer the hulking, dynamic and domineering figure he once was, strode hesitatingly to the microphone and spoke in his muted and strangely croaking voice."[6] Ruth told the crowd, "I am proud that I hit the first home run in this stadium. I am thrilled. It is a marvelous privilege to come back here and to see 13 men of 1923 playing together again. It makes me proud."[7] As he walked away from the microphone, tears ran down his face, joining the tears of others on the field and in the stands.

Ruth went back into the clubhouse while two teams of Yankee old-timers played a two-inning exhibition game preceding the regularly scheduled game between the Yankees and the Indians. While he sat in the clubhouse, former teammate Joe Dugan came in after a short appearance in the game. As the two sat talking and having a drink together, Dugan asked him how he was doing. Prophetically, Ruth told him, "Joe, I'm gone. I'm gone, Joe." Both men broke down and cried.[8]

Thirteen days after "Silver Anniversary Day," Ruth entered Memorial Hospital on East 68th Street in New York for radium treatments. He made only one more public appearance, when he went to the Astor Theater on July 26 for the premier of *The Babe Ruth Story,* starring William Bendix as Ruth and Claire Trevor as his second wife, Claire. But he was so weak that he was able to stay for only 40 minutes.

Some of the others present probably wished they had left early, too. A mixture of fact and fiction—when the script had been read to the ailing Ruth months before, tears ran down his face and he asked, "Gosh, did all those things happen to me?"[9]—the film was a corny, highly romanticized portrayal of the nation's greatest sports hero, depicting him as a combination diamond demigod, clown, and faith healer of sick little boys. One critic called it one of Hollywood's "unmitigated stinkers," and many others panned it as the worst baseball movie ever made, which, considering the competition, was quite an accomplishment.[10]

As he got progressively worse, Ruth put his affairs in order, talked with a priest, and prepared for the end. On Thursday, August 12, a hospital bulletin described his condition as "critical," and in the next 48 hours the hospital was deluged with telephone calls and some 10,000 letters, telegrams, and cards. On Friday night, 60,000 fans at Yankee Stadium stood in a silent prayer for the stricken hero. By Monday morning, it was obvious that death was near, and that night, at 8:01, he passed away. Reverend Thomas H. Kaufman, who administered last rites to Ruth about 30 minutes before the end, told reporters, "The Babe died a beautiful death. He said his prayers and lapsed into a sleep."[11] He was 53 years old. Within minutes the radio networks interrupted their regular broadcasts to relay the news to the nation.

An autopsy revealed that the cancer had originated in the nasal pharynx, spread to nerves emerging from his brain, and then advanced to his neck, lungs, and liver. Although Ruth's family, friends, and most reporters knew that he had cancer, Ruth was never told because his family felt that the news would devastate him. But Dulaney later said, "Babe knew, I believe, that he was suffering from cancer. . . I must have told him 100 white lies to keep him from that certain knowledge. But he knew."[12]

No athlete ever received such an outpouring of grief. Mrs. Ruth received expressions of sympathy from President Truman and from dozens of other figures from the political, entertainment, and sports world. On the night of Ruth's death and for several days afterward, special tributes to him were held in major and minor league parks across the country. Flags were lowered to half mast, and players, managers, coaches, umpires, and fans stood in silent prayer. In Fenway Park, where Ruth began his major league career 34 years earlier, the lights were dimmed and for several minutes 33,000 people stood in respectful silence. In Philadelphia, before the Dodgers-Phillies game, a large number "3" was placed in center field and, while everyone in the park stood, the lights were turned out and players Del Ennis, Richie Ashburn, and Granny Hamner put a torch to the figure. In Cooperstown, flags were flown at half mast and a black crepe was draped over a bronze plaque of the home run king. In Japan, where Ruth had been immensely popular ever since his barnstorming tour there in 1934, his death was big news, and in ballparks all across that baseball-mad land that had only recently been defeated by American military forces, games were halted and a moment of silent tribute observed for "Babu Russu."

In America's newspapers, Ruth's death and funeral were front-page news for days as writers outdid themselves in deifying him. Newspapers and magazines all across the nation carried stories and cartoons about "the Babe hitting his last home run," being "safe at home," being called out by the "Great Umpire in the Sky," or being struck out by "the Grim Reaper." In the four days following his death, New York newspapers alone carried a total of 490 eulogistic columns on Ruth. As *Time* wrote, "No death since Franklin Roosevelt's had moved the people—and the press—to such maudlin excess."[13]

On Tuesday afternoon, the day after Ruth's death, his coffin was taken to Yankee Stadium and placed in the great rotunda just inside the press gate. Banks of flowers surrounded the rotunda, and on the concrete wall behind the open coffin was a photographic mural of Ruth striking out and hitting a home run. For the rest of Tuesday and Wednesday, as his body lay in state at the stadium, people from all over the city, the state, and the nation came for one last view of the home run king.

At times the lines waiting to get inside encircled the stadium and went for a block down 157th Street, while inside the stadium vendors sold hot dogs, soft drinks, photographs of Ruth, and other souvenir items, just as at a regular baseball game. An estimated 75,000–100,000 mourners and curiosity seekers filed past his coffin, at the rate of 50 per minute. Most were talking quietly, and some were weeping. Young boys stood on tiptoes to peer inside the coffin. Adults holding children in their arms or by the hand were heard saying, "That's Babe Ruth," and others were heard telling their companions or even total strangers when and where they had seen the Babe play and how far his home runs had gone. One man kept saying over and over, "I loved that man," and an elderly woman told a policeman, "I don't know why I came. I just wanted to see him." As many of those present remarked, nobody could draw a crowd like Ruth.[14]

A requiem mass, presided over by Francis Cardinal Spellman, was held at 11:00 A.M. on Thursday, August 19, at St. Patrick's Cathedral on Fifth Avenue. Some 250 policemen were used to handle the crowds and the procedures. There were over 50 honorary pallbearers, headed by Mayor O'Dwyer, Governor Thomas A. Dewey, Joe DiMaggio, and other prominent public figures. Over 6,000 people crowded into the Gothic cathedral, while another 75,000 stood in the rain outside and down several blocks of Fifth Avenue between 46th and 57th Streets. It was hot and humid inside the cathedral, and during the service Joe Dugan whispered to Waite Hoyt, another old teammate of Ruth's, "I'd give a hundred dollars for a beer." Hoyt replied, "So would the Babe."[15]

The 25-car funeral cortege then made the 30-mile trip to the Gate of Heaven Cemetery in Mt. Pleasant, while an estimated 100,000 people waited reverently and patiently in the rain for it to pass by. Many others looked out from windows and rooftops. The cortege reached the cemetery at 1:43 P.M., where a crowd that had begun gathering early that morning had grown to an estimated 6,000. Since the Ruth family had not chosen a final burial plot, his coffin was placed in a temporary burial vault. At the end of the graveside service, hordes of souvenir hunters took sprigs of gladioli, and the crowd melted away. Ruth's last public appearance was over.

On the day of the funeral, baseball life went on. The game at the Polo Grounds between the Giants and league-leading Braves was rained out by the same rain that marred Ruth's funeral, but elsewhere the Pirates edged the Cubs, the Cardinals shut out the Reds, the Athletics defeated the Red Sox, and the Yankees beat the Senators for the third straight day. Joe DiMaggio flew from the funeral in New York to Washington, arrived at Griffith Stadium in time to suit up for the third inning, then stroked a single in the fourth to ignite a six-run rally. But like everyone else in the league, the Yankees had to look up in the standings at the Cleveland Indians, who led the pack by 2½ games.

That the Indians were sitting atop the league in the middle of August was largely due to the baseball savvy of the team's 34-year-old owner, Bill Veeck, Jr., who headed a 10-man syndicate that bought the club for $2.2 million in the middle of the 1946 season. Veeck was no stranger to baseball. Son of a former sportswriter who served as the president of the Chicago Cubs from 1919 until his death in 1933, he practically grew up at Wrigley Field. By the age of eight he was accompanying the players to spring training, and soon he was roaming the park selling scorecards, peanuts, and other concessions and working in the office. He become the treasurer of the Cubs in 1940, and in June of the next year he and Charlie Grimm joined forces to purchase the Milwaukee Brewers, a Cub farm team in the American Association, for $100,000. Inheriting a team that was $85,000 in debt when he and Grimm took it over, Veeck resorted to a wide variety of promotional gimmicks to lure fans into the park. Attendance skyrocketed, and the Brewers became one of the most successful franchises in minor league baseball, allowing Veeck and Grimm to sell the club in 1945 for a handsome profit.

Cleveland had not won a pennant since 1920 and had never drawn a million fans in one season. The club had its own small facility, League Park, built in 1910, which the owners used for weekday games while renting Cleveland Municipal Stadium, with its 75,000 seating capacity, for weekend and holiday games. After Veeck was able to draw over a million fans in 1946, the Indians rented the municipal stadium for the entire season in 1947 and 1948.

The young owner was a flamboyant maverick and showman who enjoyed being regarded as the P.T. Barnum of baseball. A flouter of tradition and convention, he usually appeared in public wearing an open-necked sports shirt, casual slacks, and open-toed sandals, and he saw no need to wear a hat, coat, or tie to even the most formal of occasions. At 6 feet 1 inch and 200 pounds, he was a man of great energy, in spite of various physical ailments, including a right leg that had been severely damaged by a wound he suffered while he was a marine fighting on Guadalcanal during World War II. In November of 1946 the leg was amputated below the knee and replaced with a wooden leg, which he sometimes used as a place to snuff out his cigarettes.

Veeck brought his baseball philosophy with him to Cleveland. "Baseball has generally been too grim, too serious," he said soon after he took over the club. "It should be fun, and I hope to make it fun for everyone around here."[16] He believed that baseball owners had not realized that the world around baseball had changed and that baseball had to change along with it. Baseball was a sport and a business, but it was also entertainment, and if it expected to prosper in the competitive market of the postwar world it would have to merchandise itself just like the movies, television, and other rivals for the entertainment dollar. Veeck often said that as a gate attraction nothing could beat a winning season, but he felt that fans of less successful clubs would still come out to the park if they would have a good time. The trick, he said, is to make sure that at the ballpark "every day is Mardi Gras and every fan is a king."[17]

From the time he arrived in Cleveland in 1946 until he sold the club in 1949, Veeck treated the fans like kings, providing them with swimsuit competitions, spectacular fireworks displays, tumblers, five-ring circuses, clowns, vaudeville acts, barber shop quartets, and a wide variety of gifts, including lobsters, rain capes, and ice cream. To attract female fans, he held "ladies' days," when women were allowed in free or at a discount, given nylon stockings or other gifts, even orchids flown in from Hawaii. He spent $20,000 to build a nursery so that women who wanted to get away from the house and children could come to the park, deposit their children in the free nursery, and let someone else look after them while they watched the game. During games, Veeck roamed the stands, sitting and chatting with fans and soliciting their ideas on what they liked to see when they came to the ballpark. He also devoted a lot of time to what he called "the mashed potato circuit," speaking to civic clubs and other groups in Cleveland and nearby cities and towns, drumming up interest in his ball club.

One of Veeck's favorite gimmicks was his special nights, such as the one he had honoring all the mayors in Ohio or the one for Joe Early, a night watchman who had written a letter-to-the-editor in the *Cleveland Press* asking why special days and nights were held for celebrities who did not need the money or gifts instead of for ordinary working fans like himself who did. The letter was signed, "Good Old Joe Early." This was too good an opportunity for Veeck to pass up. "Good Old Joe Early Night" was held in 1948. Early was first presented with a series of gag gifts—a swayback horse and other livestock, an outhouse, and a Model-T circus car that backfired, lost its fenders, and performed several other tricks. Veeck then rolled out the real prizes of the night—a new Ford convertible, a washing machine, and several other gifts donated by local merchants. The happy night watchman was overwhelmed.[18]

The promotions worked. Attendance, which stood at 289,000 when Veeck took over in midseason in 1946, skyrocketed to 1,057,000 by the end of the year, an increase of 89 percent over that of 1945 and 144,000 more than the previous single season high of 912,832 set back in 1920. And this was for a club that finished in sixth place, 36 games behind the leader. Attendance climbed to 1.5 million in 1947, when the club moved up to fourth. In 1948, the club set major league attendance records for a night game (65,781), doubleheader (82,781), and for a season (2.6 million).

Veeck's promotions were not popular with most of the other owners, the baseball commissioner, and many reporters. He was widely regarded as a dangerous maverick who did not respect the traditions of the game and was undermining its dignity and integrity. He would later claim in his autobiography, *Veeck—As in Wreck*, that Clark Griffith and many of the other owners "looked upon my little entertainments as a disgrace to the game and insult to their own persons—although I never noticed any of them, Mr. Griffith in particular, looking quite that insulted when I handed them their share of the receipts."[19]

While Veeck's gimmicks helped to sell the Indians to the fans, the performance of the club proved the old axiom that nothing keeps the fans coming through the gates better than a winning team locked in an exciting pennant race. The 1948 Indians were a good team, well-run from the front office and on the field. To help operate the club, Veeck hired Hank Greenberg, who purchased $100,000 worth of Indians stock and joined the club as vice president and batting coach. On the field, the club was run by 31-year-old shortstop Lou Boudreau, now in his seventh year as player-manager.

Boudreau had one of his best years in the majors, hitting .355, second only to Ted Williams's .369, and winning the MVP Award. His strong hitting was backed up by the slugging of left fielder Dale Mitchell (.336), second baseman Joe Gordon (.280 with 32 homers), third baseman Ken Keltner (.297 with 31 homers), and right fielder Larry Doby, who came in to his own with a .301 average and 14 home runs. The pitching staff was superb. Bob Feller won 19 games. Gene Bearden, a knuckleballer acquired from the Yankees at the end of 1946, won 20, as did Bob Lemon, who broke in to the majors with Cleveland in 1941 as a third baseman but was converted into a pitcher after he returned from service in 1946. And then early in July, in the midst of the hot pennant race, Veeck added Satchel Paige to the mound corps.

When Veeck signed the Negro leagues' most famous pitcher, reportedly paying him a full year's salary of $40,000, far more than most major leaguers were making, the baseball world was either amused or outraged. Paige was at least 42 years old. While Veeck claimed that he hired Paige because he needed additional relief pitching to win the pennant, many agreed with J. Taylor Spink, editor of the *Sporting News*, who looked upon the signing as just another one of Veeck's promotional stunts. "To sign a hurler of Paige's age is to demean the standards of baseball in the big circuits," Spink wrote. "Further complicating the situation is the suspicion that if Satchel were white, he would not have drawn a second thought from Veeck."[20]

Only a hustler like Veeck could realize the value of adding another great hustler like Paige to the Cleveland roster. Paige was one of the most colorful personalities to ever wear a baseball uniform for any club at any level. A native of Mobile, Alabama, he began playing professional baseball as a teenager and had played on at least 30 teams—black and white semipro teams, minor and major Negro league teams, barnstorming teams, touring all-star teams—and made special paid appearances for perhaps over 200 other clubs. He often played year round, sometimes appearing in as many as 250 games a year. He performed not just in the United States but in several South American countries, the Caribbean, and Japan, frequently making upwards of $35,000 a year. When Veeck signed him in 1948, he was playing for the Kansas City Monarchs.

From the earliest days of his career Paige had been a superb pitcher. Many major league managers, scouts, and players who had watched him play said that he was the best pitcher, black or white, they had ever seen. In postseason exhibition games against major league all-star teams he regularly baffled some of the greatest hitters in the game, fanning 22 in one game, striking out Rogers Hornsby five times in another and Jimmie Foxx three times in still another. Joe DiMaggio, who once managed just one hit off Satchel in a five-game exhibition series, called him "the best I ever faced, and the fastest."[21] No less a pitcher and ego than Dizzy Dean frequently said that Paige was the best pitcher he ever saw. In 1934, in a game against major league all-stars, Dean and Paige engaged in a pitching duel for 13 innings before Paige finally emerged with a 1–0 victory.

In his early years Paige was primarily a fastball pitcher, so fast that one hitter who went down on a called third strike is supposed to have turned around to the umpire and asked, "That last one sounded a little low, didn't it, ump?"[22] With his characteristic showmanship, Paige claimed to have a "bee ball" (so-called because it hummed) and several other kinds of fastballs, among them the "Long Tom" and the "Little Tom," the "jump ball," and the "trouble ball." He also claimed to have a "blooper," a "two-hump blooper," a "bat dodger," and a variety of other pitches. In later years he did add several kinds of slow curves, a knuckleball, a screwball, and a change to his repertoire.

But Paige was more than a superb pitcher. Tall and skinny (6 feet 4 inches and 180 pounds), with long arms and pencil-thin legs, he was also a natural clown and showboater. Early in his career he began the practice of calling in his outfield when he had the game won and having them sit down while he pitched the last out or two. In other games, he would announce that he was going to strike out the side—and then proceed to do it. He used a variety of windups, his delivery ranged all the way from overhanded to sidearm to submarine, and he developed what he called a "hesitation pitch," in which he paused momentarily between his windup and delivery, upsetting the hitter's timing.

He was also a shrewd promoter of his own reputation and legend. He gave conflicting accounts of his age and of the origins of his nickname, Satchel. He often gave his age as "somewhere between thirty and seventy," and sometimes claimed that he did not know his age because the family Bible it was recorded in had been eaten by a goat. He was fond of saying, "Age is a question of mind over matter; if you don't mind, it don't matter." He gave at least three different accounts of the origins of his nickname, but the one he repeated the most often was that his mother and neighborhood kids gave him the name when he was a small boy working at the train depot in Mobile carrying passengers' satchels and bags for a dime apiece. He carried a bottle of liniment he claimed to have acquired from a Sioux Indian girl in North Dakota in 1935 which he used to rub on his arm to keep it forever young by sending "curative sensations vibrating about the muscles," and he often entertained his teammates and reporters with his endless repertoire of tall tales about his barnstorming days.

Paige was a remarkable physical specimen who played top caliber baseball far longer than most men have been able to. When asked the secrets of his longevity, he cited his famous six rules for staying young:

1. Avoid fried meats which angry up the blood.
2. If your stomach disputes you, lie down and pacify it with cool thoughts.
3. Keep the juices flowing by jangling around gently as you move.
4. Go very light on the vices, such as carrying on in society—the social ramble ain't restful.
5. Avoid running at all times.
6. And don't look back. Something might be gaining on you.[23]

No wonder Tom Meany wrote at the time of Paige's signing that "the Satchmo has been a baseball legend for a long time, a Paul Bunyan in Technicolor. . . . Like Dizzy Dean, he told interviewers what he thought they wanted to hear and wanted to write."[24]

On July 9, two days after he signed a contract, Paige made his debut as the American League's first black pitcher and the major league's oldest rookie in a game against the visiting St. Louis Browns. At the beginning of the fifth inning, he got the call to relieve Bob Lemon. The first batter he faced, first baseman Chuck Stevens, rapped a single, but Paige retired the next three batters. In the next inning he again allowed a lead-off single before retiring the side. He was then lifted for a pinch hitter. As expected, he had employed his favorite pitches, and he threw overhanded, sidearmed, and underhanded. The crowd loved every minute of it. When asked after the game if he thought he could stick in the majors, he replied, "Plate's the same size."[25]

When the Indians traveled to Philadelphia on July 15 for a double-header, so many fans mobbed the ticket office that the contest sold out long before game time and an estimated 20,000 disappointed ticket-seekers had to be turned away. In the second game of the doubleheader Paige relieved Bob Lemon in the sixth and pitched a three-hitter the rest of the way to gain his first major league win, 8–5. After six more relief appearances, he got his first starting assignment in a night game on August 3 against the Senators. Over 72,000 fans, a new record for a night game, turned out to watch him weave his magic. Although he left for a pinch hitter in the last of the seventh, he got credit for the 4–3 win.

For much of July and August, Paige was the pitching sensation of the majors, performing effectively as a starter and reliever and bringing black and white fans alike through the gates. In his second start he attracted 73,382 fans, still another record for a night game, bringing the total attendance for his first three starts to over 200,000. But in September he ran into trouble. He was knocked out of the box early in two games and fell out of favor with Boudreau, who quickly tired of his habit of being late for workouts, trains, and curfew, and decided that in the pennant stretch he would rather use experienced pitchers. After September 20, Paige did not pitch at all.

Still, at season's end, he had compiled a remarkable record for a rookie of any age. He had started 7 games, relieved in 14 others, won 6 (including two consecutive shutouts) lost 1, and compiled an ERA of 2.48. His performance vindicated Veeck's faith in him as a pitching artist and gate attraction, and it caused many to wonder just how great he could have been if he had been brought to the majors twenty years earlier. Paige, of course, did not wonder. In later years, recalling his rookie season in his autobiography, *Maybe I'll Pitch Forever*, he would say, "Now everybody could see how ten years ago I could have won thirty-five or forty games a season in the majors. They could see if I'm kept out of the Hall of Fame it won't because of lack of ability, but because of organized baseball's color line."[26]

Even before Paige put on a Cleveland uniform, the American League race was the most exciting in years. For most of the season, it was a four-way race between the Yankees, Red Sox, Indians, and Athletics. As late as August 8, these teams were virtually tied for first, separated by only a few percentage points. The four-way battle continued until late August, when the Athletics lost eight consecutive games and dropped out of contention, leaving the remaining three teams to fight right down to the wire. The Yankees, still managed by Bucky Harris under the new ownership of Dan Topping and Del Webb, who had bought out Larry MacPhail at the end of the 1947 season, were led by Joe Dimaggio, as they had been for so many years. DiMaggio would finish the season with a .320 average while leading the league in homers (39) and RBIs (155). As always, he was a clutch player, delivering the hit or defensive play when the club needed it the most.

The Red Sox had moved Joe Cronin from field manager to general manager and persuaded former Yankee skipper Joe McCarthy to come out of retirement to manage the club. McCarthy, who had won nine pennants and seven World Series with the Cubs and Yankees, had managed the

Yankees for 15 years before quitting after 36 games in 1946 because of quarrels with Larry MacPhail. McCarthy's crossover from the Yankees to the Red Sox made the race even more interesting, as did the fact that it also pitted Joe DiMaggio against his brother, Dom. Late in the season when Joe called his mother in San Francisco, she told him that Dom planned to get married on October 7 unless the Sox played in the World Series, which would delay the wedding until October 17. Joe kiddingly told her, "Mama, I'll see that Dom is free to get married on the seventh."[27] Dom would be free to marry on the seventh, and Joe would have the time to attend the wedding, too. For it was the Indians, not the Sox or Yankees, who wound up in the October classic.

On September 24, with nine days left in the season, the Indians, Red Sox, and Yankees were locked in a tie with identical records of 91–56. Not until October 2, the next-to-the-last day of the season, did the ranks thin out further, when the Red Sox eliminated the Yankees by beating them 5–1 in Fenway Park. Going into the last day, the Indians led the Sox by one game and could clinch the pennant if they could defeat the Detroit Tigers in Cleveland Municipal Stadium. But Hal Newhouser notched his 21st victory as the Tigers beat the Indians by the score of 7–1, while the Red Sox dealt the Yankees another defeat, 10–5, to end the season in a tie with the Indians and force the first playoff in American League history. A flip of the coin by league president Will Harridge dictated that the one-game playoff would be held the next day in Boston.

Hoping to play in their second World Series in three years and to avenge the 1946 humiliation by the Cardinals, the Red Sox put their playoff hopes on the right arm of 36-year-old Denny Galehouse (8–8), while the Indians countered with left-hander Gene Bearden (20–7), who had been their clutch pitcher all year. Bearden responded with a five-hitter, while Boudreau hit two homers and two singles. Even the despondent Red Sox fans gave the shortstop a standing ovation in the ninth after he got his fourth hit. The Indians won the game, 8–3, to take their first pennant in 28 years and just their second one in history. The Red Sox had to settle for second place and the league batting champion, Ted Williams, who took his fourth crown with a .369 average. Cleveland was ecstatic, and no one was happier than Bill Veeck, who in just two and a half seasons had taken the Indians from sixth place to first. Earlier in the year he had promised that if the Indians did not win the flag he would jump off the "highest bridge in Cleveland."[28] Whether he would have kept that promise now became a moot point.

Over in the National League the pennant race, while close much of the season, was much less dramatic. The Dodgers were unable to repeat their pennant-winning ways, but a team that had both Leo Durocher and Jackie Robinson was bound to get more than its share of publicity.

The Dodgers returned to Florida for spring training in 1948, in spite of the problems it might pose for Robinson and for rookie catcher Roy Campanella, and it led to one of the most demeaning incidents of Robinson's career. While the rest of the team went to an all-white restaurant for dinner after a game with the Indians, Robinson and Campanella had to wait in the team's bus for road secretary Harold Parrott to bring their food. When Parrott appeared, he was politely thanked by a seething Robinson, whom Campanella was trying to calm. "Let's not have no trouble, Jackie," Campanella said. "This is the onliest thing we can do right now, 'lessen we want to go back to them crummy Negro leagues." The famished catcher devoured the food Parrott had brought, but Robinson sat quietly, refusing to eat.[29] It was a bitter moment for the man who in the previous year had won the Rookie of the Year Award and helped lead his team into the World Series.

Robinson's trips around the banquet circuit during the off-season caused him to report to training camp 25 pounds over his playing weight, and it took him several weeks to get into playing shape. On March 6, the Dodgers had traded Eddie Stanky to the Boston Braves, paving the way for Robinson to move to second base to team up with Pee Wee Reese to anchor the middle of the infield. After a slow start, Robinson put together a good year, batting .296, hitting 12 home runs, scoring 108 runs, driving in 85, and stealing 22 bases. He was also hit by pitches seven times, more than any other player in the league.

Many of the experts felt that Rickey's club had a good chance of repeating in 1948, but the Dodgers were a troubled team. Many fans were angry because Rickey had traded Dixie Walker to the Pirates for Elwin "Preacher" Roe and Billy Cox, sold Stanky to the Braves, and raised ticket prices at Ebbets Field. Having served his suspension, Durocher was back at the helm, but he and Rickey were feuding behind the scenes over some of the trades and the way Durocher was handling the team. Near the end of May the club lost eight consecutive games, and on May 25 dropped into the cellar, where it remained as late as July 2. The team's morale was low, and angry fans were staying away from the park.

As the Dodgers foundered, Rickey began to think about bringing back Burt Shotton, who seemed to win pennants without generating the controversy Durocher seemed to thrive on. Hoping to avoid the public outrage that would occur if he fired Durocher, Rickey sent Parrott to persuade Durocher to resign. Not unexpectedly, Durocher exploded when Parrott brought him the suggestion. "Hell, no, I won't resign," he told Parrott. "He's going to have to fire me and he's going to have to do it man to man."[30]

Rickey backed off from a direct confrontation, but behind the scenes, in discussions with Giants' owner Horace Stoneham and league president Ford Frick, he quietly paved the way for Durocher's departure. Stoneham wanted to replace Mel Ott, who had been a popular player but ineffective manager, so after getting permission from Rickey and Frick to talk with Durocher, Stoneham lured the Lip to the Polo Grounds. On Friday, July 16, the Giants announced that Ott had resigned to take a front office job and that Durocher would take over as the manager. Durocher, who had coined his phrase, "nice guys finish last," in reference to Ott, now had the chance to show that a not-so-nice guy could lead the Giants to the front of the pack. Shotton returned to manage the Dodgers.

Rarely had New York baseball fans been as shocked as they were after the events that transpired on what many were now calling "Black Friday." Leo Durocher the manager of the Giants? Impossible. Dodger fans hated to see him cross over to join the despised Giants, while Giant fans, after detesting Durocher for so many years, could hardly bear the thought that he would now be the manager of their beloved team. For many Giant fans, the situation was made even worse by the fact that he was replacing Mel Ott, a hero to Giant fans since joining the club as a player in 1922. "That settles it, brother. I'm through," one Giant fan told an Associated Press reporter. "I'll never enter the Polo Grounds again."[31]

Neither the Giants nor the Dodgers were able to recover from their early season problems. When the switch in managers was made on July 16, the two teams were tied for fourth place. The Dodgers improved after the managerial switch, and at the end of August moved into first, but only briefly. In early September they lost six games to Durocher's Giants and faded to third place, 7½ games off the pace. The Giants finished the season in fifth, 13½ games behind. Their hot bats of 1947, when they hit a record 221 homers, cooled off, except for Johnny Mize, whose 40 homers tied him with Ralph Kiner of the Pirates for the home run championship for the second year in a row.

The National League pennant winner in 1948 was not the Dodgers or the Cardinals, as many had predicted, but the Braves, who took their first flag since 1914. The Braves were managed by Billy Southworth, who had won three consecutive pennants at St. Louis (1942–1944) before coming to Boston in 1946 to take over a club that had finished in the second division for 11 consecutive seasons. After finishing sixth in 1945, they rose to fourth in Southworth's first year and to third in 1947.

The Braves got good pitching from right-hander Warren Spahn and southpaw Johnny Sain. Sain led the National League with 24 victories, and he and Spahn combined to win 39 of the 91 games the club captured in route to the flag. The effective alternating of these two aces led to the popular jingle, "Spahn and Sain, two days of rain, then Spahn and Sain again." The Braves also got a big boost from the play of rookie shortstop Alvin Dark, who hit .322, and from sophomore first baseman Earl Torgeson, third baseman Bob Elliot, and the early season play of Eddie Stanky, who was hitting .320 before a broken ankle forced him out of the lineup in July.

The National League race was tight well into September, and with the American League race going right down to the wire, fans were being treated to an exciting finish in both leagues. As *Life* said in early September, "It was a season when no man who ever pretended to be a fan would dare go to bed before the last out of the last inning of the last night game."[32] The Braves gradually pulled ahead and finished 6½ games ahead of the Cardinals and 7½ ahead of the Dodgers. The Cardinals got 20 wins from Harry Brecheen and an amazing performance from Stan Musial, who had perhaps his best year in the majors and captured his third MVP Award. Musial led the league in hitting (.376) and RBIs (131), and missed the home run crown—and the Triple Crown— by finishing just one homer behind Kiner and Mize. Musial also led the league in doubles, triples, runs, and hits. In some games he was virtually unstoppable. In games against the Dodgers on May 18 and 19 he went 9-for-11, banging out one home run, one triple, three doubles and four singles. On September 22, playing against the Braves, he got five hits in one game for the fourth time that year, tying a record held by Ty Cobb since 1922. With both wrists taped because of injuries, Musial decided before the game that he would swing no more than necessary. Five swings produced a home run, a double, and three singles as the Cardinals downed the Braves, 8–2.

The 1948 season brought still another record in major league attendance, which rose to 20.9 million. With the Indians leading the way, the American League drew 11.1 million, while the National League attracted 9.8 million.

The World Series opened on October 6 in Boston. It had been a long dry spell for both clubs. The Braves had not been to the series since 1914, the Indians since 1920. The Indians took the Series in six games, with Bob Lemon picking up two wins and Gene Bearden and Steve Gromek winning the other two. Satchel Paige pitched two-thirds of an inning, becoming the first black pitcher to appear in a World Series game. Among the most disappointed players was Bob Feller, who had waited 10 years to pitch in his first World Series game. Feller hurled a superb two-hitter in the opener but lost 1–0. In game five he gave up eight hits and seven runs before departing in a losing effort in the seventh inning. Spahn and Sain captured one game each, but there was not enough rain this time.

The Indians made the overnight trip from Boston to Cleveland after the last game in a train overflowing with champagne provided by their happy owner. The next morning the returning champions rode in a parade through the streets of the city accompanied by the cheers of an estimated half million fans who turned out to welcome their conquering heroes. It was a great moment for the city and for a franchise that had gone so long between world championships.

Thanks to the huge crowds (238,493 in three games) that flocked into Cleveland's Municipal Stadium, the Series set a new attendance record of 358,493 for a six-game series. Individual players' shares were $6,722.07 for the winners and $4,570.73 for the losers—both hefty bonuses at a time when few players made over $15,000 a year.

Many fans in both cities saw the games on television, which continued to spread rapidly in 1948. As the World Series approached, television dealers in the two competing cities and in others within range of a television station could not meet the demand for sets. In Toledo, Ohio, a department store that had been selling 10 sets a week early in the summer was selling 40 sets a day as Cleveland moved in on the pennant. The series was telecast to several cities on the East Coast and in the Midwest. An estimated 7.7 million fans viewed the games on television, almost 20 times the number that saw them in the parks. Philco installed a television set in a Capitol Air Lines plane for the second game in Cleveland, the Baltimore and Ohio Railroad put a television set in one of its passenger trains for one of the games, and RCA Victor and Gillette combined forces in Boston to spend $25,000 to install 100 sets on the Boston Commons. An estimated 15,000 viewers showed up there each day to watch the action.

By November of 1948 there were some 718,000 television sets in the United States and the number was growing by almost a thousand sets a day, while the number of commercial stations had jumped from 16 to 46. Many television and sports pundits were crediting the televising of major sports events as one of the main factors behind the boom in television sales. Madison Square Garden President John Reed Kilpatrick claimed that within "a year or so" sporting events would be televised nationwide and that each evening television stations would carry brief pictorial summaries of the day's major sporting events. Many predicted that this would cause a boom in attendance in almost all sports.[33]

One who disagreed was President Frank Shaughnessy of the International League. Blaming television for the alarming attendance declines being suffered by some minor league clubs within reach of telecasts of major league games, he predicted that television had the potential to destroy the minor leagues, the source of major league talent.[34] His voice would be joined by hundreds of other minor league officials in the next few years.

6. Mighty Casey Establishes a Dynasty (1949)

The 1949 season began under a cloud. The reserve clause, which most of established baseball regarded as essential to the health and future of the game, was under serious attack again, just three years after 18 players had jumped to the Mexican League and Robert Murphy had tried to unionize major league players. The Mexican League quickly folded, and Murphy's union attempts failed, but out of that turbulent year came one of the most serious challenges ever to the reserve rule.

It was mounted by Danny Gardella, one of those marginal players given a chance to star during the manpower-starved war years. A bench-warmer with the New York Giants in 1944, Gardella won a regular outfield position in 1945 and went on to compile a .272 batting average, with 18 home runs and 71 RBIs. A high-spirited maverick who often quarreled with management and played outrageous practical jokes on his teammates, he was sometimes called "Dangerous Dan," partly because of his antics and partly because of the problems he had playing the outfield. Reporters made sarcastic references to his catching a fly ball "unassisted," and one wrote in 1949 that "whenever a fly ball was struck in his direction, the fans shut their eyes and murmured prayers. Some of them prayed that Danny would catch the ball; the initiated prayed that he wouldn't get killed by it."[1]

What made Dangerous Dan even more dangerous was his decision to mount a lawsuit against organized baseball. Dissatisfied with team rules and the $5,000 contract offered by the Giants for the 1946 season, Gardella had accepted the Pasquels' offer of $10,000 to join the Veracruz club. After just one disappointing season there, he toured with Max Lanier's All-Stars, played semipro baseball, and worked as a hospital orderly. Then, in 1947, he decided to go to court to get back his old job with the Giants. His lawyer, Frederic Johnson, filed suit in the Southern District Federal Court in New York against the reserve clause, the Giants, Happy Chandler, and the major and minor leagues. Asking for $300,000 in damages, the suit claimed that the growing practice of telecasting games across state lines had brought baseball into interstate commerce and therefore subject to the antitrust laws, that the reserve clause gave professional baseball a monopoly over its product and its personnel, and that it prevented Gardella from pursuing his livelihood. Several other players, including Max Lanier, filed similar suits totaling $2.8 million, but Gardella's case was the most celebrated and persistent.

When the Southern Federal District Court dismissed the case without a trial on the grounds that the 1922 Supreme Court decision upholding the reserve clause removed the case from its jurisdiction, Gardella took his grievance to the Second Circuit Appellate Federal Court in New York, which ruled on February 11, 1949, that Gardella's case had enough merit to justify a trial and ordered the lower court that had dismissed it to try it. The appellate court argued that the growing practice of broadcasting and televising baseball games had given baseball "an interstate character that brings it within the provisions of the Anti-Trust laws and that, therefore, the ballplayer had a cause for action." Justice Jerome Frank said that the reserve clause was "something resembling peonage of the baseball player" and that "only the totalitarian-minded will believe that higher pay excuses virtual slavery."[2]

Gardella's new trial was set for November of 1949, and now there was the distinct possibility that *Gardella v. Chandler* would be heard in court and that Gardella would emerge victorious. Baseball officials were getting nervous. Soon after the appellate court's decision, Chandler said, "No major leaguer makes less than $5,000 a year and some make up to $100,000. If you call that peonage, then a lot of us would like to be in it."[3] In April, speaking at a luncheon of advertising executives in Baltimore, Branch Rickey even went so far as to claim that people who opposed the reserve clause had "avowed Communistic tendencies."[4]

The impending trial finally forced the baseball commissioner into a countermove. On June 5, over two years ahead of schedule, Chandler reinstated all players "who were placed on the ineligible list in 1946 for breaking their player contracts and jumping to Mexico." In explaining his decision, Chandler said, "I feel justified in tempering justice with mercy." Not long after his announcement, he called Mickey Owen and told him, "Get your bag packed, boy, and get to your club right away."[5]

But Roy Campanella now held Owen's old catcher's spot, so Owen signed with the Cubs. For the rest of his career, first with the Cubs and then with the Red Sox, with whom he ended his career in 1954, he was a part-time player. Among the few Mexican League players who were able to regain their old jobs was Sal Maglie, who rejoined the Giants in 1950 in time to enjoy some of the best years of his career. One of the few defectors who never regretted heading south, Maglie would later say, "They offered to double my salary to sixteen thousand. I not only made good money for two years, but I learned how to pitch."[6]

Chandler's decision weakened Gardella's case, and in early October he settled out of court, accepting a cash award and a release from his contract with the Giants. Although he and his lawyer agreed not to reveal the details of the settlement, there were rumors at the time that the payoff was $80,000 and that the sum was raised by the 16 major league clubs donating $5,000 each, hoping to keep the case out of court. Gardella would disclose in 1966 that he had received from the Giants a cash settlement of $60,000, half of which went to his lawyer.

Gardella managed to catch on with the Cardinals for the 1950 season. He was only 29 years old, but he had not played a major league game since 1945 and his skills and enthusiasm had declined. He had only one plate appearance, as a pinch hitter, and he flied out. He was soon sent packing to the minors, where he ended his career in 1951 and faded into obscurity. The owners would enter the 1950s with the reserve clause intact and in firm control of their players. But even though Gardella was gone from the major league scene, the controversy over the reserve clause would rear its head several times in the decade to come.

In spite of the controversy raging off the field, the 1949 season saw two of the most exciting pennant races in history. The year also marked the debut of a new Yankee manager but familiar baseball figure, Charles Dillon "Casey" Stengel, who had been hired at the end of the 1948 season by Yankee owners Dan Topping and Del Webb and general manager George Weiss, formerly the director of the Yankee farm system. Stengel replaced the easygoing Bucky Harris, who was popular with the Yankee players and fans but was regarded by Topping and Webb as a weak disciplinarian who mishandled his players on and off the field and made the mistake of finishing third in 1948.

The announcement of Stengel's appointment had been made on October 12, the day after the end of the 1948 World Series, and the Yankees' choice surprised almost everyone. Many were expecting a young man with a proven managerial track record in the majors, but instead it was a 58-year-old former major league player who in nine years as a major league manager had never finished in the first division and was widely regarded as a practical joker and clown. Sportswriter Dave Egan of the *Boston Daily Record* probably expressed the sentiments of many other reporters when he wrote, "The Yankees have now been mathematically eliminated from the 1949 pennant race."[7]

Stengel came to the Yankee job with nearly forty years of experience as a player and manager. A native of Kansas City, he played with several minor league clubs before joining the Brooklyn Dodgers in 1912, where he was dubbed "Casey," for K.C., the initials of his home town. His other nickname, "Professor"—later "the Old Professor"—came from his brief stint as a college baseball coach with faculty status. In his 14-year career as a big league player, he was well-traveled, playing for the Dodgers, Pirates, Phillies, Giants, and Braves and compiling a lifetime batting average of .284. He played in three World Series, one with the Dodgers and two with the Giants.

Beginning his managerial career in 1925 with Worcester (Massachusetts) in the Eastern League, Stengel managed five minor league clubs and two major league teams before he came to the Yankees. He won three pennants in the minors, but in three years (1934–1936) with the Dodgers and six (1938–1943) with the Braves he never finished higher than fifth. When he was picked to run the Yankees in 1948, he had just completed a pennant-winning season at Kansas City, a Yankee farm club.

Stories about Stengel the clown had been circulating since he broke in with the Dodgers shortly before World War I. He once came to the plate with a sparrow under his cap, and as the fans booed him when he stepped into the batter's box, he bowed and tipped his cap, allowing the sparrow to fly away — Stengel's unique way of giving the bird to hostile fans. In the 1923 World Series he gave the opposing Yankees the finger as he rounded the bases after hitting a home run. While managing the Braves, he once showed his discontent at the umpires' decision to play a game on a rainy, dark afternoon by taking his starting lineup to the plate while dressed in a raincoat and carrying an umbrella and lantern. There were dozens of other stories that had followed him through the years, some true, some false, most embellished with the telling and the retelling. In his years with the Yankees, he would add even more. Having become a legend, he began to promote his reputation deliberately. He enjoyed being famous, being laughed at, and being touted as a wit and baseball sage.

An accomplished mime and raconteur, Stengel had also become a master of a particular kind of double talk and stream of consciousness conversation that became known as "Stengelese." Once he began telling a story or even answering a simple question there was no predicting where the conversation would go and when — if ever — it would end. He said whatever came to mind, jumped from point to point or from subject to subject without any apparent connection between them, digressed, quickly jumped from the present to the past and then back again, leaving the listener bewildered and unsure of what the original question or point had been. Stengel's words were all given emphasis by facial contortions and gestures with the arms or hands or fingers. He often ended his obfuscations with the phrase, "you could look it up," but of course this was usually impossible because it was difficult to determine exactly what he had said. Actually, his Stengelese was often a device for evading a question he did not want to answer or for giving his audience a good story and a good laugh. As some of his players could attest, when he wanted to be direct and clear, he could be, and there was no mistaking what he said or what he meant.

Knowledgeable baseball men knew that the undistinguished managerial record he brought to the Yankees was due more to the quality of the players he worked with than to his omissions as their field leader. Behind his clowning lay a great knowledge of baseball history, techniques, strategies, and subtleties of the game, derived from his long experience as a player and manager. He loved baseball and he lived it all year long; he had few outside interests. He seemed to have an instinctive genius about the game, knowing when to make the right moves. Though he knew the book on baseball strategy, he often violated it by doing the unexpected and the unpredictable. More often than not, his gambles paid off.

Stengel viewed himself as a teacher who could draw on his experience to show his players how to make the most of their mental and physical skills. He often criticized his players because he thought it would help them to recognize their mistakes and learn how to correct them so they could play better. He was not popular with some of his players who did not like to have their mistakes pointed out to them, especially when, as was often the case, he did it in public and humiliated them with his biting sarcasm. Some thought he really was nothing more than a clown, and often complained and second-guessed him behind his back.

Stengel would win ball games for the Yankee management, but he would not turn out to be the strict disciplinarian they wanted. In his days as a player he had been a hard-drinking night owl who was certainly no model for the other players, and as a manager he rarely reproached his players for drinking or violating curfew or other club rules unless it affected their performance on the field. In the 1950s he sometimes protected Whitey Ford, Billy Martin, Mickey Mantle, and others who had partied too much the night before by sitting them down for all or part of a game, telling reporters that they had a "slight injury" or they needed "a rest." He once remarked, as he watched Bob Turley struggling on the mound, "Look at him. He don't smoke, he don't drink, he don't chase women, and he don't win."[8] He did caution players that "it ain't sex that's troublesome, it's staying up all night looking for it,"[9] and that "you gotta learn that if you don't get it by midnight, chances are you ain't gonna get it, and if you do, it ain't worth it."[10] The players found him hard to outwit, for as he told one Yankee squad, "You can't fool me. I pulled every stunt that was ever thought up, and I did them fifty years before you even got here."[11]

In January of 1949 at the annual New York Baseball Writers dinner, Stengel said, "I've been hired to win, and I think I will. There is less wrong with the Yankees than with any club I've ever had."[12] When he heard that most sportswriters were expecting his club to come in third again, trailing Boston and Cleveland, he said, "Third ain't so bad. I never finished third before."[13]

The club he had to work with was a team in transition, a mixture of veterans like Joe DiMaggio, Charlie Keller, Tommy Henrich, Snuffy Stirnweiss, and Phil Rizzuto, and of young players like Yogi Berra, Gene Woodling, Jerry Coleman, Hank Bauer, and Bobby Brown. He had good pitching, led by Vic Raschi, Allie Reynolds, Tommy Byrne, Ed Lopat, and reliever Joe Page. But many of the veterans who had played under Harris and McCarthy were dismayed at Stengel's hiring, believing that the job was too big for him and that he was just an interim manager while the team was rebuilding. Some even felt that he was just holding down the job until DiMaggio was ready to retire and take over.

It was a very difficult year for the new manager, for the Yankees were struck by one injury after another. DiMaggio missed the first 65 games because of bone spurs in his heel, Berra lost close to a month with a broken finger, Henrich sat out several games with two fractured vertebrae, and Johnny Mize, the left-handed slugger acquired from the Giants in August, played only a week before suffering a shoulder separation. For the year the Yankees suffered a total of 72 injuries.

Faced with these problems, Stengel had to resort to juggling his lineup to find nine healthy men to put on the field at one time. As he did, he was unveiling the practice he would become famous for — platooning. The word was first used to describe what he was doing by *New York Herald Tribune* sportswriter Harold Rosenthal in a column in May of 1949. Besides running men in and out of the lineup because of injuries or for defensive purposes, Stengel alternated players in the lineup to load it with left-handed or right-handed hitters depending on the opposing pitcher. Of course, the practice had existed as early as the first decade of the century. But it had never been used as extensively as Stengel employed it, and it had declined in the twenties and thirties until he revived it and it was copied by other managers in both leagues.

Although Henrich played regularly in right field, Stengel platooned outfielders Johnny Lindell, Hank Bauer, Gene Woodling, and Cliff Mapes, while in the infield he alternated Bobby Brown and Billy Johnson at third base and Jack Phillips and Dick Kryhoski at first. He did not platoon everybody. When they were healthy, star players like DiMaggio, Berra, and Rizzuto played on a regular basis no matter who was pitching, and of course when switch hitter Mickey Mantle came to the club in 1951 his bat could be used in the lineup every day no matter who was on the mound. Some players did not like being platooned, but Bauer, who resented being platooned with Woodling, later said, "When you're walking to the bank with that World Series check every November, you don't want to leave. There were no Yankees saying play me or trade me."[14]

Stengel surprised the experts. The Yankees got off to a fast start and by the end of April, riding a 10–2 record, were firmly established in first place, while Joe McCarthy's Red Sox were mired in sixth with a 5–6 mark, 4½ games out. By July 4, the Red Sox were 12½ games behind Stengel's injury-ridden team. But then Boston recovered from its dismal start. Led by the hitting of Ted Williams, Johnny Pesky, Bobby Doer, Dom DiMaggio, and Vern Stephens, and the pitching of Mel Parnell and Ellis Kinder, who would combine for half of the club's 96 victories, the Red Sox turned the race into one of the most stirring pennant battles in history. They undoubtedly would have won it all, had it not been for Stengel's genius in juggling his injury-ridden lineup and for the inspiring play of Joe DiMaggio, who returned from what appeared to be a career-ending injury to lead the club to the flag.

DiMaggio's contract in 1949 was for $100,000, making him the first player to ever reach that plateau and reinforcing his stature as the top player in the game. But his career had been riddled with injuries and other medical problems, and in 1949 he had to go on the injury list once again. He had undergone surgery for bone spurs on his left heel in January of 1947 and then on his right heel in November of 1948. After his last surgery his doctors had assured him that he would be ready to play by opening day, but when he reported to spring training his heel was still so tender that he found himself hobbling around the outfield and humbled at the plate. He left the team, and after consulting with doctors he decided to give the heel more recuperative time. He went to his hotel apartment in New York, where he stayed off his feet as much as possible while hoping that the inactivity would cause the pain to go away.

It was a difficult time for the Yankee Clipper. He was the team leader, and as he lay in bed watching games on television or trying to sleep, he worried about letting the team down and wondered if he would ever play again. Every morning when he got out of bed he put his foot on the floor hoping there would be no pain, but every morning the pain was there. On top of these problems, his father died in May. It was the low point in his career.

Then one June morning he got up and put his right heel on the floor, expecting to feel the usual pains. There were none, and as he walked around the room they still did not return. When the Yankees returned from a road trip he rejoined the team, and after working out for about a week, he told Stengel that he was ready to play. He was out of shape, but the most important thing to his teammates and to Yankee fans was that Joe DiMaggio was back.

DiMaggio returned to the lineup on June 28 as the Yankees opened a crucial three-game series in Fenway Park, where the Red Sox had won 10 of their last 11 games. Although he had missed all the regular season so far and had to wear a special orthopedic shoe, he began to play as if he were in mid-season form. In his first at bat, he hit a single over the shortstop's head, then in his second appearance he hit a three-run homer. Players on both benches joined the fans in standing and watching the Yankee superstar as he ran out the blast that announced his return to the pennant wars. The Yankees went on to win, 5–4. The next day he hit two more home runs as the Yankees came back from a 7–1 deficit to take a 9–7 victory. In the final game of the series he hit still another home run to help the Yankees win 6–3 and sweep the series. In just three games, and after such a long layoff, he hit 4 homers, drove in 9 runs, and made 13 putouts in the outfield. The Yankees left town eight games ahead of the Red Sox. A few days later, after sweeping a July 4 doubleheader from McCarthy's men in Yankee Stadium, the Bronx Bombers left their rivals 12 games behind and seemingly out of contention.

DiMaggio's comeback was the talk of the season. He dominated the sports pages of the newspapers and was on the cover of *Life* magazine, which called his return "one of the most heart-warming comebacks in all sports history" and featured a cover story under his byline entitled, "It's Great to Be Back."[15] With his spectacular return, DiMaggio resumed his role as the leader of the Yankees. He helped carry the team from late June until late August, then missed several more games because of a sprained left shoulder and a bout with viral pneumonia that drained his energy and kept him out of the lineup until the last two games of the season. At season's end, he had played in only 76 games, but he had managed 94 hits, 14 homers, 67 RBIs, and a .346 batting average. No one was surprised when the Associated Press voted him the "Comeback Player of the Year."

While DiMaggio was making his comeback, the Red Sox were making one of their own. In the second half of the campaign the team jelled and made an incredible run for the pennant. They won 19 of 23 games during one hot streak and took 24 of 32 games in August. But the injury-plagued Yankees still managed to play well enough in September to maintain a slim lead over the Red Sox until the next to the last weekend of the season, when they lost three in a row to their rivals and fell out of the lead for the first time all season. With only one week to go, the Red Sox, declared dead by many observers at the Fourth of July mark, led the Yankees and dreamed of going to the World Series and avenging the humiliation of 1946.

The Red Sox held on to their narrow lead over the next five games. On Saturday, October 1, they came into Yankee Stadium with a one game lead with just two games left to play. It was also "Joe DiMaggio Day," a special event that had been planned long before it was known that on this day the two teams would be battling for the pennant. Among the 69,551 in attendance were some 700 fans who came in from New Haven in a special nine-car train called "The Joe DiMaggio Special." DiMaggio's mother, Rosalie, and his son, Joe, Jr., were also present for the ceremonies. With Joe playing for the Yankees and Dom for the Red Sox, Mrs. DiMaggio was guaranteed to have one son in the World Series.

The Yankee Clipper, still weak from his battle with pneumonia, was given a new Cadillac and several other gifts, along with $50,000 in cash, which he donated to his favorite charities. Visibly moved by the honors accorded him on this special day, he had to fight back the tears as he stood at home plate with his brother Dom by his side. Speaking into the microphone, he said, "I'd like to thank the good Lord for making me a Yankee," standard crowd-pleasing words that he sincerely meant. He praised the Red Sox, who had given him a plaque autographed by the players and his old manager, Joe McCarthy, as a "grand team and a great bunch of guys" and said "if we don't win the pennant I'm happy that they will."[16]

With the festivities out of the way, the crucial next-to-the-last games of the season began. The Yankees had their backs to the wall, for they had to take both games to win the pennant while the Sox needed only a split. The Red Sox initially looked as if they would wrap the pennant up on "Joe DiMaggio Day," as they took a 4–0 lead early in the game. But the Yankees came back to tie the score at 4–4 in the fifth, then went on to win 5–4 on a home run by Johnny Lindell in the eighth. Joe Page, who relieved starter Allie Reynolds, pitched brilliantly, giving up just one hit and no runs in 6⅔ innings. He ended the year with 13 wins and 8 losses and led the league in games (60) and saves (27).

Now tied with identical records of 96–57, the two teams met the next day before another large crowd of 68,055. The Red Sox put their hopes behind 23-game-winner Ellis Kinder, while the Yankees countered with Vic Raschi, who at 20–10 was having his best year yet. The Yankees scored early and held a 5–0 lead going into the ninth, when the Sox rallied and scored three runs before Raschi recovered and preserved his 21st victory. As the final out was made, a pop foul by Birdie Tebbetts to Henrich behind first base, coach Bill Dickey got so excited that he jumped up off his dugout seat and hit his head on the roof, and collapsed, unconscious. It was, some said, the seventy-third Yankee injury of the year. Stengel had won his first pennant, and it was, he said, "the greatest thrill of my life."[17]

The Red Sox seemed jinxed. Like the Dodgers, they always seemed good enough to be also-rans but not good enough to win the big ones–the American League pennant and the World Series. They had lost the 1946 World Series in the seventh game on Slaughter's famous score from first, had come off second best in the 1948 playoff with the Indians, and now they had squandered the 1949 pennant on the last two days of the season. For Ted Williams, the end of the season brought a double disappointment. Not only did his team lose the pennant on the last day, but he also lost the batting crown and the Triple Crown on the same day. He took the home run crown (43) and tied teammate Vern Stephens for the RBI title (159), but after battling George Kell of the Detroit Tigers down to the wire for the batting title Williams went 0-for-2 in his last game while Kell went 2-for-3 to win by .3429 to .3427, just .0002 of a percentage point. However, for his contributions to the Red Sox pennant drive, Williams won his second MVP Award.

The defending champions, the Indians, finished in third place, eight games behind the Yankees, but they still managed to draw 2.6 million fans. As always, owner Bill Veeck had treated the fans to bread and circuses even if he could not give them a pennant, and after being mathematically eliminated from the race he gave them one of the most bizarre stunts yet. On the night of September 23, before a home game with the Detroit Tigers, he staged a mock funeral to bury the 1948 championship flag.

With Veeck dressed like a mortician and several club officials dressed as pallbearers, the flag was solemnly taken down from the flagpole and placed in a pine coffin, which was then loaded into a hearse. Veeck drove the hearse around the field, and as it passed by the Cleveland dugout the players came out and joined the procession. He stopped the hearse behind the wire fence in center field at the flagpole. As business manager Rudie Schaffer read the last rites from the Baseball Bible, the *Sporting News*, Veeck wiped his eyes with a white handkerchief. The coffin was slowly lowered into the grave, then covered and decorated with flowers. An imitation tombstone inscribed with the words "1948 Champs" was put into place. The solemn occasion was completed with the playing of taps by a bugler. When the ceremony was over, the Indians went out, and appropriately, were buried by the Tigers, 5–0.[18]

It was Veeck's last year in Cleveland. He was getting restless, looking for new worlds to conquer, and he had been threatening all year to sell the club. "I have to have a challenge," he said. "That's why I've been playing tennis every afternoon. One-legged men aren't supposed to play tennis. I have to prove that I can do it."[19] At the end of the season he sold the club for $2.2 million to a group of Cleveland businessmen. But he would not be gone from baseball for long. In 1951, he would resurface as the owner of the St. Louis Browns.

The National League race would be just as dramatic as the American League one, with the traditional rivals, St. Louis and Brooklyn, being the major contenders for the league flag. The Cardinals fielded a strong team led by sluggers Stan Musial and Enos Slaughter, the slick fielding of shortstop Marty Marion and second baseman Red Schoendienst, and the pitching of Howie Pollet. After finishing second the previous two years, Eddie Dyer's club was hoping to regain its familiar place at the top of the league.

Meanwhile in Brooklyn the Dodgers had taken on a definite Branch Rickey look. The Dodger farm system, and a few judicious trades, had produced a team that would remain at or near the top in offensive and defensive play for nearly another decade. It had Roy Campanella behind the plate,

Gil Hodges at first, Jackie Robinson at second, Pee Wee Reese (the only holdover from the MacPhail years) at short, defensive wizard Billy Cox at third, Duke Snider in center field, Carl Furillo in right, and Gene Hermanski sharing the starting role in left with several others. Rookie of the Year Don Newcombe (17–8), Preacher Roe (15–6), and Ralph Branca (13–5) led a pitching staff strengthened in August by the addition of Carl Erskine, who came up from Ft. Worth to fashion an 8–1 record in the last weeks of the race. The Dodgers had three of the major leagues' seven black players: Robinson, Campanella, and Newcombe. The other four were Monte Irvin and Hank Thompson of the Giants and Larry Doby and Satchel Paige of the Indians.

The 1949 season brought a change in the play of Jackie Robinson. For three years he had kept his promise to Branch Rickey, tolerating the grossest insults and avoiding ugly incidents that might jeopardize the continued integration of organized baseball. Now that he and integration were firmly established in the major leagues, Rickey told him, "You're on your own now."[20] With this new freedom, he was more aggressive than ever at the plate and on the base paths. Around the keystone he made all the plays he was supposed to make and some that it seemed nearly impossible to make. He was quick to dispute an umpire's call, to lash back at harassing opponents, and to stand his ground against players who had tormented him in the past. He told Ben Chapman, his old nemesis, "You SOB . . . . You've been on me for two years. If you open your mouth one more time, I'm gonna . . . kick the shit out of you."[21] As the season progressed he gained a reputation as a hothead, a man with a chip on his shoulder who overreacted to real and imagined offenses. But as he would later write, "It felt good to be able to breathe freely, to speak out when I wanted to."[22]

The 1949 season would be Robinson's best year in baseball. He led the league in hitting (.342) and stolen bases (37), was second in RBIs (124) and hits (203), scored 122 runs and hit 16 homers. And he got the recognition he deserved. He became the first black player to play in the All-Star Game (Campanella, Newcombe, and Larry Doby also appeared), and was named the National League MVP. At season's end he would sign a contract for 1950 for $35,000, seven times the salary he had received as a rookie just three years before.

In this perennial battle between Brooklyn and St. Louis, the Cardinals got off to a slow start in the spring but managed to work their way into the lead by the last week of June. They would stay there for most of the remainder of the season, though the Dodgers always managed to within striking distance. On September 25, the Cards led by 1½ games with five games to go, while the Dodgers had four games remaining. The Cardinals then stumbled, losing three in a row, and as the two teams entered the last weekend of the season the Dodgers had crawled on top by one game with a record of 96–56, the exact same lead and record the Red Sox held in the junior circuit. It had been a very dramatic season in both leagues, and now it all boiled down to one final weekend.

On Saturday, October 1, while the Yankees were honoring Joe DiMaggio and beating the Red Sox, the Dodgers lost to the Phillies and the Cardinals fell to the Cubs, delaying the decision until the very last day. On Sunday the Cardinals finally ended a four-game losing streak by beating the Cubs, 13–5, then awaited the outcome of the Dodgers-Phillies game. The Dodgers forged a 5–0 lead behind Don Newcombe, then allowed the Phillies to knot the score at 7–7 and carry the game into extra innings. But in the 10th, the Dodgers scored two and held the Phillies scoreless to emerge with a 9–7 victory and the National League pennant, just 36 minutes after the Yankees had clinched the American League flag. Distressed over the Cardinal collapse in the final week, manager Eddie Dyer said, "We just ran out of gas, that's all."[23]

After one of the most exciting seasons in baseball history, the Dodgers and Yankees opened the World Series in Yankee Stadium on October 5. The Dodgers had a much better team than the one that had lost to the Yankees in seven games in 1947, and Burt Shotton was hoping to capture the first flag ever for the team from Flatbush. The Yankees seemed vulnerable, especially with DiMaggio still recuperating from viral pneumonia. On the day of the first game, the *Brooklyn Eagle* ran the headline, "NEXT YEAR IS HERE."

But it was not the fabled next year. DiMaggio did have a poor Series, managing just one single and one homer in 18 at bats, but the rest of the team picked up the slack. The clubs split the first two games and went to Ebbets Field, giving the Dodgers the crucial home field advantage in the next three contests, but the Yankees swept all three to wrap up the championship. The Dodgers were humiliated, especially Don Newcombe, who was saddled with two of the losses. But Brooklyn players and fans could take heart in the knowledge that there was always next year and that the Dodgers had a young team that would undoubtedly have another shot at the world title.

An estimated 78 million people listened to the Series on the radio, beating the 1947 record of 72 million, while close to 20 million watched on television, another record. Gillette was again the sponsor, shelling out $350,000 for television and radio rights.

With all the major league clubs except Pittsburgh televising their home games, and with a red hot pennant race in both leagues, more and more fans had bought sets so they could watch one of baseball's most exciting seasons from the comfort of taverns or from their armchairs at home. Perhaps that helped explain why, after four consecutive record-breaking years, major league attendance declined from 20.9 million in 1948 to 20.2 million in 1949.

During the 1949 season, while fans had their eyes on the exciting pennant races, tragedy came to Eddie Waitkus, one of the stars of the third-place Philadelphia Phillies. A young, good-hitting slick-fielding first baseman, Waitkus was nearly killed in a brief encounter with a psychotic female admirer.

Organized baseball had been troubled by "camp followers"—also known as "Baseball Sadies" or "Baseball Annies"—for decades. Usually young teenage girls with adolescent crushes on their idols, older women looking for a husband, or young women looking for blackmail opportunities, they sent letters and telegrams to players, telephoned them, sat behind the dugout, and hung around train stations, hotels, restaurants, and bars frequented by the players. Most players were well aware of the problems of getting involved with these women—the potential for embarrassing publicity, harassment, violence, paternity suits, blackmail, and marital problems and messy divorces. Most avoided contact with these women, and those who did not sometimes found more trouble than they had anticipated.

A native of Cambridge, Massachusetts, Waitkus was a World War II veteran who went unscathed through four invasions of the Pacific Islands. He had played just 12 games with the Cubs in 1941, his first year in the majors, but he returned from service in 1946 to claim the first base job, which he held until he was traded to the Phillies at the end of the 1948 season. In his first 54 games with the Phillies in 1949, the 30-year-old left-handed slugger hit .306, with 41 runs and 28 RBIs. But then he made the mistake of going to Ruth Ann Steinhagen's Chicago hotel room.

A 19-year-old typist for a Chicago insurance company, Steinhagen was a neurotic young woman who had been obsessed with movie star Alan Ladd and other celebrities until 1946, when she first saw Waitkus, then the first baseman for the Cubs. What began as a teenage crush quickly developed into a strong infatuation and eventually a psychotic obsession. She ate baked beans because he was from Boston, began to study Lithuanian because she had read that he was of Lithuanian descent, and made her room in her parents' home into an Eddie Waitkus shrine, crowded with pictures of the young star, game programs, press clippings, rain check stubs, and other memorabilia. She went to as many games at Wrigley Field as she could, standing with other bobby-soxers to watch the players pass by and sitting in the stands near first base so she could worship her hero at close range.

When Waitkus was traded to Philadelphia at the end of the 1948 season, she immediately transferred her loyalty to the Phillies and tried to see every game the team played in Chicago. Her mental state steadily deteriorated. On June 13, 1949, she drew all her money ($85) out of the bank and went to the room she had rented in the name of Ruth Ann Burns at the Edgewater Beach Hotel, where the Phillies stayed while they were in town to play the Cubs. She carried along 50 pictures of Waitkus and a .22 caliber rifle she had bought at a pawnshop. The next afternoon, she and her girlfriend went to the Cubs-Phillies game, but she left in the seventh inning and went back to her hotel, where she dressed up, ordered three drinks sent to her room, and gave the bellhop $5 to take a note to Waitkus's room. Handwritten on hotel stationery, the note said, "We're not acquainted, but I have something of importance to speak to you about. . . . As I am leaving the hotel the day after tomorrow, I'd appreciate it greatly if you could see me as soon as possible. My name is Ruth Ann Burns. Room 1279-A."[24]

When Waitkus returned to his room shortly after 11 o'clock that night he found the note the bellhop had left on his bureau. He had never met Steinhagen, but he telephoned her because he had some friends in Chicago named Burns and he thought it might be important. When she said that she would rather not discuss the matter over the phone, he agreed to come to her room. After he came into her room and sat down, she told him, "I have a surprise for you," then went to her closet and got the rifle. Waving it in his face, she motioned him toward the window, saying, "For two years you've been bothering me, and now you're going to die." Startled, Waitkus only had time to yell "What in the world goes on here?" before she shot him in the chest. As he lay on his back on the carpet, he looked up at her and said, "Oh, baby, what did you do that for?" She knelt beside him, took his right hand, and said, "You like this, don't you? But why in the name of heaven did you do this to me?"[25]

Steinhagen had planned to kill herself, but she lost her nerve and blacked out. When she came to, she called the hotel operator and told her that she had shot a man. The police and an ambulance soon arrived, and Waitkus was hurried to a hospital, where surgeons found that the bullet had pierced his lung and lodged in the muscle tissue near his spine, barely missing his heart and spine. At first one of his doctors reported that "it's touch and go whether he'll live,"[26] but fortunately he had youth and an excellent physical condition on his side. The bullet was removed and he was soon out of danger, but his doctors told him that his 1949 season was over.

Steinhagen was examined by psychiatrists at the Behavior Clinic of the Criminal Court of Cook County. When asked why she had shot Waitkus, she replied, "It's a mixture of things. First of all I think I shot him because I liked him a great deal and I knew I never could have him and if I couldn't have him neither could anybody else. Secondly, I had the idea that if I shot him I would have to shoot myself. In the third place I wanted publicity and attention for once." When asked about the future, she said, "If I ever get out of here I'll kill him if he ever got married. He's the only one worth shooting. I wouldn't shoot anybody else."[27]

After extensive tests and several court hearings, she was declared insane and sent to the Kankakee State Hospital, where she was to remain until she was cured of her schizophrenia and other mental problems and posed no threat to herself or to anyone else. In 1952 hospital authorities declared that she was cured and released her, in spite of the opposition of Waitkus, who argued that she might try to harm him or his family. But she never contacted him or any members of his family.

Waitkus's brush with death at the hands of a "Baseball Annie" received a great deal of publicity. What many fans did not know was that the Phillies' star was not the first major league player to be shot in a Chicago hotel room by a female admirer. Seventeen years earlier, Cubs' shortstop Bill Jurges had been shot three times during a scuffle with a 21-year-old showgirl. In 1952, Bernard Malamud would draw upon the Waitkus and Jurges incidents, along with fact and fiction surrounding Shoeless Joe Jackson and Babe Ruth, in his baseball novel, *The Natural*, which would be made into a popular movie starring Robert Redford in 1984.

The publicity over Waitkus's shooting did nothing to end the activities of "Baseball Annies." Joe DiMaggio had often received letters from women wanting to meet him and promising to attend to all of his needs. Not long after Waitkus was shot, DiMaggio, who was recovering from bone spurs in his hotel room, began to receive letters from an admirer who threatened to commit suicide if he did not return her love. She even tried to visit him at the hotel but was turned away before she got to his room. The Yankee management, mindful of the Waitkus case, assigned a bodyguard to the Yankee Clipper and brought in the police to investigate. They finally arrested a young woman who, after being interrogated by the police and examined by psychiatrists, was released to her family's care on the condition that it seek further treatment for her and prevent her from harassing DiMaggio. Police and hospital authorities did not reveal her identity to the press, and theorized that her actions may have been triggered by the publicity surrounding the Waitkus case.[28]

Waitkus spent the rest of the season recuperating while his team finished in third place. In 1950, he, and the Phillies, would come back to give the "City of Brotherly Love" a long-awaited pennant.

7. Heroes, Bonus Babies, and Whiz Kids (1950)

The United States entered the fifties in an apprehensive mood. Everything seemed to be going wrong. The Cold War between the Communist world and the West had taken on new dimensions in the latter half of 1949 when Russia developed the atomic bomb, ending the American monopoly of that terrible weapon, and when China, containing nearly one quarter of the world's people, fell into the hands of Communist leader Mao Zedung after a long civil war.

In the first few months of 1950, the headlines seemed to bring bad news every day. Alger Hiss, a former high official in the Roosevelt and Truman administrations, was convicted of perjury in a sensational treason trial. President Truman, citing the new danger posed to Americans by the development of Russian atomic weapons, announced the inauguration of a crash program to build a bigger, better weapon — the hydrogen bomb — and Americans began to worry more and more about atomic attacks on the United States. An espionage ring was uncovered in Canada and the United States, resulting in the arrest of several Americans, including Julius and Ethel Rosenberg, on charges of passing atomic secrets to the Russians. Senator Joseph McCarthy began his rise to power with his wild charges that the State Department and other government agencies had been infiltrated by Communists. Then on June 25, North Korean forces invaded South Korea, plunging the United States into a long, bloody, and divisive conflict. Less than five years after the end of World War II, America was at war again.

On April 18, two months before the outbreak of the Korean War, major league baseball began still another season in its long history when Truman took time from his busy schedule to throw out the first ball at Griffith Stadium. It was his fifth consecutive appearance at the Washington opener. Although it began to rain in the sixth inning, Truman donned a light jacket and stayed until the end of the game, which Washington took from the Athletics by an 8–7 margin. The American League was off to its fiftieth season and the National to its seventy-fifth, and both circuits were hoping for a banner year.

In spite of the increasing competition from television and other leisure activities, the controversy over the reserve clause, and other nagging problems, baseball was still the king of professional sports. In both the minors and the majors, the postwar period had seen huge increases in attendance. Professional football and basketball were overshadowed by the college versions of their games, soccer and ice hockey were regarded as foreign sports, and golf and tennis were still identified in many people's minds as sports of the idle rich. In the nation's pantheon of heroes, baseball players still ranked at or near the top. "Call it hero worship, if you will," Arthur Daley said in the *New York Times* in April of 1950, "but the fact remains that the baseball gods are worshipped with a fervor which is almost idolatrous." And he noted one of the factors that had made baseball so popular: "Not in fifty years has there been a rules change of any consequence. A Rip Van Winkle could awaken after a twenty-five year snooze and find the national game exactly the same as it was when he first closed his eyes. But he wouldn't recognize football, basketball, or many other sports."[1]

It was true, as Daley said, that America's favorite pastime had been a remarkably stable game. But it was changing, in subtle and not so subtle ways. It was being transformed by television, integration, the steady increase in the number of night games, and a growing reliance on airplanes for team travel. It was also undergoing alterations in strategy. The growing reliance on home runs was leading to a decline in batting averages, an increase in strikeouts and walks, and a decreasing emphasis on the stolen base, hit and run, and other fine points of the game. Meanwhile, pitching was also undergoing changes as managers began to rely more and more on relievers. Pitchers developed new weapons like the slider and used illegal pitches like the spitter to defend themselves against lineups packed with sluggers intent on knocking the ball out of the park. All of these changes would become more and more pronounced as the decade of the fifties wore on.

It was also true, as Daley wrote, that major league baseball players ranked among the greatest of American heroes, idolized for their exploits on the field and for the kind of lives they seemed to lead. For much of the 20th century, and especially since Babe Ruth appeared on the scene, major league baseball players had been regarded by much of the population as folk heroes doing something others could only dream of. Where but in the major leagues could a man play a boy's game for half a year and enjoy the adoration of millions of fans, a high salary, and an exciting lifestyle? It seemed to be the best of all possible worlds.

But as the Mexican jumpers, Murphy's union, Gardella's lawsuit, and other examples of increasing player militancy had helped to show, the baseball heroes idolized by the American public led lives that were far from idyllic. It was difficult for most fans to understand that playing major league baseball was a job, and that like most jobs it was accompanied by fatigue, boredom, insecurity, and stress. The baseball season was long, beginning with spring training in February and lasting until October. Players spent about 60 percent of this time on the road, and frequent travel brought fatigue, a constant stream of hotel rooms and hotel food, irregular eating and sleeping hours, loneliness, and long separations from families. Baseball careers were short, five years on the average, and even the stars saw their careers come to an end in their mid-thirties or, in rare cases, in their early forties. Thus when most men their age were just beginning to hit their stride and were looking forward to 20 or 30 more years of productive work, baseball players were looking for a new profession.

With only a few years to practice their trade and only 400 major league jobs, the pressure to perform or be replaced was constant. There was always the fear of being traded, sent down to the minors, or losing one's starting position to a younger or better player, to injury, or to a dispute with management. The pressure to get to the big leagues and to stay there sometimes led to nervous breakdowns, alcoholism, and other mental and medical problems. The pressure to conform to management's desires on and off the field led grown men to accept rules about shaving, hair grooming, dress, and curfew, as if they were college athletes or military recruits. If a player did not like the way he was being treated there was little he could do about it except to submit to it or quit, for the reserve clause bound him to the club in perpetuity.

There were other occupational hazards as well. As public idols, players were prime targets for "Baseball Annies," deserved or undeserved paternity suits, blackmail, and physical threats from pranksters and psychotics. Jackie Robinson received dozens of death threats in his early years in the majors, and even as late as 1953 he received a letter saying, "No use crying for the cops — you'll be executed gangland style at Busch Stadium." In that same year, Mickey Mantle received a letter containing a threat to kill him when the Yankees came to Boston for a doubleheader at Fenway Park. Sometimes the letter writers were trying to extort money. In August of 1951, Ralph Kiner received a letter demanding $6,200 "or I'll shoot you and you make a good target in left field."[2] Although club authorities and police believed that most threatening letters or telephone calls were hoaxes, they had to take them seriously and provide police and sometimes even FBI protection for the targeted player.

The salaries of players were generally above those of the average American worker, but most players did not make the huge salaries much of the public thought they did. The only players to reach the $100,000 plateau between 1945 and 1960 were Ted Williams, Joe DiMaggio, and Stan Musial. Most players made far less. In 1950, the 10 highest paid players ranged from Ted Williams ($125,000) and Joe DiMaggio ($100,000) at the top to George Kell, Jackie Robinson, and Pee Wee Reese—each earning $35,000—in the last three spots. These were excellent salaries for that time, but the average player made around $13,000.

Salaries did rise in the fifties. By 1957, the average salary was $15,000, with Williams ($100,000 or more), Musial ($80,000), and Mantle ($65,000) leading the way. Nearly 75 percent of the 400 major leaguers made between $10,000 and $25,000, but only 40 players made $25,000 or more and only 10 made over $50,000. Minimum salaries had risen, too. The first minimum salary was established in 1947 at $5,000, and it rose to $6,000 in 1954 and to $7,000 in 1960. For those players lucky enough to play in the World Series, October brought an extra bonus. The winning share for each player was $3,750 in 1946, and rose steadily thereafter, to $8,300 in 1953 and $11,200 in 1959.[3] But these figures tend to obscure the real problems with salaries. When adjusted for inflation, the real wages of major leaguers declined by about 10 percent between 1945 and 1963. And there were great disparities among individuals and teams. Team salaries of successful clubs like the Yankees, Dodgers, and Giants in some years were in the $500,000 to $600,000 range, while the Reds, Pirates, and other second division clubs had total payrolls of $300,000 or less. After a poor team finish, a bad year at the gate, or a decline in performance, players' salaries were often cut, even those of star players like Mantle. And hampered by the reserve clause and the absence of agents to help with the negotiations with the club owners, most players had little bargaining power when presented with a take-it-or-leave-it contract. A star player might succeed in getting his salary adjusted by a few thousand dollars, but dramatic pay raises were out of the question. The owners had the players over a barrel—"play for us or you don't play at all."

Most of the players of the fifties supplemented their baseball salaries with off-season jobs. Contrary to the belief of the fans, very few players were able to spend the winter playing golf, fishing, hunting, or traveling. Some used the time to pursue college degrees, but most had to find employment, often at jobs that allowed them to capitalize on their status as folk heroes. Many found positions as salesmen in furniture, clothing, or sporting goods stores or as hosts or greeters in restaurants. Jackie Robinson once worked as a television salesman in an appliance store. Yogi Berra of the Yankees and Ralph Branca of the Dodgers worked for the same men's clothing store in Newark, New Jersey. Some owned their own businesses. Jim Konstanty owned a sporting goods store, Granny Hamner and his brother operated a service station, Roy Campanella ran a liquor store, and Ted Williams was a "consultant" to Wilson Sporting Goods Company, receiving a check twice a month, even when he was flying jets in Korea. Many had less glamorous jobs; for example Hank Bauer worked as a pipe fitter, and Robin Roberts as cardboard box salesman.

Some players picked up extra cash by making television and radio appearances and endorsing consumer products. Stars made more money from public appearances and endorsements than lesser lights, and white players made more than black players, who usually got few chances to pick up extra cash hawking shaving cream or other products. As the decade progressed, more and more players hired agents to handle these activities, but this was all the agents did; they did not conduct contract negotiations for their clients with their major league club. It was not until 1971 that owners allowed players to use agents in salary negotiations.

Unfortunately, major leaguers of this era played before the salary explosion of the 1970s and 1980s, so most retired from baseball but not from working. Some found employment in baseball as managers, coaches, scouts, front office executives, or broadcasters, but most had jobs that had little direct connection with the game they loved. Jackie Robinson became a corporate executive, Bobby Brown became a physician (and later president of the American League), Wilmer "Vinegar Bend" Mizell went into politics and even made it to Congress, and DiMaggio, Williams, and other stars continued to make money on their past fame by endorsing various consumer products. But many found work far removed from the glamor of their baseball days, such as bartenders, construction workers, factory workers, and other menial jobs. In the 1970s, when Roger Kahn interviewed several Dodger greats for his book, *The Boys of Summer,* he found George Shuba working for the post office, Preacher Roe running a supermarket, Carl Furillo laboring as a construction worker installing elevators in the World Trade Center, and Billy Cox bartending at a private club.

When they reached the age of 50, many players of this era were eligible for a pension. It was hardly enough to live on. The first plan, adopted in 1947, made all coaches, players, and trainers on the payrolls of the 16 major league clubs on opening day eligible for a pension of from $50 to $100 a month after they had reached the age of 50 if they had played for five years or more. The pension would be based on the age and years of service and ranged from $50 to $100 a month. The pension plan was gradually improved, and in 1957 a new plan increased the range of the pension to between $175 and $550 a month, depending on the player's age and years of service. The 1957 plan was partly funded by the players, who contributed $2 a day to the plan, and primarily from the team owners, who agreed to put 60 percent of the fees they received from radio and television rights to the All-Star and World Series games. In 1957, these rights cost $3.4 million. The increased cost of this plan was the main factor behind the decision to hold two All-Star games each summer between 1959 and 1962.

As baseball began play in 1950 it was facing a potential manpower shortage. Of the 559 players on the 16 major league rosters in 1945, only 30 were still playing for major league clubs in 1950. World War II had interrupted the flow of talent from the high schools, colleges, and farm clubs, and in the postwar period teams were faced with the problem of restocking their rosters with young men to take the place of aging and retiring veterans who had come back to the game after years of military service. This shortage of talent encouraged some teams to follow Brooklyn's lead in tapping the previously ignored pool of black talent and forced many teams to engage in a wild bidding war for the talent that was around. This gave rise to the "bonus babies"—young players, often no more than 18 or 19 years old, signed out of high schools and colleges for large bonuses designed to get them to put their name on the dotted line. Young men who could throw hard or rattle the fences with their bats quickly found a host of big league scouts on their doorsteps, promising bigger bonuses and a faster trip to major league stardom than the competition could provide.

The practice was extremely rare prior to the 1940s. Before then, players usually received little or no bonus for signing with a major league club—just getting the chance to play major league ball was incentive enough. Some who went on to become major league stars had signed for as little as $500 or $1,000. Bob Feller signed with the Indians in 1935 for $1 and an autographed baseball.

Six years later came the first bonus baby, outfielder Dick Wakefield, who was a baseball star at the University of Michigan when the Detroit Tigers gave him an unprecedented $52,000 bonus and a new car to sign with them. Few bonus babies were recruited during the war years, but in the late 1940s and 1950s the major league teams paid millions of dollars for untried players. In the 1950s, nearly 100 bonus babies were signed, 37 of them in the boom year of 1955.

Most of these gambles did not pay off. The first of this breed, Wakefield, appeared in just 638 games in his nine-year major league career and managed a lifetime average of .293 with 56 homers and 315 RBIs. The Tigers also paid $75,000 for catcher Frank House in 1948, and he too had an undistinguished career—a .248 batting average in 653 games spread over a 10-year career with the Tigers and two other clubs. The Red Sox signed pitcher Frank Quinn for almost $60,000 in 1948, but arm trouble reduced his major league career to just 24 innings spread over two years. The White Sox paid pitcher Constantine "Gus" Keriazakos $67,000 in 1949, and he eventually played for three teams and left the majors for good in 1955 after appearing in only 28 games with a 2–5 record. And one of the biggest mistakes of all was the $100,000 the Pirates paid pitcher Paul Pettit, whose major league career would consist of just 12 games and a 1–2 record. The list of failures was a long and expensive one.

The practice of signing bonus babies created still other problems. These highly-paid rookies spent most of their time hugging the bench instead of developing their skills by playing every day in the minors. They were often resented by veterans who had played regularly for years and had not yet hit the $20,000-a-year mark, far less than what many of the new recruits were paid just to sign a contract. At a time when the average salary was $13,000 and the minimum was $6,000, veterans bitterly resented the huge sums doled out to untested teenage players.

In spite of the problems, most major league teams continued the practice of handing out large sums to untried teenage prospects. "What else can you do?" Cleveland executive Hank Greenberg asked in 1952. "When there's a kid you really want — when baseball men whose judgment you respect say that he has everything — you have to meet the competition if you expect to stay in business. If a boy is going to be a star, why there's hardly any limit to how much he's worth. He'll be a bargain at almost any bonus."[4] And there were examples of players whose performance matched their bonuses — Alvin Dark ($45,000 from the Braves), Jackie Jensen ($75,000 from the Yankees), Curt Simmons ($65,000 from the Phillies), Robin Roberts ($25,000 from the Phillies), Harvey Kuenn ($55,000 from the Tigers), Al Kaline ($35,000 from the Tigers), and Johnny Antonelli ($75,000 from the Braves).

Fears that bidding wars could inflate payrolls and allow the richer clubs to monopolize young talent led the major leagues to try to regulate the practice of signing bonus babies. In 1946, a bonus rule was put into effect requiring that players given $6,000 or more to sign a contract and then sent to the minors for seasoning had to be placed on the major league roster after one year or become eligible for drafting by another team. In the 1950s, attempting to correct some of the worst abuses in the bonus baby wars, the owners made several additional modifications in the bonus rules, such as defining a bonus player as anyone given more than $4,000 to sign a contract, and requiring major league clubs to carry bonus players on their 25-man roster for at least two years. However, the practice of giving large bonuses to untried players would continue virtually unabated into the 1960s, when the owners went to an amateur draft system in an attempt to end the bidding wars and escalating salaries.

One of the teams that benefited the most from the bonus baby practice was the Philadelphia Phillies. The club had been managed since 1948 by scholarly Eddie Sawyer, who was a Phi Beta Kappa graduate of Ithaca College, had a master's degree from Cornell, had been a college biology professor during World War II, and had never played major league baseball. He led a young team that had been assembled by Du Pont heir Robert M. Carpenter and his son Bob, who was named club president after his father purchased the team in 1943. Trying to make a pennant winner out of a moribund franchise, the Carpenters had spent close to $2 million on players, including nearly a half million for bonus babies, the most valuable of whom were pitchers Robin Roberts and Curt Simmons. In 1948 the Phillies finished sixth, but in 1949 they rose to third, their first upper division finish since 1932.

The Carpenters' attempt to buy a pennant finally paid off in 1950. With most of their players in their twenties, the Phillies had the youngest starting team in the majors. At first base was Eddie Waitkus, who at 30 was the oldest starting player on the club. He had fully recovered from the shooting by a deranged fan the year before and came back in 1950 to play in all 154 games, hit .284, and lead all league first basemen in putouts with 1,387. Not surprisingly, the Associated Press gave him the Comeback of the Year Award. Second baseman Mike Goliat (age 24), shortstop Granny Hamner (23), and third baseman Willie "Puddin' Head" Jones (24) rounded out the infield, while the outfield was made up of Dick Sisler (29) in left, Richie Ashburn (23) in center, and Del Ennis (25) in right. Catcher Andy Seminick (29) handled a pitching staff led by Robin Roberts (23), who wound up the year with a 20–11 record, and Curt Simmons (21), who compiled a 17–8 record before his Pennsylvania National Guard unit was called to action in the Korean War. Jim Konstanty, the old man on the club at 33, would make a record 74 appearances, gaining 16 wins and 22 saves and becoming the first reliever to win the MVP Award. The Phillies' youth, along with memories of a basketball team of a few years before, led the press to dub the club the "Whiz Kids."

With so many young players, the Phillies naturally attracted a large group of "Baseball Sadies." In early 1950 one Philadelphia player had received a note saying, "Either make a date with me or I'll shoot you."[5] After what had happened to Waitkus, such threats had to be taken seriously.

Many of the experts picked the Phillies to finish fourth in 1950, behind the Dodgers, Cardinals, and Braves. In the first half of the season these four teams seemed to be evenly matched, with each team resting in first place for at least part of the time, and as late as July 17, only one game separated the leader from the fourth-place club. But then the Phillies began to play like world champions. After falling to as low as sixth place in late April and again on May 6, they took the lead on July 26 and kept it. In August they pulled away from the other contenders by winning 20 of the 28 games, and by September 1 they were six games in front of the second-place Dodgers.

The Phillies were the surprise of the league in 1950. They had not won a pennant since 1915 and had long been the doormat of the league. They had the worst record of all the National League teams between 1900 and 1949, having won only 3,202 games while losing 4,325, and they began the season holding the dubious record for last place finishes (17). It was no wonder that the city of Philadelphia paid little attention to the Phillies when they hovered in the first division for most of the first half of the season. In a town that boasted the lowly American League Athletics as well as the

Phillies, few fans could get excited over a few winning streaks at the beginning of the season.

But after the club took over first place in late July, the Phillies became the talk of the country and the darling of the City of Brotherly Love. When the team returned from a winning road trip on September 3, some 30,000 fans came out to the airport to welcome the players home. By now there was a fan club for practically every player on the team, and the club was selling player photographs, sketchbooks of the players, and other souvenirs as fast as they could be manufactured. Sensing that this team was different from the contingents of the past 35 years, fans and sportswriters were now talking about "the Miracle at Philadelphia."

On the morning of September 19, the Phillies had a 7½-game lead over the Braves and a 9-game lead over the Dodgers, and Philly fans were making plans to go to the World Series. But then the Whiz Kids squandered their lead in a late September collapse. Curt Simmons had been lost to the army on September 10. Pitchers Bubba Church and Bob Miller suffered injuries that left them ineffective for the rest of the season, forcing Sawyer to try to stagger the rest of the way home with Robin Roberts and Jim Konstanty. And stagger the Phillies did. They lost 8 of their next 11 games, including a two-game series to the Dodgers on September 23–24 and a disastrous four consecutive games to the Giants in back-to-back doubleheaders on September 27–28. Meanwhile the Dodgers won 12 of their next 16, and on the same days that the Phillies were swept by the Giants, the Dodgers split doubleheaders with the fading Boston Braves, who were in the process of losing 11 of their last 16 games of the season. Then on September 29, while the Phillies were idle, the Dodgers, playing their fourth doubleheader in five days, swept the Braves to pull within two games of the Phillies. The season had come down to the final weekend of the season, a two-game series between the Dodgers and the Phillies.

As the Phillies and the Dodgers squared off, everything seemed to favor the Dodgers. They had the experience, the momentum, and the home crowd, while the collapsing Phillies appeared exhausted and demoralized. Dodger hopes for a second consecutive pennant rose in the first game on Saturday when Duke Snider and Roy Campanella hit home runs to stake young Erv Palica to his thirteenth victory and pull the Dodgers to within one game of the leaders. For the second consecutive year, the National League race would be decided on the last day of the season.

On Sunday, October 1, over 35,000 fans jammed Ebbets Field, hoping to see their Dodgers force a playoff. Both teams started their aces. The Dodgers went with a well-rested Don Newcombe, a 19-game winner who had started only one game since he had notched his last victory on September 19. The Phillies had no choice but to go with Robin Roberts, starting his third game in five days and, like Newcombe, looking for his twentieth victory. Ironically, these same two pitchers had dueled on the opening day of the season, with Roberts coming away the victor.

The game was scoreless for the first five innings. Both teams scored a run in the sixth. Though the Dodgers threatened in the ninth, the game remained knotted at 1–1 at the end of nine innings. The game went into the tenth with both starting pitchers still on the mound. With Waitkus and Ashburn on base and the count at 2–1, Dick Sisler drove a Newcombe fastball into the left field bleachers to give the Phillies a 4–1 lead. Among those few Philly fans in the stands was Sisler's Hall of Fame father, George Sisler, former first baseman for the St. Louis Browns, who in 1950 was a scout for the Dodgers. In the Dodger half of the inning a tiring Roberts held on to the lead, getting Campanella to line out to left field, striking out Jim Russell, and getting pinch hitter Buckshot Brown to foul out to Waitkus. Sisler was the hero of the day, overshadowing Roberts's twentieth victory, which made him the first Philly pitcher to win 20 games since Grover Cleveland Alexander captured 30 in 1917.

There would be no playoff, no Dodger miracle. Once again for Flatbush fans it was "wait until next year," while the Phillies celebrated their first pennant since 1915. Bob Stevens of the *San Francisco Chronicle* wrote, "The Philadelphia Phillies, the incredible Whiz Kids, today became of age." But he also predicted, as did many others, that the Yankees "will probably eat them alive."[6]

The Giants finished in third place, five games back. Ever since taking over the team in 1948 Durocher had been assembling what he called "my kind of team," trading off aging sluggers like Johnny Mize and acquiring scrappy players and good pitchers. In December of 1949, he traded four players to the Braves for Alvin Dark and Eddie Stanky, who in 1950 formed a keystone duo second only to Reese and Robinson in Brooklyn. He welcomed Mexican jumper Sal Maglie back into the fold, and Maglie responded with 18 wins and 4 losses. He purchased Jim Hearn from the Cardinals in June, and Hearn proceeded to win 11 consecutive games and lead the majors with a 2.49 ERA. The Giants would be a team to be reckoned with in 1951.

In spite of the pitching of Warren Spahn and Johnny Sain—who won 21 and 20 games respectively—the Braves folded in the second half of the season and finished in fourth place, eight games behind the Phillies. The Cardinals finished fifth, the first time they had finished out of the first division since 1938. The only Cardinal regular to hit .300 or better was Stan Musial, who won his fourth batting title with a .346 average.

The Reds, Cubs, and Pirates brought up the rear. The Pirates were the doormat of the National League, but for the fourth straight year they went over the million mark in attendance, primarily because of the slugging feats of young Ralph Kiner. The fans came to see him, not the hapless Pirates.

In the seventh and eighth innings of most games, there was usually a mass exodus of fans after Kiner had completed what would apparently be his last turn at bat. Kiner hit 47 homers in 1950 to become the first National League player to hit 40 or more home runs in four consecutive seasons.

The American League race would be exciting for the third consecutive year. In spite of Stengel's success in his freshman year, most baseball writers picked the Red Sox to win the pennant. But Stengel was ready to show that his 1949 world championship was no fluke. He had proven to his team and to the rest of the baseball world that he was more than a clown, that he could take a good ball club and win with it. He now became the real leader of the club, becoming confident, even arrogant, quick to give orders to his players and to criticize them when they made errors.

He was also getting some new blood. In June he brought Ed "Whitey" Ford up from the minors, and the 21-year-old left-hander won nine straight and wound up with a 9–1 record. Ford joined Vic Raschi (21–8), Allie Reynolds (16–12), Ed Lopat (18–8), and Tommy Byrne (15–9) to make up one of the most respected pitching staffs in the league. Stengel installed Johnny Mize, who had been acquired from the Giants during the 1949 season, at first base, and the old slugger hit 25 homers, drove in 72 runs, hit .277, and seemed to have the knack of delivering the clutch hit when the club needed it most. And Stengel had Phil Rizzuto. The little shortstop batted .324, scored 125 runs, and won the MVP Award, leading Stengel to say, "He's got that extra something which you can't blame me for."[7]

One of the biggest disappointments for Stengel was the performance of Joe Page, nicknamed "the Fireman" for his role as the premier relief pitcher of the late 1940s. Page was not the first relief pitcher in baseball history, but he was the first modern relief pitcher in the sense that he was the first to appear in 50 or 60 games a year, to be used in critical situations rather than as a mop up specialist, and to be paid like a star. Primarily a fastball pitcher, Page could warm up with only 10 pitches. A mediocre starting pitcher, he found his niche on the Yankee team after being placed in the bullpen by Bucky Harris in 1947, when he appeared in 56 games, was 14–7 as a reliever, and though the statistic was not kept at that time, saved 17 games. In 1948, he was 7–8 with 16 saves in 55 appearances, and in 1949 improved to 13–8 with 27 saves in 60 appearances. He also pitched well in the 1947 and 1949 World Series, winning one game and saving one in both classics.

In 1950, Page signed a contract for the upcoming season for between $30,000 and $35,000, believed to be the highest salary any Yankee pitcher had ever received and much higher than what the majority of the other 400 major league players were making. An obviously pleased Page told reporters that this was "something new. I believe this is the first time a relief pitcher has been paid like a starter."[8] But his best years were behind him, for he slipped to a 3–7 record in 1950 and then disappeared from the majors until 1954, when he appeared in just seven games with the Pirates in an unsuccessful comeback attempt.

The relationship between Stengel and DiMaggio, never a warm one, cooled even further in 1950. After playing just half the season in 1949, DiMaggio got off to a bad start in the spring with a prolonged batting slump. His average dropped to .220 in May, and stayed below .300 for most of the season. As DiMaggio's slump deepened, Stengel dropped him from fourth to fifth in the batting order, and on August 11 even went so far as to give him a "rest," marking the first time in his career that he had been benched for poor hitting rather than for an injury or illness. Stengel also tried installing him at first base, but DiMaggio balked after just one attempt at the new position. All of these incidents angered the sensitive veteran, who was moody and frustrated and barely speaking to his manager. But on August 18 he returned to the lineup and went on a tear for the rest of the season, finishing with a .301 batting average, 32 homers, and 122 RBIs, and won several key games with his bat and glove. Once again, he was a key player in another Yankee pennant drive.

In the first part of the season it was a four-way battle between New York, Boston, Detroit, and Cleveland. The Yankees got off to a good start and during one stretch in May won nine in a row before faltering and losing the lead to the surprising Tigers. With four regulars—George Kell (.340), Walter Arthur "Hoot" Evers (.323), Vic Wertz (.308), and Johnny Groth (.306)—hitting over .300, and Art Houtteman (19–12), Fred Hutchinson (17–8), Hal Newhouser (15–13), and Dizzy Trout (13–5) providing good pitching, the Tigers kept the lead for most of the rest of the season, in spite of losing their ace hurler, Virgil Trucks, to arm trouble early in the year. But on September 16, the Yankees took over the lead and sprinted to the finish line three games ahead of the Tigers. It had been a close race all season, and ended with just six games separating the first and fourth place clubs. But Stengel had defied all the prognosticators and won his second consecutive pennant.

The Red Sox finished third, four games out. The club could blame part of its woes on an injury to Ted Williams, who began the season as baseball's greatest active hitter (.353) and highest paid player with a salary of $110,000, some $10,000 more than Joe DiMaggio. However, Williams fractured his elbow trying to make a catch during the All-Star Game and appeared in only 19 more games the rest of the year. Playing in just 89 games for the season, he hit 28 homers and drove in 97 runs, but his average fell to .317, the lowest since he entered the majors. The Bosox's leading hitter was utility player Billy Goodman, who captured the league batting crown with a .354 average.

Led by third baseman Al Rosen, who took the league home run crown with 37, the Indians finished fourth, just six games out. Their pennant hopes had been dashed during a September series when they lost four consecutive games to the St. Louis Browns. The winning streak for the seventh place Browns was a fluke, for they seemed to be competing with the Athletics for the reputation as the worst team in baseball. In one two-day stretch early in the season, their pitchers gave up 49 runs. The Red Sox beat them 20–4 on June 7, then followed that thrashing the next day by banging out 28 hits, including seven home runs, a triple, and nine doubles en route to a 29–4 victory, setting a new major league record for most runs scored by one team in a nine-inning game. Browns manager Zack Taylor called it an "unmerciful beating, totally uncalled for," and accused Joe McCarthy of leaving his starters in to run up the score and embarrass his club.[9]

It was an exciting season in both leagues, and as it ended it seemed that it would probably be remembered as the year of the home run. From opening day on, sluggers in both leagues had been knocking the ball out of the park at a record pace. On June 23, 30 homers were hit in the majors, with a record 11 of them coming in just one game, a slugfest in Detroit that saw the Tigers hit 6, one of which was a grand slam by pitcher Dizzy Trout, to outlast the Yankees by a 10–9 margin. Three weeks later, on July 16, another record was set when 37 home runs were hit around the two leagues. Then on August 31, Dodger first baseman Gil Hodges hit four homers in one game in a lopsided 19–3 victory over the Braves at Ebbets Field. Hodges became the second major leaguer to hit four homers in a nine-inning game. (Lou Gehrig was the first, back in 1932.) By year's end, 1,100 homers had been hit in the National League and 973 in the American—both new records—for a total of 2,073. This broke the 1949 record of 1,705 homers, which had in turn snapped the previous mark of 1,571 set back in 1940.

The outbreak of the long ball raised the perennial cry that the ball was livelier than it had been in previous years. But *Popular Science* magazine and several other agencies tested several balls in 1950 and concluded that the 1949 and 1950 balls were essentially the same, as did the A.G. Spalding and Brothers Company, which had made the official ball for the major leagues since the turn of the century. But the arguments over the alleged rabbit ball would continue for most of the 1950s.

On Wednesday, October 4, the 1950 World Series opened in Shibe Park, the home of both the Phillies and the Athletics. It had not hosted a World Series since 1931, when the Athletics lost to the Cardinals in seven games. Only the Phillies and their most diehard fans really expected the Whiz Kids to win. The day before the Series opened, manager Eddie Sawyer said, "I don't go along with the experts who pick the Yankees to win in four or five games."[10] But in the last month of the season his club had collapsed, winning only 13 of 29 games. The young and inexperienced club had only two hitters over .300, Del Ennis (.311) and Richie Ashburn (.303), and the pitching staff was in shreds. Curt Simmons was in the army, Bubba Church and Bob Miller were hurting, and Robin Roberts had made three starts in five days. The Yankees were loaded with sluggers and pitchers and experienced in World Series play.

The Phillies never knew what hit them. The first two games were pitching duels, with Vic Raschi beating Jim Konstanty 1–0 in game one and Allie Reynolds taking a 2–1 win over Robin Roberts in game two with the help of a tenth inning home run by Joe DiMaggio. As the Series moved to New York, fans and the press were calling the demoralized club the "Fizz Kids," the "Wuz Kids," and the "Wheeze Kids." Cartoonist Willard Mullin said that the Phils were suffering from a bad case of "The Yanks"—a malady that had afflicted many a player and team over the years. Phillies' fan Dr. Lauren H. Smith of Pennsylvania Hospital said that his team was "scared and tight—like a prizefighter who knows something is going to hit him and starts ducking before the other fellow swings."[11]

On Friday, October 6, the Phillies came into Yankee Stadium hoping to bounce back from the two losses in Philadelphia. Sawyer was reduced to starting left-hander Ken Heintzelman, who had a 3-9 record, while Stengel went with Ed Lopat. When the Yankees won 3–2 for their third consecutive one-run victory, the stage was set for a sweep, a humiliation the Yankees had imposed on opponents in five previous Octobers. They made it six. The Yankees chased started Bob Miller from the mound in the first inning, while Whitey Ford pitched magnificently, carrying a 5–0 lead into the ninth and, with a little relief help from Allie Reynolds, coming away with a 5–2 victory. Just five days after Dick Sisler's exhilarating home run took the pennant away from the Dodgers, the Phillies had been mowed down in four games. They had played well, losing three games by one-run margins, but they were embarrassed by the sweep.

The Whiz Kids faded quickly after 1950. In spite of the huge sums that the club had shelled out for bonus babies, they were not able to compete with the great clubs in New York, the Giants and the Dodgers. They fell to fifth place in 1951, climbed back to fourth in 1952 and to third in 1953, then spent the rest of the decade mired in fourth or deep in the second division. The franchise had waited 35 years to be in the World Series, and now it would have to wait 30 more before making it to the fall classic again. In 1980, they would take the measure of the Kansas City Royals in six games.

At a luncheon press conference in Philadelphia a week and a half after the World Series, Cornelius Alexander McGilicuddy, better known as Connie Mack, Mr. Mack, and Mr. Baseball, announced that he was retiring as manager of the Philadelphia Athletics and turning the club over to two of his sons, Roy and Earle. Jimmy Dykes would take over as manager. In making his announcement, the 88-year-old Mack said, "I'm not quitting because I'm too told, but because I think the people want me to." However, he promised to remain as president of the club.[12]

As Red Smith wrote in the *New York Herald Tribune* the day after Mack retired, "There never was another like Connie. There never will be."[13] After playing professional baseball for 11 years (1886–1896) as a catcher, managing the Pittsburgh Pirates from 1894 to 1896, and helping establish the American League, Mack had managed the Athletics for 50 years. Directing the club in street clothes from the dugout, he had led the Athletics to nine pennants and five world championships and established several records which seem to be unbreakable, including most years managing in the majors (53), most years managing one club (50), manager of most games (7,878), and the oldest manager. As he had so many times (17) in the past, his club finished last in the American League in 1950. It had been a long time since the last pennant (1931) and world title (1930).

Mack's resignation was only one of several managerial changes made during and after the 1950 season. Joe McCarthy of the Red Sox retired early in the year because of health reasons and was replaced by Steve O'Neill. At the end of the year Paul Richards, manager of the minor league team in Seattle, took over the reins of the White Sox from Red Corriden, and Al Lopez became manager of the Cleveland Indians, replacing Lou Boudreau, who went on to the Red Sox as a player in 1951 before taking over as manager in 1952. In the National League, Marty Marion became the Cardinal pilot after Eddie Dyer resigned at the end of the season, while in Brooklyn Chuck Dressen replaced Burt Shotton. The Dodgers also underwent a major shift in the front office. In October Branch Rickey, who had lost a power struggle with Walter O'Malley, sold his share (25 percent) of Dodger stock to O'Malley and Mrs. John Smith for $1,025,000. Never one to be out of a job for long, Rickey was appointed general manager of the Pittsburgh Pirates in November. Pirate executives and fans were hoping that he could bring to Pittsburgh some of the magic he had worked in St. Louis and Brooklyn.

The winter of 1950–1951 was a terrible time for the nation. The Korean War was going badly, for in November the People's Republic of China entered the war, sending 200,000 troops into North Korea to drive the United Nations forces out of North Korea and back across the 38th parallel. American soldiers were being killed in such large numbers and were having to retreat so quickly that they sometimes could not even collect their dead and had to bury them hurriedly in mass graves. On December 15, Truman appeared on television to declare a national emergency and to call for the mobilization of the nation's military and economic power to meet the

Communist threat in Korea. "Our homes, our nation, all the things we believe in are in great danger," he told the American people. The army would be increased to 3.5 million men and economic controls would have to be imposed on the economy.[14]

As the war worsened, American entertainers went to Korea to lift the spirit of the soldiers fighting there. Among them was Joe DiMaggio and his close friend, Lefty O'Doul, the manager of the San Francisco Seals. The two men visited 18 military hospitals in 17 days, shaking hands with the wounded, sitting on the bed and talking, passing out cigarettes, and posing for photographs that would be proudly kept by the bedside or sent home to family and friends as proof that they had actually met the great Joe DiMaggio. They then went on to Japan, where they saw part of the Japanese World Series, visited military hospitals, and had lunch with General and Mrs. Douglas MacArthur. When he returned to San Francisco, DiMaggio, who lost seven pounds during the whirlwind trip, told reporters that morale was good but that the soldiers resented the view back in the States that they were just fighting a "police action" rather than a real war. "It looked like an all-out war to me," he said, "and the boys want the people in this country to know that they're not just a police force. They want credit for what they're doing, and I don't blame them."[15]

Professional baseball had been worrying about the impact of the Korean War even before Truman's alarming December 15 speech. On December 7, the ninth anniversary of Pearl Harbor, Commissioner Chandler had predicted in a banquet speech before National Association officials in St. Petersburg, Florida, that the Korean War might have a serious impact on baseball, similar to World War II. He warned that the majors might even have to suspend play until the wartime crisis had passed. He said that he hoped that the game would be given a green light as it had been in World War II, but he warned, "I do not know what is coming. I do not know if we are to have total mobilization, or what we would do if it came. However, we are living in terrible times. All of you in baseball must make your plans accordingly. We have got to be ready for emergencies."[16]

Baseball was ending the year in a troubled atmosphere. The worsening Korean War was the main threat on the horizon, but there were others. Chandler and the owners were at odds over several matters, and they had already voted not to renew his contract, which was scheduled to expire in May of 1952. That dispute would come to a head in 1951 and force his early resignation.

Major league attendance had also declined for the second year in a row. After dipping slightly in 1949, it fell to 17.5 million in 1950, a drop of 2.7 million. The minor leagues suffered even greater losses. After riding the crest of postwar prosperity and popularity to a peak of 42 million in 1949, their attendance dropped to 34.5 million, a drastic decline that would only worsen as the fifties progressed and television and other diversions robbed them of their customers.

Perhaps the one bright spot for professional baseball as the year came to an end was the inking of a new, lucrative television contract. On December 26, Chandler announced that he had signed a six-year agreement with Gillette and the Mutual Broadcasting Company, giving them exclusive television rights to the World Series and All-Star Games from 1951 through 1956 for a total cost of $6 million, a far cry from the $65,000 paid by Gillette and Ford for the first World Series telecast just four years before. Gillette had already obtained radio rights to these events from 1949 to 1956 at a total cost of $1,195,000. Most of the television and radio revenues were earmarked to go to the players' pension plan.

Although the majority of the club owners approved of the new television deal, some felt that the television advertising situation was changing so rapidly that it was unwise for Chandler to sign such a long-term pact. Warren Giles of the Cincinnati Reds said, "It will probably take six years to tell whether it's a good deal or a bad deal."[17]

The national pastime was obviously entering a period of uncertainty and trouble, though the nature and extent of its problems would not be fully realized for a few more years and would be largely hidden by the upcoming battle in New York between the New York Giants, Brooklyn Dodgers, and New York Yankees. New York was the center of the baseball world, and in 1951 it would have its most exciting year ever.

8. The New York Game

The New York Yankees' 1950 world championship had been another blow to Yankee haters all across the country. Once again, the Bronx Bombers had shown that they were the best team in baseball. From 1921 through 1950, they had won 17 pennants and 13 World Series, finished either first or second 23 times, and finished in the second division only once. They were the most successful franchise in major league history, arousing the admiration and hatred of players and fans of other clubs and causing some critics to claim that the domination of the men in pinstripes was hurting baseball.

How had they managed to win so consistently? Some said that it was money—that the Yankees had made huge profits during the Ruthian era and kept plowing them back into the business, acquiring the best players money could buy. "The Yankees traditionally dominate baseball by sheer economic might," a *Life* magazine article, "I Hate the Yankees," said in April of 1950. As evidence, it pointed to the fact that since Yankee Stadium opened in 1923, it had drawn close to 30.5 million customers. From 1940 through 1949 alone, the team had attracted nearly 14.5 million fans, 3.5 million more than their closest rivals, the Cleveland Indians. Besides paying millions of dollars for tickets, these fans had paid millions more for food, beverages, and souvenirs. On top of that, additional revenues had poured into Yankee coffers from the sale of radio and television rights.[1]

It was clear, though, that money alone could not explain the phenomenal success of the Yankees. They had prudently built one of the best farm systems in the majors, with some of its Triple-A clubs, such as Oakland, Newark, and Kansas City, fielding teams that were as good, some baseball men claimed, as some of the lower division teams in the majors. This talent-rich farm system supplied the Bronx Bombers with a steady stream of good players. Front office executives and the scouts out in the field somehow seemed to have the knack of finding much of the best talent in the land, and to find it at just the right time. When Ruth hung up his spikes, the Yankees signed Joe DiMaggio to assume his place as the team star and national hero, and in 1951 as DiMaggio's career came to an end the Yankees came up with his replacement, Mickey Mantle.

Then there was the Yankee mystique that enabled a team rich in pride and winning tradition to transform players and managers into champions. The Yankees seemed to make winning look easy, to play as if they expected to win, and to show little emotion when they did. Ed Lopat once said, "The Yankee clubhouse had a bell. It rang five minutes before a game stated. We went through the door. We were ready. The Yankees were always ready."[2] And just putting on that pinstripe uniform, many said, could turn a mediocre performer into a star or inspire a player at the end of his career to have one or two more good seasons.

Whatever the explanation, the Yankees did reign over baseball in the middle of the twentieth century, but they were just part of a larger domination of the game by the city of New York. The largest city in the nation, the center of finance, trade, publishing, theater, radio and television, and so much else, it was also the center of baseball. It was the only city with three teams and with two teams in the same league. This intracity rivalry brought an annual battle for games, pennants, world championships, players, fans, and media coverage. From the beginning to the end of the baseball season, and during the off-season as well, fans argued baseball at school, at work, in cabs and subways, on street corners, and at restaurants. Fans often got to see their players close-up, for many players lived in homes, apartments, or hotel rooms near the ballparks and took a taxi or subway to the games. These provided the perfect ingredients for intense rivalries between teams, players, and fans.

The intracity competition was heightened by the frequent crossovers of personnel. Larry MacPhail served as an owner and executive for both the Dodgers and the Yankees, and among those who played or managed for two or more of the New York teams were Casey Stengel, Leo Durocher, Chuck Dressen, Eddie Stanky, Johnny Mize, Sal Maglie, Hugh Casey and Ralph Branca. Announcer Russ Hodges was one of the voices of the Yankees before he moved over to announce the Giants' games, and Dodger diehard Red Barber left the Bums to join Mel Allen on the Yankee airwaves in 1954. And in 1951, Horace Stoneham even lured head Dodger groundskeeper Matty Schwab to the Giants with a better salary and a new rent-free, two-bedroom apartment underneath the left field grandstand in the Polo Grounds.

Not surprisingly, the most intense rivalry for the pennant and the loyalty of the fans was between the two teams in the same league. Barber, who followed the rivalry close-up for many years, once said, "Whenever the Dodgers and Giants played you had both factions in the stands. In other words, it wasn't a rivalry just on the ball field, with a home crowd rooting for their team and booing the visitors. At the Dodger-Giant games in Ebbets Field and the Polo Grounds, you had a constant back-and-forth roaring from the first pitch to the last, *for* both teams and *against* both teams."[3]

Possessing the kind of excitement usually reserved for the World

Series, Dodger-Giant games usually lasted longer and had more dramatic events, rhubarbs, and fights than the average major league game. Giant Monte Irvin once said, "When you walked onto the grass at Brooklyn in your gray flannel road uniform with New York printed across its front, the feeling of hatred focused at you was so thick you could cut it with a knife."[4] Andy Pafko, traded from the Cubs to the Dodgers in 1951, soon found out that playing with the Dodgers against the Giants was a lot more dangerous than playing with the Cubs against the Giants. "Nobody bothered me with the Cubs," he said. "But Brooklyn has a Murderer's Row with Hodges, Campanella, Snider, and Furillo. When someone ahead of me hits a home run, the next pitch comes at my head. That isn't fun. Dodger-Giant games aren't baseball — they're civil wars."[5]

The two teams were fairly evenly matched in their long rivalry with one another. In a baseball war dating back to 1900 and lasting until the two teams pulled up stakes and moved to California at the end of the 1957 season, the Giants won 650 games and the Dodgers 606. In the most intense years of their opposition, from 1947 through 1957, the Dodgers won 136 and the Giants 109.

Second to the rivalry between the Dodgers and Giants was their own rivalry in October with that team in that other league, the Yankees. In the period between 1945 and 1957, the Giants and the Yankees played each other for the world championship only once, in 1951, when the Giants lost in six games. More frequent, and happening so often that some fans and sportswriters thought that it was getting to be a bore, was the traditional Yankee-Dodger World Series. The Dodgers had already played and lost one world championship to the Yankees before the postwar period, and from 1945 to 1960 they lost to the Yankees five times while beating them just once.

While fighting one another, the three New York teams dominated the majors in the postwar period. The Cubs and Tigers took the pennants in 1945 and the Cards and Red Sox in 1946, but over the next 11 years, it was a near-monopoly for New York teams. In this stretch the Yankees won nine pennants and seven world championships, including a record five in succession. The Dodgers won six pennants and one World Series, and the Giants won two pennants and one Series. Seven of the Series between 1947 and 1957 were "Subway Series" between the New York teams. When the Dodgers and Giants left town at the end of 1957, the Yankees carried on the New York — and Yankee — tradition by winning the pennant and World Series in 1958 and then ending the decade with still another pennant and dramatic loss to the Pirates in the 1960 Series.

The New York teams dominated in other ways as well. Between 1947 and 1957, players from New York teams won the Rookie of the Year Award eight times, the MVP Award thirteen times, the home run title seven times, and the batting title four times. With their team and individual records, coupled with the publicity that came from playing in New York, it was not surprising that the New York clubs had the most popular stars. Players toiling for the less successful clubs had to have the talent of a Musial, Williams, or Kiner to get the kind of publicity that came quite easily to New York players.

Not surprisingly, the home of three major league teams and the national center of radio and television broadcasting had some of the nation's top baseball voices, led by Mel Allen and Red Barber. Both had gained their experience and fame during the golden age of radio broadcasting in the forties and then went into television when the new media came along. They would eventually have the honor of being the first two announcers elected to the Hall of Fame.

As the play-by-play radio announcer of the Yankees, Allen's voice betrayed his sympathies for the home team. In his Alabama drawl and famous lines — such as "It's going, going, gone!" and "How about that!" — he dramatized the game, making the listener in some remote part of the country imagine that he was at the game itself. He received nearly one thousand fan letters a week, and his sponsors liked him too, especially when he referred to home runs as "Ballantine Blasts" or "White Owl Wallops." Before he was fired by the Yankees in 1964, he had announced 20 World Series and 24 All-Star Games, along with numerous regular season baseball games, football bowl games, heavyweight fights, and sports features on Movietone Newsreels. At his peak, *Variety* magazine said that he had one of the "twenty-five most recognizable voices in the world."[6]

Some critics claimed that Allen talked too much, and sometimes he did. At one game he was working with Phil Rizzuto, he noticed two teenagers kissing in the center field bleachers. "That's interesting," he said. "He's kissing her on the strikes, and she's kissing him on the balls." Trying to cover up the gaffe, Rizzuto could only say, "Mel, this is just not your day."[7]

Allen's rival at Ebbets Field was another Southern-born announcer, Walter "Red" Barber, "the Old Redhead." The voice of the Dodgers from 1939 through 1953, Barber combined a deep knowledge of the game with homespun humor and a knack for coining phrases that became famous all across the country — "Bedford Avenue Blasts," (home runs hit into Bedford Avenue), the bases are "F.O.B." (full of Brooklyns), "sitting in the catbird seat," "oh, doctor," the "rhubarb patch," and his promise that Old Gold cigarettes gave "a treat instead of a treatment." When Barber left the Dodgers at the end of the 1953 season and joined Allen in the Yankee broadcast booth, many Brooklyn fans felt abandoned and betrayed.

In 1950 New York acquired another popular announcer. He was Dizzy Dean, the former Cardinal pitching star who became the radio voice of the Cardinals and the Browns in 1941 after a bad arm forced him to retire from baseball at the age of 30. In the St. Louis broadcast booth, he was a hit from the beginning. A natural comic and showman, he developed a folksy, breezy, and irreverent style punctuated by deliberate and unconscious use of bad grammar (he had only a second grade education), malapropisms, and outrageous neologisms. He became famous for saying such things as the runner "slud," the runners returned to their "respectable bases," the batter is standing "confidentially" at the plate, the hitter "swang" at the ball, and the pitcher threw that "old patata." He dropped the "g" at the end of most words (runnin', hittin', playin'), used Southern colloquialisms (dunno, dawgone, umpaar, shore, hisself, gonna, Pod-nuh), and coined words such as "spart," which he claimed meant "pep" or "gumption." He talked about food, hunting, and fishing, launched into singing "The Wabash Cannonball," and told his listeners, "Don't fail to miss tomorrow's game."

His use—or rather, misuse—of the English language offended some listeners, and in 1946 even led the English Teachers Association of Missouri to complain to the Federal Communications Commission that he was having a bad effect on young students' writing and speaking habits and should be taken off the air. When Dean heard that the teachers had complained about his syntax, he reacted with his typical disarming humor, "Sin-tax? Are them jokers in Washington puttin' a tax on that too?"[8] Many fans felt that he had a better knowledge of the game than most broadcasters and found his candor and running chatter humorous and entertaining. Dean survived all outside pressures to get him off the air, but he lost interest in broadcasting "them sloggish Browns" and the Browns' management tired of his frank criticisms of the hapless club. When he got the offer in 1950 to move on to New York, both he and the Browns were relieved.

At the age of 39, then, "Ol' Diz" went big time, taking over as the color commentator on Mel Allen's telecasts of Yankee games over New York station WBAD, part of Dumont's television and radio network. When some New Yorkers predicted before the season started that it would be difficult for them to understand Dean's country language, he told reporters that it just evened things up, because "I never could make out what folks around here was sayin', either." He also promised, "I'm gonna talk the way I always talked. Maybe I won't learn the fans no English, but I'm gonna learn them a lot of baseball."[9] In 1950 he was paid $30,000, which, he said, "is more than I ever made pitchin' baseballs."[10]

Dean was popular with the New York fans, who liked his baseball knowledge and humor. He received thousands of fan letters and phone calls. In 1951 his salary was raised to $40,000, and he was expected to make another $35,000 from his Texas farm and other businesses and investments. A highly sentimentalized movie of his life, *The Pride of St. Louis*, appeared in 1952, and the following year he was inducted into the baseball Hall of Fame, an occasion he marked by observing that "the Good Lord was good to me. He gave me a strong body, a good right arm and a weak mind."[11]

Working in New York provided Dean many opportunities to gain additional income and notoriety by appearing on other radio and television shows. He was also a popular after-dinner speaker in New York and other cities, and everywhere he went he continued to play the role of the dumb country boy. But he knew what he was doing. As his close friend, White Sox manager Paul Richards, said, "If Diz ever gets smart, he's through."[12]

In 1953 Dean moved on to bigger pastures. On June 6, he made his debut on Falstaff's "Game of the Week" on the ABC television network. Two years later, the Saturday afternoon show moved to CBS, where it stayed for 10 years. For most of the fifties Dean's sidekick on the program was Buddy Blattner, who left the show at the end of 1959 and was replaced by former Dodger shortstop Pee Wee Reese. But no matter who his "Pod-nuh" was, Dean was always the star of the popular show, which added a Sunday afternoon game in 1957. A rival Saturday game was started by NBC, and in 1959 it added a Sunday game as well, but it always came in second to Dean's show in the ratings.

Dean would reach his peak on CBS's "Game of the Week." Part natural and part put on, this shrewd entertainer was the main attraction, with his cowboy hat, string tie, slang, fractured grammar and diction, and candor. He was as irreverent as ever, mispronouncing the names of the players and managers and saying what he pleased about the game, the players, managers, coaches, and his own sponsors. He once called NBC's "The Dinah Shore Show" "the best variety show on TV," and although American Airlines and United Airlines bought commercial time on CBS, Dean would come out with such statements as "Pod-nuh, I hate to fly, but if you have to, Eastern is the best."[13] And on one Saturday afternoon as he broadcast a one-sided game, he told his viewers that the Dodger-Giant game on NBC was a better contest to watch. He often aroused the ire of his network and sponsors, but he got away with it because his show drew large audiences and made a great deal of money for CBS. By 1957, he was being paid $62,500 a year by the network, and was making thousands more from other television appearances and outside investments and appearances. He stayed on until 1965.

But it was the players who made New York the center of baseball, and in 1951 New York had some of the best-known players in the nation, led by the incomparable Joe DiMaggio. The eighth of nine children born to Sicilian immigrants living in San Francisco, DiMaggio spent three years with the San Francisco Seals before joining the Yankees in 1936 as the most publicized rookie in the history of the game. Only 21 years old, he was a natural and complete ballplayer in his rookie season, collecting 206 hits, belting 29 homers, compiling a .323 batting average and a .978 fielding average, and leading American League outfielders in assists with 22. Brothers Vince and Dom would later follow him into the majors, but they always played in Joe's shadow. But then, so did most of the other players of the day.

Not long after he arrived in New York, DiMaggio's talent and the adulation of the press allowed him to take over Ruth's place as the nation's premier sports idol. He was the subject of "Joltin' Joe DiMaggio" and several other popular songs and of countless photographs and articles in the daily press, the *Sporting News,* and other sports and general interest magazines of the day. When *Life* and other publications polled their readers on which Americans they admired the most, DiMaggio's name was usually near the top of the list.

DiMaggio was a great all-around player — many think the best who ever played the game. A natural hitter, he stood erect, far back in the batter's box, with his feet firmly planted about 36 inches apart. A picture of relaxation at the plate, he held the bat over his shoulder, moving the bat very little, waiting until the last fraction of a second to swing, then taking a short stride and swinging smoothly, with great wrist action, to meet the pitch. And meet the ball he usually did, striking out only 369 times in 13 seasons, an incredibly low figure for a power hitter. In 1941, when he compiled his 56-game hitting streak, he struck out only 13 times the entire season. As a right-handed pull-hitter, he was handicapped by the spacious outfield dimensions of Yankee Stadium, which was built for left-hander Babe Ruth and was known as one of the toughest parks in the majors for right-handers. Still, he managed to hit 361 homers and compile a lifetime batting average of .325. DiMaggio was also a fast, smart baserunner and one of the top defensive center fielders of all time. The smooth way he covered the outfield, the way he seemed to glide under the ball after a graceful, seemingly effortless run, earned him the nickname of the "the Yankee Clipper," to go along with his other one, "Joltin' Joe," made famous by the popular song. He rarely made a mental or physical mistake in the field. In his entire career, he made just 105 errors.

At bat and in the field, he was a controlled, disciplined, unemotional player, always seeming to be above the roar of the crowd. He was never thrown out of a game by an umpire and never had a serious argument with a teammate or opposing player. Although he compiled impressive individual statistics, he was a team player who very early in his career emerged as the leader of the proud Bronx Bombers, inspiring them not by pep talks and constant chatter on the field but by the example of his own professionalism and performance. Joe Page, his roommate on the road, once said, "As long as I can remember, when the Yankees took the field, they all waited for Joe to make the first break. Nothing was said about this ritual, but everybody held back and waited for Joe to lead us out."[14] It was more than just a coincidence that the Yankees won 10 pennants and 9 world championships during his 13 years with the club.

This public hero was a very private man. Hank Greenberg once said that "if he said hello to you, that was a long conversation,"[15] and newspaper columnist Jimmy Cannon, who had known DiMaggio since 1936 and was one of his closest friends, once wrote that DiMaggio was "the shyest public man" he had ever known.[16] A loner who did not make friends easily on or off the field, he was admired by his teammates yet never got close to most of them. He rarely showed emotion, rarely complained of injuries or personal problems or engaged in locker room pranks. He was also courteous, well-mannered, soft-spoken — a real gentleman, it was often said.

DiMaggio wanted to maintain a private life off the field, but he found this very difficult to do. He was the most famous baseball player of his time, and as his career progressed, Joe DiMaggio the baseball star quickly became Joe DiMaggio the cultural hero and national idol. Easily recognized, he was often mobbed when he tried to go out in public. In New York he virtually stopped taking the subway and buses and took taxis instead, to keep from being mobbed. "He couldn't even eat a meal in a hotel restaurant," pitcher Ed Lopat once said. "The fans just wouldn't let him. He led the league in room service."[17]

This son of a hardworking Italian fisherman was paid very, very well. He realized his value to the Yankees, insisted on being paid a high salary, and engaged in frequent contract disputes with management. After being paid $8,000 in his rookie season, his salary steadily rose, until in 1949 he became the first major league player to receive $100,000 in salary alone. By the time he retired, he had made a total of $704,769 from baseball and another $250,000 from product endorsements and radio and television appearances.

It was natural that the fans, players, and writers would often compare DiMaggio with his counterpart in Boston, Ted Williams. Natives of California, both were great athletes playing on teams that were often the hottest rivals in the American League. Actually, their careers overlapped only part of the time, for DiMaggio broke into the majors three years before Williams did and retired nine years before the Splendid Splinter. Both lost three valuable years to military service during World War II and Williams was destined to lose nearly two more during the Korean conflict. Many felt that Williams was the better hitter, both for average and for power, and their lifetime statistics would bear that out — Williams retired with a .344 lifetime average and 521 homers, while DiMaggio wound up with a lifetime average of .325 and 361 homers.

But most contemporary observers felt that DiMaggio was the better all-around player — at bat, on the base paths, in the field, and as team leader. DiMaggio was a team player who regularly led his club into the World Series, while Williams was often considered to be interested only in his individual statistics and played in only one World Series. DiMaggio also played in the media center of the nation, was popular with the fans and sportswriters, and became a national hero. Williams played in Boston, which was not the fishbowl New York was, and he was frequently at war with the fans and the writers who controlled the publicity he received. DiMaggio was said to have class, Williams to be surly and rude and sometimes even crude. This is an argument without end, but what is clear is that they were two of the greatest ever to play the game. In 1941, they provided the fans with two extraordinary feats that are unlikely ever to be equaled — DiMaggio's 56-game hitting streak and Williams's .406 batting average.

When DiMaggio signed his third consecutive $100,000 contract in February of 1951, he told reporters, "I intend to play ball for as long as my body holds out, and for as long as Casey Stengel wants me to play on the Yankees." But when spring training came around, he seemed to realize that his 36-year-old body, worn down by passing years, injuries, and pain, could no longer do what he wanted it to. In March, he told reporters in Phoenix that "this might be my last year. . . . I would like to have a good year and hang them up."[18]

DiMaggio's retirement talk caught Yankee executives by surprise and led them to speed up their efforts to turn a young, switch-hitting shortstop from Oklahoma into a center fielder. Mickey Mantle was just 19 years old, but he was already being trumpeted by the press as the successor to Ruth and DiMaggio. A native of Spavinaw, Oklahoma, he had played football, basketball, and baseball at Commerce High School, where he had been accidentally kicked in his left shin during football practice, resulting in an injury that led to osteomyelitis, a chronic bone infection. The first of many leg injuries Mantle would suffer over the years, it was the primary reason he received the 4-F draft classification that kept him out of the Korean War, but it also hampered and shortened his career.

Just three weeks after he graduated from high school in 1949, Mantle was offered a $1,400 bonus by Yankee scout Tom Greenwade, who later recalled that while he was scouting Mantle he said to himself, "Now I know how Paul Krichell felt when he first saw Lou Gehrig."[19] In this era of "bonus babies," this was surely the best bargain ever struck. Mantle played shortstop for the Yankee Class D farm club in Independence, Missouri, in 1949, then in 1950 he was sent up to the Class C Joplin, Missouri, club in the Western Association, where he hit .383, bashed 26 home runs, and drove in 136 runs. It was impossible to hide the find the Yankees had made, and reporters were already calling him the best major league prospect to come along in years.

When Mantle was invited to join the Yankees in spring training in 1951, Stengel had planned to send him to the Bronx Bombers' Triple A farm club in Kansas City for one more year of seasoning before he was brought up to the big time, but DiMaggio's retirement talk and Mantle's spring performance changed that. In exhibition games he hit 9 home runs, drove in 31, and hit .402. In batting practice and in exhibition games he hit long home runs from both sides of the plate, causing other players and the press to stand and watch with their mouths gaped open in amazement. He was fast as a rabbit, too, running from home to first in just a little over three seconds. Stengel told reporters that "the kid is the kind of player a manager runs into about once in his career if he is lucky." But the wise old baseball man also worried about all the publicity the young player was getting. "The kid is just about that—a kid," he reminded reporters. "And we should not place on his shoulders responsibilities which he could not carry."[20]

After Branch Rickey saw Mantle during spring training, he hurriedly scribbled a note to Yankee owner Dan Topping. "With this," he wrote, "I make my first official bid to buy Mickey Mantle for the Pirates. Name your own price, but for goodness sakes be reasonable." Topping informed Rickey "The very lowest price would be Ralph Kiner and $500,000." Rickey made no further offers.[21]

Mantle was given a contract for $7,000, just $1,000 above the major league minimum, and since he was not yet ready to dislodge Rizzuto from shortstop or DiMaggio from center field, he was put in Babe Ruth's old position in right. Tommy Henrich and DiMaggio coached him in the art of playing the outfield, and he caught on quickly, though he was still far from being the great defensive outfielder he would later become.

Standing a little over 5 feet 11 inches tall and weighing 175 pounds, Mantle would eventually fill out to a muscular 190 to 195 pounds, adding even more punch to the homers he knocked over the walls in stadiums around the league. He seemed to have all the tools needed to be a superstar—strength, speed, power from both sides of the plate, and a good arm. He also had the right looks to attract publicity. With his youth, blue eyes, blond hair, and fetching grin, he was a prototype of the good-looking All-American boy of the fifties.

In the opening game in Yankee Stadium against the Red Sox on April 17, Mantle was in the starting lineup in right field, playing beside his boyhood idol, DiMaggio, before 44,860 fans. "At first I was scared silly," he later said. "I was afraid I'd bump into DiMaggio and make a fool of myself. . . . But then the game started and everything was all right. I was too busy to worry."[22] He grounded out, flied out to the shortstop, singled in a run, and handled three chances in the outfield flawlessly.

Two weeks later he hit his first home run, a booming shot in Chicago. By May 15, he was hitting near .300, but then the pressure, inexperience, and major league pitching began to get to him, and his batting average began to drop. On Memorial Day, he struck out in five consecutive times at bat in a doubleheader in Boston. After the fifth, he came into the dugout and kicked the water cooler. Casey came over to him and said, "Son, that water cooler ain't striking you out." Mantle sat down and burst into tears, telling Stengel, "You'd better take me out of there and put in somebody who can hit."[23] Stengel took him out, and a few weeks later, on July 15, when Mantle's average had dropped to .260, sent him to Kansas City for more experience.

When he got to Kansas City, Mantle considered quitting baseball altogether. But he was talked out of it by his father, Mutt, who was now suffering from incurable Hodgkin's Disease but traveled to Kansas City to shore up his son's confidence and courage. "Baseball is no different from any other job," Mutt told him. "It takes guts, not moaning, to make it. And if that's all the guts you have . . . come on back to Commerce and . . . the mines."[24]

Mantle stayed. Regaining his confidence and batting eye, he played in 40 games, hitting .361 with 11 homers and 50 RBIs. He rejoined the Yankees on August 24, and by season's end had played in 96 games, garnered 91 hits, hit 13 home runs, scored 61, and driven in 65. He still had trouble at the plate, striking out 74 times and managing only a .267 batting average. But he was back in the majors for good.

Mantle's major league debut coincided with that of another center fielder destined for greatness. He was Willie Howard Mays, born in Westfield, Alabama, on May 6, 1931, just five months before Mantle. Mays began his professional career with the Birmingham Black Barons when he was only 17 years old, playing full time during the summer and on weekends when school was in session. When he graduated from high school in 1950, he was given a $4,000 bonus for signing with the New York Giants, who sent him to their Class B team in Trenton, New Jersey, where he hit .353 in 81 games. In 1951, he was elevated to the Giants' Triple A club, the Minneapolis Millers, in the American Association. Playing in just 31 games, he hit .477, stroked eight homers, stole eight bases, and made spectacular catches in the outfield. He was the darling of the local fans and of crowds around the league.

But the Giants could not let him stay; they were slumping badly and needed his glove and bat in New York. In the last week of May, he was called up to the majors, joining the club in Philadelphia on May 25 as it opened a three-game series in Shibe Park. Barely 20 years old, he got off to a dismal start. Put into the lineup the night he arrived in Philadelphia, he went hitless in five trips to the plate and ran into Monte Irvin in the outfield, allowing a routine fly ball to fall in for a double. He went hitless the next day, and the next. But in his fourth game, making his debut at the Polo Grounds, he hit a towering home run off Warren Spahn.

At first that homer appeared to be a fluke, for Mays continued to be embarrassed at the plate, often swinging wildly at bad pitches. In his first 26 trips to the plate, the homer was his only hit. Like Mantle, he was having his troubles, and like Mantle he went to his manager with doubts about his ability to hit major league pitching. After the young rookie had suffered through one particularly dismal night with the bat, Durocher found him crying in front of his locker. Mays told Durocher that he was hurting the team and should be sent back to the Millers where he belonged. Durocher put his arm around Mays and told him, "As long as I'm here, Willie, you're going to play center field. Tomorrow, next week, next month. As long as Durocher is manager of this ball club you will be on this ball club because you are the best ballplayer I've ever seen."[25]

Mays was too good a hitter to be stymied by major league pitching for very long. He recovered from the early slump, and with his hitting, fielding, and baserunning, became the spark plug of the 1951 Giants, hitting 20 home runs, driving in 68, and batting .274. For his efforts he would be named Rookie of the Year. The Giants, mired in fifth place with a 17–19 record the day Mays joined the team, went on to win the pennant.

Even as a young rookie, Mays showed that he was something special, electrifying his teammates and fans with his spectacular hitting, fielding, throwing, and running. At 5 feet, 10½ inches and 175 pounds, he could hit for average and power, bunt, sacrifice, and execute the hit and run. Like Jackie Robinson, he was always a serious threat when he got on base. He could steal, go from first to third on a single, score from first on a double, and force the pitcher to worry more about him than the batter.

He was a superb defensive player. He was fast, had quick reflexes, and an intuition that told him where the ball was going as soon as it came off the bat. He made one-handed catches, diving and sliding catches, and over-the-shoulder catches. One of his most spectacular grabs came in a 1951 game against the Pirates in Forbes Field. Rocky Nelson slashed a ball that headed to deep center field as Mays ran back looking over his shoulder. As he got to the warning track, nearly 457 feet from home plate, the sinking ball hooked away from his glove. On the dead run, he reached down and caught it at knee level with his bare hand. Branch Rickey, always appreciative of talent even if it were used against his team, sent a note to Mays in the dugout saying, "That was the finest catch I have ever seen . . . and the finest catch I ever hope to see."[26]

Mays also had a strong, accurate arm. On at least three occasions in his career he threw the ball on one hop to the catcher from over 400 feet from the plate. One of his most celebrated throws occurred on August 15, 1951, in a crucial game with the Dodgers. In the eighth inning, the game was tied at 1–1 with one out and Billy Cox on third base when Furillo hit what looked like a routine sacrifice fly to Mays in center field. After the catch, Cox tagged up and headed for home with an apparent 2–1 lead for his team. But in one motion Mays caught the ball and spun around and pegged it to catcher Wes Westrum, who caught it and tagged Cox, who was so sure of scoring that he had not even bothered to slide. An incredulous Chuck Dressen said, "He'll have to do that again before I believe it."[27] For many years around the National League, players and fans would talk about what came to be known simply as "the throw."

Mays had all the skills needed for stardom, but one of the things that endeared him to the fans was his infectious love of the game. Whether he was at bat, on the bases, or in the outfield, he always seemed to enjoy the national pastime, and he played it with a flair that has rarely been equaled. He was an intense, dramatic player. No wonder he was one of the biggest gate draws of his time.

DiMaggio, Mantle, Mays. The aging veteran and the two young rookies received a lot of attention from the New York press in 1951, and all three were destined for the Hall of Fame. So was the slugger and ballhawk roaming center field in Brooklyn, Duke Snider. As the 1951 season began, the 24-year-old Duke of Flatbush had finally, after four years in the majors, found the strike zone. In 1950 he had finished first in the league in hits (199), third in batting average (.321) and triples (10), fifth in homers (31), and sixth in RBIs (107). He was a superb baserunner and an outstanding defensive center fielder capable of coming in to make shoestring catches or racing back to the wall to pull down what had looked like a sure home run. When DiMaggio retired at the end of the 1951 season, allowing Mantle to move to center field, it would set the stage for one of baseball's biggest debates in the 1950s: who was the best center fielder in New York, indeed, in all of baseball—Mantle, Mays, or Snider?

New York also had catchers Lawrence "Yogi" Berra and Roy Campanella, two other future Hall of Famers and frequent topics of "who's the best?" debates. A native of St. Louis, Berra grew up in the "Hill," the Italian section of town, on the same street with his lifelong friend, Joe Garagiola. Signed by the Yankees for a $500 bonus in 1943, Berra played for the Yankee farm team at Norfolk before going into the navy. Discharged in the spring of 1946, he spent the season with the top Yankee farm club, the Newark Bears in the Triple A International League, where he hit .314 while bashing 14 homers.

Near the end of the 1946 season, Berra was one of several minor league players brought up to the Yankees for a little major league experience. Playing in seven games, he hit two home runs, one in his first at bat in the majors, and wound up with a .364 average. In 1947, the 22-year-old rookie played in 83 games, hitting .280 with 11 home runs, but gained a reputation for chasing too many bad pitches and for making too many fielding and throwing errors. However, with each passing year his hitting and his fielding improved as his playing time increased.

In his 19 years (1946–1965) in the majors, Berra never won a major batting title, but he was often among the leaders, finishing his career with a .285 average, 358 home runs, and 1,430 RBIs. He had a reputation as a bad ball hitter, but generally a good and dangerous one, and he was one of the greatest clutch hitters of all time. In 1950 his defensive weaknesses caused him to tie the major league record for passed balls, but he eventually became a top-notch defensive catcher, adept at handling pitchers, outsmarting hitters, throwing out base runners, blocking bad pitches, and guarding the plate against runners. His career fielding average was .989, and he ranked high among catchers in games played, double plays, chances accepted, and other offensive and defensive categories. From July 28, 1957, through May, 10, 1959, he would set a record by catching 148 consecutive games without an error. In 1951 he became the first American League catcher to win the MVP Award since Mickey Cochrane of the Philadelphia Athletics in 1934. He would win the award again in 1954 and still again in 1955.

Berra was fortunate enough to play in 14 World Series, and he set several records: most games (75), at bats (259), hits (71), and doubles (10). He also hit 12 homers (third), scored 41 runs (second), and drove in 39 (second), and set a record by throwing out 36 would-be base stealers. He hit the first pinch-hit homer in World Series history in 1947, hit the fifth grand slam in Series history in the second game of the 1956 fall classic, and caught Don Larsen's no-hitter in game five of that same Series. He always seemed to perform best at World Series time.

Berra was a mainstay of the great Yankee teams of the Stengel era and one of the most colorful and popular players in the game, attaining fame not just for his playing but for his wide grin, wisecracks, and malapropisms. Some of the sayings credited to him and stories told about him were true, some were exaggerated, others were made up and attributed to him by Joe Garagiola and others. Many of them centered on his alleged dumbness, but in actuality he was a shrewd man who enjoyed putting people on and having a reputation as a colorful, humorous character.

Berra's public reputation as a humorist was first promoted in 1947 in a speech he made in Sportsman's Park in St. Louis, where his home-town fans gave him a special night near the end of the season during the Yankees last trip into town to play the Browns. He had memorized a brief appreciation speech written by teammate Bobby Brown, but as he stood before the microphone his nervousness caused him to make a slip that would be forever remembered when his malapropisms were recalled. "I want to thank everyone for making this night necessary," he said. This was his first major public malapropism, and it brought laughter and thunderous applause.

As Berra's baseball records grew, so did his reputation as a coiner of "Berraisms" or "Yogiisms" that became almost as famous as the "Stengelese" of his manager. He referred to a player on an opposing team as "the main clog in their machine," said that because of the late summer sun and shadows in left field in Yankee Stadium "it sure gets late early out there," claimed that one of his classmates "was so popular in school, nobody could stand him," and once explained that he took an early subway to Brooklyn for a World Series game because "I knew I was gonna take the wrong train, so I left early." And there were many others over the years: "It's deja vu all over again," "ninety percent of this game is half mental," "this is the earliest I've ever been late," and, after being introduced to Ernest Hemingway and told that he was a writer, asked, "What paper you write for, Ernie?" Of course almost everyone had heard his "it ain't over 'til it's over," and perhaps everyone should have heard his claim that "I really didn't say everything I said."[28]

Berra's main rival for the title of the best catcher in New York—indeed, in all of baseball—was Roy Campanella. Born in Philadelphia in 1921 to a black mother and white father of Italian descent, Campanella began to play professional baseball in the Negro leagues when he was only 14 years old. For years he played with the Negro leagues in the spring and summer and with Latin American teams in the winter, sometimes catching two or three games in a day. After being signed to a Dodger contract in 1946, he played for three Dodger farm clubs before being called up to Brooklyn in May of 1948 as a nearly 27-year-old rookie. Campanella quickly established himself as a major leaguer, showing that he could hit, handle pitchers, and play a better defensive game than most veteran catchers. In 1949 he became the regular Dodger catcher, and was one of the team's leaders during the successful pennant drive, hitting 22 homers, driving in 82 runs, and compiling a .287 batting average. He followed this performance in 1950 with a .281 batting average, 31 homers, and 89 RBIs.

Campanella's physical appearance belied his true athletic prowess. At 5 feet, 9 nine inches and 200 pounds, he looked obese, and indeed reporters frequently called him "roly poly," "burly," and "husky." But he was muscular, a deceptively fast runner, quick and agile behind the plate, and had a rifle arm that cut down many a base thief. He hit for average and power and could usually be counted on in clutch situations. His best year was 1953, when he batted .312, hit 41 home runs, led the league in RBIs with 142, and scored 103 runs. His 41 homers would be the most by a catcher until Johnny Bench hit 45 in 1970.

Friendly, easygoing, gregarious—his teammates called him "the Good Humor Man,"—Campanella was liked and respected in both leagues. He loved baseball, and his attitude toward the game was shown in his often-repeated claim that "you got to be a man to play baseball for a living, but you got to have a lot of little boy in you, too."[29] On the field he was always chatting and joking with his teammates and with opposing players. Rookies on opposing teams quickly learned that one of the main purposes of his chatter when they came to the plate was to prevent them from concentrating on the business of hitting Dodger pitching.

Campanella never voiced any hatred of the racism that had kept him out of the majors for so many years. Rather, he was glad for the chance to play, even if it came late. He once said, "Knocking around the Negro leagues for ten years and playing winter ball in Latin America was good training for me. It taught me to appreciate what I'm getting now. Up here in the big leagues you play on fine diamonds, the clubhouses are nice and you stay at the best hotels. How can you call that work? This is a breeze compared to the old days."[30]

Campanella was of a different temperament from his fiery teammate, Jackie Robinson. A believer in gradual integration, he thought that Robinson sometimes pushed too hard, too fast and held back the advancement of blacks by arousing white hostility. On one occasion, when a seething Robinson was about to get into a feud with umpires, Campanella helped to calm him down, telling him, "Come on Jackie, don't be like that. Let's not take any chances. It's nice up here."[31] The two men were never close friends, in spite of their racial bond and years spent as roommates while the Dodgers were on the road, but Campanella had great respect for Robinson as a pioneer and as a player. In later years he would say, "I thought he was the greatest ballplayer, considering all the obstacles he had to face. . . . Nothing could stop this man, and the more you would ride him the better he could play. This is the kind of man he was."[32]

In 1951, Campanella would hit 33 home runs, drive in 108, and compile a .325 batting average. Although the Dodgers would lose the pennant to the Giants, he won the MVP Award, like his counterpart with the Yankees. He would win the award a second time in 1955, when the Dodgers finally broke the jinx and won the World Series.

DiMaggio. Mantle. Mays. Snider. Berra. Campanella. Robinson. These were only a few of the players making New York the baseball capital of the world at the beginning of the 1950s. And in no other year would this be truer than in 1951, when all three teams finished in first place on the last day of the regular season, forcing the Giants and Dodgers into a dramatic playoff to determine who would face the hated Yankees in the World Series.

9. The Year of the Midget and the Giants (1951)

On February 2, 1951, around 600 people from the baseball world, including 15 of the 23 living members of the Hall of Fame, gathered at the Broadway Central Hotel in New York to celebrate the 75th anniversary of the founding of the National League. The league president and master of ceremonies, Ford Frick, read a warm letter from President Harry Truman, who at that time was being assailed from all sides for the catastrophic losses the American forces were suffering in the Korean War. Congratulating the National League and lauding baseball as "our national sport," Truman said, "Baseball has made great contributions in peace, and in war it has asked for no special favors, nor will it in our present preparedness program." He concluded with the words, "May the sun never set on American baseball."[1]

The president's letter caused some concern among many of those in the audience. Although he had praised baseball, he certainly did not confer the green light that Roosevelt had given the game during World War II and that organized baseball was hoping for as the nation approached the end of the eighth month of the Korean conflict, which seemed to worsen with each passing day.

Professional baseball was already facing potential manpower shortages as the draft dipped into the pool of young men across the nation. "If the war situation gets any worse," Philadelphia Phillies owner Bob Carpenter moaned, "there won't be anybody left to play for my club but me. Practically all my players are in the vulnerable age bracket."[2] There were problems in other areas of the game as well. Shortages were driving up the price of wool, rubber, and other ingredients used in the manufacture of baseballs, and government regulations had frozen the use of horsehide and decreased the allotment of crude rubber to manufacturers of sports equipment. Although there was some fear that a shortage of baseballs might develop, A.G. Spalding and Brothers Company officials said they should be able to supply baseballs to the majors in 1951 but warned that temporary shortages might develop at the lower levels.

Korean War or not, the baseball season began on schedule. On April 20, President Truman made his customary journey to Griffith Stadium to throw out the ceremonial first pitch. It was his first public appearance since he had fired General Douglas MacArthur, the commander of the American and United Nations forces in Korea, for disobeying orders and challenging the president's constitutional position as the commander-in-chief of the armed forces. On April 19, the general had made an impassioned speech to Congress, replete with such MacArthuresque phrases as "there is no substitute for victory" and "old soldiers never die, they just fade away."[3] Later in the day he made a triumphant journey down Pennsylvania Avenue, and on April 20, the day of Washington's home opener, he rode at the head of a four-hour parade down Broadway in New York before a crowd estimated at over 7.5 million people.

With MacArthur capturing the love and sympathy of the nation for the moment, Truman's popularity had dropped to one of its lowest points ever. Not surprisingly, when he made his appearance at Griffith Stadium he became the first president to be booed at a baseball game since the depression when Herbert Hoover had been given the treatment at the 1931 World Series in Philadelphia. But Truman never let on that he heard the boos or the cries of "Where's MacArthur?" Before the game, he predicted that the home team would defeat the hated Yankees by a 5–3 score, and after throwing out the first ball he and Bess settled down to watch the game, eat hot dogs, and drink hot chocolate. Just as he predicted, the Senators won, 5–3. And just as he predicted, MacArthur would soon fade away.[4]

In the American League, most sportswriters picked the Red Sox to take the flag, in spite of the two consecutive world titles Stengel and the Yankees had won coming into the 1951 season. Yankee haters all across the nation were hoping the pundits were right. Early in the season, a Cleveland fan even tried to derail Stengel's pennant drive by putting a jinx on the Bronx Bombers. Carrying a black cat, he bolted out of the stands, ran toward the mound, waved the feline in Ed Lopat's face, then dropped it at the hurler's feet. He and the cat were quickly escorted off the field by stadium police.

For much of the season, the jinx seemed to work, for the Yankees had to battle the White Sox, Red Sox, and Indians for the top spot. The White Sox got off to a slow start, then reeled off 14 consecutive victories in May, captured first place, and held it from May 28 through July 1. But after the All-Star break they faded from contention almost as quickly as they had risen to the top. Then it was the Red Sox's turn to hold the lead, but after 12 days they were swept aside by the Indians and the Yankees, who would battle one another for the pennant for the rest of the season. By August 23 the Indians had a three-game lead over the Bronx Bombers, and their fans were talking World Series for the first time since 1948.

It had been a problem-ridden season for the Old Professor. Whitey Ford had been drafted, several players were sidelined with injuries, Joe

DiMaggio was having the worst year of his career, and rookie Mickey Mantle seemed to be striking out more often than he made contact with the ball and had to be sent to Kansas City for seasoning. But Stengel never gave up. Faced with these personnel problems, he drove his club hard and went to platooning even more than he had in his first two years at the helm, running rookies and veterans and healthy and injured players in and out of the lineup with an almost bewildering regularity.

Somehow it worked, and the Yankees began to gain on the Tribe. On September 16, sporting a one-game lead over the Bombers, the Indians came to New York for a two-game series. The Yankees won both contests to take over first place, which they never relinquished. The Indians stayed within striking distance, but the Yankees won 9 of their last 12 games and finally clinched the pennant on September 28 by taking both ends of a doubleheader from the Red Sox in Yankee Stadium. The first game was won by Allie Reynolds, a Creek Indian who celebrated American Indian Day with an 8–0 no-hitter, making him only the second major leaguer to toss two no-hitters in one year. The other was Johnny Vander Meer, who turned the trick for Cincinnati in 1938. The Yankees had won a record eighteenth pennant in 31 years, and they did it with only one starter, Gil McDougald, hitting over .300, and with no one driving in 100 runs or more. McDougald's .306 average and play at third base earned him Rookie of the Year honors, while teammate Yogi Berra won the Most Valuable Player Award with a .294 average, 88 RBIs, and 27 homers. Vic Raschi and Ed Lopat captured 21 games each, and Allie Reynolds won 17.

Finishing five games behind, the second-place Indians had three 20-game winners. Bob Feller led the league with 22 victories and also picked up a no-hitter, while Mike Garcia and Early Wynn each won 20. But the excellent pitching could not make up for a team batting average of .256, seventh in the American League. The top American League batting titles were captured by Ferris Fain and Gus Zernial of the sixth-place Athletics. Fain's .344 topped the league in average, while Zernial led in home runs (33) and RBIs (129).

In the years to come, few fans would remember the details of the 1951 American League race. It would be overshadowed by the National League campaign, and by one single game in the American League schedule — the day Bill Veeck sent a midget up to bat.

Two years after he sold the Cleveland Indians, Veeck returned to the majors on July 5, 1951, when he and several associates bought controlling interest in the St. Louis Browns for $2 million. Many of the other owners were sorry to see him, fearing that he would resume his unconventional promotional gimmicks. The Browns certainly needed promoting. Since entering the American League in 1902, they had finished last eight times, in the second division 38 times, and first only once — in 1944, during the talent-depleted war years. Poor play had naturally brought low attendance over the years. In 1950 the club had drawn only 247,131 fans, and in July of 1951 the team seemed destined to have another dismal year on the field and at the gate. It had a record of 21–49, was 23½ games out of first, and was sinking fast.

Veeck quickly proved that he was his old self. Not long after he took over, he happened to answer the switchboard when a fan called in wanting to know what time the day's game started. "What time can you get here?" Veeck asked.[5] He resurrected many of the gimmicks he had used at Cleveland and also introduced some new ones. One was "Grandstand Managers' Day," held on August 24, when 1,115 fans were chosen to sit behind the dugout and indicate by boos and applause or "Yes" and "No" cards what they wanted the Browns to do. While manager Zack Taylor sat in a rocking chair near the dugout smoking a pipe and reading a newspaper, two coaches held up a large sign asking the grandstand managers what they would do in crucial situations: "Bunt?" "Pinch Hitter?" "Steal?" and so on. The majority ruled. The Browns beat the Philadelphia Athletics 5–3, with Ned Garver picking up his fifteenth victory as he headed toward a 20–12 season. After the game Veeck announced that the practice would be discontinued because it was best "to quit while you're ahead."[6]

Veeck also hired baseball comedian Max Patkin as a coach and brought back another comic figure and proven crowd-pleaser, Satchel Paige, who had been forced to go back to barnstorming when Veeck sold the Indians at the end of the 1949 season. When he signed Paige to a Browns' contract, Veeck said that "everybody kept telling me he was through, but that was understandable. They thought he was only human."[7] Paige appeared in 23 games and compiled a 3–4 record.

But Veeck's greatest stunt came when he sent a midget up to bat in an official major league game. Most reporters claimed that he must have gotten the idea from a James Thurber short story, "You Could Look It Up," published in the Saturday Evening Post in 1941. However, Veeck always insisted that the genesis of the scheme dated back to when he was a small boy and heard about a short, hunchbacked man that manager John McGraw had kept around the Giants' clubhouse for good luck and often threatened to send to the plate.

Whatever its origin, Veeck decided to carry out an idea that Thurber and McGraw had only dreamed of. He engaged the services of 26-year-old Eddie Gaedel, a 42-inch, 65-pound midget who worked as a Chicago newspaper office boy and often hired himself out for promotional stunts or private parties. Veeck brought him to St. Louis, signed him to a contract, and paid him $100 for one day's work. But he kept his plans secret from everyone except his wife, manager, and a few other club officials.

The date chosen for the stunt was August 19, when the Browns were playing a doubleheader against the visiting Detroit Tigers. The games were promoted as a celebration of the fiftieth anniversary of the founding of the American League and as a birthday party for Falstaff Brewery, which sponsored the radio broadcasts of the Browns' games and paid for the party. Over 18,000 fans showed up, the largest Brownie home crowd in four years, and they certainly got their money's worth. They were given a free can of Falstaff beer, ice cream, and other prizes, and after the first game they were treated to the traditional Veeck entertainment — bands, jugglers, acrobats, dancers, and other elements of a three-ring circus. Then a seven-foot-high birthday cake was wheeled onto the field, accompanied by "Sir John Falstaff," an actor dressed in Elizabethan clothing. Falstaff tapped the top of the cake and out popped Eddie Gaedel, wearing elf shoes and a baseball uniform with the number ⅛ sewn on the back.

When the second game began, most fans thought the stunts were over, but Veeck was saving the best for last. In the bottom of the first inning, Gaedel emerged from the dugout and headed for the plate, swinging a toy bat, to pinch hit for center fielder Frank Saucier. Home plate umpire Ed Hurley went over to the Browns' dugout to protest, but Taylor jumped off the bench and showed him Gaedel's contract and a carbon copy of the telegram he had sent to American League President Will Harridge informing him that Gaedel had been added to the roster. Hurley reluctantly ordered the game to resume.

As the fans laughed and cheered, Detroit catcher Bob Swift went out to the mound to confer with Bob Cain on how to pitch to a 42-inch midget with a miniature strike zone. When he took his position behind the plate, Swift got down on his knees and held the glove in a position for a low strike. Gaedel crouched, planted his feet wide apart in an imitation of Joe DiMaggio, and tried to look as menacing as possible. He did not dare swing at the ball. Veeck had told him, "I've got a man in the stands with a high-powered rifle, and if you swing at any pitch, he'll fire."[8] This was typical Veeck bombast, but Gaedel obeyed, while Cain, struggling to control his laughter, served up four consecutive high fastballs.

Gaedel ran down to first base, where he put one foot on the bag and the other in the infield as he awaited the pinch runner, outfielder Jim Delsing. After patting Delsing on the rear and shaking hands with the first base coach, he jogged across the infield on the way to the Browns' dugout behind third base, stopping to bow and to wave his hat to the crowd, savoring his special moment for as long as he could. It was the high point of the little man's life. After the game, he told one reporter, "For a minute, I felt like Babe Ruth."[9] A week later, when he was arrested for public intoxication in Cincinnati, he proudly informed the police that his occupation was "major league baseball player."[10]

The fans at Sportsman's Park loved the Gaedel stunt, but the league president and other baseball owners denounced it as just another attempt by Bill Veeck to make a mockery of the national pastime. The day after the game, claiming that the use of Gaedel was "not in the best interest of baseball," Harridge decreed that no midget could ever appear in an American League game again. Veeck protested that there was no maximum or minimum height requirement for major league baseball players and that Harridge's actions were arbitrary and discriminatory. Gaedel was incensed. "Harridge is ruining my baseball career," he told reporters. "This is a conspiracy against all short guys. This is a strikeout against the little people."[11] The ban remained, but so did Gaedel's inclusion in the standard baseball record books, along with the other immortals who have played the game. He achieved what millions of American males could only dream of—for a few minutes, he was a major leaguer.

While the Yankees were continuing their winning ways and Veeck was staging stunt after stunt to draw paying customers into Sportsman's Park, the National League was enjoying the most dramatic pennant battle in baseball history. Before the season began, the members of the Baseball Writers Association of America predicted that the race would be a toss-up between baseball's two greatest rivals, the Giants and the Dodgers. As usual, Leo Durocher left no doubt as to where he stood on the upcoming pennant campaign. During the offseason he said that the Giants' strong finish in 1950 had shown that "I can win anywhere when I have my kind of team," and he predicted that 1951 would be the year "the Giants take it all."[12]

But in the first half of the season, the Giants played as if they were seeking last place, not first. After winning their first two games, they lost 11 in a row and fell into the cellar. Five of the losses were to the hated Dodgers, led by baseball's fiercest competitor, Jackie Robinson, who had been feuding with Durocher ever since "the Lip" left Brooklyn. In the first six games the two teams played early in the season, Robinson hit .409, slammed three homers, drove in eight runs, and constantly taunted his former boss.

On April 29 at Ebbets Field, Robinson led the Dodgers to their fifth consecutive win over the Giants. Tempers flared on both sides, and the bench jockeying was as heated as at any time in the two teams' long rivalry. Don Newcombe kept yelling at Durocher, "Eat your heart out. Eat your heart out," causing Durocher to turn white and shake with anger.[13] In the fourth inning, Larry Jansen knocked Duke Snider down with a high inside fastball, a pitch the Dodgers habitually called "the Durocher pitch." Snider got back into the box and hit another Jansen offering into the parking lot across Bedford Avenue, a favorite resting place for many of his home runs.

In the sixth, with the score tied 2–2, Jansen hit Robinson in the side. As he ran down to first, Robinson taunted Jansen all the way, shouting, "You've got some nerve to try and scare a guy with that stuff. Go ahead and do it again."[14] Jansen seemed to lose his nerve, or at least his concentration. He quickly served up a home run to Gil Hodges, a double to Bruce Edwards, a single to Pee Wee Reese, and a double to Billy Cox. By the time the inning was over, Jansen had departed for the showers and the Dodgers had taken a 5–2 lead. Snider later hit another home run as the Dodgers went on to a 6–3 victory and dealt the Giants their eleventh consecutive loss.

The next day the two teams played their sixth game of the young season. It was another vicious, hard-fought contest. In one incident Robinson tried to extract revenge against "the Durocher pitches" by laying down a drag bunt along the first base line, hoping to draw pitcher Sal Maglie over to field it so he could bowl him over in the base path. The ball rolled foul, but Robinson managed to bump Maglie anyway. After the game, Durocher called it a "bush stunt," prompting Robinson to retort, "If it was a bush stunt he is a bush manager, because he taught me to do it."[15] The Giants won, 8–5, to end their 11-game nightmare.

April had been a disaster for the Giants, who finished the month at the bottom of the standings. The hitting, pitching, and fielding had all fallen apart, and the club was demoralized by the long losing streak. Many of the Giants' fans seemed to think that the Polo Grounders were already out of the race, and so did many writers. "It would take a miracle for them to win the championship now," Arthur Daley wrote in the *New York Times* on May 1. Although the Dodgers were in third place, one game back of Boston and a few percentage points behind St. Louis, Daley felt that "the team that's sitting prettiest right now is Brooklyn."

The Dodgers boasted one of baseball's best teams in years. They had experienced, solid players at every position: Campanella behind the plate, Hodges at first, Robinson at second, Reese at short, Cox at third, and Furillo and Snider in the outfield. The one weak spot, left field, was filled in the middle of June when Andy Pafko was acquired from the Chicago Cubs. This superb defensive team also made up a murderers' row of sluggers to match that of the 1927 Yankees, leading the league in home runs (184) and batting average (.275). The team had a good pitching staff headed by Don Newcombe (20–9), Preacher Roe (22–3), Carl Erskine (16–12), and Ralph Branca (13–12). The club was piloted by Chuck Dressen, who had been hired by owner Walter O'Malley to replace Burt Shotton after Shotton's boss and mentor, Branch Rickey, sold his Dodger stock in 1950. Dressen was a former infielder who had managed the Cincinnati Reds from 1934 to 1937, served as a coach for the Dodgers and the Yankees, and piloted the Oakland Oaks in the Pacific Coast League in 1950 before being tapped for the Dodger job.

Dressen's club started the season with a 5–1 record, took over first place on May 13, and marched steadily toward the pennant. On July 5, after taking three straight from the Giants in Ebbets Field, the Dodgers fattened their lead to 7½ games. "We knocked 'em out," Dressen boasted after the sweep. "They won't bother us anymore."[16] The Dodgers kept rolling along, fashioning one win streak of eight games, another of 10, and at one point taking 17 out of 20. On August 9, after completing still another three-game sweep of the Giants at Ebbets Field, the Dodgers enjoyed a lead of 12½ games. "It seems such a cinch that nobody but nobody can beat the Dodgers," sportswriter Joe King wrote. "Only through a cataclysmic blowup could they allow an inferior competitor to sneak in, and this Dodger team is so well balanced and so deep in great men, and so zestful in spirit that it hardly can collapse."[17]

The completion of the Dodger sweep of the Giants on August 9 marked the Dodgers' twelfth victory over the Giants in 15 meetings that year. The Dodgers were naturally exuberant, but they made the mistake of taunting the downtrodden Giants. As the two teams showered in adjoining dressing rooms after the sweep, the Giant players could hear their tormentors celebrating their huge lead and planning for the World Series. Making sure the Giants could overhear, the Dodgers were yelling over and over, "Eat your heart out, Leo! So that's your kind of team?" and singing, "We've got the Giants on the run." Captain Al Dark later told a reporter that "human beings can only take so much and we had a belly-full. . . . You just can't treat human beings like they treated us and get away with it."[18] Weeks later, the Giants would look back on this locker room incident as the spark that set them off on a 16-game winning streak that turned what looked like a Dodger cakewalk into the fiercest pennant battle in major league history.

On August 11, two days after the locker-room celebration, Branca pitched the Dodgers to an 8–1 victory over the Braves in the first game of a doubleheader at Ebbets Field, putting them 13½ games in front of the Giants. Carried by CBS, this was the first major league game ever telecast in color. Although the Dodgers dropped the second game by an 8–4 margin, their lead still stood at 13 games. The season still had 6½ weeks to go, but with a 70–36 record and only 48 games left, the Dodgers were counting their World Series money.

But the Giants never gave up. After the dismal losing streak at the first of the season, Durocher had said, "There is a long way to go before the season is over. We'll show them yet."[19] The Giants had rebounded from that disastrous start, winning 14 of their next 21 and improving their record to 17–19 by May 25, the day Willie Mays joined the club. Although he could not buy a hit for several games, he sparkled in the field and gave new life to a demoralized team. After his arrival, the Giants won three straight and went over the .500 mark for the first time all year.

The Giants played respectable ball from then on, but on August 11 they were still 13 games out. Then the miracle began to unfold. The next day, they captured a doubleheader from the Philadelphia Phillies, with Maglie taking the first game by a 3–2 score and rookie Al Corwin winning the second, 2–1. Few people saw any significance to this double victory, but the Giants won the next game, then the next, finally stretching their winning streak to 16, including a three-game sweep of the Dodgers, before they were stopped on August 28 by Pirates' left-hander Howie Pollet, 2–0. The Giants played like a team on fire, making the right play at the right time, getting clutch hits, coming from behind to win in late innings, and taking eight games by just one run.

Everyone seemed to come through when needed, especially the young Mays, who recovered from his initial troubles at the plate and gave the club a lift in morale and in the league standings with his hot bat and glove. When the streak was finally snapped, Durocher told reporters, "When he arrived in late May we were still floundering around in sixth place. We couldn't do anything right. But once he came and we put him out there in center, things began to happen. Willie transformed the whole lineup."[20] He often claimed, "I wouldn't trade him for Stan Musial, Ted Williams, or Joe DiMaggio. They've been great ballplayers, but Willie's only 20 and he's the best-looking rookie I've seen in my 25 years of baseball."[21]

Mays's exploits quickly got the attention of the press. Reporters searched for words to describe the play of the young rookie, and came up with "incredible," "impossible," "spectacular," "unbelievable," "miraculous," "fantastic," and most often, "amazing." By the middle of the summer the "Amazing Mays" was being heralded as the spark plug of the rampaging Giants and a cinch for Rookie of the Year honors.

Mays was not the whole story, of course. Durocher himself deserved much of the credit for the rebirth of the Giants. All season long he had been yelling encouragement, telling his men not to give up, trying to convince them that they were a good team that would eventually get back on track. He also made several key personnel changes. On May 21 he decided to have left fielder Whitey Lockman and first baseman Monte Irvin switch positions. Irvin had spent most of his career in left field, had never liked first base, and played better in the field and at bat when he was put back in his old spot. Lockman also responded well to the change, playing good defensive ball and finding the range at the plate. Then on May 25, Durocher brought Mays up to take over center field from Bobby Thomson, who was hitting well below .250 and was being booed by the fans for his miscues in the field. After riding the bench for awhile, Thomson was installed at third base when Hank Thompson suffered a spike injury and had to come out of the lineup. It was a brilliant move. A .237 hitter when the change was made on July 20, Thomson hit .357 for the remainder of the season and wound up with a .293 average, 101 RBIs, and 32 homers.

Finally, the pitching staff jelled at midseason. It was led by Maglie and Jansen, who tied for the league lead in wins with 23 each. Maglie, who was often called "The Barber" because of his ever-present five-o'clock shadow, the close shaves he gave opposing hitters, and Durocher's claim that he "looks like the guy at the third chair in the barber shop,"[22] was always at his best against the hated Dodgers. Jim Hearn contributed 17 victories, Al Corwin came up from Ottawa on July 18 and posted a 5–1 record, and George Spencer and Dave Koslo pitched well in relief. After playing lackluster ball for much of the season, in the last seven weeks the Giants found good pitching, good hitting, good managing, and the lucky breaks that had eluded them earlier in the season.

The Dodgers played .500 ball and refused to panic as the Giants whittled away at what had once looked like an insurmountable margin, but they were relieved when the Pirates snapped the Giants' streak on August 28 while they beat the Cincinnati Reds to increase their lead to six games. For the first time in several days, the Dodger players sang in the showers. As Pafko looked around at his happy teammates, he said, "It looks like the World Series."[23]

The Dodgers' celebrating was premature. They kept winning, but so did the Giants, keeping the pressure on the leaders and staying within striking distance. The Dodgers were showing the strain. They were grim, tense, playing to keep from losing rather than playing to win. Still, as the two teams returned from road trips on September 20, the Dodgers had a 92–52 record and a 4½-game lead with only 10 games left to play, while the Giants had an 89–58 record with only seven games remaining. The advantage seemed to lie with the Dodgers, who could win the pennant by winning only half their games even if the Giants won all of theirs.

But the Dodgers could not seize the opportunity. Feeling acutely now what sportswriter Bill Corum called "the Creeping Terror of the Giants,"[24] the Dodgers staggered to the finish line, making foolish mistakes and blaming one another for bad plays. They were coming apart at the seams while the Giants were as unified as perhaps any team had ever been. The Giants won all seven of their remaining games, while the Dodgers managed to drop six of ten, including a disastrous doubleheader loss to the Braves on September 25, by 6–2 and 14–2 scores.

They came back to beat the Braves the next day, but lost a close game to them the following day, 4–3. The game turned on a disputed call at home plate in the eighth inning, when Campanella thought he had tagged Bob Addis out but umpire Frank Dascoli called him safe with what turned out to be the winning run. Campanella and coach Cookie Lavagetto argued so vigorously that they were thrown out of the game. The Dodger bench continued to heckle Dascoli, who, unable to single out the worst offenders, cleared the entire bench except for Dressen and coach Jack Pitler. Among those ejected was outfielder Bill Sharman, recently brought up from Ft. Worth. Sharman had never appeared in a major league game and never would, making him the only player to be ejected from a major league game without ever playing in one. He would go on to become a basketball star with the Boston Celtics and eventually make it to the Basketball Hall of Fame.

On Sunday, September 30, the last day of the season, the Dodgers and Giants were tied for the lead. The Dodgers were playing the Phillies in Shibe Park, while the Giants were taking on the Braves in Boston. The Giants had the easiest time. Playing before a crowd held to around 13,000 by unseasonably cool weather, Durocher's onrushing club won by a score of 3–2 on Thomson's homer and Jansen's five-hitter.

Meanwhile, in Philadelphia the game had not gone well for the Dodgers, who were trailing 8–5 in the seventh when the final Giants-Braves score was posted on the scoreboard to the roar of the 31,755 fans. Desperately trying to stave off defeat, the Dodgers rallied in the eighth to tie the score at 8–8. Newcombe and Robin Roberts were locked in a grim duel, each holding the other side scoreless in the ninth, tenth, and eleventh innings. By the beginning of the twelfth it was beginning to get dark and fans and players alike were having trouble following the ball, but league rules prohibited the lights from being turned on for a Sunday game. In the twelfth, with the score still tied, Eddie Waitkus smashed a low liner to the right of second base. Somehow in the darkness, Robinson picked up the flight of the ball, ran over, and made a seemingly impossible diving catch, snaring the ball just inches off the ground. He fell hard on his shoulder and collapsed. Robinson's teammates gathered around his slumped body while he struggled to regain his breath. After several minutes, he got up and, still groggy, walked hesitantly toward the dugout as the crowd cheered his tremendous effort.

Neither club scored in the thirteenth, but in the fourteenth, with two outs and a 1–1 count, Robinson saved his club again by tagging Roberts for a home run into the left field bleachers to give the Dodgers a 9–8 victory. The World Series would have to wait. After 154 games, the Dodgers and Giants had identical 96–58 records.

The three-game playoff opened at Ebbets Field on October 1. Behind the five-hit pitching of Jim Hearn and home runs by Thomson and Irvin, the Giants won the opener 3–1. The win sent the series to the Polo Grounds, where the Dodgers would now be faced with the task of winning two games in hostile territory. With their backs to the wall, they roared back with a vengeance. Rookie Clem Labine held the Giants to six hits, while his teammates pounded out 13, including four homers, en route to a 10–0 drubbing of the home team.

The third and indisputably last National League game of the season was played on Wednesday, October 3. It was an overcast day, with rain threatening, which helped to account for the less than capacity crowd of 34,320, about evenly divided between Dodger and Giant partisans. The lights had to be turned on in the third inning. The game began with New-combe and Maglie on the mound, and for seven innings it was a pitcher's battle between the two 20-game winners, with the Dodgers scoring one run in the first and the Giants finally knotting the score at 1–1 in the seventh. But in the eighth the Dodgers managed to score three runs by stringing together four singles, a wild pitch, and a walk. Newcombe set the Giants down in order in the bottom half of the inning. After Maglie was lifted for a pinch hitter, Jansen came on in relief in the ninth and got the Dodgers out in one-two-three fashion.

The Giants still had one more time at bat, but they were down by three runs with only three outs to go. With Newcombe still on the mound, it looked hopeless. But hope slowly returned. Lead-off hitter Alvin Dark got an infield single off the glove of Hodges at first, then scampered to third when Mueller drove a Newcombe pitch through the hole between first and second. The next hitter, Irvin, who had hit 24 home runs and led the league in RBIs with 121, fouled out to Hodges. Just two more outs and the Dodgers would be in the World Series and the Giants' miracle surge would be nothing more than a bad memory. While the Dodgers were holding a meeting at the mound to discuss how to pitch to Whitey Lockman, an announcement was made in the press box: "Attention, press. World Series credentials for Eb-bets Field can be picked up at 6 o'clock tonight at the Biltmore Hotel."[25] But Lockman doubled to left, scoring Dark and allowing Mueller to ad-vance to third, where he sprained his ankle as he slid into the bag. The game was delayed for about 10 minutes while he was attended to and finally car-ried off the field on a stretcher. Clint Hartung came in to run for him.

With the score at 4–2, Bobby Thomson headed toward the plate with Durocher's words — "Bobby, if you ever hit one, hit one now" — still ringing in his ears.[26] Although he had contributed to the Giants' victory in game one with a homer and driven in three of the five runs the Giants had scored so far in the playoffs, he had struck out with the bases loaded in the second game and was the main candidate for the goat of game three. He had helped to snuff out a Giant rally in the second inning with boneheaded baserun-ning, and had let two balls get by at third that he should have caught. But in the past seven weeks he had been the Giants' hottest hitter, and 7 of his 31 homers had come off of Dodger pitching. Because of his success against the Dodgers, many expected Dressen to walk him, loading the bases to set up the double play, and pitch to the inexperienced rookie, Willie Mays.

But Dressen made a decision that would be second-guessed for years to come. Newcombe was obviously tiring, so Dressen looked to the bullpen, where Erskine and Branca were warming up. When Dressen called, coach

Clyde Sukeforth told him that Erskine was not as sharp as he should be and that Branca had the best stuff. Dressen told him to send in Branca, a fastball pitcher who had yielded 10 homers to the Giants in 1951, including two to Thomson, one during the regular season and the other in the first game of the playoffs. As Branca walked in from the bullpen and onto the infield grass, he passed Reese and Robinson. Trying to ease the tension they all felt, he asked, "Anyone have butterflies? If you haven't, I have." When he reached the mound, Dressen handed him the ball and said simply, "Get this guy out!"[27]

After taking his warm-ups, the 13-game winner wound up and threw his first pitch, a called strike on the inside of the plate. His second delivery was a waste pitch, a high and inside fastball designed to set Thomson up for the next pitch, a curveball. But there would be no next pitch. The Scot swung, and sent a long drive to left field. Sitting in the dugout with an injury, Campanella was thinking, "Sink, you devil, sink," and so were the rest of the Dodgers.[28] It did sink, and for a brief moment looked as if it might fall into the glove of Pafko, who was racing to the wall, or bounce off the wall, scoring Hartung and Lockman to tie the game. Thomson also thought it would hit the wall, but as he got halfway to first he heard the crowd roar and saw Pafko standing underneath the 315-foot marker watching helplessly as the ball soared over his head and cleared the wall by about six inches. The year of miracles had come to an end with the most improbable miracle of all, a four-run rally in the ninth that gave the Giants a 5–4 victory and the pennant.

Dazed, Thomson leaped and danced his way around the bases, while up in the broadcast booth Giants' radio announcer Russ Hodges was screaming over and over again, "The Giants win the pennant . . . the Giants win the pennant. . . ."[29] The fans easily eluded the police barriers and poured onto the field. Eddie Stanky came running out of the dugout and jumped on the back of Durocher, who was coaching at third base. As Thomson rounded third, Durocher half-dragged Stanky toward home plate, where the entire Giant team awaited. When Thomson touched home his teammates pounded him on the back and hoisted him on their shoulders for a victory ride, then ran toward the clubhouse in center field with hundreds of frenzied fans in pursuit.

Stunned, the Dodgers seemed frozen in place on the field. Branca was thinking, "Oh, God, why me, why was I the one?"[30] Then all the players except Robinson began the long, agonizing walk to the clubhouse in center field. Always the die-hard competitor, Robinson stood with his hands on his hips, watching to make sure that Thomson touched all the bases. Then he, too, began the long trek to the losers' clubhouse.

One of the happiest men in the park when Thomson hit the home run was the on-deck hitter, Mays, who was excited about the win but relieved that he did not have to come to bat. As he crouched in the on-deck circle he was praying, "Don't let it be me. Don't make me come to bat now, God."[31] Reporter Joe Flaherty later wrote that as Thomson's homer sailed over the fence Mays jumped up and down, "acting like a man who had just received the midnight call from the governor."[32]

Some of the fans who had attended the game at the Polo Grounds heard the dramatic finish on their car radios; they had given up on the Giants and had left in the ninth to try to beat the rest of the traffic out of the parking lot. Among them was Yogi Berra, who had come to the game with several other Yankee players to scout the two teams. "I never saw it," he said later. "But I heard it on the car radio. I left in the ninth—I wanted to beat the crowd."[33] The famous phraseologist, often quoted as saying that "it ain't over till it's over," left before it was over.

Thomson's pennant-winning home run marked an incredible comeback for the Giants, who had been pronounced dead on August 11 when they were 13½ games out. The playoff win was their ninth victory in their last 10 games, the fourteenth in their last 16, and the thirty-ninth in their last 47. It was a miracle finish, likened to that of the 1914 Miracle Braves, who had come from last place on July 4 to win the pennant and crush the Philadelphia Athletics in four straight games in the World Series. It was the Giants' first pennant since 1937.

Thomson's home run was quickly immortalized in print as "The Shot Heard 'Round the World" and "The Miracle at Coogan's Bluff." Sportswriter Roger Angell would call it "the greatest moment in the history of mankind,"[34] and could perhaps be forgiven, as a Giants fan, for such hyperbole. Arthur Daley wrote in the *New York Times* that "a demented Hollywood script writer in the last throes of delirium tremens would not have dared pen anything so completely fantastic as the way this dizziest of pennant races has finished."[35] But perhaps the most eloquent tribute came from one of the nation's premier sportswriters, Red Smith, in "The Miracle at Coogan's Bluff," penned for the *New York Herald Tribune* and widely reprinted: "Now it is done. Now the story ends. And there is no way to tell it. The art of fiction is dead. Reality had strangled invention. Only the utterly impossible, the inexpressibly fantastic, can ever be plausible again." He noted that at the end of the game, "Ralph Branca turned and started for the clubhouse. The number on his uniform looked huge. Thirteen."[36]

After the greatest comeback in baseball history, the Giants' clubhouse was bedlam. Players were shouting and spewing champagne on one another and the press, while thousands of cheering fans had gathered outside, refusing to leave until their heroes came out for curtain calls. Several Dodger officials and players came over to congratulate their conquerors. Robinson went over to Maglie, with whom he had feuded all year, shook his hand, and said, "It's all over. No hard feelings."[37]

The Dodger clubhouse resembled a wake. Several players showered and dressed quickly, eager to flee the scene of their humiliation. Some sat around in gloomy silence, while others were sobbing. Dressen quietly answered reporters questions, patiently explaining why he had not walked Thomson to pitch to Mays. "I thought of it," he said. "Five times this year I walked the winning run, and got away with it every time. But Thomson? The guy behind him — Mays — could have hit a home run, too."[38]

Most of the Dodgers still could not believe it. A 13½-game lead had vanished. A 4–2 lead with two outs to go, then one pitch, one swing, and their season was over, while the Giants were going to Yankee Stadium to battle for the world title. It was a bitter defeat for a team that had a reputation for blowing the close ones in pennant races and the World Series. For the second year in a row they had lost the pennant in the last inning of the last game of the season. They had also participated in the only two playoffs in National League history — against the Cardinals in 1946 and now against the Giants — and had lost both of them.

Branca was inconsolable. He came into the clubhouse and sprawled on the steps leading up to the training room, sobbing. Later, after showering and answering a few questions from reporters, he left and went to his car, where his fiancée was waiting. As he drove off, he was still asking, "Why me?"

Branca always seemed to be in the wrong place at the wrong time. He was the losing pitcher in the first game of the 1946 playoffs and in the first and third games of the 1951 playoffs. He had made only two pitches in the final playoff game, and was destined to go down in history as one of baseball's biggest goats, mentioned in the same breath as Mickey Owen and "Bonehead" Merkle. No wonder he kept asking himself, "Why me?"

The young pitcher eventually learned to live with the stigma of being the goat of the 1951 playoffs. He often said that "if it hadn't been for that homer, who would remember Ralph Branca?"[39] But he hated being reminded of it, and felt that it was unfair that he would be remembered for that one pitch rather than for his other accomplishments on the mound, including winning 21 games in 1947 at the age of 21. In 1987 he said, "For 25 years, I'd have to say I tolerated going through that ordeal. I had had it. I was tired of being introduced as the guy who threw the home run pitch . . . . A guy commits murder and he gets pardoned after twenty years. I didn't get pardoned."[40]

Branca did not realize it in 1951, but his baseball life was practically over, even though he was only 25 years old. In an eight-year career stretching back to 1944, he had won 76 games and lost 56. But over the winter of 1951–1952, he fell out of a chair and injured his pelvis. Although he eventually recovered, he was never able to throw as well as he had before the injury. Playing for the Dodgers, Tigers, and Yankees before retiring in 1956, he managed to win just 12 more games while losing an equal number.

Thomson's career and reputation would follow a much different course. With just one swing of the bat he had gained instant hero status and a permanent place in baseball history. A native of Scotland who moved to the United States with his parents when he was a small child, the "Staten Island Scot" had played for the Giants since 1944 and acquired a reputation as a good hitter but mediocre fielder. He would play for nine more years, wearing the uniform of the Giants and four more clubs before finally retiring in 1960, but he never had a moment anywhere near the one he had on October 3, 1951. His .270 lifetime batting average and 264 home runs were not enough to get him into the Hall of Fame, but in baseball history his name and deed are far more familiar than the names and deeds of many of those enshrined there.

The rest of the league's teams were overshadowed by the drama surrounding the Giants-Dodgers race. Under new manager Marty Marion, the Cardinals finished third, 15½ games out, with Stan Musial capturing his fifth batting title with a .355 average. The Braves finished fourth, followed by the Phillies, Reds, Pirates, and Cubs. Ralph Kiner of the Pirates again led the league in homers with 42.

After one of the most exciting seasons in history, many fans would have agreed with *Life* magazine's lament that "it's too bad summer can't last forever."[41] Fortunately, more fans were able to follow the game than ever before, for with the installation in late summer of the coast-to-coast coaxial cable, millions of fans on both coasts and in dozens of cities in between were able to watch the Dodger-Giant playoff and the World Series that followed. Televised baseball had finally spanned the continent.

The Giants' players and fans had no time for a breather. On Thursday, October 4, less than 24 hours after Thomson's home run, the World Series opened in Yankee Stadium. For once, the fall classic seemed like the anticlimax to the season. What could possibly top the Giants' pennant miracle? "A year from now, or a hundred years from now," the *Chicago Daily News* wrote on October 3, "nobody will remember how they came out against the Yankees, even if they win."

The Giants' late season surge seemed to continue on into the Series, at least briefly. After splitting the opening games in Yankee Stadium, Durocher's team went back to the Polo Grounds hoping that the home-field advantage would enable them to wrap up the Series. They did take the first of the three-game home set by a 6–2 count, but the fourth game was postponed by rain, and it seemed to cool off the miracle workers from Coogan's Bluff. DiMaggio's last major league home run helped the Yankees win the fourth game, 6–2, and the next day the Yankees obviously had the Giants on the run as they clobbered them, 13–1. The two teams returned to Yankee Stadium, where the Bronx Bombers wrapped up the title in the sixth game when Hank Bauer tripled home three runs in the sixth and preserved the Yankees 4–3 lead with a sensational catch in the ninth.

But the Giant players and fans were not crushed by the loss of the Series. As Monte Irvin later said, "We didn't feel that badly let down. We were still thinking about the playoff against the Dodgers. That was our year, right there, when Bobby hit that ball."[42]

Although the World Series was overshadowed by the pennant races it did have drama. It marked the first Series appearance of Willie Mays and Mickey Mantle and the last game in the career of Joe DiMaggio. It saw rookie infielder Gil McDougald, with his schoolgirl stance, hit a grand slam in game five, putting him in the elite circle that at that time included only two others — Tony Lazzeri of the Yankees (1936) and Elmer Smith of the Indians (1920). It saw Monte Irvin, who hit .458 in a losing cause, execute in game one the first steal of home in a Series game since Bob Meusel of the Yankees did it in 1928. It also witnessed the appearance of the first all-black outfield in major league history — Monte Irvin in left, Willie Mays in center, and Hank Thompson in right — playing against a lily-white Yankee team that would hold the line against black players until 1955.

The Series was also the stage for a tragic injury to rookie Mickey Mantle. In the fifth inning of the second game, Mays led off with a fly ball to right center field. As Mantle and DiMaggio ran toward the ball, Mantle tripped over a wooden sprinkler cover and crumpled to the ground with a torn ligament in his right knee. DiMaggio, who made the catch, later said, "I thought he had been shot." Mantle was carried off the field on a stretcher and taken to the clubhouse, where his knee was packed in ice. The next morning he was taken to Lennox Hill Hospital to undergo the first of four knee operations he would have to endure over the years. Years later he would claim, "It was never right again. . . . So far as I'm concerned that was the worst thing that could ever have happened to me. It forced me to retire early, and I know that I could have set a lot of records that I didn't get a chance to because of my legs."[43]

Young Mays and Mantle were at the beginning of their careers, DiMaggio was at the end of his. After starting off poorly in the World Series, going 0–12 in the first three games, he regained his batting eye, getting six hits, including a home run, in his last 12 at bats. In his last trip to the plate, in the eighth inning of the last game, he doubled off the right center field wall. After the game, many of his teammates came up to his locker to shake his hand and ask for autographs and souvenirs.

Throughout the season it had been painfully obvious that DiMaggio was not the player he had been in his prime or even in 1950. He could not pull the ball like he wanted to, his arm was weak, and he often played in pain. He disliked playing under Stengel, and he could see that Mantle was making rapid progress and that his youth and phenomenal ability would inevitably dislodge him from center field. The Yankee Clipper's .263 batting average (lowest of his career), 12 homers, and 71 RBIs were obvious signs that he was slipping, and slipping badly.

DiMaggio had also been angered and embarrassed by the publication of a late-season scouting report done on the Yankees by the Dodgers' Andy High. After their playoff defeat, the Dodgers passed it on to the Giants, and it eventually fell into the hands of *Life* magazine, which printed excerpts from it in its October 22 issue. When Durocher first read High's document, he told the press, "It's great. Never saw a report like it. It has everything— all the little details." Indeed it did, including some damning passages on DiMaggio, claiming, "He can't stop quickly and throw hard. You can take the extra base on him if he is in motion away from the line of throw. He won't throw on questionable plays and I would challenge him even though he threw a man or so out." Furthermore, the report said, "He can't run and won't bunt, . . . his reflexes are very slow and he can't pull a good fast ball at all."[44] The report embarrassed and angered many of his teammates and his large circle of friends among the sportswriters. "Andy High couldn't carry DiMaggio's jock, even now," one reporter said.[45] But High's description of DiMaggio's declining skills was close to the mark.

At the close of the World Series, DiMaggio told Yankee owner Dan Topping that he planned to retire, but Topping offered him another $100,000 contract and convinced him to delay a final decision until he had returned from a barnstorming trip to Korea and Japan. DiMaggio did not change his mind, and the decision that almost everyone in baseball expected was announced at a crowded press conference held on the afternoon of December 11 in the Yankee offices on Fifth Avenue.[46]

Standing in front of a photographic mural of himself as a young player, DiMaggio, who had turned 37 on November 25, read a prepared statement announcing that "I've played my last game of ball." Telling those gathered there that he had made up his mind to retire back in the spring, he said, "I only wish that I could have had a better year. But even if I had hit .350, this would have been the last year for me." He reminded them that he had "had more than my share of physical injuries and setbacks during my career. In recent years these have been much too frequent to laugh off. When baseball is no longer fun, it's no longer a game. . . . I feel that I have reached the stage where I can no longer produce for my ball club, my manager, my teammates and my fans the sort of baseball their loyalty to me deserves."

After reading his statement, he sat down. In response to reporters' questions, he said that night ball had taken two years off his career and that his greatest baseball thrill was his 56-game hitting streak in 1941. Asked who he thought was the greatest active player, he said, without hesitation, "Ted Williams. He is by far the greatest natural hitter I ever saw."

DiMaggio's career had been a relatively short one—just 13 seasons—but what a career it had been: 1,736 games, 2,214 hits, a .325 batting average, 361 homers, 1,537 RBIs, and only 369 strikeouts. Hitting for both average and power, he won the American League batting crown twice, dropped below .300 in only two seasons, averaged 28 homers a year, led the league in homers and RBIs twice, and captured three MVP Awards. He was the leader of the Yankee teams that won 10 pennants and 9 world championships during his years on the major league diamond. In World Series competition he played 51 games, a record when he retired in 1951, compiling a .271 batting average with 8 home runs and 30 RBIs.

Unlike Ruth and some other stars who tried to hang on too long, DiMaggio knew when to quit. He could have played another year or so and pocketed his $100,000 salary, but he had too much pride to subject himself to the embarrassment of being an over-the-hill player misplaying fly balls in the outfield and swinging futilely at the offerings of pitchers almost half his age. Perhaps his brother, Tom, who ran the family restaurant in San Francisco, understood better than most why his brother gave up the game he played so well. Joe quit, Tom said, "because he wasn't Joe DiMaggio anymore."[47]

10. Old Timers, Women, and the Russians (1952)

The hottest topic in the hot stove league over the winter was the sensational finish of the 1951 National League pennant race. As the story was told and retold, Thomson's dramatic home run was already beginning to take its place in baseball lore as the single most dramatic event in the history of the national pastime. The Giants were becoming entrenched in the record books and memories as one of the greatest miracle teams of all times, Bobby Thomson was taking on the aura of one of baseball's greatest heroes, the Dodgers were becoming even more firmly established as one of baseball's greatest choke teams, and Ralph Branca was taking his place among baseball's greatest goats. Rarely had one swing of the bat brought such dramatic consequences.

The 1952 season would be played under a new commissioner, Ford Frick, who had taken office at the end of the previous campaign after a prolonged battle between the baseball owners and Happy Chandler. After succeeding Judge Kenesaw Mountain Landis in 1945, Chandler had enjoyed a brief period of popularity with many of the major league owners, but as time passed they began to find fault with the man many began to call the "Hillbilly Commissioner" and the "Bluegrass Jackass." Many thought his handling of the Mexican jumpers had helped to precipitate the Gardella case and drag the reserve clause into the courts where it could have been overturned. Some did not like his suspension of Durocher in 1947, his opposition to Sunday night games, his support of Jackie Robinson and the integration of baseball, the television contract he signed in December of 1950, or his folksy manner, which they thought detracted from the dignity of the office. Some also felt that his statement in December of 1950 that baseball might have to cease operations during the Korean conflict had unduly raised anxieties among players and fans. But underlying all these quarrels with Chandler was a more fundamental one — he wanted to be a strong commissioner like Landis, while the owners wanted a figurehead who would simply administer their decisions.[1]

Chandler had helped to pave the way for his own dismissal near the end of the 1950 season when, with two years left on his contract, he asked the owners to give him a vote of confidence by extending it for another seven years. The move backfired; when the owners held their winter meetings in St. Petersburg, Florida, in December of 1950, a group led by Fred Saigh of the Cardinals, Lou Perini of the Braves, and Dan Topping and Del Webb of the Yankees began a move to oust him. When a poll of the owners in December and again in March of 1951 failed to yield the three-fourth's vote necessary for the renewal of his contract, Chandler decided to cut his losses and run. He informed the owners that he would resign on July 15, 1951, but that he expected to be paid for the duration of his contract, which expired on April 30, 1952. The owners agreed, and as promised, Chandler stepped down shortly after the 1951 All-Star Game.

The search for Chandler's successor began almost as soon as talk of his ouster surfaced in late 1950. Nearly 40 candidates were considered, including General Douglas MacArthur and other prominent figures outside the baseball world, but the choice ultimately boiled down to a race between Warren Giles, the president and general manager of the Cincinnati Reds, and Ford Frick, president of the National League. Finally, on September 20, 1951, in a joint major league meeting in Chicago lasting through 16 ballots and nine hours of deliberations, the owners settled on Frick, who began his official duties on October 16. Giles got the consolation prize, succeeding Frick as president of the senior circuit.

The new commissioner was a member of the baseball fraternity, not an outsider like Landis or Chandler. A native of Indiana and a graduate of DePaul University, Frick had worked as a high school and college teacher, a *New York Journal* sportswriter, Babe Ruth's ghostwriter, a radio announcer, and, since 1934, president of the National League. As league president he had generally concentrated on administrative matters, letting the owners run the game. This track record undoubtedly made him very attractive to the owners.

Only the third commissioner in the history of the major leagues, Frick turned out to be just the man the owners wanted. He served primarily as a promoter of the game, a mediator in disputes between owners and between owners and players, and an administrator who buried himself in the business of enforcing the rules and regulations made by the men who paid him. A pliant tool of the owners, he tried to avoid court battles and any controversy that might reflect negatively on the game or cause its practices to be called into question, or worse, into court. He resisted all outside interference in baseball matters, taking refuge in the argument that all baseball problems and issues were "league matters." Bill Veeck once said that when Frick wrote his autobiography it should be entitled, "Armageddon Is a League Matter."[2] Serving during troubled times, Frick was popular with most of the owners, but many players thought he was pro-owner and anti-player. He would serve two seven-year terms before retiring in 1965.

Many of the problems that Frick would have to deal with during his stint as commissioner were already surfacing in 1952. Baseball was in trouble, facing falling attendance at both the minor and major league level, a decline in the number of minor leagues and teams, competiton from other sports and amusements, attacks on the reserve clause and other business practices, and a host of other problems. Naturally, there was no dearth of critics who felt that they knew what was wrong with the game and how it could be fixed. One of them was Ty Cobb, the crusty, opinionated, and arrogant Hall of Famer who never minced words or backed away from a fight, verbal or physical. In the spring of 1952, while the teams were in spring training, he provoked a controversy over the relative merits of the oldtimers and the players of the fifties in a two-part series in *Life* magazine entitled, "They Don't Play Baseball Any More."

Cobb, who was paid $25,000 for the interviews the articles were based on, claimed that the main reasons for baseball's decline as the national pastime were that modern players were not as good as those of his day and that the emphasis on the home run had turned baseball into a boring sport that was driving the fans away from the parks. Stan Musial and Phil Rizzuto, he said, were "the only two players in the major leagues today who can be mentioned in the same breath with the oldtime greats." As for the others, "Most players don't learn the fundamentals. Most of them don't practice. They don't even train. The sole object, encouraged by the lively ball and the shortened fences, is to make home runs. But even the home run, becoming commonplace, has lost its thrill." Cobb lamented, "Any athlete, if he has just picked up the knack of pulling the modern lively ball to the fence, can get into the big leagues." Pointing to Ralph Kiner and Gus Zernial as examples, he claimed that the modern player "needn't be too good a fielder. . . . He needn't even be in top physical condition, for hitting a baseball 350 feet is mostly a feat of sheer momentary strength like carrying a piano up a stairway."[3]

Cobb felt that there were few good baserunners, few catchers or pitchers who could stop a good baserunner, and few really good hitters who could bunt, hit and run, hit to the opposite field, or sacrifice. Except for Bob Feller, "the one pitcher in the game today whose record stacks up with the oldtimers," Cobb did not think much of modern pitchers, either, calling them "a particularly fragile lot . . . who are always getting sore arms and bone chips, and mysterious growths in the shoulder joints."[4]

He did not spare two of the game's best known players from his criticism. Ted Williams and Joe DiMaggio, he said, "have limped along on one cylinder. Playing the same way in the old days, they would never have hit the top." Williams was a good hitter but was too lazy to learn to hit to the opposite field to foil the "Williams shift." As for the Yankee Clipper, "perhaps the greatest natural ballplayer who ever lived," he did not like to hit to the opposite field and did not train hard enough to keep himself in top shape during the regular or off-season. "He will never know how great a ballplayer he might have been — or how many more years he might have lasted — if he had taken care of himself,"[5] Cobb said.

As could be expected, most of the old time baseball players agreed with Cobb's criticisms of the game. But not Clark Griffith, the 82-year old president of the Washington Senators. "Those old fellows who get out of the game should keep their mouths shut," he said. "The ballplayers of today are just as good as they were in Cobb's day or mine." Washington manager Bucky Harris, who had played second base and managed the Senators in the 1920s as the "Boy Manager," said that "Ty Cobb is nuts. . . . As great as he was, Cobb couldn't carry DiMaggio's glove in center field . . . or hit with the same power that Joe did."[6] And Leo Durocher growled, "These old guys make me sick, always talking about how it was in the old days. . . . But it's always been like this. Even when I came up they used to tell me how great the old-timers were and that the guys around the league in my time couldn't carry the old guys' gloves."[7]

Ralph Kiner, incensed about Cobb's comments on his physical condition and his emphasis on home runs, asked a reporter, "Why do old-time ballplayers always live in the past? I have a size 32 waist and I defy any athlete in baseball my size to show me a smaller waist." Ralph's mother, Beatrice, also took up for her son. At a Pirate exhibition game she told reporters, "They tell me this is the age of specialization, isn't it? Ralph specializes in home runs."[8] DiMaggio turned down a $25,000 offer from a national magazine to respond to Cobb, but he did tell reporters, "I just don't see why I should get into that with Cobb. I never saw the old-timers." He added, "I don't know if Cobb had a tendency to get fat, but each man knows his own life. I never trained between seasons. I needed a rest."[9] Williams claimed that he was not upset at Cobb's remarks. "At least he . . . said some nice things about me," Williams said. "That's more than the Boston writers say."[10]

Manager Bill Meyer of the Pirates and shortstop Vern Stephens of the Red Sox were among the many members of the baseball fraternity who thought it was foolish to make the kind of sweeping judgments Cobb had made. "You can't compare the two eras. Too many things have happened," Meyer said. Stephens agreed. "Did Cobb ever have to play a twi-night doubleheader? Did Cobb ever have to play a doubleheader the day after a night game? Conditions are different today than they were in Cobb's time."[11]

It was an argument without end, the stuff of which baseball is made. Cobb apparently was not familiar with an article that appeared in the *Spalding Base Ball Guide* back in 1916, when he was at the midpoint of his career, hitting .371 but coming in second in the batting race to Tris

Speaker's .386. "Baseball today is not what it should be," a former player and manager wrote. "The players do not try to learn all the fine points of the game as in the days of old, but simply try to get by . . . . It's positively a shame, and they are getting big money for it, too."[12]

The controversy surrounding Cobb's article was still raging on April 15 when President Truman threw out the first ball at Griffith Stadium for the seventh consecutive year, and his last. His presence did not help the home team, which lost 3–0 to the Boston Red Sox. That night, a fan attending the opening game at Crosley Field in Cincinnati had an experience he would not soon forget: he got locked in the park when the game was over. It was a cool April evening in Cincinnati, and the captive fan, James McElhaney, a milk wagon driver, later explained that he had gotten so cold by the ninth inning that he went to the men's room to try to get warm. "I fell asleep and when I awoke it was 11 P.M. and the place was locked up tight," he told police. "I tried every exit and hammered on every door I could find, but couldn't open one or make the night watchman hear me." He finally found a telephone and called friends, but they did not believe his story and refused to come to his aid. He then called police and explained his predicament. They finally showed up with a ladder. After passing it to McElhaney over the left field wall, they helped him climb to freedom.[13]

The new season would be played without some of its familiar stars. DiMaggio had retired, and as the Korean War dragged on with no end in sight, the military draft continued to dip into the pool of young men playing minor and major league baseball. Among those departing for military service in 1952 were Don Newcombe of the Dodgers, Jerry Coleman of the Yankees, and two of the biggest gate draws in the majors, Willie Mays and Ted Williams. The Splendid Splinter, recalled into service by the Marine Corps, made the most dramatic departure from the game. On April 30, in his last at bat before reporting for duty, he smashed a 400-foot, two-run homer into the right field stands at Fenway to help the Sox defeat the Tigers, 5–3.

Both the Dodgers and the Giants went to spring training in 1952 still thinking of the 1951 race. The Giants were hoping to repeat their pennant-winning ways, while the Dodgers were bent on atonement and revenge. At the club's training camp in Vero Beach, Jackie Robinson said, "I think every player on the team will be putting out a little more this year because he feels that we let the team down in bad finishes in the two previous years."[14] Ralph Branca, still smarting over the humiliation of 1951, had always denied that he was superstitious about his uniform number (13), but in 1952 he switched to number 12.

The Dodgers would have to beat the Giants with a team that was not quite as good as the one that had blown the 13½-game lead the year before.

It was impossible to find a starting pitcher to replace Don Newcombe, who had won 56 games in the last three years, but the Dodgers did come up with a jewel of a reliever in 6-feet 2-inch, 220-pound right-hander Joe Black, who made the squad in spring training as a 28-year-old rookie. The rest of the team that took the field was the same one that carried the club in 1951 — Campanella, Hodges, Robinson, Reese, Cox, Furillo, Snider, and Pafko.

Fortunately for the Dodgers, the Giants were also hurting. Mays departed for the army on May 28, Eddie Stanky left to become the manager of the Cardinals, and Monte Irvin broke his ankle while sliding into third during an exhibition game in spring training. Sal Maglie and Larry Jansen, both 23-game winners the year before, developed back trouble, which contributed to Maglie's record dropping to 18–8 and Jansen's plummeting to 11–11. It would have been an even worse year for the Giants if they had not found reliever Hoyt Wilhelm to back up a thin starting rotation.

Like Joe Black of the Dodgers, Wilhelm was 28 years old before he got his first chance to pitch in the majors. In his major league debut against the Braves on April 23, he seemed to be a slugger as well as a pitcher; he hit a home run in his first at bat and a triple in his second appearance. However, these were destined to be the only triple and homer of his 21-year career.

In his rookie year Wilhelm appeared in a league-leading 71 games, winning 15 while losing only 3, picking up 11 saves and leading the league with a 2.43 ERA. During his long career he played in both leagues and for over half the clubs — nine teams in all paid for his services before he retired on July 21, 1972, just five days before his 49th birthday. The hitters found his knuckleball baffling, as did most of his catchers. He recorded 1,610 strikeouts, walked only 778, had a lifetime ERA of 2.52, and was the only pitcher to win the ERA title in both leagues. When he retired he held numerous records, including most games (1,070), most relief wins (123), most saves (227), and most games finished (651).

In spite of their problems, the Giants got off to a good start, winning 16 of their first 18 games and boasting a 26–8 record and a half-game lead over the Dodgers on May 28, when Mays played his last game before leaving for the army. They then lost 8 of their next 10, relinquishing the lead to the Dodgers in early June. The Dodgers stayed on top for most of the rest of the season, but they did manage to give their fans several scares in the second half of the campaign. After winning 60 of their first 82 games, they barely played .500 ball (36–35) for the rest of the season. They held a 10½-game lead over the Giants as late as August 25, but let that lead shrink to as low as three games on September 13. Players on both teams, along with their fans, recognized that the Giants were in an even better position than they had been in 1951, and some wondered if another Dodger collapse and Giant miracle were in the works. But the Giants then lost three straight to Philadelphia and faded from contention. With almost a week to go in the season, the Dodgers clinched the pennant on September 23. For the first time in four years, they would not have to play the last game of the season with the pennant hanging in the balance.

The Dodgers won 96 games, the same number they had won during the 1951 regular season. One of those victories was a 19–1 trouncing of the Cincinnati Reds at Ebbets Field on May 21. In the game they scored 15 runs in the first inning and set several records, including most runs scored in one inning (15), most men sent to the plate in one inning (21), most consecutive men to reach first base (19), and most runs scored after two outs (12). Pee Wee Reese set an individual record by reaching first base three times in one inning.

But for the season the team batting average was 13 points below the 1951 level, with Hodges, Snider, Campanella, and Furillo all slipping in home runs, batting average, and RBIs. With Newcombe gone, the top Dodger starter was Carl Erskine, who posted a 14–6 record, including a 5–0 no-hitter over the Cubs on June 19. Fireman Joe Black appeared in 56 games, winning 15, losing 4, and saving 15, good enough to make him the third Dodger to capture the Rookie of the Year Award since its inception in 1947.

Elsewhere in the National League, rookie manager Eddie Stanky brought his Cardinals home in third place. Stan Musial won his third consecutive batting crown with a .336 average. Ferris Fain took his second consecutive crown in the American League with a .327 average, giving major league baseball its first batting crown repeaters since Ty Cobb of the Tigers and Jake Daubert of the Dodgers turned the trick back in 1913 and 1914. Fain's average was also the lowest winning mark in either league since 1945.

The Phillies ended in fourth place, 9½ games out. But they had the league's only 20-game winner, Robin Roberts, who had a phenomenal year to finish with a 28–7 record. The Cubs finished fifth, with left fielder Hank Sauer, the National League's MVP winner, leading the league in RBIs (121) and sharing the home run crown (37) with Ralph Kiner. The Reds, Braves, and Pirates brought up the rear.

Since leaving the Dodgers in 1950, Branch Rickey had expanded the Pirate farm system and acquired bonus babies in an attempt to build the Pirates into the kind of winners he had established in St. Louis and Brooklyn. His efforts had not paid off. Kiner set home run records and pulled in the fans, but Rickey wanted more. When Kiner, one of the highest paid players in the majors ($75,000), asked him for a hefty raise at the end of the season, the tight-fisted owner refused. "I know you hit all those homers, but remember, we could have finished last without you," Rickey told him.[15]

Not only did the Pirates finish last, they won only 42 games and finished 54½ games out, one of the worst records in baseball history, and established themselves as one of baseball's all-time worst teams. Their longest win streak was two, their team batting average was only .231 (22 points below the league average), and their team ERA was 4.65, almost a run higher than the league average. They also led both leagues in errors with 182, and that of course did not count the numerous mental errors the club seemed to make in every game. "If there was a new way to lose," catcher Joe Garagiola later said, "we would discover it."[16]

The presence of 13 rookies on the Pirate roster undoubtedly accounted for some of the inept play and for the problems the team had in keeping up with the manager's and coaches' signals. During a game with the Cardinals, the Pirate runner on first base kept missing the "steal" sign from the third base coach. Finally, second baseman Red Schoendienst walked over to the runner and asked, "When are you going to run? They've given you the signal three times and I'm tired of covering second base."[17]

In 1952 Rickey believed that he had found one of the solutions to the Pirates' pitching problems in the phenomenal right arm of 20-year-old Ron Necciai. Playing for Pirate farm clubs at Bristol (Tennessee) and Burlington (North Carolina), Rocket Ron struck out 19 batters in one game, 11 out of 12 in another as a reliever, 11 in a row in another, then an incredible 27 in still another, a no-hitter. Perhaps too soon, he was called up to the Bucs by Rickey, who once said, "There have been only two young pitchers I was certain were destined for greatness. . . . One of those was Dizzy Dean. The other is Ron Necciai."[18] But as a major leaguer, Rocket Ron was a bust. Control problems, ulcers, and a sore arm limited his 1952 season to just 12 games, a 1–7 won-loss record and a 7.08 ERA in 54.2 innings. He never pitched in the majors again.

Unfortunately for Rickey, the Pirates would have to muddle through seven more seasons before his dream of a world title came true.

The American League campaign opened with Casey Stengel hoping to take his fourth consecutive pennant. But he had his problems. Mickey Mantle had undergone surgery at the end of the 1951 season, and no one knew how his repaired knee would hold up. Whitey Ford still had another year to go on his hitch in the army, which had also taken infielders Jerry Coleman and Bobby Brown and pitcher Tom Morgan. No wonder many writers and baseball men around the league favored Al Lopez's Cleveland Indians, who were led by sluggers Al Rosen and Larry Doby and the best pitching staff in either league, made up of Early Wynn, Mike Garcia, Bob Lemon, and Bob Feller.

But the Old Professor responded to the challenge. He placed Gil McDougald at third full-time instead of alternating him between third and short, and Billy Martin at second base to replace Coleman. Martin was a spark plug who fired up the team with his words and actions and often fought with umpires and opposing players. With his available talent scarcer than usual, Stengel resorted to juggling the lineup more than ever. Before the year was over, he had used 41 different players and 98 different starting lineups. His ingenious platooning was the talk of the league, but one of the reasons for the Yankee success had little to do with the manager. That reason was the play of sophomore Mickey Mantle.

Coming back from knee surgery, Mantle was still learning how to play the outfield and still struck out too often — a league-leading 111 times — but his hitting began to live up to the rave reviews it had received before he ever put on a Yankee uniform. Playing in 142 games, he led the Yankees in batting average (.311), hit 23 home runs, drove in 87 runs, and scored 94. The 75 walks he received were a tribute to the respect given him from pitching staffs around the league.

Still only 20 years old, Mantle was hitting long shots from both sides of the plate. In July, when he was wielding the hottest bat in either league, teammate Ed Lopat said, "As long as I've been in baseball I've never seen anybody who could hit a ball as far as Mantle, either way." "I'm not just talking about switch hitters. I mean I've never seen any right-handed hitter hit 'em as far as Mantle does righthanded and I've never seen any left-hander hitter hit 'em as far as he does left-handed."[19] On July 26, Mantle hit the first grand slam homer of his career. Three days later, he hit his second, but he fell one short of the major league record of three grand slams in one month.

Gene Woodling (.309) was the only Yankee player besides Mantle to hit over .300. Berra's average dropped to .273, but he led the club in RBIs (98) and homers (30). The pitching staff had its troubles, too. Lopat, a 21-game winner in 1951, developed shoulder problems and wound up with a 10–5 record. But veteran Allie Reynolds came through again with 20 wins and led the league in strikeouts (160) and ERA (2.06). Vic Raschi finished with 16 wins and Johnny Sain with 11.

Sporting an 18–7 record by the end of May, the Yankees reeled off 10 victories in their next 11 games and took over first place on June 10. By July 19 they had built a 5½-game lead, their biggest of the season. For most of the summer, they fought off challenges from the Indians, Athletics, and White Sox. After being in first place for most of June and July, they slumped in August, allowing the Indians to go in front by 2½ games by Labor Day. But the Bronx Bombers regrouped, regained the lead in mid–September, and held on to finish two games ahead of the Tribe. It was Stengel's fourth consecutive flag, putting him in an elite group with former Yankee manager Joe McCarthy and former Giant manager John McGraw.

For Al Lopez and the Indians, it was a bitter disappointment. The Indians had lost to a team that, on paper at least, did not seem to be as good as they were. The Indians had three 20-game winners (Wynn, Garcia, and Lemon), the league's leader in home runs (Larry Doby, with 32) and RBIs (Al Rosen, with 105), and three regulars who hit .300 or better (Dale

Mitchell, Rosen, and Bobby Avila). But their defense undermined their offensive and pitching prowess. They made 155 errors, tying the Browns for the lead in that unhappy department, and finished last (141) in double plays.

Trailing the Yankees and Indians at season's end were Chicago, Philadelphia, Washington, Boston, St. Louis, and Detroit. The surprise showing of the Athletics was partly due to the arms of little left-hander Bobby Shantz, who won the MVP Award with his 24–7 record, and his teammate, Harry Bird, who was named Rookie of the Year on the basis of his 15–15 mark. The Tigers, who won only 50 games and finished 45 games behind the Yankees, did turn in the league's only no-hitters. Virgil Trucks (5–19), pitched two no-hitters, joining Johnny Vander Meer and Allie Reynolds in the record books as the only pitchers to pitch two in one season.

One of the saddest stories of the season was the strange case of Jimmy Piersall, a young Red Sox player. A native of Waterbury, Connecticut, Piersall appeared in six games in 1950, spent 1951 in the minors, and rejoined the Red Sox in 1952. He was a young, talented outfielder with good speed, a good arm, a good glove, and the potential to be a good hitter. But he was also a high strung, complex young athlete who suffered from severe headaches, an extreme fear of failure, paranoia, temper tantrums, and other emotional problems that were magnified by the pressures of trying to stick with a big league ball club. His troubles were made even worse by manager Lou Boudreau's attempts to turn him into a major league shortstop. Beginning the season at shortstop but later switched to right field, he played in 56 games and hit .267.

Piersall's performance was overshadowed by his antics on and off the field. He had fistfights with teammates and opposing players, with the most notable incident coming in late May in a pregame battle with Billy Martin in the runway leading from the dugout to the dressing rooms at Fenway Park. After coaches from both clubs broke up the fight, Piersall went to the clubhouse to change the shirt he had ripped during the fight. There he got into another fight, this time with teammate Mickey McDermott.

But fighting was not his only problem. He screamed and yelled at umpires over routine calls, performed hula dances and other antics during the pregame warm-ups and between innings, bowed after making a catch, and did comic imitations of his teammates and opposing players. As the Sox ran in from their defensive positions, Piersall fell in behind center fielder Dom DiMaggio, dogging his steps and imitating his run. When he ran out to take his position in the outfield, he took off his hat and bowed to the fans and then played catch with teammates in the bullpen in right center field. When Boudreau took him out of the lineup for a rest, he badgered him to let him start the game. On one occasion, after Boudreau refused to insert him into the lineup, he broke down in the dugout and wept uncontrollably for several minutes, in clear view of his teammates, opposing players, and fans.

The fans loved his clowning, but his manager and teammates had trouble dealing with him, the umpires felt he was making a travesty of the game, and his wife worried about his mental health and baseball future. On June 28, fed up with Piersall's behavior, Boudreau shipped the troubled rookie to the Birmingham Barons, telling him to work on his hitting and to get control of his emotions. But the demotion only made his problems worse. He stayed 22 days with the Barons, again puzzling his teammates and the fans with his antics, then flew back to Boston to get his wife and children. While he was in Boston he broke into unrestrained yelling and fighting and had to be taken to a hospital. The 22-year-old player had suffered a serious mental breakdown.

Piersall woke up in the violent room of the mental hospital, tied to his bed. Over the next few months, through medication, shock treatment, counseling, support from his wife, and reliance on his religious faith, he gradually recovered from his illness. But he remembered little that had happened between the middle of January and the time he woke up in the violent room in August. It was all a blank that had to be filled in through conversations with his wife and doctors and by a detailed scrapbook his wife had kept of magazine and newspaper articles about his baseball playing and clowning. He spent the rest of the year recovering from his illness and looking forward to his return to baseball in 1953.[20]

The 1952 World Series opened in Ebbets Field on October 1 with the Dodgers' eternal hope that this would be "next year." It was a see-saw battle, with the Dodgers winning games one, three, and five and the Yankees games two, four, and six. By the seventh game, played in Brooklyn on October 7, players on both teams were tired. In this subway series no time was alloted for travel and there had been no rain outs, so the two teams were playing their seventh game in as many days. It had been a dramatic, nail-biting series, with all but the second game, which the Yankees won 7–1, decided by only one or two runs. Game five had gone 11 innings before the Dodgers finally won 6–5 behind the superb pitching of Carl Erskine. The gutsy pitcher was starting with only two days rest yet he went the distance and retired 19 Yankees in a row after giving up five runs in the fifth.

The seventh game, matching Ed Lopat against Joe Black, was a hard-fought contest. It was tied 1–1 in the fourth, 2–2 in the fifth. The Yankees went ahead 3–2 in the sixth when Mantle hit a solo homer. Mantle came through again in the seventh, driving Rizzuto home with a single to up the lead to 4–2. But in the bottom of the inning, the Dodgers threatened, loading the bases with only one out and Duke Snider and Jackie Robinson the next two scheduled hitters. Stengel went to reliever Bob Kuzava, who ran the count to 3–2 on Snider before getting him to pop up to McDougald at third.

This brought up Robinson, who had not hit well in the Series but was always a dangerous competitor, especially in clutch situations. Again the count went to 3–2. As Kuzava threw the next pitch, all three runners were going. Robinson swung hard and lifted a high pop fly between the mound and first base. For a second or two it looked as if it might fall in safely, for Kuzava stood frozen on the mound and first baseman Joe Collins lost the ball in the sun. At the last possible moment, after two Dodgers had already crossed the plate with what looked like the tying runs, Billy Martin ran in from second with his glove extended and made a seemingly impossible catch at knee level. The side was out, and the two runs that had crossed the plate erased. Kuzuva held the Dodgers scoreless in the eighth and ninth to preserve the win and clinch the Series.

The Series was characterized by good pitching, good hitting, and sparkling defensive play on both sides. Raschi and Reynolds won two games each, while Black, Erskine, and Preacher Roe picked up the Dodger wins. The hitting stars for the Yankees were 39-year-old first baseman and pinch hitter Johnny Mize, and Mickey Mantle, barely half Mize's age. Mize hit .400, clubbed three homers, drove in six runs, and scored three. Mantle hit .345 and led his team with 10 hits, including two homers, a double, a triple, and three RBIs. Martin hit only .217, but he hit one homer, drove in four runs, scored two, and made the game-saving catch in the final contest.

For the losers, Duke Snider was clearly the batting star. He hit .345, and his 10 hits included four homers, two doubles, and eight RBIs, most at crucial points in the games. Shortstop Pee Wee Reese also managed 10 hits and a .345 average, but subpar performances were turned in by Robinson (.174), Furillo (.174), Campanella (.214), and worst of all, Gil Hodges, who went hitless in 21 consecutive times at bat.

The biggest flake in the Series was Dodger pitcher Billy Loes, who told a reporter before the Series that the Yankees would win in seven games. When confronted by an angry Chuck Dressen on this indiscreet remark, Loes said that he was misquoted. "I picked 'em in six," he said.[21] In the seventh inning of the sixth game he committed a balk by dropping the ball as he went into his stretch, and later in the same inning he let a ground ball bounce off his knee for a single. After the game he told several reporters that the ball slipped out of his hand because it had "too much spit on it" and that he missed the grounder because "I never saw the ball at all. I lost it in the sun."[22]

The Dodger players and fans were heartbroken, having gone to the well and come up dry six times in World Series competition. This one hurt even more than most; it came just one year after the 1951 collapse and after the Dodgers had the Yankees on the ropes three games to two with the last two games scheduled in Ebbets Field. As the fans filed out of Ebbets Field after the seventh game, organist Gladys Godding played "This Nearly Was

Mine," "You Got Me Crying Again," and "What a Difference a Day Makes."

For the fourth consecutive season, Stengel had proven the preseason predictors wrong. He had won four consecutive world championships, a feat accomplished by only one other manager. Joe McCarthy did it with the Yankees in 1936–1939. It was the Yankees' fifteenth championship and the American League's sixth straight victory.

In many ways, 1952 was a year of controversy for the game off the field. Cobb had started it with his "They Don't Play Baseball Any More" articles in March. Then a minor league team created an uproar in June by signing a female player, the Russians outraged many Americans in September by claiming that they had invented baseball, and Jackie Robinson created a stir in November with his charges that the Yankees were prejudiced against black players.

The controversy over the female player arose when the Harrisburg (Pennsylvania) Senators of the National Association signed Eleanor Engle, a 24-year-old stenographer and 132-pound shortstop, to a contract on June 21. The next day she was in uniform, taking infield and batting practice with the team. But as soon as news of the signing circulated, a storm of protest came from throughout professional baseball. The signing was condemned by Commissioner Frick, National Association President George M. Trautman, and several league umpires. Harrisburg manager Clarence "Buck" Etchison, who had not been consulted prior to the signing, reacted by claiming, "She'll play when hell freezes over." The manager of the rival Allentown club, Whitey Kurowski, said that he would launch a protest if she played, and umpire Bill Angstadt said, "If she ever comes up to bat, I quit." But the club president, Dr. Jay Smith, refused to back down. "We've signed her and that's that," he said. "She can hit the ball a lot better than some of the fellows on the club."[23]

Engle was not the first woman to sign a professional baseball contract. Several had made brief, one-time appearances in exhibition games against major and minor league teams in the 1930s, and at least two had appeared in a regulation minor league game. In 1898, Lizzie Arlington had pitched part of an inning for Reading in the Atlantic League, and in 1936 Frances "Sonny" Dunlap played an entire game in the outfield with the Arkansas Bears in the Class D Arkansas-Missouri League.

Engle never got a chance to show if she could really play as well as the men on the club. After talking with several baseball officials, Trautman issued a statement saying, "I am notifying all clubs that signing of women players by National Association clubs will not be tolerated and clubs signing, or attempting to sign, women players will be subject to severe penalties." He said that he had talked with Ford Frick and that "he asked me to express his concurrence in the view that it is just not in the best interest of professional baseball that such travesties be tolerated." Most of the baseball establishment agreed with this stance, including the *Sporting News*, which felt that "as far as Organized Baseball is concerned, a woman's place always will be in the grandstand."[24]

A disappointed Engle went back to her office job, but she considered trying out for a position with a girls' baseball team. "I think baseball is making a big mistake," she told reporters. "I love the game. More women should be playing. I'm sure that I would have been able to remain as a player with the Senators."[25]

For Engle and other women aspiring to play professional baseball, the ban on female players left only one other alternative—the All-American Girls Professional Baseball League (AAGPBL), established by Phil Wrigley in 1943 and then sold to Arthur Meyerhoff in 1944.[26] Most of the league's managers and coaches were former major and minor league players and even included such notables as Jimmie Foxx and Max Carey. A hybrid game that borrowed from both baseball and softball, the AAGPBL had nine players on each side, used regulation baseball gloves and bats and a ball smaller than a softball but larger than a baseball, allowed base runners to take a lead, steal bases, and slide, and generally provided a faster brand of play than that of girls' softball teams.

Players were chosen on the basis of skill, looks, and character, and were required to act as ladies on and off the field. On the diamond, they wore conservative blouses and flare skirts. Off the field they were forbidden to wear masculine hair cuts or tight shorts and were discouraged from wearing tomboyish clothing such as dungarees or slacks. They were given training in posture, dress, and the application of makeup, and were forbidden to smoke, drink, or use profanity. Female chaperones traveled with each club, approved the girls' dates, choice of living quarters and restaurants, and enforced a strict 12:30 A.M. curfew. Any player associating with "persons of questionable character" could be banned from the team and from the league.

Playing a grueling, four-month schedule in Midwestern cities, the young women were paid between $50 and $85 a week, though some stars with proven gate appeal made over $100 a week. Among the most famous were Dottie Kamenshek, an outstanding hitter and fielder for the Rockford Peaches; Sophie Kurys, who became known as "Tina Cobb" for her base-stealing skills with the Racine Belles; and Dottie Schroeder, a sure-handed shortstop for the South Bend Blue Sox and later the Fort Wayne Daisies. Schroeder's defensive abilities caused fans to dub her "Honey Wagner" and led Chicago Cubs General Manager Jim Gallagher to claim, "If that girl were a man she'd be worth $50,000 to me." Overhearing this remark about a player widely known for her beauty as well as her diamond skills, Connie Mack quipped, "If I were sixty years younger, I'd take her as she is."[27]

The AAGPBL enjoyed considerable success for nearly a decade. By 1948, it had 10 teams, all in the Midwest, and drew over 900,000 fans. This rapid growth led league officials to make plans to expand all across the nation. But it was not to be. Like the minor leagues, girls' baseball profited from the general sports boom of the immediate postwar years, then began to suffer at the gate due to competition from television and other amusements of the affluent 1950s. By 1952, the league was down to six teams, and two years later it folded. But it was not forgotten. In 1988, the Hall of Fame opened a long-overdue exhibit honoring women in baseball, with much of it devoted to the AAGPBL and the close to 500 women who played in it during its 12-year history.

Near the end of the season the propaganda battle between the United States and the Soviet Union invaded baseball again. The Soviet leaders had long been boasting that Russia had invented nylon shirts, the airplane, radio, television and many other marvels that the United States and other Western democracies laid claim to. In September the Russian magazine *Smena*, a publication of the Young Communist League, extended those claims to baseball as well. "Let us leave to one side the national origin of this game," the magazine said. "It is well known that in Russian villages they played *lapta*, of which baseball is an imitation. It was played in Russian villages when the United States was not even marked on the maps."

In shamelessly copying *lapta*, the magazine claimed, the Americans had brutalized and commercialized it, turning it into a highly competitive, capitalistic game which often brought serious injuries and even death to fans and players alike. As an example, the article pointed to the aggressive nicknames ("Piratov" and "Tigrov") of the teams, and showed a picture of Cardinal catcher Del Rice being carried off the field after being hit by a ball. Besides turning the sport into a "bestial battle, a bloody fight with murder and mayhem," the team owners held their players "in a condition of slavery . . . bought and sold and thrown out the door when they are no longer needed." The average career of a major league player lasted only six or seven years, *Smena* said, "after which, with ruined health and often also crippled, he increases the army of American unemployed."[28]

Summaries and denunciations of the *Smena* article appeared in the *New York Times, Time* magazine, and several other American periodicals. Most players and fans dismissed the article with ridicule, but the Eisenhower administration even went so far as to charge the Soviet leaders with deliberately trying to stir up ill-feelings between the American and Russian people. The high-brow literary magazine, the *Saturday Review of Literature,* which often added features on baseball and foreign affairs to its literary coverage and certainly was not found around many dugouts or locker rooms, felt the affair was serious enough to invite St. Louis Cardinal manager Eddie Stanky to reply to the Russian charges.

Stanky, who had been traded frequently, said that each time he had been "thrown out the door" he had benefited, picking up fat World Series checks with the Dodgers, Braves, and Giants and a partial share as manager of the third place Cardinals in 1952. "If that's slavery, I'm sure there are two hundred million Russians who would like to trade places with me," he said. Labeling the *Smena* article "a phony," he claimed, "Baseball, with its team play, its rhubarbs and its beefs, its umpire-baiting, the freedom of the fans to decide when to boo or applaud is the big game of a free people."[29]

The controversy over the *Smena* article waned as the season ended, but this was not the last time the Russians would lay claim to the national pastime. As late as the summer of 1987, when Soviet leader Mikhail Gorbachev was making headlines with his startling reforms of Soviet domestic and foreign policy, *Izvestia,* the official government newspaper, repeated the old argument that baseball was another one of the Soviet Union's many inventions. This time, in the waning years of the Cold War, the claim caused hardly a ripple.

Controversy always seemed to stalk Jackie Robinson, and as the memory of the World Series faded and the American people's sports interest turned to football and basketball, the outspoken Dodger landed on the front pages of the newspaper sports sections. On Sunday, November 30, he appeared on the radio and television program, "Youth Wants to Know," where he was asked by a young male, "Do you think the Yankees are prejudiced against Negro players?" With his typical candor, Robinson answered, "Yes, I think they are," hastening to add, "I don't mean the players—they are a fine bunch of fellows and sportsmen.... But I think the Yankee management is prejudiced. They haven't a single Negro on the team and very few in the Yankee organization."[30]

The Yankee management hotly denied Robinson's charges. George Weiss claimed that the Yankees had several good black prospects in their farm system and that "our attitude has always been that when a Negro comes along who can play good enough to win a place on the Yankees we will be glad to have him—but not for exploitation." Dodger president Walter O'Malley tried to downplay Robinson's comments, arguing that he had been put on the spot and had the right to express his opinion. O'Malley also said, "The only feud we want with the Yankees is that one in October."[31]

He would get it, but once again, he would not like the results.

11. Same Old Story (1953)

As the 1953 baseball season approached, the nation was still settling in under a new president, Dwight D. Eisenhower, who had defeated his Democratic rival, Adlai E. Stevenson, by a wide margin in the 1952 elections. The new president was very popular, and would remain so throughout his eight-year presidency, but he got off on the wrong foot with organized baseball before the first season played under his administration even began.

On April 2, when Clark Griffith made his customary trip to the White House to give the president a gold-plated season's pass to the Senators' home games and to invite him to attend the opener, Eisenhower told him that he would not be able to make it because he would be traveling to Augusta, Georgia, on the morning of April 13 for a week-long golfing vacation. Griffith told reporters, "I will admit that I'm a little disappointed, but if that's the President's will it certainly is all right with me.... Mr. Eisenhower was very nice about it."[1]

When news of Eisenhower's decision to forego the opener reached the newspapers on the morning of April 3, it created quite a stir. Ever since President Taft began the practice in 1910, presidents had missed only 12 out of 43 openers. Many of these had been during the war years when understandable pressing business prevented them from going out to give their official blessing to the game. Franklin Roosevelt had attended eight openers, in spite of his preoccupation with the Depression and World War II, and Truman, after missing the 1945 lid-lifter, had attended seven consecutive openers.

The reaction to the president's decision was not long in coming. The day after the meeting between Eisenhower and Griffith, the sports editor of the *Washington Post*, Bus Ham, wrote that Eisenhower's decision left him "a little shocked and quite sorry" and speculated that the new president had violated an American tradition primarily because "he had been out of the country for many years before he was elevated to the Presidency. He was out of touch with baseball and some other American customs." Washington bartender Edward Luckett undoubtedly expressed the feelings of many fans when he said, "Can you imagine turning down the chance to throw out the first ball on opening day in favor of playing golf?" Another fan from

Philadelphia said, "I don't think he's smart breaking political tradition. . . . It looks like a political blunder."[2]

Eisenhower had indeed made a political blunder, and on April 4 Vice-President Nixon tried to take some of the heat off his chief when he announced that he was ready to substitute for him on opening day. Confessing to reporters that he was a "real fan but a lousy ballplayer," he said that when he played as a child "I was usually stationed any place on the field where the ball was not likely to come. . . . That was usually right field." He tried to inject some humor into the situation by quipping, "I've been getting in a little golf to get loosened up for the big day."[3]

As planned, Eisenhower flew to Augusta on Monday, April 13, for a working vacation. He was scheduled to play with Ben Hogan, who had just won the Master's Tournament on Sunday, Byron Nelson, and several other professional golfers. The president was so eager to get to the links that when he walked off the plane in Augusta he was carrying his golf shoes in his hand, and a few minutes later he was on the warm-up tee practicing his swing and getting a few tips from Hogan. His obvious obsession with golf was duly noted by the press and many baseball fans.

But bad weather intervened to make it possible for the president to make a token appearance at the Senators' opening game after all. Rain postponed the game until Thursday, and after working and playing golf in Augusta for three days, he flew to Washington on Thursday to deliver a scheduled luncheon speech. Afterwards, he went out to Griffith Stadium to carry out his civic duties. It was a chilly afternoon and he wore a topcoat for most of his short stay. After 1½ innings, with the Yankees holding a 4–0 lead, he boarded a plane and headed south to the links in Augusta. But in the future, he would make an effort to ensure that his busy calendar reserved a place for the annual opening game.

The season would begin with the first franchise shift since the turn of the century. Ever since the end of World War II, pressure had been mounting for a realignment of the major leagues. The population was growing rapidly, from 140 million in 1945 to 180 million in 1960, and increasing by some 29 million in the 1950s alone. Regional population patterns were changing, as people left the older cities of the northeast for warmer weather and jobs in California, Texas, Florida, and other sunbelt states. There were also population shifts within cities, as many in the middle and upper class left the inner city for the pleasures of suburbia. Most of the major league parks were in the inner cities and were now often in undesirable neighborhoods having more than their share of crime. To make matters worse, many of these parks were aging structures with too few seats and parking spaces and inadequate rest rooms and concession stands.

Some cities with two clubs were having trouble supporting an entry in each league, and even New York, the nation's largest city and premier baseball town, was having trouble sustaining three teams. Further to the south and west loomed bustling cities promising new stadiums, spacious parking, big television markets, large crowds, and big profits. Air transportation was becoming faster and safer, with transcontinental flights from New York to Los Angeles taking less time than it took to travel by train between many major league cities. Owners might claim that baseball was a sport and not a business, but the economic benefits of pulling up stakes and moving halfway or all the way across county were becoming more and more obvious.

There were many cities anxious to land a major league team. Acquisition of a major league franchise would be a sign that the city had joined New York, Chicago, Philadelphia and other large cities in the ranks of the big time, and it would provide a big economic benefit. The team, players, and fans from the city and from surrounding areas would bring millions of dollars into the city, which would become a more popular attraction for vacationers and conventioneers. No wonder so many cities in the fifties were promising that they would use tax money or bond issues to finance the construction of major league stadiums and parking lots if a team agreed to relocate in their area.

There had been plans even before World War II to shift franchises. In late 1941, St. Louis Browns' owner Donald Barnes was planning to move his team to the West Coast, but the idea was shelved after Pearl Harbor. After the war, there were many who felt that the most likely place for expansion would be to California, which was booming in the forties and fifties and was destined to pass New York as the most populated state by 1963. Besides, the Pacific Coast League, a Triple A league, was noted for its high caliber of play and the large number of fans the teams drew through the turnstiles.

But the first franchise shifts in half a century occurred in the Midwest, not California. The first team to try to move was the Browns. The Browns were the most dismal team in baseball at the gate and on the field, and owner Bill Veeck was hoping that a change of scenery would improve the team's economic and playing fortunes. But on March 16, the American League owners turned down his request to move the team to Baltimore or Milwaukee, citing the club's recent attendance gains and the problems involved in moving a franchise just a few days before the new season began. However, the real stumbling block was the opposition of Braves' owner Lou Perini, who had plans of his own for his minor league franchise in Milwaukee. Many of the owners also saw Veeck as a troublemaker and hoped that if his bid to move the team were rejected he would be forced to sell the team and get out of baseball altogether.

Just two days later, the National League and American Association owners agreed to Perini's request to transfer his Braves to Milwaukee and to move the Braves' Milwaukee Triple A club, the Brewers, to the open city of Toledo. The news came as a shock to the city of Boston and to Braves fans everywhere. The Braves had been a charter member of the National League in 1876, and to many it seemed inconceivable that in just a few days Eddie Mathews, Warren Spahn, Lew Burdette, and the rest of the Braves would be opening the home season in Milwaukee instead of Boston. The day after the announcement, the *Boston Daily Record* carried the headline, "It's Official, Braves Go To Milwaukee," surrounded by a mourning band. In Milwaukee, of course, the mood was different. There the *Milwaukee Sentinel* headlined, "We're Big Leaguers Now."[4]

Perini really had no choice. Boston could not — or would not — support two major league teams. As Perini said at the time of the move, "I definitely feel that since the advent of television Boston has become a one-team city, and the enthusiasm of the fans for the Boston National League Club has waned."[5] In the previous eight years, the Red Sox had consistently outdrawn the Braves, usually by a wide margin. When the Braves won the pennant in 1948, they drew 1.5 million fans, but after that attendance declined steadily to a low of 281,278 fans in 1952 when the club finished in seventh place. "We were playing to the groundskeepers," said manager Charlie Grimm.[6]

After losing $207,718 in 1951 and some $600,000 in 1952, Perini's head was turned by Milwaukee officials' promises of a new county-financed stadium and other amenities. Milwaukee County Stadium, the first major league park to be financed by the taxpayers rather than private investors, had 35,911 seats and 10,000 parking spaces. So Perini took his club and left town, predicting, "This is the start of the realignment of baseball that has been talked about so often."[7]

Milwaukee welcomed the Braves with parades and packed stands. In the team's first 13 games at home, it drew more fans than it had in all of its home games the previous year, and for the year it drew a club record of 1.8 million, bringing Perini a handsome profit of $637,798. Over the rest of the decade, the Braves would outdraw all the other major league clubs.

The St. Louis Cardinals began the season under new ownership. After being convicted of income tax evasion, ordered to pay over a half million dollars in back taxes, fined $15,000, and sentenced to 15 months in prison, Fred M. Saigh was forced to sell his club. The buyer was Anheuser-Busch, the prominent brewery, for $3,750,000. The new president, August Busch, also purchased Sportsman's Park from Veeck for $800,000 and renamed it Busch Stadium. Busch had plenty of money to plow into developing his club and drawing St. Louis baseball fans through the gate, giving Veeck another reason, if he needed one, to move his Browns.

The oldest professional baseball club, the Cincinnati Reds, did not change owners or cities in 1953, but it did try to change names. With the United States in the midst of the war in Korea and a Cold War in much of the rest of the world, and with Senator Joe McCarthy of Wisconsin still creating headlines with his "Red Scare" tactics, club officials decided to change the team's name to Redlegs. But the new name would not stick. Fans and reporters did not like it and refused to use it. The publisher of the *Cincinnati Inquirer* told his reporters to continue to use the name "Reds" in the sports section. "Let the Communists change their name," he said. "We were here first."[8]

Most sportswriters and other baseball experts picked Brooklyn to repeat as the National League champions in 1953. But in the first half of the season the flag seemed up for grabs, with the Phillies and the transplanted Braves challenging the Dodgers for the top rung. As late as mid–May the Dodgers were in fourth place. Then they won 10 in a row to take over the lead on May 31, only to relinquish it to the Braves for most of June. But on June 21, the Braves began an eight-game losing streak, including three to the Dodgers, and after that the Braves never held first place again and the Dodgers never lost it. The race stayed close until the All-Star break, which saw the Dodgers on top by two and the Yankees up by 6½. According to tradition, the clubs resting in first place at the All-Star break were destined to win the pennant, and more often than not that had held true; since 1901, 34 American League pennant winners and 32 National League winners had held the top rung on Independence Day.

Tradition held in 1953. After the National League took its fourth straight All-Star Game by a 5–1 score in Cincinnati, the Dodgers caught fire. They reeled off 16 victories in their next 19 games to build an eight-game lead, then launched a 13-game winning streak on August 7. From July 16 through September 1, the Dodgers won 41 of 50 games for a spectacular .820 percentage, and kept on going. On September 12, with two weeks left in the season, Carl Erskine beat the Braves 5–2 to give the Bums their seventh pennant, their fourth in seven years, and the first back-to-back pennants in the National League since the Cardinals took three consecutive flags during World War II. They clinched the flag in their 142nd game, the earliest in National League history.

Although the Giants were really not in the running for the pennant, games between the Polo Grounders and the men from Ebbets Field were as heated as ever. As the Giants' fortunes sagged on the field, Durocher seemed to take out his frustrations on umpires and opposing players. His heated arguments with umpires finally led National League President Warren Giles to call him into his office for a reprimand. Durocher apologized publicly for his criticism of the men in blue, somehow managing to keep a straight face as he said, "In all my years of baseball I've never questioned the integrity of umpires."[9]

On September 6, Durocher got into a fight at the Polo Grounds with

Dodger Carl Furillo, who was leading the league in batting with a .344 average. The Reading Rifle had long thought that his old manager had been ordering his pitchers to throw at him, and as he stood at the plate facing Giant pitcher Ruben Gomez, Furillo heard Durocher yell from the dugout, "stick it in his ear."[10] Gomez's aim was a little off: he hit Furillo on the wrist. Furillo made a movement toward the mound, then changed his mind and began walking down the line toward first. On the way to the bag he exchanged some words with Durocher, who was in the dugout.

As Furillo stood on first, Durocher continued to taunt him and, as Furillo later told it, beckoned for him to come on over to the dugout to settle things. Furillo stood on first while Gomez threw two pitches to the next hitter, then called time and ran toward the Giants dugout. The 48-year-old Durocher, who loved a good fight as much as anybody in baseball with the possible exception of Billy Martin, ran out to meet the charging right fielder. Furillo swung at Durocher but missed, and the two men wrestled on the ground while players from both clubs ran out to either join in the fray or to try to separate the two. Duke Snider later claimed that as he stood near the pile of players who had jumped on the two men, he could hear umpire Babe Pinelli yelling, "Kill him, Carl. Kill him."[11] Somehow in the scuffle, somebody stepped on Furillo's left hand and fractured a metacarpal bone. His hand had to be put in a cast, and he missed the last 22 games of the season. Ironically, Furillo had played seven years in the majors without being ejected from a game or being in a serious argument with another player.

Still furious after the fight, Furillo told reporters, "I'm gonna get him. I'm gonna get him the first time I see him. . . . He has crossed me once too often." But four days after the fight Giles telephoned Furillo and told him that after studying the incident he was convinced that Gomez had not tried to hit him and that if he followed through on his threat, he would be disciplined by the National League office. Furillo assured Giles that the threat was made in anger and that he wanted the argument ended. Giles then considered the matter closed, and it was.[12]

The 1953 Dodgers were perhaps the best of all the postwar Brooklyn teams in an era when the Flatbushers fielded so many good ones. It was an experienced, stable team fashioned in the postwar period by Branch Rickey from the Dodger farm system and aggressive signing of black players. It led the league in batting average, hits, and slugging average, and topped the league in home runs, RBIs, and runs for the fifth consecutive year, and in stolen bases for the eighth consecutive year. The team scored a record 955 runs, an average of 6.16 per game, and over 200 more than the second-place Braves and 154 more than the Yankees. In a game against the Phillies on May 24, the Dodgers held a 3–2 lead when they came to bat in the eighth. They then proceeded to score a record 13 runs, all without the benefit of a home run, before the Phillies could get them out.

Five Dodger regulars hit .300 or better, six scored 100 runs or more (a major league record), and three drove in over 100 runs. The club hit a total of 208 homers, second to the record of 221 held by the 1947 Giants. Snider hit 42 and Campanella 41, making the Dodgers the only National League team to ever have two players hitting 40 or more homers. Campanella's homers, .312 batting average, league-leading 142 RBIs, and superb defensive play made him a clear choice for the MVP Award, which he won for the second time. Furillo robbed many hitters of hits and extra bases with his glove and arm, considered the best in the majors, and he won the batting crown with a .344 average while sitting out the last three weeks of the season with his injured hand.

Second baseman Junior Gilliam hit .278, led the league in triples with 17, scored 125 runs, stole 21 bases, and became the fourth Dodger in seven years to win the Rookie of the Year Award. The man he replaced at second, Jackie Robinson, hit .329 while playing almost half the season in left field and filling in at first, second, short, and third whenever needed. At third base was light-hitting Billy Cox, considered by many to be the best defensive third baseman of the era.

Devastating on offense, sure-handed on defense, fast on the bases, the Dodgers' main weakness was their pitching staff. Their big ace, Don Newcombe, was still in the army, and Ralph Branca, the hard-luck hurler who had not won a game since June of 1952, was traded to Detroit in July. Carl Erskine had a 20–6 record, but no other pitcher won 20, and the entire staff compiled only 51 complete games. Reliever Joe Black had a disappointing season, appearing in 34 games, compiling a 6–3 record with five saves, and seeing his ERA soar to 5.33.

The surprising Braves, who had finished seventh just one year before, finished second, 13 games out. They had been strengthened by trades that brought sluggers Joe Adcock from Cincinnati and Andy Pafko from the Dodgers, and they had one of the league's best pitching staffs, with Warren Spahn tying Robin Roberts for the league's wins at 23 and leading the league with a 2.10 ERA. The Braves led the league in team ERA with 3.30. Twenty-one-year-old third baseman Eddie Mathews led the league in home runs with 47, breaking Ralph Kiner's string of seven consecutive years capturing or sharing the home run title. Kiner, suffering from back problems, was traded to the Cubs in June, and fell off to only 28 homers.

The Cardinals and Phillies tied for third place, followed by New York, Cincinnati, Chicago, and Pittsburgh. Playing under new manager Fred Haney, the Pirates won eight more games than they had in 1952 but still lost 104 games and finished a dismal 55 games off the pace.

During spring training, Casey Stengel told reporters, "We're out to win a fifth straight pennant, something no club has yet been able to do in the major leagues."[13] Most sportswriters thought he would be able to pull it off. For the first time since he took over the Yankees, the Baseball Writers Association chose them to take the flag.

Stengel had tested, solid players at almost every position: Joe Collins at first, Billy Martin at second, Phil Rizzuto at short, Gil McDougald at third, Yogi Berra behind the plate, and Mickey Mantle, Hank Bauer, Gene Woodling, and Irv Noren in the outfield. Johnny Mize could be counted on as a trusted pinch hitter. Whitey Ford was back from the military, and the 24-year-old left-hander was ready to become one of the pillars of an otherwise aging Yankee staff led by Allie Reynolds (38 years old), Ed Lopat (35), Johnny Sain (35), and Vic Raschi (34). Martin, with a full-year's experience under his belt, would become the scrappy leader of the team, but Mantle would emerge as the star.

Mantle was still a shy, inarticulate country boy adjusting to the spotlight and to life in the big city. Only 21 years old, he was a big gate attraction at home and on the road. He was receiving around 1,200 fan letters a week, was eagerly sought for radio and television appearances and as a banquet speaker, had written (with Ben Epstein) *The Mickey Mantle Story,* and was raking in thousands of dollars from endorsements of Wheaties, Camel cigarettes, and several other products. His baseball salary was around $18,000, but these outside commercial activities swelled his total income to around $30,000. Although his homer total was far off the pace of league leader Al Rosen's 43, Mantle showed that he could hit home runs as far or further than anyone who had ever played in the majors. On April 17, hitting right-handed against left-hander Chuck Stobbs at Griffith Stadium, he drove the ball over the 55-foot-high left-field wall, and it finally came to rest in the backyard of a home at 434 Oakdale Street, 565 feet from home plate. No one else—not even Ruth, Gehrig, or Foxx—had ever hit a ball over the left field wall at Griffith on the fly. Questioned about the drive, Mantle said, "I unloaded it. I guess it was the longest ball I ever hit in my life."[14] This is still the longest measured homer in major league history. The ball, along with Mantle's bat, was sent to Cooperstown to be displayed in the Hall of Fame.

It was natural that the talent-laden Yankees would receive plenty of publicity for their play, but in a game with the Browns early in the year, the Bronx Bombers also made big headlines by being involved in the biggest rhubarb of the season. Catcher Clint Courtney and several of the Yankee players had been feuding for two years, had already been involved in one fight, and on April 28 they went at it again. In the beginning of the tenth inning of a hotly contested game, McDougald gave the Yankees a 7–6 lead when he scored from second on a single by bowling over Courtney at home plate, causing him to drop the ball. When Courtney came to bat in the Browns half of the inning, he told Berra, "Someone is going to pay."[15]

Courtney singled to right, but instead of stopping at first he made the turn and headed for second and for Phil Rizzuto, who was covering the bag. He slid into Rizzuto with his spikes high in the air, severely gashing the little shortstop's right leg. Bauer ran in from right field to join Reynolds and the Yankee infielders as they pounced on Courtney. Somehow in the melee, Reynolds managed to pin the scrappy catcher's arms while Martin punched him in the face, bloodying it and knocking his glasses to the ground, where they were promptly stepped on by first baseman Joe Collins. Players from both teams swarmed onto the field, Brownie fans pelted the Yankee out-fielders with bottles and garbage, and umpire John Stevens suffered a dislocated shoulder trying to break up the 17-minute melee. Later, American League President Will Harridge fined two Brown players and four Yankees a total of $850, the highest ever levied in a single incident up until that time.

The Yankees won the game, 7–6, holding onto first place. But the Indians were pressing hard, and managed to take over first place early in May. The Yankees then regained the lead on May 11, and on May 27 they began an 18-game winning streak that was not broken until they were beaten on June 16 by the Browns, who happily snapped their own 14-game losing streak. After losing to the Browns, the Yankees won five of their next six to fatten their lead to 12.

But then they collapsed. From June 21 until July 1, they lost nine in a row, their longest losing streak since 1945, and saw their lead melt to only five games. Most of the club took the losses in stride, but not their manager, who became progressively grouchy and defensive. Near the end of the streak, he barred all reporters from the clubhouse, virtually shutting the door in their faces. One angry reporter said, "The Yankee action came as no surprise. . . . They are the most arrogant oufit in baseball. This is just typical."[16]

Not long after the losing streak was finally snapped, Stengel told Arthur Daley of the *New York Times*, "When we lost those nine straight, everything fell apart at once. Our battin' wuz bad, our fieldin' was bad, our pitchin' wuz bad, and our managin' wuz bad. And judgin' by what I read in the newspapers, the Yankee writers wuz in a slump, too. They didn't do so good, either."[17]

During the Yankee collapse in late June the White Sox temporarily replaced the Indians as the main threat to Stengel's fifth pennant. Mired in fifth place, 13 games out, in the middle of June, Paul Richards's club captured 29 of their next 35 games to pull to within four games of the Yankees. But on July 19 the Yankees took a doubleheader from the Pale Hose by the scores of 6–2 and 3–0, and after that they never looked back. They built their lead to eight games by August 8, then to 13 by September 14, when, like the Dodgers, they wrapped up the flag with almost two weeks left in the season. The Bronx Bombers coasted on to a 99–52 season, winding up 8½ games ahead of the second-place Indians.

Woodling (.306) and Bauer (.304) were the only regulars to hit over .300, but the Yankees led the league in team hitting (.273) and runs (801). While Mantle's slugging feats (a .295 average, 21 homers, 92 RBIs) got the most publicity, Berra led the team in homers (27) and RBIs (108). Forty-year-old Johnny Mize, playing his last season, was a valuable pinch hitter, garnering a .250 average, 4 homers, and 27 RBIs. The Yankee staff led the league in team ERA (3.20) and saves (39), but none of the pitchers had a 20-game season. Ford, finishing at 18–6, came the closest. Trailing him were Lopat (16–4), who led the league in winning percentage (.800) and ERA (2.42), and Sain (14–7), Raschi (13–6), and Reynolds (13–7).

The Indians finished second for the third straight year. They paced the league in home runs (160), and their leading hitter and MVP winner, Al Rosen, topped the league in homers (43) and RBIs (145) and barely missed the triple crown by falling one point short of Senators' first baseman Mickey Vernon's league-leading .337 average. Vernon's teammate, Bob Porterfield, led the league in victories (22) and shutouts (9).

Ted Williams returned to major league play in August, having served in the Marines since May of 1952. On his first combat mission, his F-9 Panther jet had been hit in a bombing run over North Korea, forcing him to fly his burning plane to an Allied base, where he crashed-landed it on its belly after the landing wheels failed to descend. He walked away without injuries, and the next day he was back in action, bombing North Korean supply lines near Pyongyang, the North Korean capital. In all, he flew 37 missions and won three air medals. But he suffered from viral pneumonia and from a recurring ear infection that hampered his flying. Near the end of July, as the Korean War came to an end, he was given an early medical discharge.

Williams joined the Red Sox on July 29, telling his teammates and reporters, "I don't feel a day older than when I first saw Fenway Park."[18] Gradually working back into shape, he was first used as a pinch hitter, managing one hit in five at bats. But on August 9, three weeks before his 35th birthday, he drove one of Mike Garcia's fastballs over the bullpen in Fenway Park for his 325th home run. The crowd gave him a tremendous ovation, while across the field in the Indians' dugout another old veteran, Bob Feller, marveled at Williams's talent and claimed that "he made me feel young again."[19] Playing in just 37 games, Williams hit 13 homers and finished with a .407 average. Red Sox General manager Joe Cronin told him "Ted, you've just set spring training back 20 years."[20]

Recovered from his nervous breakdown, Jimmy Piersall also returned to the Red Sox starting lineup in right field. Playing in 151 games for the fourth-place club, he had a .272 batting average and made several sparkling catches as he established himself as one of the premier defensive outfielders in the game. Teammates, opponents, and the press all praised him for his courageous recovery from his debilitating mental illness of the year before, while several organizations and publications awarded him comeback of the year awards. Perhaps Harold Kaese said it best when he wrote in his *Boston Globe* column, "More than any other player, the comeback big leaguer of 1953 is Jim Piersall. . . . He came from farther back than any of them."[21]

Piersall would spend most of the rest of the decade in the Boston outfield, and although he was still an intense ballplayer who occasionally lost his temper, yelled at umpires, and resorted to clowning or showboating, he did not lapse back into the nightmarish mental state of 1952. He would play with several clubs in both leagues before winding up his career in 1967 with a lifetime batting average of .272, 104 homers, 591 RBIs, and 115 stolen bases.

In the 1950s mental illness was still looked upon as a moral failure or some other character fault rather than a legitimate illness that should be treated as openly and sympathetically as a physical one. Having learned to deal with his illness, Piersall linked up with sportswriter and radio commentator Al Hirshberg to present his story to the public. The result was a two-part article entitled, "They Called Me Crazy and I Was," which appeared in the *Saturday Evening Post* early in 1955, and the book it was taken from, *Fear Strikes Out: The Jim Piersall Story,* published later in the year. In 1957, Tony Perkins starred as Piersall in the motion picture *Fear Strikes Out*, which received some critical and popular acclaim, but Piersall later called it "a lot of bullshit, just a heap of fiction. . . . The whole movie was dreamed up in Hollywood."[22]

In June the Red Sox dealt the sixth place Detroit Tigers the worst back-to-back defeats of 1953—or any year. Playing in Fenway Park on June 17, the Red Sox pounded Tiger pitchers for 20 hits and a 17–1 victory. The next day was even worse for the Tigers, who were trailing by only 5–3 before the bottom fell out in the seventh. In a 48-minute nightmare for Detroit, the Red Sox sent 23 men to the plate, tallied 14 hits, received 6 walks, and scored 17 runs, a new record for the most runs ever scored in one inning. Fifteen other major league records were also set, including most hits in one inning (3), set by Gene Stephens. The Red Sox went on to win 23–3. In the two-day period, the Tigers had been outscored 40–4.

The Browns could boast of having the majors' only no-hitter of the season, and it was recorded by a very unlikely pitcher, Alva Lee "Bobo" Holloman, a reliever who had spent the previous 10 years toiling in the minors. On May 6, on a cool, rainy evening that helped keep the crowd down to only 2,473, Holloman had a glorious night, the highlight of his career. Not only did he become the first rookie to pitch a no-hitter in his first official start, he also hit two singles and drove in three of his team's six runs. This game was in essence his major league career. He won two more games that year, but this was his first and last complete game. The rest of the year was all downhill, and on July 24 he was sold to Toronto—never to pitch in the majors again.

Holloman was lucky—he at least got to play part of one major league season. There were others who came up in 1953 and played only one game or none at all. After six years in the minors, catcher Dick Teed was brought up in July to bolster the Dodger catching staff when Rube Walker, Campanella's backup, was injured. Teed came in to pinch hit against the Braves, and was struck out by Max Surkont. Soon he was back in the minors for good, with the memory of that one unsuccessful major league at bat.

Then there was Yankee shortstop Frank Verdi, who did get to play in one game but never got to bat. Almost 27 years old, Verdi had spent seven years playing in the minors before he was brought up to the talent-rich Yankees. On May 10, he finally realized his lifetime dream of getting to play in a major league game. In the last of the sixth inning of a game against the Red Sox in Fenway Park, he was sent in to play shortstop, and in the top of the seventh, after the Yankees had taken a two-run lead and loaded the bases with two out, Verdi walked up to the plate, anxious to take his first cuts in the majors. But as he stepped into the batter's box to hit against Ellis Kinder, the Red Sox called time so they could bring in a relief pitcher, Ken Holcombe. Verdi stepped out of the box while Holcombe took his warm ups, then stepped back in. But now Stengel called time, and as Verdi looked toward the Yankee bench he saw Bill Renna loosening up to hit for him! Verdi went back to the dugout. A week later, still looking for his first major league at bat, he was shipped down to Syracuse, his short major league career over. He was philosophical about it all. "At least I got in the batter's box twice," he said. "A lot of guys only got in once."[23]

When Bill Veeck took over the St. Louis Browns in 1951, he called them "the worst collection of ballplayers I've ever seen,"[24] and their play since then had done little to change his mind. The club finished last in 1951, seventh in 1952, and last again in 1953. Veeck did not have the players or capital to compete with the more popular and successful Cardinals, but he had managed to improve the club's attendance from 247,131 in 1950 to 518,796 in 1952. But in 1953, the uncertainty surrounding the Browns future, along with their 23–54 record at home and total of 100 losses, caused the attendance to dip to 310,914.

Veeck spent most of the 1953 season trying to find a place to move the Browns. In September as the season was drawing to a merciful close for the Browns, he again tried to move the team to Baltimore. Once again, the other owners turned him down. They clearly wanted to get rid of this maverick, not move him to another city. After losing close to one million dollars in less than three years, Veeck had no choice but to give up the club. At the end of the season he sold his controlling interest in the Browns for $2.5 million to a Baltimore syndicate headed by attorney Clarence W. Miles, who secured the other American League owners' permission to move the team to Baltimore. The city's municipal stadium, constructed in 1950, was upgraded by the addition of a double deck that would make it the major league's fourth largest stadium, trailing only the parks of the Cleveland Indians (73,500), New York Yankees (67,000), and New York Giants (55,000). The team was named the Baltimore Orioles.

Once again, Veeck packed his suitcase. But he told reporters that his departure did not mean that he was leaving baseball. "In fact," he told reporters, "like a bad penny, I'll probably turn up again somewhere."[25] Most of the American League owners were hoping it would not be in their league.

Veeck's exit also brought the end of the active major league career of Satchel Paige, who had been brought into the majors by Veeck at Cleveland in 1948 and then at St. Louis in 1951. Used as a starter and reliever, Paige won 3 games in 1951 and 12 in 1952, and in 1953, when he was the highest-paid player on the Brownies with an annual salary estimated at $25,000, he pitched in 57 games, compiling a 3–9 record and a 3.53 ERA. Stengel chose Paige for his 1953 All-Star pitching staff. He pitched one inning, becoming the oldest (he was probably 47) player to ever appear in an All-Star contest. It was a great honor for the old hurler, although the National League hitters tagged him for three hits and two runs en route to a 5–1 victory.

It was estimated that by 1953 Paige had pitched in at least 2,500 games, an average of 125 a year. Catcher Clint Courtney claimed that he still had his incredible pinpoint control and that "his fast ball still burns my mitt when he lets it go, which is whenever he needs it." He was still highly respected by some of the game's top hitters, including Mickey Mantle, who early in the season had a lifetime record of one hit in ten at bats against Paige and said that he would "rather face any other pitcher in the league in a pinch situation."[26] Mantle's manager, Casey Stengel, had respect for him, too. Every time he saw Paige warming up in the bullpen, he would tell his players, "Get the runs now! Father Time is coming."[27] But when the new owners moved the team to Baltimore for the 1954 season, they did not ask Paige to go along.

One of the more interesting sidelights of 1953 was a revival of the old argument about whether a pitcher's curveball actually curved or not. Credit for inventing the curveball is usually given to Arthur "Candy" Cummings, who played minor and major league baseball in the Civil War era and supposedly developed the curve in the late 1860s. It won him a spot in the Hall of Fame in 1939, but that still did not silence the critics who claimed that the ball actually did not curve. As far back as the 1880s newspapers in

Buffalo and Chicago dismissed the idea that a player could actually make a ball curve, with some even suggesting that batters who claimed that a pitcher was throwing curves must be drinking.

One of the most famous studies of the curveball was done in 1941 by *Life* magazine, which concluded from its scientific photographs that the curveball was an "optical illusion."[28] This study, and others reaching similar conclusions, prompted baseball players to joke that the pitch they hit for a home run was "a hanging optical illusion" and led Lefty Gomez to complain after one particularly rough day on the mound, "I guess I've lost my optical illusion."[29] In 1953, *Life* did another study, using the latest improvements in high speed photography and wind tunnel experiments. This time, *Life* reported that its studies had shown that a curveball curved "in a gentle arc" but did not "break," and maintained that the hitter's belief that the ball broke dramatically was an "optical illusion" caused by the fact that the ball was within 10 feet of the plate when it curved. *Life* compared this illusion to the one a man sees as he watches a train coming toward him. The train seems to be moving slowly when it is far away, but the closer it gets the faster it appears to travel.[30]

These and other studies continued to evoke derisive comments from baseball people. Yogi Berra said, "If anybody wants to find out what a ball does at the plate, I'd say throw away the camera and get back there with a mask, chest protector and glove. Maybe two gloves — one for each hand."[31] Ex-Cincinnati pilot Luke Sewell said, "Isn't it strange that the optical illusion only happens when someone tries to throw a curveball, and never when a fast or straight ball is attempted?"[32]

The debate continued throughout the decade, and finally even the U.S. government lent its authority to the controversy. In 1959, Dr. Lyman J. Briggs, an avid baseball fan and director emeritus of the National Bureau of Standards, turned to the bureau's wind tunnels to conduct a study using Washington Senators' manager Cookie Lavagetto and pitchers Pedro Ramos and Camilo Pascual. Briggs concluded that "there's no question about it. A baseball curves." Furthermore, he claimed, it curved as much as 17½ inches between the mound and the plate. Baseball men took an "I told you so" attitude, and one of them said, "If he found out it could curve 17½ inches with pitchers like Ramos and Pascual, what would have happened if he'd made the tests with Warren Spahn?"[33]

Briggs's study, as well as others done by scientific magazines such as *Popular Science*, did prove to most people that baseballs, like old cannon balls and modern missiles, created small whirlpools of air as they rotated and moved through the air and that the changing pressures did, indeed, cause the object to curve. Of course, hitters never doubted it.

In October, millions of Americans were hit once again by that annual malady, World Series fever. It was a special time, when even those who were not normally fans of the game got caught up in the battle to determine major league bragging rights. For a few days in early fall, as the sun cast long shadows on the field, baseball seemed to unite the nation in a great civic celebration. Some fans were beginning to say that it was getting a little boring, seeing the Dodgers and Yankees play in the fall classic almost every year. But others disagreed, including the inmates at the Massachusetts State Prison, who were finally allowed to see the games on television after they threatened to riot unless the warden gave in and let them watch the Yankees and Dodgers go at one another.

On September 30, the two teams gathered in Yankee Stadium for the fifth postseason meeting between the two clubs, with the Dodgers still looking for their first title in seven attempts. It was also the diamond jubilee of the classic, which had started back in 1903 (no Series was played in 1904) when the Red Sox beat the Pirates five games to three. Six members of that historic Series were present as the guests of honor, and 86-year-old Cy Young, the starting pitcher for Boston in the first game a half century before, threw out the first ball to Yogi Berra.

Dodger fans and players were fully expecting to win. After all, they had one of the most powerful hitting clubs in history and they had that extra ingredient of revenge. This had to be their year. But the Yankees took the first two games in Yankee Stadium by scores of 9–5 and 4–2. The Dodgers were against the wall as they returned to Ebbets Field for the next three encounters, knowing that no team had ever won the Series after losing the first two contests. Back on friendly turf, Carl Erskine stopped the Dodger skid with a 3–2 victory and broke the old World Series record of 13 strikeouts by fanning 14 Yankees, including Mantle and first baseman Joe Collins four times each. The Dodger comeback continued in game four, when they drove Whitey Ford from the mound in the first inning and went on to win by 7–3. But thanks to a grand slam from Mantle, the Yankees took the fifth game by a 11–7 margin and then wrapped up the Series back in Yankee Stadium with a 4–3 win behind Ford. There would be no seventh game, and no joy in Flatbush. It was "wait until next year" time again.

Casey Stengel had captured an unprecedented fifth consecutive world championship, and the Yankees their sixteenth title in their last 20 attempts, dating back to 1927. For the American League, it was the seventh consecutive championship and the thirty-third in the history of the classic. The Yankees had almost half of those 33 victories.

Dodger fans just could not understand how they could have lost again. Led by Gil Hodges, who rebounded from the 0–21 humiliation of 1952 with a .364 average, five Dodgers hit .300 or better in the Series while only four Yankees did. As a team, the Dodgers outhit the Bronx Bombers .300 to .279. In home runs, the two teams were nearly equal, with the Yankees hitting nine and the Dodgers eight, setting a new record for total homers in a World Series. But the Yankees outscored their opponents 33–27, made only one error to the Dodgers' seven, and had a deeper pitching staff, a critical advantage in a subway series played on consecutive days with no travel time or rain delays. The Dodgers also left too many men on base, stranding 22 in the first two disastrous games in Yankee Stadium.

The individual star of the Series was Billy Martin. A .257 hitter during the regular season, Martin hit an even .500 during the series. His 12 hits set a new record for a six-game classic. His 2 homers, 2 triples, double, and 7 singles gave him 23 total bases, breaking the 6-game Series record (19) set by Ruth in 1923. Martin also drove in eight runs. He got the Yankees off to a good start in game one with his bases loaded triple in the first inning, tied the score in game two with a home run, and drove in the winning run with a single in the last of the ninth in game six. A disappointed Chuck Dressen moaned at the end of the Series that "we were beaten by a .257 hitter" and claimed that "if I'd had Don Newcombe, we'd have beat 'em."[34]

The day after the Series ended, Stengel told reporters in his suite at the Essex House in New York that he planned to take his sixth World Series in 1954. Denying reports that he was thinking of retiring and traveling, the 64-year-old manager said, "I had all the traveling I want when I was younger. I tell my wife, who is travel-minded, to get some travel films."[35]

The Old Professor was not through yet.

12. A Changing, Troubled Pastime

For much of its history, major league baseball had been one of the most stable of American sports. Changes, when they occurred, had come at an evolutionary, rather than a revolutionary pace. In the early 1950s the national pastime still bore a close resemblance to the game of the 1920s or even of the late 19th century. But in the postwar period it had been changing faster than ever before and, as the circumstances surrounding the movement of the Braves' and Browns' franchises in 1953 had shown, it was also in trouble.

The greatest change occurring in the postwar period was integration. By 1954, there were 25 black players on major league rosters, and finally, in 1959, 12 years after Jackie Robinson opened the door, the Boston Red Sox added Elijah "Pumpsie" Green to their roster, giving all 16 clubs at least one black player. In the summer of 1959 *Ebony* magazine wrote, "More than half a hundred colored players are cavorting over the big league diamonds from New York to Los Angeles, with World Series dreams riding high on the shoulders of the Negro stars. . . . Today, Negro players are bought, traded, sold and given bonuses. Fans cheer them or boo them on their merit and not on their skin color."[1]

While the fans were not as colorblind as *Ebony* wanted to believe, it was true that with each passing year, blacks were having a greater impact on the game, especially in the National League, which was far out in front of the junior circuit in the signing of black players. Such black stars as Robinson, Mays, and Aaron helped the National League to outpace the American League in attendance and to reverse its dominance of the All-Star Games and World Series. After winning just four All-Star Games between 1933 and 1949, the National League took nine of the contests played between 1950 and 1960. In the second half of the fifties, the National League began to gain on the American in World Series titles, winning five from 1954 to 1960. From 1947 through 1960, black players captured nine Rookie of the Year Awards, eight MVP Awards (all in the National League), four batting crowns (all in the National League), and five home run titles (four in the national league), and frequently appeared among the leaders in other categories. When given a chance, black players showed that they could, indeed, play major league ball.

Gradually, black players had been accepted by the fans, who saw how much they added to the game and realized that many of the old fears, such as the belief that blacks would take over the field and the stands once the door was opened, had not materialized. But black players still met with problems on and off the diamond. They were tormented by racial slurs from the stands and opposing dugouts, sometimes tagged harder than necessary on the base paths, were frequent targets of high-flying spikes and hard slides at second and third base, and were sent sprawling into the dirt by brushback pitches more often than white players were. Robinson was hit 9 times in 1947, a new record for a National League rookie, Luke Easter was hit 10 times in 1950, Minnie Minoso 65 times between 1951 and 1954, and Cincinnati Reds rookie Frank Robinson 20 times in 1956.

Off the field, the problems of black players began every season in spring training and in the exhibition games played in the South and West. Throughout the 1950s Jim Crow laws continued to bar them from the hotels, restaurants, rest rooms, swimming pools, golf courses, and other public and private facilities open to their white teammates. These abominable conditions followed them to some of the major league cities, particularly St. Louis, Cincinnati, and Baltimore. The teams themselves perpetuated prejudice and discrimination by giving black players side-by-side lockers or assigning them to room with one another, with black sportswriters, or with Latin players on road trips.

The integration of the minor leagues followed close on the heels of the opening up of the majors. Even more than Robinson and other black pioneers in the majors, black minor leaguers faced hostility on the field, from the stands, and from the communities they lived in while they were with the club. In the South this hostility actually increased in the second half of the fifties as whites closed ranks to fight back against the civil rights decisions of the U.S. Supreme Court. Curt Flood, who played in the Carolina League before coming up to the Cardinals in 1956, once said, "My teammates despised me and rejected me as subhuman. I would gladly have sent them all to hell."[2]

Second to the black revolution in its effect on postwar baseball was the continuing acceleration of the shift in strategy that began back in the 1920s with the powerful bat of Babe Ruth—a decreasing reliance on the bunt, sacrifice, hit and run, and stolen base and an increasing emphasis on putting men on base and knocking them in with the home run. While purists might long for the good old days of pitching duels and low scoring contests, the fans liked the "big bang" style with its emphasis on homers and high-scoring games.

Aided by the livelier baseball introduced during the Ruthian era, the annual total of homers in both leagues, which stood at 631 in 1920, increased to 1,350 in 1929 and to 1,571 in 1940. In the period from 1940 to 1949, the National League hit a total of 6,635 homers, an average of 1.07 per game, while the American League hit 6,323 for a 1.02 average. Then came the explosion: From 1950 to 1959, the sixteen major league clubs hit a combined total of 20,860 homers, an average of 1.69 homers per game. The peak year for the National League came in 1955 with 1,263 homers, while the American's best year was 1959, when it hit 1,091. The team record for a season was 221, tallied by the 1947 Giants and 1956 Reds.

Almost every team tried to load its lineup with as many sluggers as possible. To make it easier for them to hit homers, they brought the outfield fences in, moved home plate closer to the outfield fences, or put in outfield bleachers. In 1950, the rules committee aided the big bang style by narrowing the strike zone, which had previously been defined as from the top of the shoulder to the top of the knee, to the area from the armpits to the top of the knee. Players of the period were taller, heavier, and stronger than those of 20 years before, and many of them went to lighter and thinner bats, so they could get around quicker and with more power. And of course many hitters were swinging from the heels. They looked at the big salaries of the home run kings and decided that the maxim attributed to Ralph Kiner—"home run hitters drive Cadillacs, singles hitters drive Fords"—explained the major league salary schedule.

One inevitable consequence of the emphasis on the home run was a dramatic increase in the number of strikeouts. While in 1920 the 16 clubs recorded 7,288 strikeouts, the number rose to 9,056 in 1940, to 9,565 in 1950, and to 12,800 in 1960. From 1953 to 1960 alone, the number of strikeouts increased by 25 percent. Increasingly, the strikeout was becoming less of an embarrassment and more of an accepted price for increased home run production.

The big bang style naturally led to a decreasing emphasis on stolen bases. Why risk having a runner thrown out trying to steal when the lineup was loaded with men who could drive him in with the long ball? The annual number of stolen bases declined from 1700 in 1920 to 650 in 1950, and hovered in the 700–800 range for most of the fifties. Then in the late fifties, thanks partly to the influx of black players and of speedy players from Latin America, the stolen base began a slow revival. In 1960, when Luis Aparicio of the White Sox stole 51 and Maury Wills of the Dodgers stole 50, both leagues combined for 923. But for most teams in the fifties, the stolen base was not a big part of the game plan.

The postwar period also saw a steady drop in batting averages. During the late 1920s and 1930s, the batting averages of both leagues generally hovered in the .280 range. In 1930, amidst charges that the ball was too lively, 66 major leaguers hit .300 or better; the National League average was .303 and the American was .288. The number of players hitting .300 or better fell to 39 in 1939 and plummeted to 17 in 1952, when both leagues managed to come up with the same puny .253 average. In the American League, Washington, St. Louis, Detroit, and Chicago had no .300 hitters in 1952, while in the National League a similar drought existed in Boston, New York, and Pittsburgh. No wonder Tom Meany would write shortly before spring training began in 1953, "A .300 hitter in major league baseball has become just about as rare as an American bison. If the decline continues at its present rate, he soon will be as extinct as the dodo."[3]

Where had all the hits gone? Many blamed the decline on the growing emphasis on the home run, which was causing more strikeouts and long outs to the outfielders as hitters sacrificed average for power. Defensive players were also taking away hits with bigger and better gloves, and many managers were putting a greater emphasis on defense than ever before. But the most important factors were the steady rise of night ball and the dramatic improvement in pitching.

From just seven nocturnal contests in 1935, the number of night games grew steadily during the war years and mushroomed in the postwar era. In 1950 409 games were played at night, about a third of all games in both leagues. The number climbed to 560 in 1959, when the Los Angeles Dodgers played 63 of their 77 home games at night and scheduled only one weekday afternoon game. By then, weekday afternoon games in most major league cities were a thing of the past, with only the Cubs, Red Sox, Yankees, and Tigers scheduling a significant number of them.

Night ball had many advantages. It was a boon to attendance, since it was more convenient for the fans, and it also brought in more revenue from television. Television producers wanted more games scheduled at night so as to take advantage of the larger audiences available. Still, there were many who did not like it. Many players complained that the reduced vision at night gave the edge to the pitcher, that the cold and dampness that often accompanied night games in the early spring affected their arms and legs and would probably shorten their careers, and that night ball upset their normal sleeping and eating routine. In 1952, Dodger shortstop Pee Wee Reese told Roger Kahn that as a youngster he had dreamed about playing big league ball, "but there were never any night games in my dreams. I'm thirty-three years old and after a night game I'm all worked up—hell, you don't calm down right away—and I have trouble falling asleep and the next day I dread the game."[4]

Besides battling night games, postwar hitters were also facing better pitching than ever before. Pitchers on the average seemed to get taller, heavier, stronger, and faster, and received better training and coaching at all levels of organized ball. More and more teams began to employ pitching coaches who took over from the manager and veteran pitchers the burden of developing the pitching staff. Pitchers, managers, coaches, and statisticians studied hitters more thoroughly and systematically than ever before, compiling a book on their strengths and weaknesses under virtually all imaginable situations. Finally, pitching was improved by the increasing use of relief pitchers and the development of new pitches.

For most of professional baseball's history, starting pitchers had been expected to complete most of the games they pitched. This gave an advantage to the hitters. If they faced the same pitcher three or four times in a game it became easier to adjust to his speed and mixture of pitches, and as he tired in the late innings he was easier to hit. Relievers were used, but they were usually rookies or other young pitchers trying to break into the starting rotation, aging veterans near the end of their careers, injured pitchers trying to work themselves back into top form, or a starter called on to relieve in crucial games.

But with the coming of Joe Page and other relievers in the late forties, the specialized relief pitcher became more and more a part of the game. With the increasing emphasis on percentage baseball, and with so many players trying to knock the ball out of the park, no team could afford to be without several relievers. Thanks to the work of Page and other relievers, such as Jim Konstanty, Hoyt Wilhelm, Roy Face, Ryne Duren, and Larry Sherry, the complete game percentage, which had stood at close to 90 percent at the turn of the century and at 46 percent between 1924 and 1946, continued to decline, falling below 35 percent in the late fifties. While in 1946, National League starters finished 493 games and American League starters 561, by the late fifties neither league could boast as many as 400 complete games. As the complete game percentage declined, so did batting averages, as hitters often had to face two or more fresh arms in the course of nine innings.

Quite naturally, the number, prestige, and salary of relievers continued to increase. In 1960, the relief pitcher had become so much a part of the game that the *Sporting News* and other record keepers instituted a new statistic, the save, that joined all those other yardsticks used to measure baseball skill and justify big salaries.

Not only were hitters facing more pitchers, they were also having to try to hit a greater variety of pitches. Most of the pitches were really not new. In the late nineteenth and early twentieth centuries pitchers had learned to make a baseball do just about everything it was possible to make it do. But in the postwar period, pitchers were experimenting with more pitches and bringing into wider use pitches that had been emphasized infrequently in the past. They were also wetting and cutting the ball in every imaginable way to cause it to curve, drop, hop, and sail. In the constant battle for games, pennants, jobs, and money, most pitchers would do anything they could get away with to get that extra edge on the hitter.

The newest and most effective pitch in pitchers' arsenals was the slider, which had been used occasionally in the twenties and thirties but did not come into wide use until after World War II. A modified curve ball thrown off the middle and index fingers without the sharp wrist action used for the regular curve, the slider was thrown with the same motion as the fastball and looked like a fastball for most of its path to the hitter, then suddenly curved three to four inches as it crossed the plate. Casey Stengel called it "a dinky curve ball thrown like a fastball."[5] Chuck Dressen said, "A slider is either a fastball with a very small slow break or a curveball with a very small fast break."[6] Many players still called it by the disparaging name of the "nickel curve," inferior to the real curve.

The *Sporting News* estimated in 1952 that some 80 percent of major league pitchers were using the slider. It was a very effective pitch, especially in the hands of such masters as Bob Lemon of the Indians and Sal Maglie of the Giants. Ted Williams, who knew as much about hitting as anyone in either league, claimed in 1956 that "the slider has made pitching at least 25 percent better."[7]

One of the most widely used and controversial pitches of the postwar period was one that was not even supposed to exist — the spitter. Moistened with saliva, Vaseline, sweat, or some other slippery substance, the spitter was thrown like a fastball and looked like a fastball until it neared the plate, when it suddenly curved and dropped. It had been outlawed in 1920, but that had not kept it from being used, and in the postwar period some of the game's most respected pitchers — including Joe Page, Whitey Ford, Sal Maglie, Don Drysdale, Lew Burdette, and Preacher Roe — were suspected of throwing it. Of course, they all denied it, sometimes with a knowing grin. In the psychological warfare between the hitter and pitcher, many pitchers found it advantageous to let opposing hitters think they were using it so that they could cross them up with their standard legal pitches. "My best pitch," Lew Burdette was fond of saying, "is the one I don't throw."[8]

One of the few pitchers who did admit to throwing the wet one was Preacher Roe, but he did so only after he retired in 1954. Roe, who pitched for the Cardinals and the Pirates before coming to the Dodgers in 1948, publicly bared his well-known secret to Dick Young in a 1955 *Sports Illustrated* article, "The Outlawed Spitter Was My Money Pitch." Roe admitted, "I threw spitballs the whole time I was with the Dodgers." But he claimed, "I wasn't the only one that did it. There are still some guys wetting 'em up right now." While refusing to name the other spitball pitchers, he did say that Leo Durocher and Alvin Dark of the Giants often complained about his spitter but "they never hollered at me when I pitched against Sal Maglie."[9]

There were many, including National League umpire Jocko Conlan and Commissioner Ford Frick, who felt that the spitter should be legalized. They claimed that it was easier to control than the knuckler and therefore not as dangerous, that it was easier on the arm than the screwball and some other legal pitches, that it was being widely used anyway, and that umpires were reluctant to call it because it was so hard to detect and to prove. Casey Stengel and others also argued that it should be legalized because the hitter was getting all the breaks—the shorter fences, lively ball, smaller strike zone, and batting helmets that gave batters the courage to dig in at the plate. "It's high time something was done for the pitchers," Stengel argued in 1955. "Let them revive the spitter and help the pitchers make a living."[10]

But many baseball executives and players disagreed. General Manager Frank Lane of the White Sox contended that "the spitter would bring back low-scoring games and cobwebs would start forming around the turnstiles." Most hitters, pointing to the rising number of strikeouts and declining batting averages, agreed with Lane. "Haven't they got enough pitches already?" Jackie Jensen asked. "They might as well take our bats away."[11] But some, like Stan Musial, simply resigned themselves to facing the spitter and joked, as he once did when he was asked how he would hit against Roe, "I'll just hit the dry side of the ball."[12]

The postwar period saw a growing reliance on "percentage baseball," a strategy in which managers relied less and less on their own experience and intuition and more and more on thick data books compiled by the club statistician. One of the earliest was Allan Roth, hired by the Dodgers' Branch Rickey in the late 1940s. Roth traveled with the club, charted every game at home and away, and kept a 200-page notebook on the Dodgers' performance against the other seven teams. Along with other information, his notebooks revealed how all the Dodger hitters performed against all the opposing pitchers in all the parks under almost every imaginable circumstance, and how opposing hitters fared against Dodger pitchers. Dodger managers relied on this information for making dozens of decisions, including filling out the lineups, choosing relievers and pinch hitters, determining whether to steal a base, whether to walk or pitch to the hitter, what to throw to the hitter, and where to position defensive players.

Roth was confident about the reliability and usefulness of his statistics, but he cautioned that percentages were only probabilities, not infallible predictions. For such a quantified game, baseball could be awfully unpredictable. "Statistics are perfectly scientific," Roth told a reporter in 1957. "But baseball is a human game. In spite of all the figures in the world, it's the men who count. In Brooklyn, it's the manager and the players—and good new men coming up from the farm system—that win ball games."[13]

Still, percentage baseball paid off more often than not, and as the fifties proceeded managers turned to it more often. This trend in strategy was helping to end the long-standing practice of having managers serve as the third base coach while their team was at bat. As the *Sporting News* wrote in 1958, the manager "has to be in the dugout to keep pace with the complicated games we have these days. There are righty-lefty switches, spitball observers, jammed bullpens, starting players, middle-distance players, lockup players, pension consideration, sympathy, understanding and above all, psychology." More and more, the newspaper concluded, "The trend seems to be to regard managing as a huge executive job, like U.S. Steel."[14]

Major league baseball was not only changing, it was also in trouble. As an article in the *Sporting News* in July of 1952 said, "Baseball . . . no longer holds a near monopoly on the leisure-time interest of the nation's sports followers. On the contrary, the National Pastime seems to be fighting a losing battle against the noisy and colorful claim for attention sounded by everything from college football to cowboy movies on television."[15]

Attendance figures for the fifties clearly showed that something was wrong. Major league attendance had nearly doubled between 1945 and 1948, when it reached a high of 20.9 million. But in 1949 it dipped slightly, to 20.2 million, and then rapidly declined to a low of 14.4 million in 1953, a drop of 6.5 million in just five years. Then, primarily because of the movement of franchises to cities with fans hungry for baseball, it began a gradual rise, finally getting back to 19.9 million by 1960. But not until 1962, when the expansion to 20 teams helped raise attendance to 21.4 million, did it pass the 1948 mark. Ironically, one of the things that helped major league attendance — the movement of franchises into new markets — only served to hurt the minor league teams in these new areas by robbing them of fans.

In the minors, the attendance declines were catastrophic. Minor league baseball had boomed after the war, reaching a peak in 1949 of 59 leagues, 464 teams, and 42 million in attendance. But then the decline came, and it came quickly and dramatically. By 1953, attendance had dropped to 22 million fans spread over 38 leagues and 284 teams, and even the surviving teams were facing great problems. On May 28, 1953, a game in the Mountain State League between Knoxville and Morristown was forfeited by the host Knoxville team because it could not come up with enough money to buy the dozen balls league rules required to begin a game. By 1960, the minors were down to 22 leagues and just under 11 million in attendance. The decline continued into the 1960s.[16]

In searching for the causes of the disappearing fans, the first culprit many pointed to was television, and it certainly played a major role. The marriage between television and baseball began early. The first sporting event ever shown on television was a baseball game between Columbia and Princeton on May 17, 1939, before commercial television programming even began. Played at Columbia's Baker Field in New York, the game was filmed by one camera, transmitted to the RCA Building, and telecast over NBC's experimental television station W2XBS.

Only a few hundred people witnessed this historic telecast, but one of those who did, Orrin E. Dunlap, Jr., the media critic for the *New York Times*, was not impressed. "Seldom are more than three players seen at one time," he complained, and argued that the fan did not get the real flavor of the game—the sun, the noise, the fans' chatter and boos, the hot dogs and peanuts and scoreboards, the smells, the grass, the dust, and all the other elements of the outdoor game. "Television is no substitute for being in the bleachers," he concluded, and mused that "to sit for two hours in a darkened room on a beautiful sunny day in May to watch a baseball game on a miniature screen stirs thoughts on the future of television in sports."[17]

Dunlap did not think that televised sports had much of a future, but closer to the mark in reading their destiny was *Life* magazine, which predicted in June of 1939 that "within ten years an audience of 10,000,000 sitting at home or in the movie theaters will see the World Series or the Rose Bowl game. . . . Thousands of men and women who have never seen a big-time sports event will watch the moving shadows on the television screen and become excited fans."[18]

In spite of technical problems and unfriendly critics, NBC's experimental station covered several other sporting events in 1939 and 1940, including the first telecast of a major league baseball game, an August 26, 1939, contest between the Cincinnati Reds and Brooklyn Dodgers. But the outbreak of the war virtually halted the development of this still experimental electronic wonder.

At war's end television faced many artistic and technical problems, but these were quickly overcome and the new electronic eye transformed the landscape of American society. Only a few thousand sets existed in 1945, but annual sales jumped to over seven million by 1950 and would average between five and seven million each year for the rest of the decade. By 1960, there were 562 stations and some 46 million households owned at least one set. In these 15 years there had also been dramatic technological and economic advances: the available screen sizes had grown from 12 to 21 inches, portable sets had been perfected, color sets were introduced, the completion of the coaxial cable made possible coast-to-coast live transmission, videotape tape had been invented, and prices had come down from the $500 to $700 range of the mid–1940s to around $200 for a black and white set in the mid–1950s.

In the early years televised baseball faced some difficult technical problems. Unlike basketball, football, and other sports which were staged on a relatively small playing area and generally had the offense going in a predictable direction, the action in a baseball game unfolded simultaneously from several directions at once. Cameras especially had trouble showing double plays, pickoff plays, the hit and run, balls hit to the wrong field, and the actions of the baserunners and defense on an extra base hit. No wonder many critics argued that the only place to see a baseball game was in the stands.

But gradually televised baseball improved in versatility and quality. The picture got clearer and bigger, and more cameras were added, usually at least three, with one positioned behind home plate, one to cover the infield, and another to capture the outfield action. Sometimes a fourth and fifth camera would be used for human interest shots in the dugouts and stands.

As the postwar seasons unfolded, the number of games available to armchair fans across the country increased dramatically. As early as 1946, the New York Yankees had become the first major league team to sell television rights to their games. By 1955, all the major league teams except the Braves, Pirates, Indians, and Athletics were televising some home games, and the Dodgers, Giants, Cubs, and Yankees were televising all their contests. ABC's "Game of the Week," the first national telecast of regular season games, began in 1953, with Dizzy Dean as the announcer. The show switched to CBS in 1955, and by 1958 Dean and Buddy Blattner were doing a game on both Saturday and Sunday. Rival NBC was also telecasting a weekly game hosted by Leo Durocher and Lindsey Nelson. By 1960, the three major networks had scheduled 123 regular season games, the All-Star Game, and the World Series, while all the major league clubs except the Giants and the Braves had scheduled a total of 687 games to local fans.

The club owners reaped huge profits from the sale of television rights. In 1952 the 16 major league teams received a total of $4 million in income from television and radio, and this figure jumped to $7 million in 1956 and kept climbing. In 1957, NBC and Gillette made sports history by signing a pact giving major league baseball $16.3 million for the rights to broadcast the World Series and All-Star Games for the next five years. In April of 1960, 29 sponsors agreed to pay $39.6 million for telecasts of major league games that year. The biggest financial windfall went to the New York Yankees, who received $900,000 in return for the rights to televise all 77 home games plus 47 road games. Televised baseball had come a long way from the humble beginnings of the late forties.

Fear of provoking antitrust action from Congress or the Supreme Court kept the baseball owners from making package deals with the networks for the televising of regular games that would have allowed all clubs to share equally in the revenues from nationally televised games. This forced the networks to negotiate contracts with the individual owners and practically guaranteed that the clubs in the larger cities with their larger audiences would demand and receive higher revenues than those in smaller ones. While professional football signed lucrative package deals early in the decade, major league baseball delayed signing a national package for regular season games until Congress passed the Sports Broadcasting Act in

1961. The act exempted professional sports from antitrust laws by allowing them to negotiate package deals with television networks and allowed baseball to sign a national contract.

⤙ The enormous success of television damaged, but did not destroy, the continuing popularity of radio broadcasts of major league games. Announcers like Russ Hodges of the Giants, Harry Caray and Gabby Street of the Cardinals, Jack Brickhouse and Harry Creighton of the Cubs, Jimmy Dudley of the Indians, Curt Gowdy of the Red Sox, Bob Prince of the Pirates, and others still enjoyed a wide following.

But the most popular radio broadcast in the 1950s was the Mutual Broadcast System's "Game of the Day," which made its debut in the spring of 1950 as the first live national broadcast of regular season games. Beginning with 312 affiliates, by 1955 it had grown to over 500 affiliates, including the Voice of America and the Armed Forces Radio Network. Broadcaster Al Helfer, a big man with a deep, homey voice, gave his millions of fans a constant stream of casual chatter about the personal lives of the players as well as a colorful play-by-play account of the games. After the grind of frequent travel led Helfer to retire in 1954, a series of announcers, from ex-players Mel Ott and Bob Feller to veteran announcers like Van Patrick, took over the show. It remained popular throughout the decade, but in 1960 it folded, primarily because of the competition from televised games and the increasing number of night games.

Whatever its other effects, television was undoubtedly good for the fans. Until the advent of television, most fans never saw a major league baseball game. Their contact with the big leagues was limited to radio broadcasts, news clips in movie theaters, newspapers, and magazines. But then, very quickly, television brought the national pastime to fans all across the country. Along with the integration of major league clubs and the movement of franchises after 1953, television helped to nationalize the game, enhance the enjoyment of existing fans, and create millions of new ones. It brought baseball into the living room, and for many the sofa or easy chair did indeed become the best seat in the house.

But then there were the negative aspects, particularly its impact upon attendance. Some pointed out that while radio had helped to promote sports and bring in new fans, television was saturating the fans with games and causing them to stay away from the parks. Frank Shaughnessy, president of the International League, claimed in 1949 that "radio stimulates curiosity. Television satisfies it."[19] The decline of major and minor league attendance coincided with the expansion of televised games, and many were quick to point an accusing finger at television.

The effect of television on major league attendance was difficult to measure. Some public opinion surveys by national magazines suggested that it was not televised ball games that kept people away from the parks.

Instead, it was the enormous appeal of other television shows, the competition from other leisure activities, the traffic and parking problems involved in going to a game, and the conditions of the parks and their surrounding neighborhoods. Some claimed that television was actually helping major league baseball by creating new fans and that television revenues helped the clubs survive the economic losses brought by declining ticket and concession sales.

The minor leagues were another matter. They were definitely hurt by the telecasting of major league games in their marketing area, especially on weekends, for weekend games were the biggest money-makers for minor league teams. One Washington Senators official, C. Leo DeOrsey, said in 1958 that weekend telecasts, especially the Sunday games, were "the time bomb that could blast minor league baseball into eternity." Lambasting "the greedy ways of major league baseball," he predicted that "if they persist, the day will come when baseball won't need large stadiums, because nobody will be at the game except the players."[20] Many fans would not come out and pay to see minor league players when they could watch Mickey Mantle, Stan Musial, and Willie Mays for free on their own televisions.

Greed and fear of Congressional and judicial antitrust action prevented major league owners and the commissioner from effectively dealing with television's devastating effect on the minor leagues. In 1940, organized baseball had implemented the policy of blacking out radio broadcasts of major league games in markets with minor league teams. This policy was extended to television broadcasts after the war. But in 1951, with both the Congress and the Supreme Court examining baseball's reserve clause and its exemption from antitrust legislation, baseball owners stopped the blackouts, fearing that Congress and the courts might find them a violation of antitrust laws and move to end baseball's unique exemption from them.

In the second half of the 1950s, major league owners did make feeble attempts to offset television's devastating impact on minor league attendance and revenues. In the fall of 1956, the owners agreed to establish a "stabilization fund" of $500,000 to help the minor leagues. Three years later, the owners introduced a new plan that would provide for a $1 million fund to aid in the development of minor league players and to promote the minor leagues. These plans provided some relief, but they did not get at the basic problems and did not halt the downward spiral of the minors.

Important as it was, television was not the only cause of professional baseball's problems. Baseball in the prosperous fifties was in competition with many other forms of entertainment — movies, college and professional football and basketball, and professional ice hockey, boxing, wrestling, and stock car racing. The growth of an automobile culture, increased leisure time, and more discretionary income were opening up a new world of recreational activities—fishing, boating, golfing, tennis, softball, hunting, bowling, water skiing, bicycling, and visiting the coast, mountains, or national parks. For those wanting to keep up with their favorite baseball team while they enjoyed these pursuits, there was always television and portable radios.

Baseball was hurt by the population shifts of the postwar years. The rapid growth of suburbia was causing a decline of the inner cities where most of the major league parks were located. When suburbanites left their job in the city at the end of the day, they were not inclined to return at night to see a big league ball game. If they wanted to watch a ball game, they could often see it in the comfort of their own living room. Why drive back to the city, fighting the crowded expressways and parking lots?

The conditions at the games themselves also kept fans away from the park. Most of the major league parks had been built between 1900 and World War I. Yankee Stadium was completed in 1923, the latest stadium in the majors. Not until the Braves moved to Milwaukee County Stadium in 1953 was there a new major league facility. The owners seemed to have forgotten about the comfort of the fans, expecting them to show up in spite of traffic and parking problems, dirty seats and rest rooms, and long lines and high prices at the concession stands. In 1956 one sportswriter described Pittsburgh's Forbes Field (built in 1913) as a "museum decorated with pigeon droppings," while in 1957 another called the Polo Grounds (built in 1891) an"antiquated museum."[21]

If the major league parks were in trouble, the minor leagues were facing disaster with their old and shabby parks, inadequate parking lots, rocky playing fields, poor lighting, dirty or broken seats, cold food and hot soft drinks, and filthy rest rooms. Al Schacht, the "Clown Prince of Baseball," who had been performing his pantomime comedy act in minor league parks across the country since 1937, said in 1954 that the minors were "fifty years behind the times" and that "the antiquated business methods, antiquated facilities and the wrong attitudes of the club owners would have led them into their present predicament even if television had never been invented."[22]

Most baseball owners at all levels were slow to realize that the game no longer had a monopoly on fans' leisure time. Many owners operated their clubs as they always had, opening the ticket booths and gates and expecting the fans to file in. Few realized the importance of aggressive marketing at a time when television and so many other amusements were actively seeking the entertainment dollars of affluent Americans. In the age of "togetherness," more and more people were seeking entertainment that the whole family could enjoy together. Bill Veeck was almost alone in realizing that baseball had to be promoted, like any other entertainment, but for his efforts he was viewed as a maverick and treated as an outsider.

There were some who felt that the game on the field had changed for the worse, and that this was what was helping to keep the fans away. Some, like Ty Cobb, whose complaints about modern players had caused such a stir in 1952, claimed that the emphasis on "the stand-around-and-wait-for-a-homer" style of play was making the game boring, but probably an equal number claimed that the homer actually made it exciting and that it was what people came to see. Some critics also lambasted the trend toward percentage baseball, which was bringing more trips to the mound by catchers and managers, more stalling while bullpen pitchers completed their warm-ups, more long walks from the bullpen to the mound, more warm-up tosses, more pinch hitters limbering up, and more conferences on the field, all while the fans sat waiting for something to happen. There were many who would have agreed with the *New York Times Magazine*'s assertion in 1950 that "a good half of the league games are prolonged, dreary bores."[23]

Nor surprisingly, the games were getting longer. Studies revealed that the length of the average game increased from an average of 2 hours and 23 minutes in 1951 to 2 hours and 38 minutes in 1960. The longest games, as might be expected, were the dogfights between the Giants and the Dodgers. In the early fifties, the typical contest between these two rivals lasted 2 hours and 51 minutes in Ebbets Field and 3 hours and 2 minutes in the Polo Grounds.

The length of baseball games did not reveal how much actual playing time was involved in a typical game. In most contests, the ball was in play less than half the time. The rest was taken up by players changing sides between innings, the pitchers picking up the resin bag or talking with their catchers, hitters walking up to the plate and stepping in and out of the box, umpires examining the ball or sweeping the plate, relief pitchers walking in from the bullpen and taking their warm-ups, and similar undramatic moments. In 1956 reporter Joe Collier of the *Cleveland Press* began to take a stopwatch to games, and he found the problem to be centered in the pitcher's box. In a single 2 hour and 5 minute game, the ball was in the pitcher's hand for 61 minutes. In another game lasting 3 hours and 16 minutes, the pitcher held the ball for 2 hours and 1 minute, almost two-thirds of the game.[24]

The slow pace of baseball games gave ammunition to those critics who felt that baseball was losing its relevance in the fast-changing world of the 1950s. In 1959, Robert Daley wrote in the *New York Times Magazine* that baseball was a game for a more pastoral time and that it was too tame for the complex and dangerous world of the 1950s. "The pitcher-batter conflict is, in this age of hydrogen bombs, and probes to the moon, no longer gripping enough," he wrote. "We long to be absorbed by the spectacle.... We want, in America, lots to watch ... not nine men standing idle while the pitcher pitches or the batter bats." This desire for action, he felt, explained the rise of professional football, "which is gaining fans even faster than baseball is losing them."[25]

There were many proposals for speeding up baseball games and making them more dramatic. Most came from journalists rather than from the players, managers, and other members of the baseball establishment. Some proposed that the time-consuming intentional walk be abolished or modified, perhaps giving two bases for it so as to discourage its use or just awarding the batter first base without the pitcher taking the time to throw four wide ones to the catcher. Others claimed that the game could be improved by permitting the use of a designated hitter for the pitcher, allowing players who had been taken out of the game to come back in after a lapse of one inning, adopting rules forcing the pitcher to stop wasting so much time between pitches, and shortening the 154-game season to make each individual game more significant.

Even the politicians got into the argument over how to fix baseball. In 1957 U.S. Representative Kenneth B. Keating suggested that the batter be given four strikes. This, he felt, would make for a more offensive game because the batter would have one more chance to hit the ball. According to Keating, "The thing that makes an exciting game is people running around the bases, double plays and home runs, lots of action."[26]

But baseball was a traditional and conservative game, and owners, managers, and players were reluctant to tamper with its time-honored customs and rules. The decade would end without any basic modifications in the way the game was played.

There were some who felt that baseball was declining because the players themselves were changing. In contrast to the players of the prewar game, they enjoyed better pay, pensions, air conditioned trains, planes, padded outfield walls, outfield warning tracks, batting helmets, better coaching, and more attention from team trainers and physicians. These and other amenities, it was said, were making players more mercenary, less competitive, and less colorful than their predecessors.

As early as the fall of 1950, Eddie Collins, the vice-president of the Boston Red Sox and a former player with the Philadelphia Athletics and Chicago White Sox, told sportswriter John Kelso, "The big difference between ballplayers today and those of other days is their attitude. Players today are businessmen first and ballplayers second. . . . They're mercenary now."[27] Many agreed with him, including respected baseball writer Roger Angell, who wrote in 1954 that except for a few standouts like Ted Williams, Bob Feller, and Stan Musial, baseball did not have the great stars and drawing cards of the past. "Better pay and working conditions have made big-leaguers prosperous and respectable," Angell wrote. He felt that the fan "longs for the screwballs—the weird and hilarious assortment of real eccentrics and simple extroverts who used to be drawn to the game and who are the subjects of most of the baseball yarns which the fan treasures."[28]

One of the most sweeping condemnations of the players of the fifties came from journalist Gay Talese in a 1958 article in the *New York Times Magazine*. In "Gray-Flannel-Suit Men at Bat," Talese charged that "baseball has been infiltrated by gentlemanly athletes." These players "would not think of tripping their mothers, even if Mom were rounding third on the way home with the winning run." Talese felt that players had become "organization men," wanting security, high salaries, and enough longevity to qualify for a pension. "What has happened," he said, "is a standardization of players.... Baseball has lost its 'characters,' its nitwits, its boneheads and, what's worse, its unpredictability and sense of humor."[29]

Ammunition for critics like Talese was provided by the public statements of some of the decade's best ballplayers. In 1956, Duke Snider collaborated with Roger Kahn for an article in *Collier's* entitled, "I Play Baseball for Money—Not Fun." In the article, the 29-year-old Dodger outfielder expressed what many other players thought but rarely voiced to anyone outside the baseball fraternity. "The truth is that life in the major leagues is far from a picnic," he said. "I'm explaining, not complaining, but believe me, even though deep down I know it isn't true, I feel that I'd be just as happy if I never played another baseball game again."[30]

Snider went on to grumble about having to endure 25 nights a year on trains, spending many lonely nights in hotel rooms, trying to work sleeping and eating into a schedule that mixed night games and afternoon games, being chewed out by managers in front of thousands of people, having fans throw beer cans and other dangerous objects at him when he was at his outfield post, having to listen to the boos of fans, and having to read the criticism of sportswriters "who know as much about baseball as my four-year-old daughter." But most of all, there was the problem of being away from his wife and children for so many days each year. Professional baseball, he said, was "like anything else. From the outside it looks great, and when you're a kid dreaming, it looks like a helluva dream. Then you grow up, you're in the major leagues and all of a sudden baseball isn't so great—and sometimes it can be a nightmare."[31]

So why did he continue to play? For the money. "With endorsements, fees, my salary and my winning World Series share, I earned about $50,000 last season. You can put up with a lot for that kind of money. I did," he wrote. For financial reasons, he hoped to play for five more years before retiring to a farm he had bought in southern California. "I'm looking forward to the day when baseball will allow me to settle down to raising avocados in the California sunshine,"[32] he concluded.

Snider's article naturally caused quite a stir in a nation that believed that baseball players led glamourous lives. Red Smith was one of several reporters who took him to task for complaining about life in the major leagues. Smith argued that most people in the country had hard jobs with low or moderate pay, whereas Snider rode the best trains, stayed in the best hotels, ate in the best restaurants, had five months vacation, and could look forward to retiring in his mid–thirties. "Chances are he hasn't more than the foggiest notion of how the other 99.99 percent lives," Smith wrote. "Somebody should tell him, gently."[33]

But Snider's complaints were shared by many players. One was Jackie Jensen, the "Golden Boy" athlete who won All-American football honors at the University of California before playing with the Yankees, Senators, and Red Sox. In 1958 he hit 35 homers, led the American League in RBIs with 122, and won the MVP Award, but in the spring of 1959 he shocked many fans with an article written with Al Hirshberg for the *Saturday Evening Post* entitled, "My Ambition Is To Quit." Jensen repeated many of the complaints made by Snider while adding that he had developed a phobia about airplanes in 1955 after experiencing a near-accident on a flight. He said that he was glad he had had such a good season in 1958, for it brought him a major salary increase and "the more money I get, the sooner I can quit." He admitted that he was not "consumed by a passion for the game, as many men are," and that "it's the money—and nothing but the money—that keeps me in baseball today."[34] Fear of flying and the desire to spend more time with his family led him to sit out the 1960 season. He returned in 1961 for one more year before retiring for good at the age of 34.

While most were not as vocal as Snider or Jensen, the players of the fifties were more concerned with off-field matters than players of earlier generations. This added to the problems of the club owners. Although the Mexican League, Danny Gardella, and unionizers like Robert Murphy were now, for most owners, bad memories from the forties, they were still facing several challenges to their monopolistic practices. Some of them came from the players themselves, while others came from Congress and the federal courts. Baseball's legal status was a difficult issue, for as Cubs' owner Philip K. Wrigley was fond of saying, baseball was unique—it was "too much of a sport to be a business and too much of a business to be a sport."[35]

With the passing of commissioner Landis in 1944, the postwar owners held more power than ever before. Under Happy Chandler and Ford Frick, they jealously guarded their territory, their players, the reserve clause, and their monopoly of the game. While some of them, such as Horace Stoneham, were knowledgeable baseball men who still derived much or all of their income from their baseball club, more and more of them had bought baseball clubs as business investments, ostentatious displays of wealth, toys that provided psychic income, or as tax write-offs. A 1951 Congressional investigation revealed that the owners of 10 of the 16 clubs derived their primary income from business interests outside of baseball. This trend would continue in the 1950s as some of the old families—such as the Macks, Briggses, and Comiskeys—sold out to wealthy syndicates. While the owners jealously guarded their financial records and employed complex accounting methods to hide their true profits from their players, the public, and the Internal Revenue Service, several studies of major league teams in the fifties showed that most owners received a good return on their investments.

But their powers and practices were coming under increasing scrutiny. In 1951, with eight antitrust cases pending against baseball, the House Judiciary Committee's Subcommittee on Monopoly Power, chaired by Emanuel Celler, a Democrat from Brooklyn and a staunch baseball fan, began to examine baseball's special exemption from the antitrust laws. Celler and most of the committee members were sympathetic to baseball's unique status. So were most of the current and former baseball players called as witnesses before the committee. Ty Cobb strongly defended the reserve clause and claimed that baseball was "a clean game and not an industry."[36] But the wife of one unhappy minor league player did write Celler a letter arguing that the reserve clause was dooming her husband to a life in the minors, because even though there was no place for him on the parent club, he could not sign with another team that could bring him up to the majors. "If baseball is not a business," she asked, "why does every team have a business manager?"[37]

Her logic failed to sway the subcommittee. Although its investigation revealed that major league baseball did have a monopoly over its markets and workers and was indeed big business—with revenues of $32 million and expenses of $25.5 million—the subcommittee refused to tamper with the status quo. In a 1,643-page report released on May 23, 1952, it declared that since the courts had previously (1922) upheld the constitutionally of the reserve clause on the grounds that baseball was a sport and not a business, "legislation is not necessary until the reasonableness of the reserve rules has been tested by the courts." The report also agreed that "professional baseball could not operate successfully and profitably without some form of a reserve clause," and argued that the baseball establishment itself, not Congress, should make any adjustment to the reserve clause that the times required.[38] Once again, Congress had treated baseball as a unique industry, allowing it to escape restrictive legislation, and thrown the ball back to the courts and baseball itself.

A year later, the reserve clause was back in the news, and this time it was in the courts. George Toolson, a pitcher in the New York Yankee farm system, sued his parent club, alleging that the reserve clause in his contract violated the Sherman Act and other antitrust laws. The case eventually wound up in the Supreme Court, now headed by new Chief Justice Earl

Warren. By a 7–2 vote on November 9, 1953, the Warren Court upheld the 1922 court case exempting baseball from federal antitrust laws and ruled that baseball could not be sued in the courts as an illegal monopoly and that the reserve clause was still legal and binding. The court reiterated that Congress had exempted baseball from the antitrust laws for 30 years, that Congress had considered changing the laws but never had, and that if the antitrust laws were to be applied it was the place of Congress to do it.[39] Toolson lost his case. Once again the Supreme Court had thrown the issue back in Congress's lap. The *Sporting News* heralded the decision with the headline "O.B. Wins the 'Big One!'" "From Commissioner Ford Frick down, baseball men everywhere were jubilant over the reaffirmation of the historic 1922 opinion," the paper said. Frick applauded the decision and promised that baseball would attack its major problems.[40] The antitrust question would come up later in the decade, but Congress and the Supreme Court would still refuse to tamper with the reserve clause and other aspects of organized baseball's monopoly.

In the meantime, the players moved ahead to try to improve their economic and legal status. In August of 1953, Ralph Kiner and Allie Reynolds, the two player representatives on major league baseball's Executive Council, hired a New York lawyer, J. Norman Lewis, to assist them in negotiations with club owners. Kiner, Reynolds, and many other players were especially concerned about the solvency and administration of the pension fund and about the possibility that the owners might try to tamper with it or even try to abolish it. Kiner and Reynolds were careful to emphasize that they were not trying to promote an adversarial relationship with the owners. "We didn't intend this to be a slap at Commissioner Frick's office or the owners," Reynolds said, "but we were in dire need of legal advice. . . . We hope there will be no animosity and we don't expect any from the owners. Our main aim is to improve the relationship between the players and the owners." Kiner was quick to add, "We are still the representatives; he's only a legal advisor."[41]

While many players applauded the hiring of a lawyer, others were afraid that it could possibly backfire by irritating the club owners and damaging any sentiment that they might have for making concessions to the players. Naturally, most baseball officials were bitterly opposed to bringing in an outsider to serve as an intermediary between the players and the owners. National League President Warren Giles claimed, "The players can do more for themselves than any outside representative, no matter how able that outsider may be." Clark Griffith argued that the players had already wrangled "more concessions from the club owners than we can afford and more than I think they should have. I don't see why they should want to get a lawyer mixed up in it who, to show that he is earning his salary, would 'ball' the whole thing up."[42]

Not surprisingly, club owners tried to avoid dealing with Lewis, refusing to invite him to a club owners' meeting in August of 1953 or to winter meetings in Atlanta in December. When Frick would not allow Lewis into the Atlanta meetings, the 16 player delegates also refused to attend. On July 22, 1954, during the All-Star Game break, the player delegates met in Cleveland and voted to form the Major League Baseball Players Association (MLBPA) and to retain Lewis as their legal counsel. Each club would elect one representative to the association, and these 16 men would choose a delegate from each league to meet with the owners. The players, their representatives, and Lewis all claimed that this was a fraternal organization and not a union. But most owners feared that it would indeed develop into a union and constitute a real threat to their authority and control over club operations and baseball in general.

Whether they liked it or not, the owners held formal and informal discussions with Lewis after the formation of the MLBPA. At a meeting on July 26, 1954, the owners and players agreed on several issues that Lewis helped to draw up and negotiate. The pension plan was revised, providing for the establishment by 1957 of a four-man pension committee and for a special fund drawn from 60 percent of the net revenues from the All-Star Games and from the receipts from the television and radio rights to the World Series. Lewis's efforts also helped bring about the increase in the minimum salary to $6,000.

In 1956, the MLBPA elected Bob Feller as its first president. Like most other players, he denied that the MLBPA was a union. "You cannot carry collective bargaining into baseball," he said.[43] For the rest of the fifties the association did operate primarily as a fraternal organization. It did not push for a major modification of the reserve clause, but instead concentrated on such bread and butter reforms as improvements in the pension fund and increases in the minimum salary. It would not change its stance until 1966, when it chose Marvin Miller as its first permanent executive director, inaugurating a new era of bitter battles over collective bargaining, the reserve clause, salary arbitration, and other matters. Until then, the owners would continue to run the game with little interference from the players.

13. The Year the Yankees Lost the Pennant (1954)

One of the most popular novels of 1954 was Douglass Wallop's *The Year the Yankees Lost the Pennant*. A selection of the Book of the Month Club, it was a lighthearted story about a middle-aged real estate salesman and Washington Senators fan, Joe Boyd, who sells his soul to the devil so that he can become Joe Hardy, a 22-year-old long-ball hitter who leads the lowly Senators to the pennant over the mighty New York Yankees. The popularity of this modern retelling of the Doctor Faustus legend was undoubtedly partly due to its appeal to the many Yankee haters across the nation, who were tired of seeing Casey Stengel's club take the pennant and the World Series year after year.

Stengel often lashed out at the anti–Yankee feelings around the country and especially around the American League. Shortly before the 1954 season began, he responded to the grumbles of some of the rest of the American League teams by asking, "Why do they knock us? Don't they want us to win the World Series for them? They ain't another damned club in the league that could win the World Series." And later in the season, bristling at the continuing anti–Yankee sentiments his team was seeing in opposing ballparks and in the press, he snapped, "What do they want us to do, try to lose? Try to give it away?"[1] His angry outbursts did nothing to reduce the widespread dislike of the Yankees, who were guilty of playing with the confidence, and even arrogance, that came with such unparalleled success. But 1954 would be different. For the first time since 1948, Stengel's team would, indeed, lose the pennant.

The new season saw the major league teams traveling by air more than ever before. During spring training, Branch Rickey announced that the Pirates had chartered a 50-passenger plane from Capital Airlines, the company that had provided flights for 13 major league teams in 1953, and that his club would become the first to travel almost entirely by plane during the upcoming season. The Pirates would use train travel only when commuting between New York and Philadelphia and between Chicago and Milwaukee — short trips that took only about 90 minutes by rail. By turning to air travel, the longest trip the Pirates would have to make would be the

3 ½ -hour flight between New York and St. Louis, which normally took close to 21 hours by rail. The Pirates could fly from Pittsburgh to any other league city in two hours or less.

The Pittsburgh example would be followed by other clubs as the decade wore on. Most owners felt that air travel was safe enough to stop worrying about losing an entire team in a crash, and the advantages were obvious. It saved time, was less tiring, and provided for easier scheduling of games, meals, and sleeping. Players could eat some meals on the plane and sleep at home or in hotel rooms at night rather than on bumpy trains. Still, the gradual passing of rail travel would have its negative aspects. As Eddie Brannick, the traveling secretary of the Giants, said in 1956, "You never forget those long, pleasant evenings and those hours of relaxation in the diners and club cars. We made a lot of friends that way.... But for a lot of reasons it is better for us now to go by plane."[2]

Most players adjusted to plane travel, but many never liked it and tried to avoid it if they could. The Yankees, still remembering some unpleasant experiences from MacPhail's attempts to transport the team by plane in 1946, stuck to the rails. Some players on other teams continued to drive their personal automobiles or take a train if the travel time between games allowed them to catch up with the rest of the team. This would become impossible, of course, when the Dodgers and Giants moved to California. Fear of plane travel forced Don Newcombe to undergo hypnosis in order to overcome it, and led others, such as Jackie Jensen of the Red Sox, to retire early.

The 1954 campaign would be played under two new rule changes. Most hitters favored the one stipulating that a player who drove in a run with a sacrifice fly would not be charged with a time at bat, but they did not like the one requiring the defensive players to take their gloves off the field when they went in to bat. The rules committee claimed that the traditional practice of leaving the gloves near the defensive spot could be a hazard to the other team's defensive players and that a game might be affected by a batted ball hitting a glove. Most owners, managers, and players claimed that the rule was unnecessary and that it would delay the game when players who had been stranded on base had to go back to the dugout to get their gloves. Clark Griffith said that he had been connected with baseball since 1887, "and only once have I seen a batted ball hit a glove lying out there. And that time it didn't affect the play. The ball was a single and ended up a single."[3] The rule caused a great deal of grumbling and threats to ignore it, but the players eventually learned to live with it.

On April 13, President Eisenhower demonstrated that he had his baseball, golf, and politics in proper perspective by showing up at Griffith Stadium to inaugurate the new season. This time he stayed the entire game, and seemed to enjoy watching the home team beat the Yankees in the tenth inning on a two-run homer by Mickey Vernon. As the first baseman made his way back to the dugout, Eisenhower left his seat and went down to the railing along the field to shake his hand.

As the season began the nation seemed to be getting back to normal as the Korean War faded from the headlines. The end of the war in 1953 had been good news for baseball; it brought the rapid return of many major leaguers to the American diamonds. On opening day, only 10 major leaguers were still in the military, with Yankee infielder Bobby Brown and Pirate shortstop Dick Groat being the best known. The Cold War draft would continue to take young players from their teams, but the worst days were over.

The Yankees were expected to waltz to their sixth straight pennant, but the first part of the season saw a tight three-way battle between them, the White Sox, and the Indians. Then, to almost everybody's surprise, Al Lopez's Tribe took over the top spot on May 16 during an 11-game winning streak. Except for a few days in June when the White Sox grabbed the top rung, the Indians held the lead for the rest of the season. The Yankees mounted a 10-game winning streak to pull to within 2½ games on August 20, but then they made a disastrous trip to Boston, where they lost three in a row. Meanwhile the red-hot Indians continued to roll, winning 26 games while losing only 6 in August to tie a major league record for the most victories in one month.

On September 8 the Indians mounted still another winning streak, this one of 11 consecutive games. On Sunday, September 12, enjoying a 6½-game margin over the Bronx Bombers, the Indians hosted Stengel's team for a crucial doubleheader in Cleveland Municipal Stadium before 86,563 fans, the largest crowd ever to watch a major league game up until this time. While consuming 100,000 hot dogs, 85,000 cans of beer, and record amounts of soft drinks, popcorn, and peanuts, they watched their favorites take both contests, 4–1 and 3–2, to extend their lead to 8½ games. "This was the way we wanted it," Lopez told reporters after the second game. "We wanted to beat the Yankees ourselves. This was the way we wanted to win the pennant."[4] Four days later, the Indians clinched the flag when Early Wynn defeated the Detroit Tigers 3–2. The Indians went on to finish the season with 111 victories, topping by one the previous American League record set by the 1927 Yankees.

In was an incredible year for the Indians, who had been relegated to third place by most of the preseason predictors. Widely regarded as also-rans, they had finished in second place three consecutive years under Lopez, who took the reins from Lou Boudreau after the 1950 season. Lopez, who would finish in second 10 times during his 17-year managerial career with the Indians and White Sox, had acquired a lot of baseball savvy crouching behind the plate for the Dodgers, Braves, Pirates, and Indians. He knew how to handle pitchers, and in 1954 he had the best pitching staff in either league.

His staff was led by the "Big Three" — Early Wynn, Mike Garcia, and Bob Lemon, all right-handers. Wynn was a ruthless power pitcher who felt that he had the right to knock down any player, especially if he crowded the plate or made a habit of hitting Wynn's pitches over the fence or back through the box. When reporters asked him if he would flatten his own mother, Wynn's stock answer was a nod and the words, "Mother was a pretty good curveball hitter." What about his grandmother? "Only if she was crowding the plate."[5] On one occasion Wynn was pitching in batting practice to his 15-year-old son, Joe Early, who hit a long drive to the outfield. The elder Wynn's next pitch sent Joe sprawling into the dirt. "He was leaning on me, and I had to show him who was boss," was Wynn's explanation for his unfatherly treatment.[6] Mickey Mantle, no easy hitter to intimidate, claimed, "That son of a bitch is so mean he'd fucking knock you down in the dugout."[7] This was Wynn's style of pitching for 23 years, and it helped bring him 300 victories and membership in the Hall of Fame.

The Tribe's opponents got no rest when Lemon and Garcia were on the mound. Lemon, who came up to the majors as an outfielder and third baseman and was converted to a pitcher in 1946, had a sinking fastball, wicked curve, and slider that had enabled him to roll up five 20-game seasons before 1954, when he and Wynn shared the league lead in victories with 23 each. Garcia, nicknamed "the Bear," intimidated hitters with his fastball and kept them honest with a good curve. He won 19 and led the league with a 2.64 ERA. Veteran Art Houtteman, acquired from Detroit in 1953, won 15. The former ace of the staff, Bob Feller, was losing his fastball, but he used control and experience to win 13, including 7 in a row, while losing only 3. These starters were backed up by a superb bullpen stocked with rookies Don Mossi and Ray Narleski and veteran Hal Newhouser.

Although the Indians' hitting did not match their pitching, they did have a strong offensive attack. Coming in fourth in team batting average at .262, they led the league in homers with 156. Bobby Avila won the batting title with a .341 average, Larry Doby hit .272 and led the league in home runs (32) and RBIs (126), and Al Rosen hit .300 and contributed 24 homers and 102 RBIs.

The second-place Yankees had their problems. Billy Martin had been called into the army, Johnny Mize had retired, and 36-year-old shortstop Phil Rizzuto was showing his age in the field and at the plate, where he managed a puny .195 average. Vic Raschi had been dealt to the Cardinals for Enos Slaughter after holding out for a better contract in the spring, while the other old reliables on the pitching staff — Ed Lopat, Allie Reynolds, and Johnny Sain — were noticeably older and less reliable in the twilight of their careers, combining for only 31 victories. Bob Grim led all Yankee pitchers with a 20–6 record, good enough for Rookie of the Year honors. Whitey Ford was second best at 16–8.

The Yankees played well. They led the league in hitting with a .268 team average. Four regulars—Irv Noren, Yogi Berra, Andy Carey, and Mickey Mantle (whose two knee operations during the off season left him with pain and reduced mobility)—hit .300 or better. Berra won the league's MVP Award. The team won 103 games, more than Stengel had ever won before and in most years more than enough to win the pennant. But it still finished second, eight games out, joining the 1909 Cubs, the 1915 Tigers, and the 1942 Dodgers as the only teams to win 100 games or more and still lose the pennant.

During the season a visitor to Stengel's office noticed that the Yankee manager had a copy of Wallop's famous book, soon to be made into the musical *Damn Yankees,* on his desk. When he was asked his opinion of the book, Stengel snapped, "I ain't read it. Some guy sent it to me the other day and it's just been laying there ever since. It ain't a true story. It's fiction."[8] Joe Hardy and his pennant-winning Senators were fiction, but the Cleveland Indians were very, very real.

The White Sox came in third, as they had in the two previous years. They won 94 games, the club's highest since 1920 and enough in many years to win the pennant, but this year it put them 17 games behind the leaders. The Red Sox finished fourth, with Williams missing all of spring training and the first 36 games of the season after he fell and broke his collarbone on the very first day of spring training trying to catch a dying fly ball hit to him during batting practice. After returning to the lineup he played in all but one of the remaining 118 games, belting 29 homers and hitting .345, but his missed games and 136 walks left him 14 short of the 400 at bats needed to qualify for the batting title.

Detroit, Washington, Baltimore, and Philadelphia made up the second division. The Baltimore Orioles began the season with high hopes and a ride through the streets in the largest parade in the city's history. But the new Orioles turned out to be as bad as the old Browns, losing 100 games, the same as Veeck's 1953 Browns. However, they did climb to seventh place, since the athletics lost 103 games. They drew 1,060,910 fans, giving the new owners a tidy profit of $643,407.

In the spring the New York Giants headed out to Phoenix, Arizona, for spring training. After the miracle finish of 1951 they had dropped to second place in 1952 and to fifth in 1953. But they were expecting 1954 to be different. Willie Mays would be back.

Discharged from the army on March 1, Mays arrived at the Giants' training camp the next day and was promptly mobbed by reporters, Giant officials, and teammates. When he first saw Mays, Giants' Vice President Chub Feeney said, "There's the pennant." Durocher was ecstatic, hugging Mays over and over and telling reporters, "There is just no saying how much

Willie means to us."[9] For the rest of spring training, the Giants were loose, with a lot of laughter and banter on the field and in the locker room. "That's what he does," Durocher told reporters. "He brings them all to life, makes everything fun."[10]

Mays came back to the game bigger and stronger than when he left. While he was in the army had had grown a half inch, added close to 10 pounds, and adopted a new defensive tactic which he had learned from another army player—catching the ball at belt-buckle level with the glove up, making it look incredibly easy. Mays claimed that he began using the basket catch because it was the most comfortable way and left him with a better balance to get off a throw quickly, not because he wanted to showboat.

Mays had not been in training camp long before he was reminded that no matter how good a ballplayer he was, he was still a black man in white America. One night after a spring exhibition game in Las Vegas he was told at a gambling casino that he could not sit at a dice table with the white gamblers. When someone in Mays's party asked the manager if he knew who Mays was, the manager angrily replied, "Yeah, I know who he is, and get that nigger away from the white guests."[11] This was just a few weeks before the Supreme Court helped spur the civil rights movement of the fifties by holding in the *Brown v. Board of Education* decision that segregated public schools were unconstitutional.

The club the Giants would have to beat for the pennant was, as expected, the Brooklyn Dodgers, who had been picked by most experts to win their third consecutive flag. The Dodgers had essentially the same team as the year before, but they were playing under a new manager. At the end of the 1953 World Series, Chuck Dressen had made the mistake of asking Walter O'Malley, who never offered pilots more than a one-year contract, to give him a three-year one. O'Malley would not budge, and when Dressen continued to press him the Dodger owner dispatched him to the West Coast to manage Oakland. While O'Malley always maintained that Dressen was "reassigned" because of the disputed contract terms, it was widely rumored that he was fired because he had lost the 1951 pennant and two consecutive World Series.

On November 24, 1953, O'Malley announced that Montreal manager Walt Alston, a 10-year veteran of the Dodger organization, would replace Dressen. Few rookie major league managers had had less contact with the big leagues. A native of Ohio and a graduate of Miami (Ohio) University, Alston had played only one game in the big time. Playing first base, for the 1936 Cardinals, he had made one error in two fielding chances and struck out in his lone time at bat. He went back to the minors, where he worked as a player and manager until he got the call to Brooklyn. Seventeen members of the 1954 Dodgers had played under him in the minors, among them Roy Campanella, Don Newcombe, Clem Labine, and Carl Erskine. Before he took over the Dodger helm he had seen Ebbets Field only once and had never been to a World Series game, not even as a spectator.

When the 42-year-old grandfather was named the Dodger manager, O'Malley gave him a one-year contract with an estimated salary of $25,000 and a promise that "the job is yours as long as you are happy with it and we are happy with you."[12] Alston and the Dodgers would be happy with one another for a long time. He would sign 22 more annual contracts, serving as the manager of one club longer than any pilot in history except for Connie Mack and John G. McGraw. When he retired at the end of the 1976 season, he had won seven pennants and four World Series, good enough to get him into the Hall of Fame.

But 1954 would not be one of his best years. Newcombe (9–8) was back from the army, but had a sore arm, and Johnny Podres (11–7) fought a two-month battle with appendicitis, leaving steady Carl Erskine (18–15) and Billy Loes (13–5) as the top pitchers. Roy Campanella's surgery for bone chips in his left wrist paralyzed a nerve and left two of his fingers numb. He played in only 111 games, and his batting average dropped over a hundred points to .207, while his home run output declined from 41 to 19, and his RBIs fell from 142 to 51. Carl Furillo, the batting champion of 1953, fell off 50 points to .294. The Dodgers still had a potent offensive attack. Four regulars— Snider (.341), Robinson (.311), Reese (.309), and Hodges (.304)—hit .300 or better, and Hodges hit 42 home runs and Snider had 40. It was still a powerful team, but not the team of 1953.

The race was close for the first month, with the Dodgers, Cardinals, Phillies, and Braves all hovering near the top. In spite of the return of Mays, the Giants started slowly, as if they were still the fifth-place team of the year before. Not until May 22 did they go over the .500 mark to stay, but in June they won 24 and lost only 4, tying the Dodgers for the lead on June 9 and then taking it over on June 15. They were still in first on July 4. After the All-Star Game (won by the American League by a score of 11–9) Mays went on a hitting tear that helped the Giants increase their lead to 7 over the Dodgers and 15½ over the Braves on July 22. Durocher's club seemed on the verge of breaking the race wide open and clinching the flag early.

But then the Giants went into a three-and-a-half-week slump, losing six in a row the last week of July and dropping seven out of eight in the second week of August. Their lead melted to just ½ game over the Dodgers and 3½ over the Braves. The Polo Grounders regrouped, however, and slowly rebuilt their lead, while the Dodgers and Braves alternated in the runner-up spot. The Braves faded after losing their leading hitter, Joe Adcock, for the season due to a wrist injury, but the Dodgers could not close the gap. On September 20, Sal Maglie beat the Dodgers on their own turf to sew up the pennant. The Giants went on to finish with a 97–57 mark, which in the American League that year would have been good enough for a third-place showing, 14 games out. The Dodgers, Braves, and Phillies rounded out the first division.

Even with Mays back in uniform, few people had expected the Giants to be a threat to the Dodgers' domination of the National League. But the Giants had made a brilliant trade when they sent Bobby Thomson to the Braves for left-handed pitcher Johnny Antonelli, a 1948 bonus baby who did not live up to his advance billings until he put on a Giant uniform. Only 12–12 with Milwaukee in 1953, he compiled a 21–7 record with New York and led the league in winning percentage (.750), ERA (2.30), and shutouts (6). Ruben Gomez won 17, while Maglie captured 14 and maintained his reputation for beating the Dodgers when it mattered most. The bullpen came through, with Marv Grissom compiling a 10–7 record with 19 saves in 56 games and Hoyt Wilhelm using his knuckleball to forge a 12–4 record with 7 saves in 57 games. Right fielder Don Mueller provided power from the left side of the plate and came in second to Mays in the National League batting race with a .342 average. James Lamar "Dusty" Rhodes contributed some of the best pinch hitting in the history of the game.

But the unquestioned leader of the Giants was young Willie Mays. After hitting just .247 with 4 home runs in his first 20 games, he finally found his batting eye. In the next 20 contests, he hit .449, with 9 homers and 25 RBIs, and he kept on streaking, getting one clutch hit after another, making dozens of sparkling plays in the outfield and drawing raves from opponents and teammates alike. "He's out there all the time stealing your ball game," Hal Jeffcoat of the Chicago Cubs marveled. "He makes the kind of plays that win ball games, and he'll do it every day."[13] And teammate Alvin Dark said, "Willie does everything, and he does it when it counts—in a game."[14]

Mays led both leagues in batting average (.345) and slugging percentage (.667), scored 119 runs, and drove in 110. He took the batting crown on the last day of the season, when he, teammate Don Mueller, and Duke Snider began the day in a virtual three-way tie. Mueller led with .3426, followed by Snider with .3425, and Mays with .3422. Mays rose to the challenge, hitting a single, double, and triple in four at bats against one of the league's best pitchers, Robin Roberts of the Philadelphia Phillies. He finished with a .345 average, while Mueller went 2-for-6 to finish at .342 and Snider went hitless and finished at .341. Not surprisingly, Mays was named the league's Most Valuable Player.

Mays was the most watched, the most talked about, the most praised player in the majors in 1954. He was compared to Joe DiMaggio, Babe Ruth, and other greats of the game, and of course to his New York rivals, Mickey Mantle and Duke Snider. In May alone he was on 15 radio or television programs, and in one weekend in early July he was on three television shows. Reporters and photographers flocked around the dugout and locker room for interviews and pictures before and after games. "It has gotten to the point in the last couple of weeks," Giants promotion direction Garry Schumacher said in July, "that Willie couldn't get into the shower without some reporters waiting to get right in with him."[15] Newspapers and magazines ran article after article recounting his hitting feats and sparkling plays, magazines ran cover stories of his life in serial form, and he was the subject of two popular songs, "The Amazin' Willie Mays" and "Say Hey, Willie."

Mays's 1954 salary was reported at somewhere around $17,500, a far cry from Ted Williams's $100,000 or even Jackie Robinson's $40,000. But he was making thousands more off of his radio and television appearances and his endorsements of Chesterfield cigarettes, Coca-Cola, and several other products. He was so beleaguered with endorsement requests that he had to hire an agent to handle his outside business interests. One Madison Avenue executive said, "Mays has become the hottest thing for us since Babe Ruth."[16]

The center of all this attention had just turned 23 in May. Having risen from poverty in Alabama, he enjoyed his new prosperity, buying a large wardrobe, a chartreuse Lincoln convertible, and records of ballads by Nat King Cole and other crooners for his record player, which he carried on road trips. He also sent part of his salary back to Birmingham to help support his 10 half brothers and half sisters. As he had when he debuted as a rookie in 1951, he was still staying at Mrs. Ann Goosby's Harlem apartment house near the Polo Grounds, renting one of her five rooms. When he was not playing baseball, he could often be found in the streets playing stickball with the neighborhood kids, using a handball, a broom handle, manhole covers for home plate and second base and fenders of parked cars for first and third.

While Mays was getting so much attention in New York, another black superstar and Alabama native, Henry Aaron, was making his debut with the Milwaukee Braves. The Braves brought the 20-year-old infielder to spring training in 1954 after he had hit .362 with 22 homers at Jacksonville the year before. They planned to convert him to an outfielder and give him one more year of seasoning in the minors. But after Bobby Thomson broke his leg sliding into second base in a spring exhibition game, Aaron was inserted into the starting lineup where he would stay for the next 23 years. In his rookie season he appeared in 122 games, hit .280, and drove in 69 runs. But there was little evidence that the new outfielder would turn into the game's most prolific home run hitter. In Busch Stadium on April 24, in his seventh game, he tagged Vic Raschi for his first home run, but he would hit only 13 for the year.

Aaron soon established a reputation as one of the most powerful and consistent hitters in either league. Curt Simmons once said that "throwing a fastball by Henry Aaron is like trying to sneak the sun past a rooster."[17] He was also a good base runner and defensive player. By staying healthy, not being called for military service, and playing consistently year after year, he piled up hits and home runs and finally broke Ruth's career record of 714 homers—a record many felt was unbreakable—in 1974. Until the latter stages of his career when he closed in on Ruth's record, he did not get the kind of media attention that Mantle, Snider, Mays, and other sluggers got by playing in New York and other large eastern cities. He was even overshadowed on his own team by Warren Spahn, Lew Burdette, and Eddie Mathews. But he was always there, quietly doing his job and accumulating spectacular statistics. When he retired, he held two batting titles, four Gold Glove awards, one MVP Award, and several hitting records, including the all-time homer record of 755.

It was a year for home runs in the National League. The eight teams averaged 158 homers each, establishing a major league record that would not be broken until the American League teams averaged 164 in 1986. The league also set a record by having six players hit 40 or more home runs. Ted Kluszewski of the Cincinnati Reds led both leagues with 49, while Gil Hodges tallied 42, Hank Sauer and Willie Mays hit 41 each, and Eddie Mathews and Duke Snider tied for fifth place in the league with 40 each. Two sluggers turned in phenomenal one-day home run performances. On May 2, tearing into Giants' pitching in a doubleheader in St. Louis, Stan Musial slammed a single and a record 5 home runs—3 in the first game and 2 in the nightcap—to drive in 9 runs and amass 21 total bases. Not even Ruth had ever had such a day. The next night the opposing pitchers walked Musial four times.

On July 31, first baseman Joe Adcock of the Milwaukee Braves hit four homers in one game, driving in seven runs, to lead the streaking Milwaukee Braves to a 15–7 victory over the Dodgers. Adcock became only the third (Gehrig and Hodges were the other two) major league player to hit four homers in a nine-inning game. Adcock also stroked a double to give him a 5–5 day and 18 total bases, a major league record for a single game. The next day he was beaned by Clem Labine, but thanks to his batting helmet, which was dented by the pitch, he was not badly hurt. After the incident, the Braves' team physician said that the helmet, which more and more players were using, probably saved Adcock from a serious injury or even death.

The top home run hitter in professional baseball in 1954 played far from the groomed playing fields, high salaries, and huge crowds of the major leagues. He was Joe Bauman, a 6-feet-5 inch, 235-pound left-handed slugger for the Roswell (New Mexico) Rockets of the Class C Longhorn League. Bauman was one of those many players in the forties and fifties who made a career out of minor league play. Some had once played briefly in the majors, were sent down for seasoning or to recover from an injury, and never made it back. Others never got the call. All across the minors these players became local favorites of the fans and carved out careers of 10, 15, or even 20 years, supplementing their meager baseball income with daytime work in factories, retail stores, service stations, and other menial jobs.

Bauman spent over a decade playing for minor league and semipro teams until injuries forced him to give up the game in 1956. For most of his career, he pumped gas and changed oil at a service station during the day and hit home runs at night for minor league clubs in Oklahoma and New Mexico. In a nine-year professional career spent at the Class A level or below, he hit 337 home runs, building up a wide fan following in the Southwest. In 1954, playing for the Roswell Rockets, he received attention from *Life* magazine and other national publications when he hit 72 home runs, breaking the professional baseball record of 69 held jointly by Joe Hauser of Minneapolis (1933) and Bob Crues of Amarillo (1948). Playing in all 138 games, the 32-year-old first baseman also led the league in batting average (.400.), RBIs (255), and walks (150). For one glorious season, Joe Bauman had a year that no slugger had ever had.[18]

In spite of the proliferation of homers, the National League was able to produce three 20-game winners. Robin Roberts led the league with 23 wins for his fifth consecutive 20-game season, and Antonelli and Spahn both won 21. The only no-hit game in either league was a 2–0 gem pitched by Braves right-hander Jim Wilson (18–2) against the Phillies on June 12.

The National League's Rookie of the Year was not a Dodger this time but Cardinal outfielder Wally Moon, who slugged a homer in his first at bat and went on to hit 11 more, drive in 76 runs, and compile a .304 batting average. To make room for Moon, the Cardinals traded Enos Slaughter to the Yankees two days before the season began. One of the mainstays of the Cardinals for 13 seasons and captain of the team since 1949, Slaughter generally batted around the .300 mark, was a good base runner, had a good glove and arm, and was the personification of the hustling, loyal team player who always gave it all he had.

When news of the trade was released, Slaughter and baseball fans across the nation were shocked. He broke down in tears when he went to the clubhouse to gather his personal belongings. Many years later he was still bitter, telling reporters, "It broke my heart. I did so much for the Cardinals over the years. . . . I didn't see how they could do that to me."[19] In the Cold War atmosphere of the time, the Russians were quick to exploit Slaughter's treatment. In the magazine *Soviet Sport,* the trade was described as "flesh-peddling in disregard of the player's wishes and rights. . . . The beizbol [baseball] bosses care nothing about sport or their athletes but only about profits."[20] There was a positive note to the trade, for it sent the battle-scarred veteran from a club that had not won a pennant since 1946 to one that had cashed more World Series checks than any franchise in baseball history. After playing in two World Series with the Cards in 13 years, he would play in three more with the Yankees before he retired in 1959.

The World Series opened in the Polo Grounds on September 29. For the first time in five years, the Yankees were not the American League representative, and it seemed a little strange. Most baseball experts thought the Indians would clobber the Giants. In Las Vegas, the oddsmakers rated the Indians 8–5 favorites. After Perry Como led the 57,751 fans in the singing of the national anthem, the Indians wasted little time in showing why they had won 111 games during the year. In the first inning, Vic Wertz, facing Sal Maglie, tripled off the right field wall to drive in Al Smith and Bobby Avila and give the Tribe a 2–0 lead. The Giants came back in the third, touching Lemon for two runs on three singles and a walk. The game went into the eighth still tied at 2–2 and the starting pitchers still on the mound.

After Maglie began the inning by walking Larry Doby and allowing a single to Al Rosen, Durocher brought in left-hander Don Liddle to face Wertz. The first baseman hit a long fly ball to deep center field that looked like extra bases and at least two runs, but Mays was off at the crack of the bat, running hard toward the wall with his back to the plate. It seemed like a futile chase. Somehow at the last possible fraction of a second, some 460 feet from home plate, Mays made a spectacular over-the-shoulder catch, lost his cap as he spun around and fired the ball to Davey Williams behind second base, and fell down. Doby tagged up and advanced to third, but no further, and Rosen had to hurry back to first to avoid being doubled up.

In the broadcast booth, Jack Brickhouse marveled that the catch "must have been an optical illusion to a lot of people."[21] It was an unbelievable play, often regarded as the best outfield catch in the history of baseball. "The Catch," as it came to be called, saved two runs, stifled the Indian rally, and was possibly the turning point in the Series. Durocher called in Marv Grissom to pitch to the next hitter. As Grissom walked up to the mound, the departing Liddle said to him, "Well, I got my guy."[22] Grissom retired the side without allowing a run. As Mays and Irvin ran in from the outfield Irvin told Mays, "That was the greatest catch I ever saw." "Had it all the way. Had it all the way," Mays assured him in his deadpan manner.[23]

The game went into the tenth, still tied at 2–2. The Indians got a man as far as third, but could not score. In the bottom of the inning, with Mays on second and Hank Thompson on first, Durocher sent in Dusty Rhodes to pinch hit for Monte Irvin. As he had been doing all year, the left-handed slugger delivered, hitting Lemon's first pitch into the lower right field stands, barely clearing the barrier 260 feet from home plate. Little more than a pop fly and nearly 200 feet shorter than Wertz's long drive back in the eighth, it hit in the first row of seats and fell back onto the field at outfielder Dave Pope's feet. The Giants had a 5–2 victory and a 1–0 lead in the Series.

In the second game the Indians drew first blood again when leadoff hitter Al Smith tagged starter Johnny Antonelli's first pitch for a home run. In the fifth, still trailing 1-0 with two on, Durocher again called on his expert pinch hitter. As expected, Early Wynn sent Rhodes sprawling into the dirt, but the fearless country boy got up and slapped a Texas leaguer into center to drive in a run and tie the score. The Giants added another run later in the inning. Rhodes stayed in the game, and in the seventh, he drilled a 400-foot home run to right to ice a 3–1 victory.

The Indians went home licking their wounds and staring at a 2–0 deficit. In the third game, over 71,000 fans came out, hoping that Mike Garcia could stop Rhodes, Mays, and company. In the first inning, Mays singled to right to drive Mueller home from second and give the Giants a 1–0 lead. In the third, the Giants loaded the bases. Durocher gave Rhodes the signal to pinch hit for Monte Irvin, who was rapidly becoming known as the man Dusty Rhodes pinch hit for. On the first pitch, Rhodes slapped a single to right to score Mueller and Mays and give the Giants a 3–0 lead. They never trailed, and went on to win easily, 6–2. When a reporter asked Rhodes after the game if he was nervous playing in his first fall classic, he replied, "What is there to be nervous about? These games with Cleveland are like exhibitions after what we went through to beat the Dodgers. That was tough, this is fun."[24]

For the fourth game, Durocher gave the nod to Liddle, while Lopez, instead of starting the well-rested Feller, decided to go with Lemon, who had only two days rest since his last start. This decision cost Feller his last chance to win his first World Series game. Once again the Indians went down to defeat. The Giants scored two in the second, one in the third, and four in the fifth to run up a 7–0 lead. The Indians mustered three runs in the fifth and one more in the seventh before quietly succumbing, 7–4. Durocher had the game so well in hand that he did not even have to call on his prize pinch hitter.

What happened? How could a team that won 111 games be swept by one that had won 14 fewer games during the regular season? For four days, the Giants simply outplayed the Indians in almost every department. As usual, Durocher had his players fired up and they played aggressive baseball, making many of their breaks and exploiting those that the Indians gratuitously sent their way. The Giants' pitching staff was stingy, emerging from the Series with a collective ERA of 1.46. The Indians' staff, which had led the league with a record 2.78 ERA during the regular season, gave up 21 runs in just four games and came out with an embarrassing 4.84 ERA.

The Giants also came out on top in offense, hitting .254 with 20 RBIs and 21 runs scored. Most of the big Giant hitters—Dark (.412), Mueller (.389), and Hank Thompson (.364)—came through during the Series just as they had during the regular season. Mays hit only .286, but he scored four, drove in three, and saved the first game with his spectacular grab of Wertz's long drive.

The big batting hero was, of course, Dusty Rhodes, who bragged after the Series that "the guy I can't hit, I ain't seen yet."[25] Coming to bat only six times, he hit .667 and drove in seven runs, only two less than the entire Cleveland team in 137 at bats. His three pinch hits tied him with Bobby Brown of the 1947 Yankees, and his six RBIs as a pinch hitter set a new World Series record. Justifiably, Rhodes was chosen the Series' Most Valuable Player. His career up until that point certainly made him a very unlikely candidate for the honor. Born in Mathews, Alabama, in that state's poor cotton- and corn-growing belt, Rhodes was buried in the minors for five years before he was brought up to the Giants in 1952. After hitting .250 in 1952 and .233 in 1953, the rugged-looking, 6-foot, 180-pound slugger came to bat only 164 times in 1954, 45 times as a pinch hitter. But he banged out 56 hits — 15 home runs, 7 doubles, 3 triples, and 31 singles, for a .341 average. And he made his hits count, driving in 50 runs, many of them in key situations. As a pinch hitter, he was 15 for 45 for a .333 average. "Every time we needed a pinch hit to win a game," Durocher later said, "there was Dusty Rhodes to deliver it for us."[26]

Durocher attributed Rhodes's pinch-hitting skills to his confidence and to his desire to come to the plate to hit in crucial situations. While other players on the bench might be praying that Durocher would not choose them to hit in a tense, crucial situation, Rhodes, according to Durocher, "would always be up on his feet, at the far end of the dugout, hefting a bat. 'Ah'm your man,' he'd call down. 'What are ya waitin' on, skip? Ah'm your man!'"[27]

Durocher would later claim that Rhodes was "the best pinch hitter, no contest, I ever looked at . . . . He was also the worst fielder who ever played in a big league game."[28] He also knew that Rhodes had a special taste for alcohol and late hours. But no matter how much he drank or how late he stayed out, he could still hit. After the 1954 World Series, Red Smith wrote, "In baseball, as in war, a man's reputation follows him around. The Giants' Leo Durocher and Horace Stoneham occasionally hear tales about Rhodes like those Abraham Lincoln heard of General Ulysses S. Grant. They make the same answer Lincoln did."[29]

After his Cinderella World Series, the Colossus of Rhodes, as some reporters were now calling him, appeared on "The Ed Sullivan Show," was the guest of honor at several dinners, was the subject of innumerable newspaper and magazine columns, and was treated to a two-mile parade in his home town of Rock Hill, South Carolina, where 40,000 people turned out to welcome him home. In the winter of 1953–1954, he had worked during the offseason for $60 a week in a local textile mill, but now he had an $11,000 World Series check to tide him over the winter.

But like Cookie Lavagetto, Don Larsen, Bobby Thomson, and several other fall heroes, Rhodes would have his one brief time in the limelight and never be on center stage again. His playing time and batting average steadily declined over the next three years, and when the Giants moved to San Francisco in 1958 he was sent back to the minors. In 1959 he returned for a brief stint as a pinch hitter with the transplanted Giants, hitting .188 in 48 at bats, but then he disappeared to the minors and eventually to retirement. In his seven-year major league career he played in only 576 games, hit 54 homers, drove in 207 runs, and compiled a .253 batting average. This was definitely not a career performance worthy of enshrinement in Cooperstown, but in baseball annals he will always be remembered for those four fantastic days in the autumn of 1954.

While Rhodes and the rest of the Giants' hitters sizzled, the Indians' bats fizzled. The team batting average was a puny .190, with only nine RBIs. The hitters seemed particularly anemic with men on base, stranding 26 in the first two games alone. Their top hitter was Vic Wertz, whose 8-for-16 performance included one homer, one triple, and two doubles but only three RBIs. As he would later say, "Willie made me famous."[30] The heart of the Cleveland order failed to produce. Avila, Doby, and Rosen combined for only seven hits, all singles, and they drove in no runs.

Leo Durocher was gracious in victory. "Everything we did seemed to be right. Everything they did seemed to go against them," he said, adding that "we got every break. The Indians didn't get any." Most of the experts agreed that the Indians were not as bad a team as they appeared to be during those disastrous four days. They had played brilliantly for 154 games, without a prolonged slump, against tough competition. Perhaps catcher Jim Hegan was correct when he said that the club won the pennant too early and too easily. "It was a great season and as soon as we won it we relaxed," he said. "Not on the surface, perhaps, but mentally. And we just never got up to the pitch we had during the season."[31] Still stunned from the Giant steamroller, Lopez said, "They say anything can happen in a short series. Well, I knew that. I just never thought it was going to be *that* short."[32] When he was asked by a reporter what had happened to the Indians, Bob Feller, still irked at riding the bench for the entire Series, snapped, "Don't ask me. I wasn't in it."[33]

In what some called "the Little Miracle of Coogan's Bluff," the Giants won their fifth Series in 14 attempts and their first since 1933. The Giants also broke the American League winning streak that had begun when the Yankees beat the Dodgers in 1947. Nonetheless, the American League still had a 33–18 advantage.

The Series had been attended by 251,507 fans, a record for a four-game Series. But it was very costly for the team owners. Since most of the profits from the first four games went to the players, the owners were hoping for a longer fall classic. It was estimated that the abbreviated Series cost them a million dollars in lost revenues.

One of the biggest baseball stories of 1954 unfolded off the field, and not long after the end of the World Series it came to a conclusion. It was the marriage and divorce of two of the nation's greatest folk idols, Joe DiMaggio and Marilyn Monroe.

After dating since 1952, they married on January 14, 1954, in a civil ceremony in San Francisco. It was the second marriage for both. DiMaggio had been married to actress Dorothy Arnold from 1939 to 1944 (she had custody of their son, Joe, Jr.), while Monroe had married aircraft worker James Dougherty at the age of 16, then divorced him just two years later. Monroe had gained fame for posing nude for a photograph that first appeared on a calendar and was later bought by Hugh Hefner and published in the first issue of *Playboy* magazine in December of 1953. In a short film career as a sex symbol she had become one of Hollywood's top box office attractions.

The marriage was short-lived. After an extended honeymoon in Japan, the DiMaggios returned to California, living first in his home in San Francisco before moving into a rented eight-room house in Beverly Hills. It did not take long for the marriage to unravel. They had strong physical attractions to one another, but they had little in common. She had never seen DiMaggio play baseball and knew and cared little about the game, while he did not like the movie roles she had as a dumb sex symbol, the way she flirted with men on and off the set, or the Hollywood environment she thrived on — the movie sets, the parties, and her friends, whom he called "phonies."

Some of the couple's friends believed that DiMaggio had delusions of turning his new bride into a happy homemaker. When he was dating her, he told his close friend, newspaper columnist Jimmy Cannon, "She's a plain kid. She'd give up the business if I asked her. She'd quit the movies in a minute. It means nothing to her."[34] She went through the motions of being a housewife, but she really did not like the role, and she resented his attempts to control her choice of friends and her social activities. She once told friends, "Joe's idea of a good time is to stay home night after night watching television."[35]

Inevitably, the two began to argue, and the marriage began to disintegrate. As it did, DiMaggio became moody, withdrawn, and uncommunicative. A turning point in their marriage apparently came during the filming of *Some Like It Hot*, when DiMaggio watched while onlookers cheered as his wife, wearing a white skirt and white shoes, stood over a subway grating at Lexington Avenue and 51st streets in New York while a wind machine under the grating blew her skirts up around her waist, showing her see-through white underpants. Embarrassed, disgusted, and angered, DiMaggio

left the scene and went to Toots Shor's restaurant. Late that night, the couple had a furious quarrel, and the marriage was all but over. Photographs
of the street made the newspapers the next day, causing DiMaggio even
more grief.

The two separated on September 27, shortly before he flew back to
New York to cover the World Series for a newspaper syndicate. On October
5, Monroe filed for divorce in Santa Monica, accusing DiMaggio of causing
her "grievous mental suffering and anguish." No details were given, and he
did not contest the divorce. During a brief hearing on October 27, Monroe
testified that to save her marriage she had even agreed to give up her movie
career. After fifteen minutes of testimony, Superior Court Judge Orlando
Rhodes issued a divorce decree. The marriage of the 39-year-old baseball
idol and 26-year-old actress and sex symbol had lasted only nine months.

News of the Monroe-DiMaggio divorce made the front pages of
newspapers all across the country, with such predictable headlines as
"MARILYN TELLS JOE: YOU'RE OUT AT HOME," "JOE FANNED ON JEALOUSY,"
"JOE STRIKES OUT," and "JOE THROWN OUT AT HOME," and other variations
of familiar baseball lingo. Humorist Oscar Levant said that the divorce
"proves that no man can be a success in two national pastimes."[36] But
DiMaggio, who once replied to the question of what it was like to be married to Monroe with the quip, "It beats rooming with Joe Page,"[37] could see
no humor in the situation. He had been deeply embarrassed by all the
publicity surrounding their wedding, separation, and divorce, and was shattered by the breakup. On November 21, he entered Franklin Hospital in
San Francisco to be treated for bleeding ulcers, an ailment he had suffered
from since the war years. He left three days later, in time to spend Thanks-
giving at home.

DiMaggio would carry a torch for Monroe for years to come. In spite
of their divorce, the two remained friends for the rest of her short life. After
she divorced playwright Arthur Miller in 1961, she and DiMaggio began to
spend more time together and rumors circulated that they were planning
to remarry. When she committed suicide at the age of 36 in 1962, DiMaggio
made all the funeral arrangements, including the decision to bar her
Hollywood friends and the press from the ceremonies. For the next 20 years
he paid a florist to put six red roses in a vase next to her crypt at Westwood
Memorial Park three times a week. In the early years after her death he also
visited the crypt a couple of times a year. In 1982, without giving a reason,
he stopped sending the flowers.

DiMaggio would never talk to reporters about Monroe after her death.
According to Roger Kahn, *McCall's* magazine once contacted him to write
a story about Monroe and authorized him to offer DiMaggio $50,000 if he
would give a 15-minute taped interview and discuss his life with Monroe.
DiMaggio refused.[38] The Yankee Clipper always did have class.

14. Next Year (1955)

In 1955, America was in the midst of the peace and prosperity of the Eisenhower years. The Korean War was now a bad memory, Senator Joe McCarthy had fallen into disgrace after being officially condemned by his fellow senators, and Eisenhower met with new Soviet Premier Nikita Khrushchev and other world leaders at the Geneva Summit Conference, a clear sign that the Cold War was thawing. American automakers produced a record 9.2 million vehicles, Ford chalked up huge sales with its sporty new Thunderbird, and General Motors became the first corporation in the world to make a billion dollars. Disneyland opened in Anaheim, California, "The Mickey Mouse Club" and "Gunsmoke" premiered on television, the new rock 'n' roll music of Chuck Berry and other singers continued to attract young record buyers, and teenage idol James Dean, who rose to fame early in the year in the film *East of Eden*, died in a spectacular wreck of his Porsche only two weeks before the release of his *Rebel Without a Cause*.

As the 1955 baseball season began, time was running out for the Brooklyn Dodgers and their fans all across the country. Seven times they had won the National League pennant, and seven times they had come up short in the World Series. After losing to the Boston Red Sox in 1916 and the Cleveland Indians in 1920, they had lost their last five Series—1941, 1947, 1949, 1952, and 1953—to the New York Yankees. The fans were tired of having to say, "wait until next year." If the Dodgers were to win the Series, it had to be soon, perhaps this year. Dodger officials were seeking a bigger stadium with more parking spaces and more profits, and they were willing to leave the borough—perhaps even metropolitan New York—to get them. Walter O'Malley was already planning to play seven home games in Roosevelt Stadium in Jersey City in 1956 while he continued to look for a site for a new stadium.

Adding even more urgency to the situation was the indisputable fact that the Dodger regulars, who had played so long and so well together, were noticeably grayer around the temples and heavier around the middle. If they did not win a Series soon, it might soon be too late. Perhaps it already was. Most of experts picked the Milwaukee Braves to win the National League flag while the Dodgers and the Giants fought it out for second place.

The Dodgers had changed little from previous years. Billy Cox and

Preacher Roe had been traded to Baltimore during the offseason, but Roy Campanella was still behind the plate and Gil Hodges, Junior Gilliam, Pee Wee Reese, and Jackie Robinson anchored the infield. Carl Furillo, Duke Snider, and newcomer Sandy Amoros, a 23-year-old Cuban with an engaging broad grin and little command of English, made up the outfield. Don Newcombe and Carl Erskine were expected to be the aces of a rather thin pitching staff, though Walt Alston was hoping for strong support from three young left-handers, Johnny Podres, Sandy Koufax, and Karl Spooner. With a 9–4 record in 1953 and an 11–7 mark in 1954, the 22-year-old Podres was expected to be even better with two years' experience behind him. Koufax, a Brooklyn native, was only 18 years old when he signed for a $20,000 bonus in December of 1954, and seemed destined for stardom if he could just control his wildness.

But the greatest young prospect seemed to be the 23-year-old Spooner, who had been called up to the club in the last month of the 1954 season after compiling a 21–9 record for Fort Worth. At the end of the month he started two games at Ebbets Field and pitched brilliantly. Going the distance in both games, he blanked the Giants 3–0 in one and the Pirates 1–0 in the other, allowing just three singles in the first game and four in the second, and striking out 15 Giants and 12 Pirates. He broke the league record for most strikeouts (formerly 13) by a pitcher in his first major league game, broke the league record for most strikeouts in two games (formerly 25), and tied a league record by pitching shutouts in two consecutive games. His sparkling performance led the Dodgers to expect great things from him in 1955.

The National League opened the season under a new rule requiring all players to wear a protective plastic safety baseball cap while they were at bat. Over the years, several major leaguers had been seriously injured by pitched balls, and in 1920 Cleveland shortstop Ray Chapman had been killed by one thrown by Carl Mays of the New York Yankees. The idea of placing a protective liner inside the regular baseball cap had first been tried out by Larry MacPhail back in 1941 when he was an executive with the Dodgers, but the idea did not catch on until the early 1950s when Branch Rickey moved to the Pirates. In 1952 Rickey ordered all his players to wear a vastly improved version of the protective headgear, which was now a special helmet made of fiberglass and polyester resin rather than just a liner. He also required them to wear it while they were on the base paths as well as at bat. The practice soon spread to other teams, to the entire National League, and in 1956, to the American League as well.

A special grandfather clause in both leagues exempted players from wearing them if they had not worn them before. Some players resisted, either out of concerns about their masculine image or because they thought the caps were too hot, obstructed their view, and made the pitchers less afraid to throw the brushback pitch. Although Oriole manager Paul Richards said in 1956 that "any player who doesn't wear a helmet is crazy,"[1] Mickey Mantle, Hank Bauer, Ted Williams, Roy Campanella, and a few others still held out. By the end of the decade, good sense prevailed and most players were wearing them and praising their virtues.

The Dodgers began the season with 10 straight victories, bettering the old National League record of 9 held by several teams. During this streak they seemed to be unbeatable, playing superb offensive and defensive baseball. Robert Creamer wrote in *Sports Illustrated,* which made its debut in 1954, "For 10 days at the start of the 1955 season they were a dream team, the best in baseball. . . . They played so well that anyone who has ever liked baseball had to like the Brooklyn Dodgers."[2]

The streak was finally broken by the Giants, who took two of three from their rivals in a bitterly-fought series. But the Dodgers recovered and promptly tore off on another streak, this time of 11 consecutive victories. Before it was snapped by the Cubs on May 11, the Dodgers had won 22 of their first 24 games and built a staggering 9½-game lead over the second-place Giants. Although they experienced several brief slumps, they continued to roll on toward the pennant, building their lead to 15½ games by the All-Star break. Still, Durocher saw, or pretended to see, a glimmer of hope for his Giants. The Dodgers, he said, "are breathing hard, and they look like they're in for trouble. If only we could be 13½ games behind instead of 15½ we might make 'em look back and wonder."[3]

The All-Star Game provided one of the best contests of the year. Played on July 12 in Milwaukee, the twenty-second annual event saw the National League give up four runs in the first and another in the sixth before rallying to knot the score with two in the seventh and three in the eighth. The game went into extra innings with the score still tied. In the top of the twelfth, the Braves' Gene Conley struck out the side. In the bottom of the inning, as Stan Musial walked up to the plate to bat against Frank Sullivan of the Red Sox, catcher Yogi Berra said to Musial, "Boy, my feet are killing me." "Relax," Musial told him. "I'll have you home in a minute." True to his word, Musial hit the first pitch into the stands for a 6–5 National League victory.[4]

After the All-Star Game the Dodgers continued their steady march toward the pennant. Finally, on September 8, they clobbered the Braves 10–2 to up their lead to 17 games and clinch the title on the earliest date in National League history. It was their eighth straight victory and their twelfth in the last 13 games. The Dodgers were in first place for all but two days of the season.

The pennant winners had a superb defensive and offensive club. Led by Don Newcombe (20–5), the pitching staff topped the league in strikeouts (773) and ERA (3.68). The big right-hander was also so good with the bat that Alston used him as a pinch hitter in 23 games. He responded with a .381 average in that role. Overall, he had a .359 average, 23 RBIs, and 7 homers (a league record for a pitcher). But when asked early in the season about his hitting, Newcombe replied, "All my hitting means to me is a better chance to win as a pitcher. That's where the money is."[5]

Clem Labine appeared in 60 games, mostly in relief, and wound up with a 13–5 record and 11 saves. At the plate, he had only three hits in 31 at bats all year, but all three were home runs. Carl Erskine, Johnny Podres, Billy Loes, Ed Roebuck, Roger Craig, and Don Bessent were the other mainstays of the staff. Craig and Bessent were both called up from the minors on July 15 and provided valuable mound support down the stretch. Karl Spooner, who had finished the 1954 season in such spectacular fashion, developed arm trouble, completed only 2 of 14 starts, and had a mediocre 8–6 record.

The Dodgers relied heavily on their big bats. They led the league in batting average (.271), home runs (201), doubles (230), runs (857), slugging average (.448), and stolen bases (79). Rebounding from his disastrous 1954 season, Roy Campanella led the club in batting average (.318), contributed 32 homers and 107 RBIs, and paced the league in putouts (672) — all good enough to bring him his third MVP Award. Carl Furillo hit .314 with 26 homers and 95 RBIs, and Gil Hodges hit .289 with 27 home runs and 102 RBIs. Hampered by age (36) and an injured knee, Jackie Robinson had the worst year of his career, hitting just .256, with only 8 homers and 36 RBIs in 105 games. With Junior Gilliam taking over his second base spot, Robinson filled in wherever he was needed in the infield and outfield.

Snider had one of his finest years, hitting .309, clubbing 42 home runs, and leading the league in RBIs (136) and runs (126). With Mays and Mantle also having stellar seasons, the "who's the best center fielder in baseball?" debate naturally heated up. Snider was often irritated by the question, and when a reporter posed it to him in the spring he replied, "It's just plain silly comparing us. I think the real fans know who's the better ballplayer." After a pause, he said, "I make more money, don't I?"[6] (He was making $35,000 to Mays's $25,000.) As he did on many other occasions when he was asked to compare himself to Mays and Mantle, he tried to brush off the question by asserting that he was not engaged in direct competition with either one and that his main job was to help the Dodgers win the pennant.

But it was natural that fans and sportswriters would want to make comparisons. Mays, Snider, and Mantle were great center fielders playing for successful clubs in the nation's media center, and they provided fans with a great opportunity to engage in one of their favorite pastimes, comparing contemporary players with one another and the greats of the past. As one reporter would write in 1972, many fans grew up in the fifties "debating whether the first person of the Holy Trinity was Mantle, Snider, or Mays."[7]

The endless dispute first emerged in 1954, when Mays returned from the army and played his first full season. All three came from home towns far from the nation's biggest city—Mays from Alabama, Snider from California, and Mantle from Oklahoma—but were quickly adopted by the New York fans as their own. All three hit for power and average and usually ended the season at the top, or hovering near the top, in the major batting categories. All three were superb defensive players capable of coming in on the ball to make a shoestring catch or going back to make a leaping catch up against the wall. All three were smart, aggressive base runners.

But it was difficult to compare them. They played in different parks and performed different roles for different managers and teams. Nationwide, Mantle was probably the most popular of the three. Young, white, and handsome, he was fast on the base paths and in the outfield and hit booming home runs from both sides of the plate for baseball's most successful ball club. Mays was popular, too, but in spite of his incredible feats in the outfield and infectious love of the game, he was still a black male playing a predominantly white game in an era of widespread racism and growing civil rights battles in the South. In 1955 alone, three blacks were lynched in Mississippi, a young black male named Emmett Till was murdered in that state for allegedly whistling at a white woman, and Rosa Parks helped instigate the black boycott of the Montgomery, Alabama, bus system when she refused to give up her bus seat to a white man.

Snider, the oldest and least colorful of the three, did not make the same kind of splash in the baseball world as his younger rivals did when they arrived in the majors at about the same time in 1951. When Snider joined the Dodgers in 1947, he received little notice, for the biggest story of the year was the debut of Jackie Robinson. Snider was slow to find the strike zone and develop his raw talent, and did not really emerge as a star until 1950. He never captured the imagination of the public quite like his two rivals did, but in one category he was better than either one—from 1950 to 1959, he hit 326 home runs, more than any player in either league during that 10-year stretch. But he never captured the MVP Award, while Mantle took it three times and Mays twice.

In the long run, Mays stayed healthier than his rivals and proved to be the most durable of the three. His career spanned 22 years (1951–1973), whereas Snider (1947–1964) and Mantle (1951–1968) played only 18. Mays led the other two in almost all offensive departments. He hit 660 homers to Mantle's 536 and Snider's 407; had a career batting average of .302 to Mantle's .298 and Snider's .295; drove in 1,903 runs to Mantle's 1,509 and Snider's 1,333; stole 338 bases to Mantle's 153 and Snider's 99; and scored 2,062 runs to Mantle's 1,677 and Snider's 1,259. In slugging percentage the three were close. Mays and Mantle each had a career slugging average of .557, while Snider closely trailed at .540. Although Mays also led in most defensive statistics, all three men were among the best defensive center fielders to ever play the game.

Many fans were attracted to Mays because of his enthusiasm for the game and for his versatility. A slugger who would wind up third on the all-time list of home runs and tenth in slugging average, he also stole more bases than Ruth, Foxx, Williams, and Ott combined. He is the only National League player besides Ralph Kiner to hit 50 or more home runs in a season on two different occasions, 51 in 1955 and 52 in 1965. He also hit four homers in one game and on two other occasions hit three in one game. He led the league in batting average once (1954), in home runs four times (1955, 1962, 1964, 1965), and in stolen bases four consecutive years (1956–1959).

Playing for the powerful New York Yankees, Mantle had the opportunity to play in more World Series (12) than Snider (6) and Mays (4) combined. In World Series play, Mantle still leads all players in home runs (18), runs (42), and RBIs (40), and he was one of the primary reasons the Yankees won 8 of the 12 Series he played in. Snider was on the winning side twice. He, too, was a clutch October performer, hitting .286 and coming in fourth among all major league players in home runs (11), tenth in runs (21), and seventh in RBIs (26). Playing in three World Series with the Giants and one with the New York Mets, Mays was on the winning side just once, with the 1954 Giants. For his World Series career, Mays managed a batting average of only .239, a slugging percentage of only .282, no home runs, six RBIs, and nine runs. But he will always be remembered for his great catch of Vic Wertz's drive in 1954.

Leo Durocher never left any doubt as to his choice of the best center fielder. During spring training in 1955, he told reporters, "I say he's the best I've ever seen right now. I'll take him over Musial and I would even if they were the same age." Warming to the subject, he went on to say, "To be great in baseball, you have to be great in five things. You must be able to hit, to hit with power, to run, to throw and to field. Willie can do them all better than anybody today."[8]

Many other baseball men agreed with Durocher's assessment. Joe DiMaggio could have been expected to cast his vote for his replacement on the Yankees, but he did not. When reporters asked him in the spring of 1955 who he thought was the greatest active player in the game, he quickly answered, "Willie Mays, without a question."[9]

Comparisons of players are difficult, and reams of statistics do not provide the full measure of a player's performance or his value to the team. Fans still debate the merits of the three great center fielders who roamed the outfields of New York in the 1950s. What is incontestable is that they were superb, exciting players who helped make the 1950s one of the greatest decades in major league history. All three made the Hall of Fame, as did that other great center fielder who retired the same year Mays and Mantle debuted, Joe DiMaggio. Long after his retirement, Snider would say, "The truth is that DiMaggio . . . was better than the rest of us. He may have been the best of all time."[10]

Mays's Giants were not even able to take second place in 1955. That consolation prize belonged to the Braves. Eddie Mathews hit 41 home runs and Hank Aaron hit .314 with 27 homers, but injuries to several key players and subpar performances by others left them 13½ games back.

The Giants finished in third, 18½ games behind. Mays led the league in homers (51) and finished second in batting average (.319), RBIs (127), and stolen bases (24). Steady Don Mueller hit .306, but Al Dark, Davey Williams, and several other key players were hampered by injuries, and pitchers Johnny Antonelli, Ruben Gomez, and Sal Maglie had off-years. The 38-year-old Maglie struggled to a 9–5 record in 23 games, quarreled with Durocher, and was sold to Cleveland after the Giants put him on waivers and no other National League club showed any interest.

It was also Durocher's last year with the Giants. Disappointed with the team's showing, owner Horace Stoneham refused to renew his contract, so on September 24 Durocher announced his "resignation." Three days later, he signed a one-year contract with NBC as a sports commentator. His place at the Giants' helm was taken by Bill Rigney, a former Giants' infielder who had played under Durocher between 1948 and 1953.

The Philadelphia Phillies rounded out the first division, 21½ games off the pace. The Phillies had the league's leading hitter, Richie Ashburn (.338), and the pitcher with the most wins, Robin Roberts (23), who enjoyed his sixth consecutive 20-game season. He also gave up 41 home runs, a new major league record. Somehow Roberts was able to keep his sense of humor in the midst of his growing reputation as a gopher ball pitcher. After he set this new record, he said, "In the long history of organized baseball I stand unparalleled for putting Christianity into practice. . . . No one has ever been so good to opposing batsmen. And to prove that I was not prejudiced, I served up home run balls to Negroes, Italians, Jews, Catholics alike. Race, creed, nationality made no difference to me."[11]

The second division was made up of Cincinnati, Chicago, St. Louis, and Pittsburgh, finishing last for the fourth straight year. The Cubs' Ernie Banks, playing his second full year in the majors, hit 44 homers, breaking Vern Stephens's old record for homers by a shortstop. Outfielder Bill Virdon of the St. Louis Cardinals was the Rookie of the Year, hitting .281 with 17 home runs and 68 RBIs.

As usual, there were several fights between players during the season, but one of the biggest brawls of the year was between two managers. On July 5 in Cincinnati, Reds' manager Birdie Tebbetts and Cardinal pilot Harry Walker got into an argument at home plate over Tebbetts's claim that

Walker and his Cardinals were delaying the game. The exchange of words got louder and louder, and finally the two men began swinging at one another, then fell to the ground, wrestling and punching like schoolboys while both benches emptied onto the field. By the time the umpires and stadium police had restored order, Walker had a bruised forehead and Tebbetts a bloody nose and a cut in his mouth. The next day, National League President Warren Giles fined both men $100.

The American League began the season with a new city in its lineup. Once the geographical stability of the major leagues had been upset by the moves of the Braves and the Browns, it became even easier for further changes to take place, especially when those two clubs were such financial successes in their new homes. On November 8, 1954, after years of declining attendance and arguments between Connie Mack's sons, Roy and Earle, over the operation of the Philadelphia Athletics, the Mack family sold the franchise to Chicago businessman Arnold Johnson, who was allowed to move the club to Kansas City. Johnson paid $3.5 million for the Athletics, acquiring the players, $800,000 worth of debts, and Connie Mack Stadium, which he promptly sold to the Phillies for $1.7 million. Announcing that "my associates and I have a million dollars to spend," Johnson promised a great future for the club.[12] On April 12 the Kansas City Athletics made their major league debut against the Detroit Tigers. Former President Harry Truman threw out the first ball, and an enthusiastic capacity crowd of 32,844 sat in the newly remodeled Municipal Stadium to watch the Athletics defeat the Tigers, 6–2. After winning only 51 games and finishing dead last in 1954, the new Athletics, playing under Lou Boudreau, who left the Red Sox to manage the club, won 63 games in their first season in Kansas City and moved up to sixth place. The attendance would also improve, jumping to nearly 1.4 million, over a million more than they had drawn at Philadelphia the year before. For the rest of the decade they would be in the rebuilding stage, and often seemed little more than a farm club of the Yankees, who bought or traded for several of their star players, including Bobby Shantz, Clete Boyer, Ryne Duren, and Roger Maris.

For most of the year the American League race was a see-saw affair between the defending champion Indians, the Yankees, the White Sox, and the Red Sox. The Indians took the lead early in the season, but were soon pushed aside by the Bronx Bombers, who managed to build a five-game lead over the Tribe by the All-Star break. But after the All-Star Game, the Yankees suffered a brief relapse, allowing the White Sox to take over first place on July 22. Between then and September 7 the four main contenders fought it out, with the lead changing hands frequently and with no team being able to build more than a two-game lead over the second- and third-place clubs. In the last week of August, the lead changed hands five times.

On the morning of September 8, with only 18 days left in the season, the Indians were clinging to first place by a half-game margin over the Yankees. The White Sox were in third, 1½ games out, and Boston was in fourth, hanging close at 3 games back. The Yankees then made their move, winning 15 of their last 19 games, including a stretch of 8 in a row. The other teams could not match this torrid pace, and on September 23, in the nightcap of a doubleheader at Fenway Park, Don Larsen beat the Red Sox to clinch the pennant. When the season ended, the Indians were 3 games out, the White Sox 5, and the Red Sox 12.

It was Stengel's sixth pennant in seven tries, and probably one of his most difficult. Injuries, Martin's absence (he was not discharged from the army until August 31), and other problems forced Stengel to juggle his lineup more and more as the season progressed. The Yankees finished fifth in team batting average (.260), with only Mantle (.306) and Bill Skowron (.319) hitting .300 or better. Mantle also led the league in home runs with 37. Yogi Berra hit .272, stroked 27 homers, and drove in 108 runs, good enough to bring him the MVP Award for the second consecutive year and the third time in the last five years.

Ten years after the signing of Jackie Robinson, the Yankees also had their first black player. He was Elston Howard, a 26-year-old catcher from St. Louis. Like so many players before him, he told reporters, "It's great to be a Yankee! It feels great to wear the Yankee uniform."[13] But with Berra at the peak of his career, Howard had to carve out a spot on a very talented team by showing his ability to hit and to play several positions in the field while he waited for the full-time catching spot to open up for him. Playing in 97 games, mostly as an outfielder or pinch hitter, he hit .290 with 10 homers and 43 RBIs.

Howard's main liability was his slowness afoot, which led Stengel to complain to a reporter, "When I finally get a nigger, I got the only one that can't run." This comment gave ammunition to those like Jackie Robinson who claimed that Stengel was a racist and that the Yankees had deliberately dragged their feet on signing black players and promoting them to the big leagues. But Howard claimed that Stengel was not a racist. "I never felt any prejudice around Casey," he said later in his career. "He treated me the same as he did any other player."[14]

Stengel's pitching staff had a new look in 1955. The familiar Big Three were gone. Raschi had been traded to St. Louis in 1954, Allie Reynolds had retired at the end of the 1954 season, and Ed Lopat, who managed only a 4–8 record in the first half of the 1955 season, was traded to Baltimore on July 30 for Jim McDonald. Bob Grim, the 1954 Rookie of the Year, developed arm trouble and fell to 7–5. Thirty-six-year-old left-hander Tommy Byrne compiled a 16–5 record, while Bob Turley (17–13) and Don Larsen (9–2), acquired from Baltimore during winter trades, made valuable contributions. The top pitcher was Whitey Ford, with an 18–7 record and a 2.62 ERA. Nicknamed "The Chairman of the Board" by Elston Howard, Ford was Stengel's kind of pitcher. "If you had one game to win and your life depended on it," Stengel once said, "you'd want him to pitch it."[15] The Yankees led the American League in team ERA with 3.23.

The defending champion Indians suffered from hitting slumps by several of their key hitters, especially Al Rosen (.244), Bobby Avila (.272), and Vic Wertz (.253), who contracted a nonparalytic form of polio and missed the last month of the season. The Indians were also hampered by the decline of their Big Three (Lemon, Garcia, and Wynn), whose total wins dropped to 46, down almost 20 from the year before. Lemon's 18 victories tied him with Ford for the league lead, but Wynn fell to 17–11 and Garcia to 11–13. Bob Feller, 13–3 in 1954, pitched only 83 innings and finished with a 4–4 record, the worst since he debuted in 1936 with a 5–3 mark. Left-handed fastballer Herb Score showed great promise with a 16–10 record, a 2.85 ERA, a league-leading 245 strikeouts, and Rookie of the Year honors.

Indian outfielder Ralph Kiner, who had spent the best part of his career in the National League with Pittsburgh and Chicago before coming to Cleveland in 1955, retired at the end of the season with a disappointing 18 homers and a .243 batting average. It was a far cry from his first seven years with the Pirates, when he won or was tied for the home run crown seven times, a major league record, and hit 51 homers in one year (1947) and 54 in another (1949). During his 10-year career he hit 369 homers, an average of 7.1 home runs per 100 times at bat, second only to Babe Ruth's 8.5.

The third-place White Sox led the league in hitting with .268 and won 91 games while losing 63 for their best record since 1920. The fourth-place Red Sox were hurt by the early season absence of Ted Williams. Although he had announced his "retirement" at the end of the 1954 season, Williams returned to Fenway in 1955. Legal problems surrounding his divorce prevented him from reporting to the team until May 13, causing him to miss spring training and the first six weeks of the season. But he reached top form quickly and led the club to a 44–16 record between June 5 and August 9, when it drew to within 1½ games of first place. But the team fell far behind the pack by playing under .500 ball (20–24) for the last 44 games. Williams was spectacular, hitting .356 with 28 homers and 83 RBIs, but with only 320 at bats, he could not qualify for the league batting title, which went to Al Kaline (.340) of the Detroit Tigers, who at the age of 20 was the youngest batting champion in major league history.

The Red Sox were also hit by a tragedy in late June with the death of their 25-year-old first baseman, Harry Agganis, who had been given a $35,000 bonus to sign with the Red Sox after he graduated from Boston

University. The "Golden Greek" seemed destined for stardom. After one year in the minors, he became the Red Sox's starting first baseman in 1954, hitting .251 with 11 homers and 57 RBIs. The young star was hitting over the .300 mark in 1955 when he developed a fever and chest pains and was hospitalized for 10 days with pneumonia. Seemingly recovered, he returned to the lineup, but fell ill again and reentered the hospital where he died suddenly on June 27 from a pulmonary embolism. "Agganis was right on the verge . . . of really doing it," Ted Williams later said. "That was a real tragedy of talent."[16]

Once again, the World Series pitted the Yankees against the Dodgers, and once again, the oddsmakers picked the Yankees. It seemed, after all, to be a safe bet. They had won 16 world championships, 5 of them under Stengel, and had not lost a Series since they were downed by the Cardinals in 1942. The Dodgers were still looking for their first championship in eight tries. Many Dodger fans believed that their team was jinxed against the Yankees, while Bomber supporters believed that the boys from Brooklyn choked whenever they were in the presence of the men in pinstripes. When Joe DiMaggio was asked by reporters his predictions for the fall classic, he picked the Yankees, claiming that they had a whammy on the Dodgers. "They can't even *say* Yankees. It's always been those blank lucky Yankees. To put it politely."[17] Former Dodgers Chuck Dressen and Billy Cox also predicted that the Dodgers would fold in the presence of Mickey Mantle and company.

Whoever won the World Series, it was sure to be a good one, since the two teams in the past had always provided plenty of drama, rhubarbs, heroes, and goats. To add additional interest to this sixth meeting between the two rivals, there were two players—shortstops Pee Wee Reese and Phil Rizzuto—who had played in all five World Series between the two clubs. Reese was hoping for a different outcome this time. In August of 1955, he told Tom Meany that the one thing he wanted most in his career was "to be on the winning side in a World Series. I've been on five losing teams. Maybe this is the 'next year' we've been talking about for so long in Brooklyn."[18]

The classic opened on September 28 in Yankee Stadium on a beautiful fall day. Conspicuously absent from the festivities was 85-year-old Clark Griffith, former player and manager, one of the founders of the American League, and part owner of the Senators since 1912. Griffith, who was suffering from neuritis and other infirmities of old age, had attended all the previous 51 World Series but was too weak to attend this one. He would die on October 27. Also missing was President Eisenhower, who had suffered a heart attack only four days before the Series opened. The fans at the stadium observed a moment of silent prayer for his recovery.

In the first two games it looked as if the Dodgers might have to wait until next year again. In the opener, matching Don Newcombe against Whitey Ford, the Yankees won 6–5, with first baseman Joe Collins clubbing two homers and driving in three and Elston Howard hitting a home run in his first at bat in World Series competition. Snider and Furillo each hit a home run in the losing cause. Two of the most exciting plays of the game came in the sixth inning, when 26-year-old Billy Martin was thrown out trying to steal home, and in the eighth, when 36-year-old Jackie Robinson stole home off Whitey Ford. The following day, the Dodgers went down to defeat again, as Tommy Byrne held them to five hits, drove in two runs with a single, and went the distance in the 4–2 victory. Yankee fans were talking "choke" and "sweep."

The Dodgers limped back to Ebbets Field on September 30, determined to become the first team to win the World Series after losing the first two games of a seven-game Series. In the third game, Johnny Podres, celebrating his twenty-third birthday, assured the Dodger faithful that there would be no Yankee sweep. Skillfully mixing his fastball, curve, and changeup to baffle the Yankee hitters, he pitched a complete game and took an 8–3 victory. Campanella had three hits, including a two-run homer, and drove in three runs. The next day, Campanella, Hodges, and Snider hit home runs to power the Dodgers to an 8–5 victory to square the Series. The momentum seemed to have shifted in favor of the Dodgers, and it continued in game five as Craig and Labine held the Yankees to three runs while their teammates scored five off of Snider's two homers and a double and Amoros's two-run homer. After being down two games to none, the Dodgers now went back to Yankee Stadium needing just one victory to claim their first world championship.

So far the home team had won every one of the games, so in game six it was the Yankees' turn. They won it early, jumping on Spooner for five runs in the first. With this big cushion, Whitey Ford held the Dodgers to just four singles and coasted to a 5–1 victory.

On October 4, with left-handers Johnny Podres and Tommy Byrne on the mound, the Dodgers and Yankees faced each other for the seventh consecutive day. The Dodgers scored in the fourth and sixth to take a 2–0 lead into the bottom of the sixth, when Walt Alson made a fortuitous defensive change. After second baseman Don Zimmer had been lifted for a pinch hitter in the top of the inning, Alston moved left fielder Junior Gilliam back to his familiar spot at second and sent Sandy Amoros in to play left field. The first Yankee hitter, Billy Martin, walked on four consecutive pitches, then took second when Gil McDougald laid a perfect bunt down the third base line for a single. This brought up Yogi Berra, who hit a lazy, high fly ball into the left field corner. Amoros, playing in left center, did not appear to have a chance to catch up to the ball, which seemed destined for extra bases. But the speedy Amoros sprinted over to the line and made a lunging, one-handed spear of the ball with his gloved hand in front of the stands.

It was a spectacular catch, one he could not have made had he not been left-handed. A right-handed outfielder, even if he caught up to the ball, would have been faced with the nearly impossible task of backhanding it or catching it with his bare hand. Certainly Junior Gilliam, a right-hander most at home in the infield, could not have caught it. After catching the ball, Amoros wheeled and rifled it to Reese, who relayed it to Hodges at first base to double McDougald, who had already rounded second base when Amoros made the catch. Hank Bauer then grounded out to Reese to end the threat.

The Yankees threatened again in the eighth when they put runners on first and third, but failed to push a run across. In the ninth, still clinging to his 2–0 lead, Podres faced only three batters. Skowron grounded out to the pitcher, Bob Cerv flied out to Amoros, and Howard hit a routine grounder to the sure-handed Reese at short. With a big grin on his face, Reese, who had waited so long for this moment, fielded the ball and threw it to Hodges, who scooped it out of the dirt for the last out. It was 4:44 P.M. on October 4. Next year was here.

After so many years of losing, the celebrating in the Dodger clubhouse was unrestrained. Players poured beer and champagne on anyone within striking distance and shouted, "To hell with Billy Cox and DiMaggio and Dressen." Carl Furillo told a newsman to "print it in big letters. Tell Billy Cox we didn't choke up. Tell him we won it—without him. Tell him to stay in that little town of his and rot."[19] Amoros sat in the clubhouse with a big grin on his face and a big Cuban cigar stuck in his mouth as players and reporters came by to congratulate him on his catch. Reporters found it virtually impossible to interview him, since he spoke little English. When asked if he had really thought he could catch Berra's fly ball, he nodded and managed to say, "I dunno. I just run like hell."[20] For him, this was the highlight of an otherwise undistinguished major league career scattered over nine seasons with the Dodgers interspersed with long stints in Montreal. But for the moment, he was happy with himself, and the Dodgers were happy with him. And well they should have been. His catch was worth $103,299.51—the difference between the World Series shares of the winners ($9,768) and losers ($5,599).

For the first time in Series history, the Dodgers did not have to make the difficult trek to the winner's clubhouse to offer congratulations. This time, the Yankees—or some of them at least—came over to congratulate them. During the friendly conversation between the rival players, Furillo spoke for many of his teammates when he told Rizzuto and Berra that "we finally beat you."[21] Someone asked Stengel if he agreed with those who said that the Dodgers deserved to win. The unflappable manager replied, "Have to tell the truth. I never figure I ought to get beat."[22]

If the Yankees wanted excuses for losing the Series, they could easily have found them, mainly by looking at the injury list. Mantle, suffering from a leg injury, played in only three games, one as a pinch hitter, and several other Yankees were hobbled by aches and pains. But the Yankees refused to make alibis. "They had more than we did," Rizzuto said. "Next year it may be a different story."[23]

The Dodgers simply outplayed the Yankees, leading them in almost all offensive and defensive departments. They also had plenty of individual heroes. There was Duke Snider, who hit .320 with 4 homers and 7 RBIs. There was Gil Hodges, the goat of the 1952 series with his dismal 0-for-21 performance at the plate, who hit .292, helped to win game four with a home run, and drove in a total of 5 runs, including both runs in the final game. There was Sandy Amoros, who hit .333 and made the catch of the year. There was Jackie Robinson, one of the team's old men, hitting only .186 but providing inspiration to the team with his hustle, his steal of home in the first game, his double and single in game three, and his 5 runs. Unfortunately, an Achilles' tendon injury he suffered in the sixth game forced him to sit out the deciding game, denying him the pleasure of being on the field with his teammates when Howard's ground out gave the Dodgers the victory he had wanted for so long. There was Clem Labine, pitching well in relief, picking up a win and a save, and Roger Craig, who allowed only four hits in six innings en route to his victory in game four. Finally, there was young Johnny Podres, who pitched two complete games, the first in game three to halt the Dodger skid and the second in game seven to give them the title. In taking his two victories he struck out 10 and allowed 15 hits, scattering them in such a way as to yield only two runs. *Sports Illustrated* named him Sportsman of the Year and *Sport* magazine chose him as the MVP of the Series and presented him with a new Chevrolet Corvette. He also picked up around $3,000 from television appearances.

The rise to fame had come quickly to the young man who had grown up in the little town (population 1,050) of Witherbee, New York, 265 miles north of New York City. He did not see his first major league game until 1949, when he and three friends drove down to watch a Dodgers-Braves game at Ebbets Field. Podres later recalled, "We sat up in the upper left field stands. Newcombe was pitching. The Dodgers had the same guys they have now: Robinson, Reese, Campy, Hodges, Furillo, Snider. I've always been a Brooklyn fan, and that day I made up my mind, I'm going to pitch for Brooklyn."[24] He signed with the Dodger organization in 1951, was farmed out, and brought up to the parent club in 1953. He fashioned a 9–4 record in 1953 and an 11–7 mark in 1954. Before the third game of the 1955 World Series, he had not pitched a complete game since the first of the summer and could boast only a 9–10 record. Bur for two days in the fall of 1955, he was the best there was.

Having been denied a World Series for so long, and coming close so often only to fall short, Brooklyn erupted in a frenzied celebration. Factory whistles blew, church bells rang, firecrackers exploded, boats in the harbor blew their whistles, and motorcades of private automobiles, taxis, busses, trucks, and motorcycles rode through the streets with horns blaring. Fans threw confetti from office windows and poured into the streets from offices, stores, bars, apartments, or wherever they happened to be at game's end. Some danced in the streets with friends or total strangers, often to the music of little bands that seemed to pop up from nowhere. Others stood on doorsteps shouting or beating pots and pans. Effigies of Yankee players were quickly fashioned and strung from lampposts. On Utica Avenue, one delicatessen owner moved his operation onto the sidewalk and gave away free hot dogs. The revelry lasted far into the night.

The press played the story for all it was worth. The *New York Times* said, "Brooklyn's long cherished dream finally has come true." Dan Daniel wrote in the *Sporting News* that the Dodger victory "will do baseball a lot of good, baseball and Brooklyn. And it isn't going to hurt the Yankees. Just give them a little more humility."[25] The *Daily News,* a New York paper with the largest circulation of any paper in the country, headlined "THIS IS NEXT YEAR" and the *New York Daily Mirror* proclaimed, "Bums Ain't Bums — Anymore."

Feelings ran high for several days. Four days after the Dodgers won the Series, Dodger fan William Christman and Yankee fan Robert Thompson got into a heated argument over the Series in a Queens bar. The two finally went out into the street to settle matters, and Thompson pulled a pistol and shot and killed Christman. Thompson was jailed for manslaughter.[26]

Late in 1955 Walter O'Malley was studying the feasibility of constructing an all-weather stadium with a controlled climate that could be used for baseball and many other entertainment events during the year. Covered by a translucent dome, the stadium, he said, "would be one of the wonders of the world. It would enclose a structure as large as St. Peter's in Rome. It would be the first thing to catch the eye as you approached New York Harbor by ship." He had even gone so far as to discuss his idea with world famous architect R. Buckminster Fuller, who had designed such a dome, which he called a "geodesic structure."[27]

Obviously, the size of such a structure dictated that it be built outside of Brooklyn, perhaps even outside of metropolitan New York. So even as the Dodgers and their fans savored their World Series victory during the hot stove league, O'Malley was looking toward abandoning Ebbets Field for greener, perhaps enclosed, pastures. The borough of Brooklyn had celebrated its first, and last, World Series victory.

15. The Mick, the Barber, and the Night Rider (1956)

Nineteen fifty-six was a memorable year in sports. It was the year Dale Long hit a home run in eight consecutive games, Rocky Marciano retired undefeated after 49 fights, and Bill Russell led the University of San Francisco to its second straight NCAA title. It was the year Notre Dame quarterback Paul Hornung won the Heisman Trophy, Johnny Unitas made his debut as the quarterback for the Baltimore Colts, and Cary Middlecoff captured the United States Open golf championship for the second time. It was the year Ken Rosewall of Australia won the United States Lawn Tennis Association singles championship in the men's division, the Montreal Canadiens took the NHL Stanley Cup, and Patrick Francis Flaherty of Chicago won the fortieth Indianapolis 500 race. It was the year of the birth of future baseball stars Dale Murphy and Eddie Murray, American gymnast Kurt Thomas, and tennis phenomenon Martina Navratilova. But most memorable, it was the year of Don Larsen's perfect World Series game.

It was also an election year, and Americans would give Eisenhower his second overwhelming victory over the challenger from Illinois, Adlai Stevenson. While some of his opponents accused Ike of "golfing and goofing" while civil rights battles raged in the schools and streets and other problems cried out for attention, the nation was at peace and millions were enjoying unprecedented prosperity.

The weather was wet and cold in many major league cities on April 17, but 226,646 fans still came out for the eight opening day games. In Washington, President Eisenhower, accompanied by his personal physician and several congressmen and cabinet members, threw out two first balls, giving photographers extra photo opportunities in this election year. Two days later, the Dodgers, who had already had an opener in Ebbets Field, staged a second opening day, this time in Roosevelt Stadium in Jersey City, where they planned to play seven home games in 1956. Jersey City Mayor Bernard Berry threw out five first balls, and as he posed for the photographers before throwing out the fifth one, an exasperated fan finally yelled, "For the love of Pete, throw the ball and let's get the hell on with the game."[1]

234

The season began with more players wearing glasses than ever before. In the early days of major league baseball, few players wore glasses, partly out of the fear of suffering an eye injury if the glasses were smashed during play and partly because of the prevailing belief that wearing them was somehow unmanly. The first modern player to wear them was Lee "Specs" Meadows, who donned them while playing for the Cardinals in 1915, but until the 1940s it was still a rare practice. As late as 1948, only 13 players were wearing them.

But in the fifties attitudes were changing dramatically. By 1956, 22 players were wearing glasses, and by 1960 the number would increase to 39, 10 of whom were with the Cardinals. Among the players wearing glasses in 1956 were Jim Konstanty of the Yankees, Jim Brosnan of the Cubs, Red Schoendienst and Bill Virdon of the Cardinals, Larry Doby of the White Sox, Roy McMillan of the Reds, and Clint Courtney of the Washington Senators, who in 1952 had become the first catcher to wear glasses. The *Sporting News* voiced its approval of the trend, saying, "If the President of the United States can wear glasses for the simple reason he wishes to improve his sight, certainly a ball player—or an umpire—has no reason to squint without them."[2]

Umpires were even more reluctant than the players to admit that they needed help seeing, but in January of 1956, American League officials decided to require all league umpires to take eye examinations. As a result, in the first few days of the new season umpires Frank Umont, Ed Rommel, and Larry Goetz appeared on the field wearing spectacles. While this brought predictable catcalls from the fans, most players took the new practice in stride. Tiger third baseman Ray Boone said, "Ball players wear 'em, and nobody thinks anything about it. Why not umpires?" Athletics manager Lou Boudreau said, "It's no disgrace to wear glasses. If it makes him a better umpire, more power to him."[3] But it was a novel practice, and it got a lot of attention in the press.

For the fourth time in five years, the Yankees and Dodgers won their league races and squared off in a subway World Series. The Yankees won the pennant easily. They began the season by capturing seven of their first eight games, took the lead for good on May 16, and coasted in, clinching the flag on September 18, with nearly two weeks left in the season. The Bronx Bombers went on to finish nine games ahead of the Indians, the widest margin yet of any Stengel team. It was the club's twenty-second pennant and Stengel's seventh in eight years, tying him with Joe McCarthy.

Although Bob Turley, Don Larsen, Bob Grim, and Tommy Byrne had off years, Whitey Ford compiled a 19–6 record and led the league in ERA (2.47), while two sophomore pitchers, Johnny Kucks (18–9) and Tom Sturdivant (16–8), came through for the Old Professor. The club lived up to its nickname of Bombers, setting a new American League record of 190 home runs, eclipsing the previous high of 182 hit by the 1936 Yankees. Berra hit 30, Bauer 26, and Skowron 23, while McDougald (.311) and Skowron (.300) joined Mantle in the .300 club. The batting star of the club was unquestionably Mantle, who became only the fifth player in history to lead both leagues in batting average (.353), home runs (52), and RBIs (130). He also became the first Triple Crown winner since Ted Williams in 1947, and only the ninth in major league history. It was an accomplishment that had eluded many other great hitters, including Babe Ruth.

Mantle had shown in his rookie season that he could hit tape-measure home runs, but it was not until 1955, when he clubbed 37, that he took his first home run crown. In 1956, he got off to his fastest start yet. In the season's opener at Griffith Stadium on April 17, he smashed two long homers over the center field fence, and from then on he hit round-trippers at a furious clip, staying ahead of Ruth's 1927 pace for most of the season. On May 30, he hit numbers 19 and 20 at Yankee Stadium, putting him 11 games ahead of Ruth's pace. With number 19, hit off of Senators' right-hander Pedro Ramos, he missed by just 18 inches becoming the first player to hit a fair ball out of Yankee Stadium. His powerful shot struck just slightly below the top of the roof cornice over the third deck, 370 feet from home plate and 117 feet above the field.

Clouting homers from both sides of the plate, Mantle continued to chase Ruth's record while the baseball world kept a homer watch. By the end of August he had 45, four games ahead of Ruth's pace. But then, like all previous challengers—Hack Wilson, Jimmie Foxx, Hank Greenberg, Ralph Kiner, and Johnny Mize—Mantle faltered in September, unable to match the Babe's prodigious feat of 17 homers in the season's last month. He hit only 7, to wind up 8 shy of the Babe's record but still 22 ahead of runner-up Vic Wertz of Cleveland.

Not surprisingly, the 24-year-old slugger was the talk of the majors and the country in 1956. Even people who were not normally baseball fans were caught up in the publicity about the young man who was hitting tape-measure home runs and challenging the legendary Bambino. Players and managers around the league were in awe of the young outfielder. Lou Boudreau, manager of the Kansas City Athletics, said, "Ted Williams could never hit as hard as Mantle," and Indian manager Al Lopez went so far as to claim that "Mantle has more power than Babe Ruth."[4] Mantle's big year brought a financial bonanza. His Yankee salary was $36,000 but he made another $59,000 from television and radio appearances and from endorsements of cigarettes, T-shirts, soap, cereal, and other commercial products. By the time his World Series shares were added in, he made over $100,000 for the year.

Many who knew Mantle felt that only two things could prevent him from becoming one of the greatest players of all time—his personality, and his fragile health. Although he was showing signs of greater maturity, he was still a shy, hot-tempered, and occasionally sullen young man prone to brooding, putting too much pressure on himself, and falling into slumps from trying too hard. The injury problem was more serious. Hardly a season went by, it seemed, when he did not experience a serious injury or have to undergo surgery. Over the years he would have operations on both knees and his right shoulder and suffer from pulled muscles, broken fingers, an abscessed hip, a broken bone in his left foot, arthritis, and groin and thigh tears.

Most fans and rival players who saw Mantle on the playing field did not fully understand the extent of his physical injuries, but his teammates, who saw him getting heavily taped before each game, did. Enos Slaughter once called him "the greatest one-legged player I ever knew."[5] Although he often played with great pain and reduced mobility, he rarely complained or made excuses. But he often wondered, as did many others, just how many records he could have set if he had been healthy and if he had taken care of himself instead of carousing late at night with Billy Martin, Whitey Ford, and other teammates.

Mantle's exploits and the Yankee waltz to the pennant overshadowed what was happening in the rest of the league. It was another disappointing season for the Indians, who finished in second place for the fifth time in Al Lopez's six-year tenure. The Tribe had three 20-game winners (Early Wynn, Herb Score, and Bob Lemon), Vic Wertz came back from his bout with polio to hit 32 homers and drive in 106 runs, and rookie right fielder Rocky Colavito contributed 21 homers, but the club hit only .244, tying Baltimore for the bottom rung in team batting. At the end of the season, having lost the confidence of General Manager Hank Greenberg, Lopez resigned. He was replaced by Kerby Farrell, manager of Cleveland's farm club in Indianapolis. Lopez was too talented to be out of a job long. On October 25, after White Sox manager Marty Marion yielded to front office pressure and resigned, Lopez was hired to manage the White Sox, who had finished third.

The Red Sox came in fourth, followed by the Tigers, Orioles, Senators, and Athletics. There were six 20-game winners, led by Frank Lary of Detroit with 21 victories. Teammate Billy Hoeft captured 20, as did Billy Pierce of Chicago and Herb Score, Early Wynn, and Bob Lemon of Cleveland. Veteran Red Sox pitcher Mel Parnell brought his career to a close with a 7–6 record and the American League's only no-hitter of the year, a 4–0 victory over the White Sox on July 14.

At 37, seemingly ageless Ted Williams had another good year at the plate, with 24 homers, 82 RBIs, and a .345 average, along with 102 walks. As usual, he still spoke his mind and let the consequences fall where they might. During spring training he created an uproar when he lambasted the draft board of Johnny Podres, the hero of the 1955 World Series. When he heard that Podres's board, which had earlier classified him 4-F because of a bad back, had reclassified him 1-A and hence subject to induction, Williams lashed out at "gutless draft boards, politicians and sports writers," claiming that "if Podres had lost the World Series games instead of winning them, he'd probably be with the Brooklyn club all season." He argued that "there's no reason why—with no war—ball players shouldn't serve their time in the off season."[6]

But the biggest problems Williams ran into in the 1956 season arose over spitting incidents. All year long he sparred with the Boston writers, and on three different occasions he had shown his contempt for them and for the fans who booed him by spitting in their direction. The spitting episode that got him into expensive trouble came on August 7 in a game in Boston with the Yankees before a sellout crowd. Throughout the game he was ridden by the fans and by the Yankee players, but the climax came in the eleventh inning of the scoreless contest when the fans booed him for misplaying a fly ball. He later ended the inning by making a spectacular catch. As he ran in from his outfield position toward the dugout, he began spitting toward the box seats behind the Red Sox dugout, then toward the press box, then in the direction of home plate and third. When the fans continued to boo him, he came out of the dugout and began spitting in all directions. Astonished at what he was seeing on the field, Red Sox announcer Curt Gowdy said "Oh, no, this is a bad scene."[7] Boston eventually won when Williams walked with the bases loaded, and as he headed toward first he threw his bat high into the air.

Listening to the game on the radio, Red Sox owner Tom Yawkey decided that these bad scenes merited some disciplinary action. An hour and a half after the game, General Manager Joe Cronin called Williams at his hotel suite and told him the club was slapping him with a $5,000 fine. According to Cronin, Williams apologized, saying, "I was sorry I did it a minute later. I just have no explanation as to why I did it."[8] The fine matched the largest in history up to that time, the one Yankee manager Miller Huggins levied against Babe Ruth back in 1925 for gross insubordination and violation of training rules.

Before the August 7 incident, Williams had said, "Nobody's going to make me stop spitting. The newspaper guys in this town are bush. And some of those fans are the worst in the world."[9] But after the fine was levied, he stopped. The day after the spitting episode, over 30,000 fans came out to see the Red Sox play the sixth-place Baltimore Orioles. As a show of support, the fans rose and gave him a five-minute ovation. Williams hit a game-winning homer, and as he crossed home plate he clasped his hand over his mouth as if he were trying to suppress an uncontrollable desire to expectorate.

The Dodgers had a much tougher time returning to the World Series than the Yankees did. For most of the first half of the season, they and four other teams—the Braves, Reds, Cardinals, and Pirates—were in serious contention. Through the end of June, the fifth-place club never trailed the front runner by more than five games. At the All-Star break, the Reds were in first, leading the Braves by 1½ games and the Dodgers by 2, while the Cardinals and Pirates were beginning to fade.

After the All-Star Game, won 7–3 by the National League and featuring homers by Mays, Musial, Williams, and Mantle, the Braves went on a rampage, winning 15 of 17 and taking over the lead on July 13. They held it for most of the rest of July and August. Then in September the defending world champions made their move, winning 15 of their last 22 games while the Braves managed only 11 victories out of their last 23. This surge allowed the Dodgers to take over first place on September 15 when Newcombe beat the Cubs and the Braves dropped a game to the Phillies. It was the first Dodger lead since the last week of April.

At this point in the race the Reds lost four consecutive games, leaving the Dodgers and the Braves to fight it out. The lead continued to alternate between the two, and they went into the last day of the season with the Dodgers desperately holding onto a one-game lead. The Braves tried to stave off elimination by beating the Cardinals 4–2, but the Dodgers, who had had more than their share of disappointing pennant playoffs in the past, made sure they would not face one this year. Playing against the Pirates in Ebbets Field, Sandy Amoros hit two home runs, while Duke Snider also hit two homers, drove in five runs, and made a spectacular catch against the center field fence to lead the Dodgers to an 8–6 victory and their ninth pennant. Don Newcombe picked up his twenty-seventh victory of the season.

The Dodgers were an experienced team that had played together through several pennant races. In the September stretch, they outplayed the Braves, refusing to buckle under the tremendous pressure of those late summer days. Duke Snider had another banner year, leading the league in home runs with 43 and driving in 101 runs. Hodges hit only .265 but slugged 32 homers and drove in 87 runs, and Furillo hit .289 with 21 homers. Suffering most of the year from injuries to both hands, Campanella tailed off to a .219 batting average, 20 homers, and 73 RBIs, while Robinson, now a utility player appearing in only 117 games, hit .275, with 10 home runs and 43 RBIs.

Although Podres spent the entire season in the military, the Dodgers still boasted one of the best pitching staffs in the league. Newcombe's 27–7 record brought him the MVP Award and the first Cy Young Award, established by the Baseball Writers of America in honor of the pitching great (511 career victories) who died in November of 1955. Carl Erskine contributed 13 wins, including the second no-hitter of his career in a 3–0 victory over the Giants on May 19 in Ebbets Field. Roger Craig had a 12–11 season, while Labine, appearing in 62 games, was 10–6 and led the league with 19 saves. But the extra pitching ingredient the Dodgers needed to nail down the pennant came from a very unexpected source. Their old nemesis, Sal Maglie, was acquired for just $1,000 on May 15 when Cleveland put him on waivers and no other team chose to gamble on an aging, seemingly washed-up, pitcher.

Dodger players and fans could hardly believe the news. Sal Maglie a Dodger? For years he had been Dodger enemy number one in the dogfights between the Brooks and Durocher's Giants. He had a lifetime record against them of 23–11. From 1950 to 1954 it had been an incredible 22–6, with five shutouts. At Ebbets Field, where he was hated by Dodger players and fans alike, he had a lifetime record of 11–3. He had sent many Dodgers sprawling into the dirt with his brushback pitches, and the Dodgers had frequently complained that he was throwing bean balls and spitters along with his fastball, sharp-breaking curve, and slider.

After they got over the shock, most Dodgers were glad to have Maglie on their side. Although he was 39 years old, suffered from back trouble, and had a 0–2 record at Cleveland that year, the Dodgers knew better than anyone else that Maglie was a "money pitcher" — the man you wanted on your mound when you had to win. Jackie Robinson, who had often done fierce battle with Maglie at the plate and on the base paths, said, "I'm only sorry he didn't come here sooner — say about five years ago." Pee Wee Reese admitted, "It'll seem a little strange to see him come walking through that door." But he added, "It's not bad having him going for you instead of against you."[10]

Maglie quickly helped the Dodger players and fans forget the past. Coming to Flatbush in the midst of a tight pennant race, he seemed to find new life, especially during the last two months of the season when he compiled a 10–2 record and a 1.88 ERA, often working with only two or three days' rest between starts. When the Dodgers needed a victory to stay close to the Braves and the Reds, he always seemed able to provide it.

On September 11 in a home game against the Braves, he drove in two runs with a single, to give his club a 4–2 victory and a tie for first place. As he took the mound in the ninth, the Dodger fans, who had so often booed him in the past, gave him a standing ovation. He was their guy now. The next day, Walter Alston said, "We wouldn't be up here now if it were not for Maglie." Campanella, who was now catching Maglie's high and tight pitches instead of ducking them, said with his usual good humor, "When that guy pitched for the Giants he looked real mean. He never shaved. Now he looks almost handsome." And Maglie was glad to be a Dodger. "Coming to the Dodgers was the luckiest break I ever had," he said. "This gave me a chance to prove to myself that I still could pitch and win."[11]

On the night of September 25, in the heat of the last week of a tight pennant race, Maglie pitched a 5–0 no-hitter against the Phillies in Ebbets Field. It was the first in his career, making him the oldest man to pitch a no-hitter since 41-year-old Cy Young turned the trick with Boston in 1908. It brought his record to 12–5 and allowed the Dodgers to hang on in the pennant race. Four days later, on the next to the last day of the season, he beat the Pirates 6–3 in a game the Dodgers had to have. He would finish the season with a 13–5 record and a 2.92 ERA.

The second place Braves were led by the slugging of veterans Joe Adcock (.291 and 38 homers), Eddie Mathews (.272 and 37 homers), and young Hank Aaron, who took the batting title with a .328 average while hitting 26 home runs. Warren Spahn (20–11), Lew Burdette (19–10), and Bob Buhl (18–8) made up a strong pitching staff, but the Braves were still one year away from fielding a championship team. At the end of 46 games, the front office dumped manager Charlie Grimm, who barely had the club above .500, and replaced him with coach Fred Haney, who guided the team to the second-place finish.

The surprising Reds ran neck and neck with the Dodgers and Braves for much of the season primarily on the basis of their tremendous home run punch. They hit 221 homers, tying the National League record set by the 1947 Giants. Left fielder and Rookie of the Year Frank Robinson hit 38 homers, while right fielder Wally Post (36 homers), center fielder Gus Bell (29), first baseman Ted Kluszewski (35), and catcher Ed Bailey (28) provided the rest of the home run power.

The Reds' fans precipitated a big controversy over the All-Star Game. Urged on by local newspaper and radio stations, they voted in large numbers for the home team, helping elect five Reds to starting positions and three others as runners-up. In an atmosphere marred by charges that Cincinnati fans had engaged in ballot stuffing, the game was played in Griffith Stadium on July 10. Led by the hitting and sparkling defensive play of Cardinal' second baseman Ken Boyer, the National League won by a score of 7–3, narrowing the junior circuit's overall lead in the event to 13–10.

Trailing the Dodgers, Braves, and Reds were the Cardinals, Phillies, Giants, Pirates, and Cubs. Robin Roberts set another record for gopher balls, serving up 46 (he would give up 502 lifetime). After six consecutive seasons with 20 or more victories he wound up with 19, losing a chance for his twentieth on the last day of the season. Roberts had excellent control and a good fastball and curve, and even pitching most of his career for the Phillies he managed a lifetime 286–245 record.

In the year of the long ball, Pirate first baseman Dale Long hit 27 homers and set a major league record in May by hitting one in eight consecutive games, breaking the previous record of six held by Lou Gehrig and

Ken Williams. The streak brought the left-handed slugger instant fame, an appearance on "The Ed Sullivan Show," a contract with a bread and milk company to endorse its products, and a raise from the Pirate management. His record stood for over 30 years, until Don Mattingly of the New York Yankees tied it in July of 1987.

The 1956 World Series opened in Ebbets Field on October 3 before 34,479 fans. It was the seventh meeting between the two clubs, and for the first time, the Dodgers were the defending champions. In spite of the claims by some that the dominance of the Yankees and Dodgers was hurting baseball and leading to another boring Series, interest was high all across the country.

With the presidential and congressional elections just a month away, it was inevitable that some of the top politicians in the country would show up for the Subway Series. President Eisenhower made a grand entrance at the opening game, being driven into Ebbets Field in a bubble-topped limousine. It was a photo opportunity not to be missed, and Eisenhower got out and shook hands with the top officials of each club and then with all the players on both teams as they stood lined up before the game. After throwing out the first ball, he sat back with Secretary of State John Foster Dulles and other government officials to watch the Dodgers, playing with the confidence befitting world champions, take the first game, 6–3. Maglie pitched a complete game, struck out 10 Yankees, and scattered 9 hits, including home runs by Mantle and Martin. After the game, the president congratulated Walter O'Malley and asked him to "tell Sal that I thought he pitched one hell of a ball game."[12]

Eisenhower's Democratic challenger showed up for the second Ebbets Field contest, which was delayed a day because of rain. As was his style, Stevenson came into the park with much less fanfare than Eisenhower, walking in like an ordinary fan and taking a seat near the dugout between New York Mayor Bob Wagner and Mrs. Averell Harriman. Like a good politician, the candidate from Illinois said, "I am for the Chicago White Sox" and wore both a Dodger and a Yankee hat during the game.[13] Along with the rest of the 36,217 fans in Ebbets Field and the millions watching on television, Stevenson was treated to a wild contest. The Dodgers blasted the Yankees 13–8 in a game lasting 3 hours and 26 minutes, a record for a nine-inning Series game. The Yankees set one record by using seven pitchers and another by giving up 11 bases on balls.

The second game brought another October humiliation for Don Newcombe, who had been dogged by the charge that he "choked up" in the big games, especially in the World Series, ever since he came up to the majors. He came into the 1956 Series with a 0–3 Series record, and now he had been knocked out of the box in the second inning after giving up six runs, including a grand slam to Yogi Berra. Newcombe left the park early, and as he departed he punched a parking lot attendant who asked him, "What's the matter, Newcombe? Can't you take it when it gets rough?" After the game a reporter asked Whitey Ford, a clutch performer who would win more Series games (10) than any other pitcher, "What about that guy? Does he really choke?" Ford replied, "I tell him that he does, but I don't believe it. I mean I'll yell 'choke' at him to try and get him mad but how the hell could he win all those games . . . this season if he's got so much trouble swallowing."[14]

The Series now moved to Yankee Stadium, where 77,977 fans turned out to watch the Yankees stop their skid with a 5–3 win over Roger Craig. Whitey Ford pitched a complete game. The margin of victory was provided by the oldest man on either team, 40-year-old left fielder Enos Slaughter, who had been described by Stengel shortly before the Series as "the only man I ever saw which plays every game as though he owns the franchise."[15] The old hustler showed his worth to the Yankee franchise by hitting a three-run homer into the right field stands in the sixth to give the Bombers the lead. The Yankees also took game four, 6–2, before 69,705 fans. Tom Sturdivant pitched a six-hitter and was supported by home runs from Mantle and Bauer.

For game five, on Monday, October 8, Alston came back with his ace, Sal Maglie, while Stengel surprised many by giving another start to Don Larsen, who had been knocked out of the box early in the second game. After a slow start early in the year, the big right-hander had come on to compile a 11–5 record and in the last month of the season had won four consecutive games in very impressive outings. In spite of his poor performance in game two, Stengel was willing to go with him again.

Larsen's career had been something of an enigma. He seemed to have all the tools necessary for becoming a great pitcher. Big and strong at 6 feet 4 inches and 215 pounds, he had a powerful arm, was an excellent fielder, and was so good with the bat that he had occasionally been used as a pinch hitter and outfielder. He would compile a lifetime batting average of .242 along with 14 home runs. Earlier in the season he had hit a grand slam off Frank Sullivan of the Red Sox. But after four years in the majors, he had won only 30 games, 10 fewer than he had lost.

Larsen had a reputation as a playboy who regarded club rules as something to be broken. His penchant for late-night carousing had long ago led his teammates to dub him "The Night Rider." Former Baltimore pilot Jimmy Dykes, who managed Larsen the year before he was traded to the Yankees, once said that "the only thing Larsen fears is sleep." The legends about Larsen grew during spring training in 1956, when his car ran off the road in St. Petersburg at 5:30 A.M., hitting a telephone pole and destroying a mailbox. When questioned about the incident, Stengel, who had broken a few rules in his day, parried reporters' questions by saying that Larsen "was mailing a letter" and that "he was either out pretty late or up pretty early." When persistent reporters asked why he did not plan to fine Larsen for the infraction, Stengel said, "Anybody who can find something to do in St. Petersburg at five in the morning deserves a medal, not a fine!"[16]

The night before his start in game five, Larsen went to a bar for a few beers, then rode back to his hotel in a taxicab with a friend, Artie Richman of the *New York Mirror*. During the cab ride he told Richman that he would like to win the Corvette that would go to the MVP in the Series. He also told him, "Maybe I'll beat Maglie tomorrow and hit a grand slam . . . . What the hell, I might even pitch a no-hitter." It was already after midnight — and after curfew — when he got out of the cab, but he bought a pizza, a Sunday newspaper, and a beer, and stayed up until after one.[17]

Monday, October 8, was a beautiful sunny day in Yankee Stadium, and 64,519 fans turned out to see the game — the 307th in World Series history — that would break the 2–2 tie. It became evident early on that they were in for a real pitcher's duel. Maglie's slider was as puzzling as ever, and his fastball was still intimidating, especially when he threw it high and inside. The 27-year-old Larsen, pitching without a windup, a technique he began late in the season in the hope that it would improve his control, had all his pitches working on the same day. His fastball had deceptive movement, his curve was sharp at different speeds, his slider looked like a fastball until it was too late for the batter to adjust to the sudden break, and his change had them swinging before the ball got to the plate.

The game remained scoreless until the fourth, when Maglie, after retiring eleven Bombers in a row and getting two balls and two strikes on Mantle, threw the Triple Crown winner an inside fastball and then watched helplessly as the ball sailed into the right field stands. Maglie gave up three singles and another run in the sixth, yielded a harmless single in the seventh, and struck out the side in the eighth. He had pitched well, allowing just five hits, two runs, and two walks through eight innings. As the game went into the ninth, he could only sit back and hope his teammates would find a way to solve the problem of Don Larsen.

But Larsen was not solvable this day. As the Dodgers came to bat trailing 2–0, he had set down 24 hitters in a row on one of baseball's best hitting teams. He had known since the seventh that he had a no-hitter going. He later recalled, "I got nervous" and became "the loneliest guy on the bench. Nobody would talk to me."[18] His teammates, of course, were just following the tradition of remaining silent so as to not invoke the jinx that had supposedly ended so many potential no-hitters in the past. Up in the broadcast booths, the radio and television announcers were also honoring the taboo. Vince Scully was saying things like "Mr. Don Larsen, through seven innings, has retired 21 men in a row," while Bob Wolff was telling his audience that "I just can't describe all that's going on as far as Larsen is concerned, but I'm sure that you who are listening are well informed."[19] The fans certainly knew. When Larsen came to bat in the eighth, he received a standing ovation.

It was a nervous Larsen who took the hill in the ninth. He was sweaty, his mouth was dry, and he later said, "I was so weak in the knees I thought I was going to faint."[20] A hush fell over the crowd. As the first hitter, Carl Furillo, stepped into the box, Berra said to him, "This guy's got good stuff, huh?" Furillo replied, "Yeah, not bad."[21] Furillo flied out to deep right field. The next hitter, Campanella, grounded out to second. Larsen had now retired 26 consecutive batters. Only one other pitcher had ever carried a no-hitter this far into a World Series game. That pitcher was another Yankee, Floyd Bevens, who in the 1947 Series, pitching to some of these same Dodgers, had held the Dodgers hitless for 8⅔ innings only to walk two and then have pinch hitter Cookie Lavagetto double off the right field wall to rob him of his no-hitter and World Series victory.

Down to one out, Alston sent Dale Mitchell up to bat for Maglie. Acquired from the Indians late in the year, the left-handed contact hitter had a .312 lifetime batting average and had struck out only 119 times in his 11-year career. Larsen worked the count on Mitchell to 1–2, then unleashed his 97th pitch of the game, a fastball, waist high, on the outside corner. At the last possible fraction of a second, Mitchell flinched as if he were going to swing, but held back. Umpire Babe Pinelli, a 24-year veteran calling his last game before retirement, thrust his right arm in the air and said, "The third strike, and you're out." Mitchell thought the ball was wide and turned around to protest, but Pinelli was already walking away from the plate. It was the 35-year-old Mitchell's last at bat in the majors, and the one that was destined to be his most remembered.

With the last out Berra ran out and jumped into Larsen's arms while the rest of the Yankee players and thousands of fans poured onto the field and swarmed toward the mound. After congratulatory hugs and pats on the back he ran off the field to the clubhouse, where a parade of visitors came by to offer their congratulations — Yankee owners Del Webb and Dan Topping, Ford Frick, and reporters seeking interviews. Maglie and Robinson came over from the Dodger clubhouse. Maglie, who had pitched a no-hitter of his own just a few days before and whose own great performance in this game was overshadowed by a better one, told Larsen, "I felt sorry for you in the ninth, Don, because I knew what was going through your mind. You were the best and there was nothing we could do about it."[22]

Not only had Larsen pitched the only no-hitter in the history of the World Series, he had pitched just the sixth perfect game — no hits, walks, hit batsmen, errors, or runs — in major league history. He had struck out seven, five of them on called third strikes. Seventy-one of his pitches were in the strike zone, and only nine fair balls were hit out of the infield. Many Hall of Fame pitchers—including Grover Cleveland Alexander, Dizzy Dean, Lefty Grove, Early Wynn, and Whitey Ford—never pitched a no-hitter in regular season competition, much less in the World Series.

Larsen's perfect game made the front page of the nation's newspapers the next day. In one of the best stories, Shirley Povich of the *Washington Post* wrote, "The million-to-one shot came in. Hell froze over today. A month of Sundays hit the calendar. Don Larsen pitched a no-hit, no-run, no-man-reach-first game in a World Series."[23]

The rest of the Series was anticlimatic. The Dodgers came back to Ebbets Field on October 9 and squared the Series with a 10-inning, 1–0 victory when Enos Slaughter misjudged a fly ball hit by Jackie Robinson, letting it go over his head and allowing Gilliam to score from second. In the seventh game, Newcombe was given another chance to redeem himself, while Stengel started 23-year-old right-hander Johnny Kucks. Burning to end his reputation for choking, Newcombe only added to it, giving up two homers to Berra and another to Elston Howard before departing in the fourth with a five-run deficit. The Dodgers never recovered, and the Yanks went on to win, 9–0, behind Kucks's three-hitter. All of the Yankee runs came off home runs—Berra hit two two-run homers, Howard a solo, and Moose Skowron a grand slam in the seventh that buried the Dodgers. Alston made no alibis, telling reporters after the game, "They beat the hell out of us. Casey did a good job—and they got some hitting."[24] After the loss, it was inevitable that comics around the country would quip, "Wait 'till last year."

In a dramatic, well-played Series, the Yankees had outplayed the Dodgers, compiling a .253 batting average to the Bums' puny .195, outslugging them 12 homers to 3, and outscoring them 33 to 25. Berra hit .360, the highest for either club, and had 10 RBIs, a new record. Slaughter had 7 hits, including a homer, and a .350 batting average. The Yankees outpitched the Dodgers, too, compiling a 2.48 ERA to the Dodgers' 4.72. For the losers, Snider and Hodges both hit .304, with Snider's tenth World Series home run in game two tying him with Lou Gehrig for second place behind Babe Ruth. Maglie and Labine both pitched well, but Newcombe was knocked out of the box in both starts and wound up with a 21.21 ERA. In his World Series career, he had started five games, lost four, won none, pitched only one complete game, and lasted a total of 14 innings in the other four. He would get no further chances to redeem himself; this would be his last trip to the fall classic.

The highlight of the Series, and the one that would be remembered long after many would forget who even won it, was Don Larsen's perfect game. For his feat, he received a $5,000 Corvette from *Sport* magazine as the series MVP, was paid $7,500 for an appearance on "The Bob Hope Show," picked up thousands more for appearances on other radio and television shows, was the subject of interviews for newspaper and magazine articles, and received more requests for paid speaking engagements than he could possibly honor. Just two years after his 3–21 record with Baltimore tagged him as the worst pitcher in major league baseball, he had gained baseball immortality. Not long after the Series Larsen said, "I know I'm going to wake up one of these days, but right now I'm still kind of numb. Here I am all of a sudden with a business manager, and a bunch of big deals, and a lot of social invites. . . . Why, I haven't even had a chance yet to have a beer in peace."[25]

Perhaps it was his penchant for late hours, or a lack of the kind of inner drive and ambition that enabled players of less talent to become stars, but Larsen never had another year that came anywhere close to matching his time in the sun in 1956. In 1959, when he was traded to Kansas City after winning a total of 45 games for the Yankees in his five-year stay in New York, Stengel said, "He should be good, but he ain't."[26] After leaving the Yankees he would pitch for six more major league clubs and in the minors before finally winding up his career with the Cubs in 1967. In 14 years in the majors, he was able to do no better than a mediocre 81–91 won-lost record. Some said he was a wasted talent. But for two hours and six minutes on that one day in October of 1956, he was the best pitcher in World Series history.

The offseason brought the end of the careers of two of baseball's greatest players, Bob Feller and Jackie Robinson.

Feller announced his retirement at a luncheon held at Cleveland Municipal Stadium on December 28. During a ceremony which saw his uniform number "19" retired, Feller said that he planned to devote his time to his insurance business but would retain his job as president of the Major League Baseball Players Association until work on a new pension plan was completed.

Thus ended the career of one of baseball's greatest pitchers, certainly one of its fastest. Manager Bucky Harris of the Washington Senators once told his young hitters that the only advice he could give them when they were batting against Feller was to "go up and hit what you see. And if you don't see anything, come on back."[27] Breaking into the majors at the age of 17 in 1936, the fireballer went into the record books with 266 wins and 162 losses. If he had not lost four years to the service during World War II he would certainly have made it into the 300-win circle. He also was credited with 3 no-hitters, 12 one-hitters, 6 seasons with 20 or more wins, 46 shutouts, and 2,581 strikeouts. He once fanned 18 batters in one game and 27 in two consecutive contests. But the biggest prize always eluded him — a World Series victory. It was one of the major disappointments of his career.

The news of Feller's retirement was overshadowed by the controversial events surrounding the closing of Jackie Robinson's career. On December 13, Robinson had been traded to the New York Giants for $35,000 and left-handed pitcher Dick Littlefield. It quickly became the most sensational baseball story in New York since Leo Durocher crossed over from the Dodgers to the Giants in the middle of the 1948 season. The trade seemed to be a good deal for both clubs. The Dodgers needed to get rid of some older players with high salaries, Junior Gilliam had already nudged Robinson out of his second base spot, and the team needed a left-handed pitcher. The Giants needed a first baseman, and Robinson would be a marvelous gate draw, especially when teamed with Willie Mays. Robinson was obviously nearing the end of his career, but in the past season there had been times when the old Robinson seemed to come to life with a clutch hit, a crucial stolen base, or a good defensive play.

Robinson was stunned at the news of his trade, which he learned about from a phone call from Buzzie Bavasi, the vice president and general manager of the Dodgers. He felt betrayed, but he also faced a dilemma. At the time he received Bavasi's call he had already decided to retire from baseball and had concluded two important business deals. He had just agreed to take a $50,000-a-year job as the vice president of personnel with Chock Full O'Nuts, a restaurant chain, and had sold exclusive rights to his retirement story to *Look* magazine for $50,000, over $7,000 more than he had ever made in one year as a player. For the article to be worth that much to the national magazine, news of his retirement would have to remain secret until the article appeared.

Caught in this awkward situation, Robinson was evasive. When contacted by reporters about the trade, he said that he was "disappointed in leaving Brooklyn" and that he hoped that "Brooklyn can win again unless the Giants can win it."[28] He also told one reporter, "I'm going to play as long as I can. I'm going to give it all I've got."[29]

The *Look* issue containing Robinson's article was received by most subscribers on Saturday, January 5, and the next morning the *New York Times* and other newspapers around the country carried the news. In the two-page article entitled simply, "Why I'm Quitting Baseball," Robinson said, "There shouldn't be any mystery about my reasons. I'm 38 years old, with a family to support. I've got to think of my future and our security. At my age, a man doesn't have much future in baseball—and very little security. It's as simple as that. . . . I'm through with baseball because I know that in a matter of time baseball will be through with me." Knowing that the secrecy surrounding his retirement would arouse considerable controversy, Robinson said, "I've always played fair with my newspaper friends, and I think they'll understand why this was the one time I couldn't give them the whole story as soon as I knew it."[30]

The news of Robinson's retirement caused as much of an uproar as the news about his trade did back in December. "I still can't believe he won't play," Giants vice-president Chub Feeney said. "I can't believe he was just misleading the newspapermen he has spoken to and told he would play." Bavasi, who had often feuded with Robinson, left no doubt as to how he felt. "That's typical of Jackie," he told reporters. "Now he'll write a letter of apology to Chubby. He has been writing letters of apology all his life." Bavasi went on to say, "This is the way he repays the newspapermen for what they've done for him. He tells you one thing and then writes another for money. You fellows will find out you've been blowing the horn for the wrong guy." Bavasi's comment brought an angry retort from Robinson, who told reporters, "After what Bavasi said, I wouldn't play ball again for a million dollars."[31]

Some members of the press felt that Robinson had deliberately deceived them and that it was unethical for him to sell his story to one publication. Many of them agreed with the *Washington Post*'s Shirley Povich, who wrote that from 1947 on, Robinson "was a big leaguer all the way, until his final act of retirement. And then he went out bush." But other sportswriters wrote that Robinson had acted the best he could in a very difficult situation and that the press owed as much to Robinson, who had provided them with so much good copy over the years, as he did to them. Al Abrams of the *Pittsburgh Post-Gazette* wrote, "I just can't get ruffled over the charge that Robinson treated newspapers unfairly in concealing his retirement plans until the magazine broke the story. Let's just say that Jackie rode out of baseball on a controversial wave, just as he rode in some ten years ago."[32]

Robinson's career had been a short one, for racism had kept him out of a major league uniform until he was 28 years old. In his decade on major league diamonds he had played 1,382 games and helped lead the Dodgers to six pennants and one world championship. He had a lifetime batting average of .311, hit over .300 six times, took the batting title in 1949 with a .342 average, hit 137 home runs, scored 947 runs, batted in 734 runs, and stole 197 bases, including 11 thefts of home (more than any post–World War II player). He led the league in stolen bases in 1947 and 1949, and his base-stealing totals would undoubtedly have been higher except for the Dodger style of play which emphasized power hitting. He was the Rookie of the Year in 1947, the National League's MVP in 1949, and drew millions of fans to tiny Ebbets Field and to parks all across the National League. In 1962 he would be elected to the Hall of Fame.

Statistics alone do not reveal Robinson's true worth to the Brooklyn Dodgers. He was a fiery competitor and leader who always played for keeps and was always regarded by opponents as the most dangerous player on the club. Leo Durocher, who supported bringing Robinson to the Dodgers and then feuded with him from 1948 on, said at the time of Robinson's retirement, "He can beat you in more ways than any player I know."[33] Teammate

Roy Campanella claimed, "Jackie could beat you every way there was to beat you. . . . I have never seen a ballplayer that could do all the things that Jackie Robinson did. . . . He could think so much faster than anybody I ever played with or against. . . . He was two steps and one thought ahead of anyone else."[34] And Duke Snider later recalled, "He could beat you with his bat, his glove, his throwing arm, his legs, and his brain—and if he couldn't do it with any of those, he could beat you with his mouth."[35]

Jackie Robinson was opinionated, argumentative, loud, aggressive, competitive, abrasive. He was often criticized for these traits, which were, incidentally, shared by Leo Durocher, Eddie Stanky, and many other white players. Roger Kahn would later write in *The Boys of Summer,* "Like a few, very few athletes, Babe Ruth, Jim Brown, Robinson did not merely play at center stage. He was center stage; and wherever he walked, center stage moved with him."[36] When number "42" retired, baseball lost one of its greatest competitors and performers.

With his retirement, Robinson disappeared from center stage but not from the public eye. An active member of the NAACP and a friend and follower of Martin Luther King, Jr., he was outspoken on civil rights and politics. But he aged rapidly, his health and energy sapped by a heart condition, arthritis, and diabetes, which gradually robbed him of his sight. He also suffered a great tragedy when his son, Jackie, Jr., born during his historic year at Montreal in 1946, developed a drug problem, was rehabilitated, and then died in an automobile wreck in 1971.

In 1972, he threw out the first ball in the second World Series game at Riverfront Stadium in Cincinnati, and was honored with a plaque commemorating the 25th anniversary of his big league debut. As he accepted the plaque, he said, "I am extremely proud and pleased, but I will be more pleased the day I can look over at third base and see a black man as manager."[37] Nine days later, at the age of 53, he was dead. Three years later, as part of the revolution Robinson had begun in 1947, Frank Robinson took the field as the manager of the Cleveland Indians.

Jackie Robinson was always more than a ballplayer. He was an agent and symbol of integration and black progress, and he forced blacks and whites to talk about racism and integration long before *Brown v. Board of Education* and the civil rights activities of the fifties and sixties. His revolutionary integration of the national pastime had helped to publicize the problems of blacks, to promote black pride, to break down prejudices and racial barriers, and to pave the way for the acceptance of blacks in other areas of American life. The Reverend King once told Don Newcombe, "You'll never know what you and Jackie and Roy did to make it possible for me to do my job."[38] More than anyone since Babe Ruth, Robinson had transformed the national pastime, and in the process had helped to transform America itself.

16. Three-Time Loser (1957)

"The pennant races should follow the usual pattern: the Yankees will run away and hide from the rest of the American League, and the Dodgers, gasping for breath, will stagger home ahead of the Braves and the Redlegs in the National League. The World Series? The Yanks will win again."[1]

So predicted noted sportswriter Tom Meany in his annual baseball preview in *Look* magazine. Picking pennant winners is a hazardous enterprise, and Meany can be pardoned for being so far off the mark. The Braves, not the Dodgers, would take the National League pennant, and then go on to deny Casey Stengel's attempt to capture his eighth World Series. But for many fans in New York and across the nation, baseball's central story in 1957 was not the pennant races but the controversy surrounding the decision of the Dodgers and the Giants to abandon their fans and move across the continent to California.

Such a move was probably inevitable. Large as it was, New York City was not supporting its three major league teams adequately. The Yankees, with their large stadium and winning ways and traditions, naturally drew the best. Over two million fans came through the turnstiles for five consecutive years, 1946–1950, before dropping off to a little less than 2 million in 1951 and to around 1.5 million from 1952 through 1956. The Dodgers, playing in the crackerbox of Ebbets Field with a capacity of around 33,000, drew over a million fans each year between 1945 and 1956. However, after reaching a peak of 1.8 million fans in 1947 their annual attendance steadily declined to just slightly over a million between 1954 and 1956. The Giants, playing in the Polo Grounds with a 56,000 seating capacity, drew over a million each year between 1945 and 1951, reaching a high of 1.6 million in 1947, a figure they could never match even during the great pennant races of 1951 and 1954. By 1956, attendance at the Polo Grounds was down to 629,179.

It was obvious that although the New York teams dominated major league baseball in the postwar period, provided some of baseball's greatest rivalries, and consistently fielded some of the game's biggest stars, support was declining. Some observers blamed it on television and other attractions that kept fans away from the parks, but they also pointed to other factors. The Dodgers and the Giants both played in aging structures with inadequate parking, seating, and other facilities. Also like other large cities, New York was suffering from an exodus of middle and upper class citizens to the suburbs. Brooklyn, especially, was changing very rapidly. In the postwar period, many middle class Brooklynites moved to the suburbs of Long Island, Staten Island, and New Jersey.

As Dodger and Giant executives began to search for a place to move their franchises, California began to look more and more inviting. The state's dramatic population growth in the forties and fifties had opened up a potentially lucrative market for professional baseball, and rapid improvements in air travel were making it easier for teams to play a coast-to-coast schedule. Such a move would likely be supported by most of the other owners. Like Commissioner Ford Frick, they felt that westward expansion would attract new fans and possibly head off any potential antitrust action by the U.S. Congress or the Supreme Court.

The leader in the move to the West Coast was Walter O'Malley, the cigar-chomping Dodger owner who had become a stockholder in the club in 1932, club attorney in 1943, part owner in 1944, and then bought out Branch Rickey's share of the team at the end of the 1950 season. A shrewd businessman, O'Malley went on to acquire controlling interest from the other owners. Running the club like a dictator, he had the look and reputation of a tough, tightfisted autocrat. Bill Veeck once described him as a man with "a face that even Dale Carnegie would want to punch."[2]

Love of profits rather than love of the game of baseball guided O'Malley's actions as a major league owner. The Dodgers were one of the most successful teams in baseball, both on the field and in the financial ledgers, but he wanted more. He looked longingly at the success of the Milwaukee Braves, Baltimore Orioles, and Kansas City Athletics, who were drawing big crowds in their new locations. O'Malley complained publicly of the Dodgers' problems and negotiated with New York City officials for a new stadium site. To underscore his concerns, he scheduled his Dodgers to play seven games in Roosevelt Stadium in Jersey City in 1956 and eight more in 1957.

Between the end of the 1956 season and June of 1957, O'Malley was a busy man. He purchased the Chicago Cubs' Pacific Coast League franchise in Los Angeles, flew to Los Angeles to talk with civic officials about the possibility of moving the Dodgers to their city, hosted Los Angeles officials at the Dodger spring training camp in Vero Beach, and purchased a 44-passenger airplane which, he said, "would prove useful if the team decided to leave Brooklyn."[3] On October 30, 1956, he announced that he had sold Ebbets Field to Marvin Kratter, a Brooklyn contractor who planned to demolish the baseball structure and erect a housing project for middle income families on its site. The Dodgers would retain a lease on the property through 1959.

All the while, O'Malley continued negotiations with New York state and city officials on an acceptable site for a new stadium somewhere in the New York City area. He also talked with Giant owner Horace Stoneham, who loved New York but was facing financial disaster as attendance at Giant home games continued to dwindle. Stoneham was already considering moving his team to Minneapolis, the home of his American Association franchise, and he lent a receptive ear to O'Malley when he described how profitable it would be to both of them if they moved their rivalry to the warmer climate and hungry fans on the West Coast.

As the 1957 season got underway, Giant and Dodger fans began to see that the impossible — the migration of the Giants and Dodgers all the way across the country — was taking shape as the inevitable. Stoneham and O'Malley were obviously looking around for greener pastures, and the other National League owners were not opposed as long as both teams moved. If only one team relocated to the West Coast, it would be too expensive for the other clubs to travel that far just to play one series in one city. In early June, the league owners met in Chicago and approved the transfer of the Dodgers to Los Angeles and the Giants to San Francisco if and when they decided to go.

New Yorkers were both angered and saddened by the news that the Giants and Dodgers might be leaving town. City leaders made new attempts to come to terms with O'Malley on a site for a new stadium. Fans formed "Keep the Dodgers in Brooklyn" committees, collecting thousands of names on petitions and distributing thousands of buttons. City newspapers also campaigned to keep the two clubs in town and lambasted O'Malley and Stoneham as greedy barons who had no love for the game or the city.

While most of the criticism was aimed at O'Malley, it was Stoneham who made the first official move. On August 19, 1957, the club's board of directors met in the Giants' office at 100 West 42nd Street in New York and voted to move the club to San Francisco for the 1958 season. In announcing the decision, Stoneham told reporters that the Giants would play most of their home games in Seals Stadium, which seated only 23,000, while the new park was being built by the city. As a part of the deal bringing the Giants to San Francisco, the city had agreed to build a new $5 million stadium and to lease it to the Giants for 35 years. The city had also agreed to construct and operate a parking lot with spaces for over 10,000 automobiles.

Still, with all these advantages, Stoneham said, "It's a tough wrench. We're very sorry we're leaving." When reporters jamming his office asked the motives behind the move, Stoneham justified it solely on economic grounds. "It was lack of attendance," he said. One reporter asked, "In other words, baseball is a business, not a sport?" Stoneham answered, "It is conducted as a sport, but it takes money to conduct it." The reporter then followed up with, "How do you feel about the kids in New York from whom you are taking the Giants?" Stoneham had an answer for this, too: "I feel bad about the kids. I've seen lots of them at the Polo Grounds. But I haven't seen many of their fathers lately."[4]

The loss of the Giants was a bitter blow to Giant fans everywhere. One of the nation's premier sportswriters and rabid Giant fans, Roger Angell, undoubtedly expressed the opinions of many of his fellow fans when he later wrote in *Holiday* magazine, "The end of the World came on Monday, August 19, 1957. . . . It was a funny way for the world to end: no trumpets, no clap of thunder, no fireball — just a brief announcement of the vote by a plump, pin-striped businessman named Horace C. Stoneham."[5]

Meanwhile, Dodger officials remained silent about their own plans. The rumors continued to fly — the Dodgers were moving to Los Angeles, they were close to an agreement with New York City officials on a new stadium site, they were going to work out a deal with the Yankees and share Yankee Stadium. There were last-ditch efforts to save the team, ranging from petitions and demonstrations to Nelson Rockefeller's attempts to help raise $3 million to enable the Dodgers to acquire a downtown site for a new stadium. In September, all negotiations between the Dodgers and city officials broke down, but by then most New Yorkers had accepted the inevitable, which would be announced during the World Series.

In the midst of all the turmoil over the westward moves, the Dodgers and Giants still had a schedule to play. It was not a banner year for either team. The Dodgers were showing serious signs of wear. *Sports Illustrated*'s Robert Creamer called them "an old team, a collection of marvelous baseball players but old ones, past their prime, prone to injury, prone to ailments, losing slowly but surely to age."[6] The club had a nucleus of young players in their early and mid–twenties, but the heart of the lineup was made up of men past their prime.

Although hampered by a bad knee, Duke Snider hit 40 homers, the fifth consecutive year he had hit 40 or more. Don Drysdale, a 20-year-old fastballer, hinted at his great future by topping all Dodger pitchers with a 17–9 record and a 2.69 ERA. But Carl Furillo (.306) was the only Dodger regular to hit over .300, a sore arm limited Don Newcombe to an 11–12 record, and Sal Maglie's 6–6 record at the end of August led the Dodgers to sell him to the Yankees for $37,000 and two minor league players.

The Dodgers would be contenders for over half the season, and in fact were only one game out of first for nearly a week in the middle of July, but they faded and were not a factor in the race during the last month. They finished in third place, 11 games out, marking the first time in eight years that they had not finished first or second. Still, they managed to draw 1,028,258 diehard fans.

The Giants had a dismal year on the field and at the gate. Willie Mays hit .333, slugged 35 home runs, and led the league in stolen bases for the second year in a row with 38. But his team won only 69 games, finished in sixth place, 26 games off the pace, and drew only 653,923 fans. One afternoon game in May with the Cards attracted just 1,604 spectators. The Giants seemed to be responding to the turmoil about their future by just playing out the string of meaningless games.

While there was unhappiness in New York, there was joy in Milwaukee, whose Braves had started the franchise shakeup in 1953 and had found new fans and new life after the move. After drawing only 281,278 paying customers in their last year in Boston, the Braves drew 1.8 million in 1953 and over 2 million each year between 1954 and 1956, setting new National League records. In this baseball-mad city, a German restaurant on Oakland Street bore a sign that read "Kalt's–29,952 Feet N.E. Of Home Plate," while a factory placed a "Special Notice" at its entrance saying that "All Requests for Leaves of Absence Owing to Funerals, Lame Backs, Housecleaning, Moving, Sore Throats, Headaches, Indigestion, etc., Must Be Handed in Not Later Than 10 A.M. On The Day of the Game."[7]

While eager fans poured through the turnstiles, the team responded with better play on the field. After finishing seventh in their last year in Boston, they finished second in 1953, third in 1954, and then second again in 1955 and 1956. After dumping manager Charlie Grimm for Fred Haney after 46 games in 1956, they had come on to finish only one game behind the Dodgers. In 1957, the players and their fans expected to take it all.

In his three years at Pittsburgh (1953–1955), Haney had had little talent to work with and suffered through three consecutive last place finishes. But at Milwaukee, he had a good, young club built around long-ball hitters Hank Aaron, Eddie Mathews, and Joe Adcock, and pitchers Warren Spahn, Lew Burdette, and Bob Buhl. In June the club also made a far-reaching trade when it sent three players to the Giants in exchange for veteran second baseman Red Schoendienst, who became the cornerstone of the infield.

Haney's team came out of the gate fast, winning 9 of their first 10 games, sparking hope that they would waltz to the pennant. But in the first half of the season the Dodgers, Reds, Cardinals, and Phillies put together long winning streaks interspersed with dramatic slumps to challenge the Braves for the lead. As late as June 30, even the sixth-place Giants were only six games out. At the All-Star break, the Cardinals were on top, but the Braves, Phils, Reds, and Dodgers were not far behind.

For the second season in a row, the All-Star contest became mired in controversy because of the actions of the Cincinnati fans. Near the end of the voting period a Cincinnati newspaper published ballots with the names of the Reds players already filled in, and within a week over a half million votes flooded in from the Cincinnati area, helping to place seven Reds on the starting team. After consulting with the league presidents, Commissioner Frick removed three Reds—George Crowe, Gus Bell, and Wally Post—from contention, saying, "The National League . . . feels that the overbalance of Cincinnati ballots has resulted in the selection of a team which would not be typical of the league."[8]

They were replaced with Stan Musial, Willie Mays, and Hank Aaron, who had been leading before the last minute balloting. This still left five Reds—catcher Ed Bailey, second baseman Johnny Temple, third baseman Don Hoak, shortstop Roy McMillan, and left fielder Frank Robinson—in the starting lineup. All five had been the leaders or strong contenders for their positions before the deluge of ballots from Cincinnati.

Played in Sportsman's Park in St. Louis on July 9, the All-Star Game was won by the American League by a 6–5 score. These would be the last All-Star teams chosen by the fans for several years. After the travesty of the Cincinnati ballot stuffing, the top baseball authorities decided that beginning in 1958, the selection of players would be turned over to the players, managers, and coaches, who could vote only for players in their respective leagues and could not choose their own teammates. This would be the selection process until 1970, when Commissioner Bowie Kuhn put the vote back in the hands of the fans.

With the All-Star Game and controversy out of the way, the National League clubs resumed their pennant wars. The Braves appeared to suffer double disasters when Adcock suffered a broken leg sliding into second base in late June, putting him out of action until early September, and speedy outfielder Bill Bruton suffered a severe knee injury in a collision with teammate Felix Mantilla in July and went on the disabled list for the rest of the year. Faced with these injuries, Haney reached down to Wichita for outfielders Bob Hazle and Wes Covington to add fielding and hitting punch and Don McMahon to shore up the bullpen. By July 29, the Braves were back on top by a half game, with only 2½ games separating them from the fifth-place Dodgers.

In August, while their opponents suffered long, demoralizing losing streaks, the Braves won 17 of 19, including 10 in a row, enabling them to build an 8½-game lead by Labor Day. But the boys from Milwaukee now seemed to unravel, losing 8 of 11, while the Cardinals, with Stan Musial coming off the injured list to hit .500 over a critical two-week period, looked like world champions as they fashioned a 10–2 record and narrowed the gap to just 2½ games by September 15. The Braves regrouped, won 8 in a row, and clinched the pennant on September 23 when Hank Aaron hit his forty-third homer of the year with one on in the eleventh inning to give the Braves a 4–2 victory over the Cardinals. At season's end, they led St. Louis by eight games and had established yet another National League attendance record of 2.2 million. It was just the third pennant in the club's history, with the other two coming in 1914 and 1948.

Over the long season, the Braves had proven themselves to be a solid club with a good starting team and a strong bench. They led the league in homers (199), triples (62), slugging average (.442), and runs (772). Hank Aaron hit .322, led the league in homers (44) and RBIs (132), and took the MVP Award. Mathews hit .292 and contributed 32 homers and 94 RBIs. While he could not entirely replace the injured Adcock, Frank Torre filled in ably at first base and contributed a .272 average, 5 homers, and 40 RBIs. Red Schoendienst proved the wisdom of the mid–June trade that brought him from the Giants by hitting .310 and setting a new league record in hits (200). Fresh from Wichita, Covington hit .284 with 21 homers and 65 RBIs.

One of the biggest contributions came from Bob Hazle, who was brought up from Wichita and installed in the lineup in late July to replace the injured Bill Bruton. The 26-year-old outfielder provided the extra spark the Braves needed in their pennant drive. A .279 hitter at Wichita, he went on a batting tear in the majors, hitting over .500 for most of August before cooling off to .317 in September. He finished the season at .403 with a .649 slugging percentage, 7 homers, and 27 RBIs, many of them in crucial situations. During Hazle's hot streak in August, Schoendienst marveled, "Right now the kid is Stan Musial, Mickey Mantle, and Ted Williams all wrapped up in one."[9] Playing in just 41 games, his torrid hitting and sparkling defensive play earned him the nickname of "Hurricane," named after the famous Hurricane Hazel that had devastated much of the East Coast in 1954.

The pitching staff was anchored by Warren Spahn, who had been one of the aces of the mound corps since his first full season in 1946. A master of the fastball, curve, slider, screwball, changeup, and sinkerball, Spahn won more games (202) than any other pitcher in the majors in the 1950s. By the time he retired in 1965, he had won 363 games, more than any left-hander in history, paced the league in wins eight times, and pitched 63 shutouts. In 1957, he led all National League pitchers with a 21–11 record, while Bob Buhl finished at 18–7, and Lew Burdette, often called "Saliva Lew," won 17. Big Gene Conley (6 feet 8 inches tall, 225 pounds), who would spend part of his career playing two major league sports — baseball with the Braves, Phillies, and Red Sox and basketball with the Boston Celtics and New York Knicks — finished at 9–9.

Led by 36-year-old Stan Musial, who won his seventh batting title with a .351 average while hitting 29 homers and driving in 102 runs, Fred Hutchinson's Cardinals made a good try at winning their first pennant since 1946 before fading near the end. Musial also established a new league record for consecutive games played when he stretched his streak to 895 before having to sit out 20 games with a shoulder injury. The old record had been 822, set by first baseman Gus Suhr of the Pirates in the 1930s.

Played in the turmoil surrounding the movement of the Giants and Dodgers to the West Coast, the National League race produced the first pennant winner from outside of New York since 1950 and only the fourth since World War II. It also brought a spate of unusual events. Pitcher Don Newcombe, in one of his lapses of concentration on the mound, was hit on the head by a new ball thrown out by the plate umpire. Fog postponed a game at Ebbets Field, the first time a major league game had ever been so postponed according to baseball reporters and historians after a hasty examination of the record books. The Cincinnati Reds paid $80,000 for a new electronic scoreboard, which seemed to work well until the Reds routed the Cubs 22–3 and the scoreboard operators discovered that it was not designed to display more than 19 runs or hits. On July 31, after Pittsburgh manager Bobby Bragan was ejected from the game for jockeying the umpires from the dugout, he strolled out on the field sipping a cup of orange juice through a straw, went up to the umpires, and offered them a drink of his juice. He was promptly banished from the park, and National League president Warren Giles followed up with a reprimand and a $100 fine for "repeated farcical acts." Three days later, Pirate officials fired him and replaced him with one of his coaches, Danny Murtaugh, who began his 15-year reign at the helm of the Pirates. Brooklyn Dodger official Red Patterson was on the mark when he said, "This year is a bizarre one. That's the word for it—bizarre."[10]

As was widely expected, Milwaukee's opponent in the World Series was the New York Yankees. To get there, the Bombers had to beat back the challenge of the Chicago White Sox, who played much of the season as if they were destined to win their first flag in 38 years. Under new manager Al Lopez, the White Sox would be labeled the "Go-Go" White Sox, relying on speed, stolen bases, the hit and run, good defensive play, and other elements of old-fashioned baseball. The White Sox won 11 of their first 13 games, stumbled and lost 5 in a row, then launched a 9-game winning streak. On May 22, they led the Yankees by three games, and by June 8 had built their margin to six.

But on June 9 the Yankees began to play like Yankees. They won 26 of their next 32 games, while the Sox went into a prolonged slump that allowed the Yankees to take over first place on June 30 and build their lead to 6 by July 19. But the White Sox continued to press the Bombers, cutting the lead to 3½ games before the Yankees came to the Windy City on August 27 for a crucial three-game set. Large crowds came out to Comiskey Park hoping to see their favorites sweep the series and pull to within a half game of first. But it was not to be. The Yankees took all three games and left town with a 6½-game cushion. After this crushing setback, the Sox could get no closer than 4½ games. On September 23, the same day the Braves clinched the National League pennant, the Yankees wrapped up the flag in the junior circuit.

The Yankees had won the twnety-third pennant in the franchise's history, the third in a row, and the eighth in the nine years Stengel had been at the helm. It was one of the weakest of the Old Professor's teams. Although the club led the league in hitting (.268) and ERA (3.00), it had only two .300 hitters (Mantle and Skowron) and no 20-game winners. Troubled by injuries, Mantle could not match his Triple Crown performance of the previous year, but he did hit .365, club 34 homers, drive in 94 runs, and capture his second consecutive American League MVP Award. Rookie of the Year Tony Kubek hit .297 and showed amazing versatility by playing two outfield positions along with shortstop, second and third base. Whitey Ford developed a sore shoulder and fell off to an 11–5 record, leaving Tom Sturdivant as the top hurler with a 16–6 mark. Bob Turley followed with a 13–6 record, and little Bobby Shantz, acquired from the Kansas City Athletics during the off season, was 11–5. Shantz won eight games in a row at one point and led the league in ERA with a 2.45 mark.

The 1957 Yankees were as famous for their brawling as for their baseball skills. The most notable incident came early in the year and far away from the baseball diamond. On May 15, six Yankee players, four of them accompanied by their wives, attended a party at a Manhattan night club in honor of Billy Martin's twenty-ninth birthday. Near midnight, several of the players got into a tussle with other guests that led to assault charges being filed against Hank Bauer. As a result, the Yankee owners fined Bauer, Mantle, Martin, Berra, and Ford $1,000 each, while Johnny Kucks got off with a $500 fine. The charges against Bauer were later dropped, and at the end of the season the Yankee owners returned all the fines.

Less than a month later, on June 9, the Yankees were involved in another brawl, this time on the field. In Detroit a free-for-all erupted after Ray Boone accused Tom Sturdivant of throwing at him. League officials found Boone and Sturdivant equally culpable and fined each $100. Just four days later, the Yankees were involved in an even more serious fray in a game with the White Sox when Yankee pitcher Art Ditmar sent Larry Doby sprawling into the dust with a brushback pitch. Doby got up, rushed the mound, and nailed Ditmar with a good left hook. Both dugouts emptied as players rushed on the field to do battle. Martin was one of the major participants in the donnybrook, as were teammate Enos Slaughter and White Sox first baseman Walt Dropo. Forty-one years old, balding, and 8 inches shorter and 30 pounds lighter than Dropo (6 feet 5 inches, 220 pounds) Slaughter exchanged several blows with Dropo before emerging from the field with his shirt nearly torn off his chest.

League officials fined Martin, Slaughter, and Doby $150 each, and

Ditmar and Dropo $100 each. The Yankee top brass decided it was time for the volatile Martin to ply his trade in some other town. Two days after the fight, George Weiss traded him to Kansas City, the second of seven clubs he would play with before his playing career came to an end in 1961.

The White Sox finished second, eight games out, their best finish since 1920. Under Lopez's brilliant managing, the Sox played inspired baseball and were in contention for the flag right up to the last month. Billy Pierce led the league with 20 wins, and Bob Keegan pitched the only no-hitter in either league, a 6–0 win over the Senators on August 20. But the Sox were hurt by the lack of a real batting punch, by injuries, and most of all, by an inability to beat the Yankees. The Pale Hose lost 14 of 22 contests to the Bombers, and the eight-game difference was exactly the number of games the Sox trailed the Yankees at season's end.

After finishing in fourth place for four consecutive seasons, the Red Sox rose to third, 16 games out. In spite of drawing 119 walks and suffering from various injuries and illnesses that limited his playing time to 132 games, Ted Williams recorded enough at bats and hits to capture the batting crown with a .388 average, the highest since his own .406 mark in 1941. At the age of 39, he was the oldest player to win the crown in the history of either league. He also added 38 homers, only 4 behind league-leader Roy Sievers of Washington.

Detroit came in fourth, while Baltimore, Cleveland, Kansas City, and Washington rounded out the second division. The team that fell the hardest was Cleveland. Under new manager Kerby Farrell they dropped from second to sixth, their worst finish in 11 years. Bob Feller had retired, and Early Wynn, Mike Garcia, and Bob Lemon combined for only 32 victories. Injuries to several players, especially the spring tragedy that hit their young star pitcher, Herb Score, clouded the Tribe's entire season.

Billed as a left-handed Bob Feller, Score had broken in with the club in 1955, sporting a 16–10 record and a league-leading 245 strikeouts, a new record for a rookie. The fireballer with the wicked curve was even better in his second year with a 20–9 record and 263 strikeouts, again leading the league. On March 17, the Indians had turned down a Red Sox offer of $1 million for the young phenomenon, and as the season began he seemed to be off to another good year when he struck out 39 hitters in his first 36 innings of work.

But on May 7, in a night contest with the Yankees, disaster struck the 23-year-old pitcher just three minutes into the game. After leadoff hitter Hank Bauer grounded to third, Gil McDougald smashed a line drive back to the mound. The ball was hit so hard that Score had no chance to duck or get his glove up to defend himself. The ball hit him in the right eye, then bounced over to third baseman Al Smith, who instinctively fielded it and threw McDougald out at first before joining his teammates in the rush to the mound. Score later recalled, "I fired it up there, heard the crack of the bat, looked up and I can remember seeing the ball coming right into my eye. Boy, it had got big awfully fast and it was getting bigger. There was really nothing I could do about it."[11]

Score fell to the ground as if he had been shot, and players and coaches from both teams rushed out to the mound. His nose and mouth were filled with blood, and he was in great pain, but he was conscious and calm. As Garcia bent over him, Score said, "Bear, you can't say I didn't keep an eye on *that* ball."[12] After ice packs were applied to his nose and eye, he was taken off the field on a stretcher and carried to the clubhouse to wait for an ambulance to transport him to Lakeside Hospital. Bob Lemon replaced Score on the mound, and Cleveland went on to win 2–1. But for players on both teams the game really did not matter. Score's injury was uppermost in their minds and overshadowed the game.

McDougald called Lakeside Hospital several times to check on Score's condition and he, Bauer, and Berra went to the hospital to see him, only to find out that the hospital had barred visitors. Not long after the game, McDougald said, "If Score loses his eye, I might quit. This isn't worth it." But Score sent word to McDougald, "Don't blame yourself. I don't blame you."[13] Score's recovery was eagerly followed by fans all across the country. One, a Whittier, California, cook named Ernest Robinson, volunteered to donate one of his eyes to Score if the young pitcher lost his. Robinson made the offer, he said, "because I love baseball."[14]

Score did not lose his eye, but it, and his pitching form, were never the same again. After sitting out the rest of the season, he returned to the mound in 1958, pitching only 41 innings and compiling a 2–3 record. In 1959, he improved to 9–11, but was traded to the White Sox at the end of the season. He appeared in only 35 games for them before retiring in 1962 to become a broadcaster. The eye injury, along with a sore arm, had cut short his promising career and limited his record to 55–46.

The 1957 World Series would be played in an atmosphere of crisis across the nation. On August 26, the Soviet Union had successfully test fired an intercontinental ballistic missile, dramatically heating up the arms race. Less than a month later, on September 24, the same day the Dodgers played their last game in Ebbets Field, President Eisenhower ordered over one thousand federal troops to Little Rock, Arkansas, to protect nine black students at Central High School from white mobs angered over this latest attempt to integrate southern schools. Then on October 4, a travel day between the second and third games of the Series, the Soviet Union stunned the world with the news that it had fired the first artificial satellite, "Sputnik," into orbit. This "technological Pearl Harbor," as some Americans called it, created a panicky feeling that the United States had lost its technological and military superiority, aroused a nationwide debate over the American education system, and sparked a crash program to catch up with the Russians in military and space technology.

On October 2, the World Series opened in New York for the seventh consecutive year. As usual, the Yankees were favored, but all across the country millions of fans were rooting for the underdog Braves. To many, a Yankees-Braves Series provided a welcome respite from the traditional Yankees-Dodgers encounters and a chance to see some new faces in the October classic. To Yankee haters, it provided the chance to watch a new challenger attempt to dethrone the Bombers.

The two teams split the opening games, with the Yankees taking the first one 3–1 behind the five-hit, complete-game performance of Whitey Ford and the Braves coming back in the second contest with a 4–2 victory behind left-hander Lew Burdette's seven-hitter. When the Series moved to Milwaukee, a delirious standing-room-only crowd of 45,804 jammed County Stadium to watch the first World Series ever played in that city. The Yankees spoiled the homecoming by wearing out six Braves pitchers en route to a 12–3 shellacking of the hosts. Leading the embarrassing rout was Yankee left fielder and Milwaukee native Tony Kubek, who dug down for a little something extra before the home folks. After hitting only three homers during the entire season, he teed off on Braves pitching with two homers and a single, drove in four runs, and scored three. But the Braves regrouped behind their aces. Spahn, the year's Cy Young winner and the only Brave veteran of the last Series the Braves played in (1948), captured a 7–5, 10-inning victory in game four. Burdette then pitched a 1–0 masterpiece in game five.

After a day off for travel, the Braves came back to Yankee Stadium needing only a split to take the Series, and they got it. Behind Bob Turley's four-hitter, the Yankees took the sixth game, a 3–2 slugfest featuring home runs by Torre, Aaron, Berra, and Bauer. Spahn was slated to start the seventh game, but he contracted the flu, forcing Haney to come back with Burdette on only two days' rest. Larsen started for the Yankees, but there was to be no repeat of his 1956 heroics. He was chased from the mound in the third inning in the middle of a four-run rally. The Braves added a fifth run in the eighth when Del Crandall homered into the left field stands. There were some anxious moments for Braves players and fans in the ninth when Burdette loaded the bases with two out and Bill Skowron lashed a hard drive down the third base line that looked as if it might go into left field for extra bases. But Mathews gloved the ball near the foul line and stepped on third for the force and the final out.

The hitting star of the Series was Hank Aaron, who carried his hot bat from the regular season into postseason play. Batting .393, Aaron had eleven hits, including three home runs and a triple, and drove in seven runs and scored five. Mathews hit only .227, but he won game four with his tenth-inning homer, drove in four runs, scored four, and made several outstanding catches at the hot corner. Wes Covington hit only .208, but had two great catches in the outfield to help preserve the Braves' victories in the second and fifth games.

For the Yankees, Hank Bauer hit only .258 but clubbed two home runs, a triple, and a double and led all Yankees with six RBIs. Jerry Coleman had the top Yankee average, .364, followed by Berra with .320. Kubek collected eight hits, including two homers, and drove in four runs, but made two costly errors in the field. Mantle hit only .263 with one home run and had to sit out the fifth and sixth games with an injured shoulder, suffered in the third game when second baseman Red Schoendienst fell on him during a pickoff play.

The hero of the Series was Lew Burdette. Ironically, he had come up to the majors through the Yankee farm system but had pitched only 1⅓ innings in two games before he was traded to Boston in August of 1951 for Johnny Sain and $50,000. In the 1957 series he pitched three complete games and gained three victories, two of them shutouts, while allowing just two runs for an incredible 0.67 ERA. He mixed fastballs, curves, sliders, sinkers, the threat of a spitter (and maybe a real one or two) to baffle the Yankee bats. He frequently brought his glove hand or right hand to his mouth, tugged at his cap, hitched up his pants, wiped his hands on his shirt — all designed to suggest that he might be wetting the ball. He did not allow a run after the third inning of the second game, giving him 24⅔ consecutive scoreless innings. He became the first player to win three complete games in series competition since Cleveland spitballer Stan Coveleski turned the trick against the Dodgers in 1920. He was also the first to pitch more than one shutout in a Series since fabled Christy Mathewson of the Giants pitched three against the Philadelphia Athletics in 1905.

The upstart Braves had defeated the Yankees for their first world championship since 1914. New York was a triple loser, letting the world championship flag fly somewhere besides New York for the first time since 1948 and losing two teams to the West Coast. New York, and baseball, would never be the same again.

On September 8, while the Yankees and Braves were closing in on their pennants, the Giants and the Dodgers had played their last game at the Polo Grounds, the final match in a rivalry that began in 1890. The Giants won this one, 3–2, on a home run by Hank Sauer. Two more contests were scheduled at the old park, both with the Pirates.

On September 29, only 11,606 fans showed up for the farewell game at the Polo Grounds.[15] Before the game began, Russ Hodges, who only six years before had yelled, "The Giants win the pennant!" six times into the radio microphone, introduced Mrs. John McGraw and several old-time Giants' players, along with Bobby Thomson, who had been traded to the Braves in 1954 but was back with his old club for the second half of the 1957 season. Thomson accommodated the fans and photographers by standing on the field and pointing to the spot where his famous 1951 homer had landed.

For the last time, fans sat in the historic stands enjoying one of the best entertainment buys in New York. A box seat along the first base line went for $3.50, a hot dog for $.20, a beer for $.35, a bag of peanuts for $.15, a score card for $.15, and a pencil for $.10. But as they had so many times that season, they had to endure another Giant defeat, this one a 9–1 beating at the hands of the last-place Pirates. The game ended when Dusty Rhodes, the great pinch-hitting star of the 1954 world champions, dribbled a ball to the shortstop and was thrown out at first base. The on-deck hitter was Bobby Thomson.

The fans rushed the field, forcing the players to run for safety in the clubhouse in center field. The crazed mob took as souvenirs anything they could get their hands on—the bases, home plate, the pitching rubber, pieces of canopy covering the Giant bullpen, rubber padding on bleacher walls, signs and telephones in the stands and bullpens, seats in the stands, and sod from the field. Several fans converged on the clubhouse and chanted for their heroes to come out for one last curtain call, but they were afraid to. Some fans shouted, "We want Stoneham—with a rope around his neck" and "We want to stone him." The object of these attacks had watched the game from the safety of the clubhouse, and understandably did not appear. The favorite chant was "Stay, team, stay," but it was too late. The New York Giants were about to become the San Francisco Giants. The mob soon broke up and went home.

The New York Giants had been one of the most successful franchises in baseball history. Since entering the National League in 1883, they had won 17 pennants (15 since 1900), more than any major league team except the New York Yankees, and five world championships. They had a legacy of great ballplayers, including Christy Mathewson, "Iron Man" Joe McGinnity, Bill Terry, Mel Ott, and Carl Hubbell, and great managers like John McGraw and Leo Durocher. They always had a scrappy team, especially when they were playing the archrival Dodgers.

The Giants had played in the Polo Grounds, located in upper Manhattan, since 1891. Built in Coogan's Hollow, under a rock cliff called Coogan's Bluff, the Polo Grounds was a four-story horseshoe-shaped stadium seating 55,987, the largest capacity of any National League stadium. With its overhanging stands built close to the playing field, the stadium gave the fans a sense of being close to the players and to the events unfolding on the field. The Polo Grounds had also been the home of the Yankees until they moved into the "House that Ruth Built" in 1923.

The Polo Grounds had been the scene of Fred "Bonehead" Merkle's 1908 boneheaded base-running, Carl Hubbell's five consecutive strikeouts (of Ruth, Gehrig, Foxx, Simmons, and Cronin) in the 1934 All-Star Game, Thomson's dramatic home run in 1951, and Dusty Rhodes's heroic pinch-hitting and Mays's catch of Vic Wertz's drive in the 1954 Series. It had also been the site of professional boxing matches, professional football games, and other sporting events. But now the old park was slated to be torn down and replaced by a high-rise housing project called the "Polo Grounds Towers."

The last Dodger game at Ebbets Field was played on September 24, and it too was against the Pirates.[16] Although no official announcement had been made, fans and players alike expected the team to move to Los Angeles during the offseason. Only 6,702 fans showed up to watch the Dodgers dispatch the Pirates 2–0 behind the pitching of Danny McDevitt. There were no special ceremonies before or after the game, but during the contest organist Gladys Godding, who had performed at Ebbets Field since 1941, played several songs especially chosen for this solemn occasion: "California Here I Come," "Thanks for the Memories," "Say It Ain't So," "So Long It's Been Good to Know You," and at the end of the game, "Auld Lang Syne."

Most fans left quietly. A few hung by the gate leading to the Dodger clubhouse with tears running down their faces. Others ran onto the field, where they pulled up home plate, grass, the bases, anything they could cart away as a souvenir from the field that had served as the home of the Dodgers for 44 years. In the Dodger clubhouse Roy Campanella threw a little party for the other players and sportswriters. The Dodgers' last game would be in Philadelphia on September 30, but for most Dodger players and fans, the season, and a way of life, ended on September 24.

The news that everyone expected came on October 8, 1957, a travel day preceding the last two games of the World Series. At a four o'clock press conference that afternoon, representatives of the National League and the Dodgers announced that the team was moving to Los Angeles for the 1958 season. In the tug of war between New York and Los Angeles, the city of the angels had won by working out an attractive land deal. In exchange for the Los Angeles Angels' park, Wrigley Field, which O'Malley had purchased earlier, the Los Angeles city council gave O'Malley a 315-acre site called Chavez Ravine, once destined for a low cost housing project. They also promised to spend $2 million to prepare the site for construction; O'Malley would build and own a $10 million stadium with a seating capacity of around 50,000. While the stadium was under construction, the Dodgers would play at the vast Los Angeles Coliseum.

Brooklynites were outraged. Many felt that O'Malley had really intended to move the club to Los Angeles all along and that his public statements and negotiations with city officials over a new site for a park were nothing but a smoke screen. Many fans and much of the press vilified him as the worst traitor since Benedict Arnold and consigned his soul to hell. *New York Times* columnist Arthur Daley condemned both O'Malley and Stoneham as greedy, uncaring businessmen: "Baseball is a sport, eh? It may be for Tom Yawkey of the Red Sox, Phil Wrigley of the Cubs, and one or two others. But the crass commercialism of O'Malley and Horace Stoneham of the Giants presents the disillusioning fact that it's big business, just another way to make a buck."[17]

When the Dodgers made their move official, the *New York Times* said, "Thus ended a colorful and often zany baseball era in Brooklyn. The Dodgers had represented Brooklyn in the National League since 1890. They had become world famous, first because of their erratic baseball and then because of their winning teams."[18]

"Colorful and zany" described only part of the Dodger story. They were among the most followed and best loved of all the major league teams, not just in New York but all across the nation. In Brooklyn itself, they were almost a religion. As the only major league team named after a borough, rather than a city, the Dodgers' fortunes and misfortunes were eagerly followed, game after game, year after year, and to many the fate of the borough itself was tied to the fortunes of the team. It was the local neighborhood team, and it inspired fierce loyalties.

Part of the charm of the Dodgers lay in their ballpark. Ebbets Field, which opened in 1913, was easily accessible to most of the population of Brooklyn by trolley, subway, or elevated railway. It was the smallest ballpark in the league, with fewer than 33,000 seats and with parking for only 700 cars. Many agreed with Red Barber, who once wrote, "There was never another ballpark like Ebbets Field. . . . You were practically playing second base, the stands were so close to the field. Everybody was in touch with everybody else at Ebbets Field."[19] It was where Hilda Chester had become famous for clanging her cowbell, a group of amateur musicians dressed in top hats and frock coats and called the Dodger Sym-Phony had serenaded the home team and razzed the visitors, and where after the umpires had decided that coats and sweaters draped over the left field railing might hinder play, the public announcer unintentionally caused a ripple of laughter by saying, "Attention, please! Will the fans along the left field railing please remove their clothing?"[20]

In spite of their crackerbox park, the Dodgers drew over a million fans a year between 1947 and 1957 and led the rest of the league in annual attendance five times. Ever since it opened as the home of the Dodgers in 1913, Ebbets Field had been the stomping grounds of many zany and sometimes great players—Casey Stengel, Zack Wheat, Dazzy Vance, Babe Herman, Pete Reiser, and the great Dodger players of the postwar era. It was where

Babe Herman doubled into a double play in 1926, where a fan ran onto the field in 1940 at the end of a game and assaulted an umpire, where Cookie Lavagetto broke up Floyd Bevens's 1947 World Series no-hitter, where Billy Martin miraculously caught Jackie Robinson's infield pop fly to end the 1952 Series, where Billy Loes claimed that he lost a ground ball in the sun, and where pitcher Russ Meyer, angry at being pulled from a game, threw the resin bag high in the air as he stalked off the mound—only to have it come down and hit him on top of the head. It was the site of half of the annual wars between the Giants and the Dodgers, of Jackie Robinson's debut in 1947, and of nine World Series.

The Dodgers were the most successful National League team in the postwar period. After winning their first pennant in 1916 and their second in 1920, they went 21 years before they won another. Between 1947 and 1956, they won six pennants. And with a break or two, their record would have been more impressive. If they had won the last game of the season in 1946, 1950, and 1951, they would have won 5 pennants in a row and 9 in 11 years. But they did not win these games, just like they lost seven consecutive World Series before finally winning the first—and only—world championship Brooklyn would ever enjoy in 1955. As one reporter wrote, the Dodgers were the most popular team in the United States because of "the team's unique ability to maintain an apparent contradiction: The Dodgers managed to remain underdogs while winning."[21]

Most of the Dodger players opposed the move to Los Angeles, but there was nothing they could do. Carl Furillo would later say, "O'Malley put the buck in front of everything else. The players thought only of baseball. We thought we'd never move. It seemed the whole team belonged to Brooklyn." Although Duke Snider was a native of Los Angeles, he later said, "I hated to leave Brooklyn. . . . Those years in New York were something, something special. . . . I wouldn't trade those years for anything."[22]

The Dodger and Giant exodus to the West Coast meant that New York City would be without a National League club for the first time since 1882 and that New Yorkers would be deprived of seeing the six other National League teams. A proud city that once housed three great baseball teams would now have only one, but many business and civic leaders were determined that this sad situation would not last for long. As soon as Mayor Wagner got the official word that the Dodgers were leaving, he announced that he was appointing a committee of concerned citizens to work to bring National League baseball back to New York. His and similar efforts by business and civic leaders would bear fruit in 1962, when the New York Mets began play. But for many New Yorkers, major league baseball ceased to exist in 1957.

17. On to California (1958)

"I love this baseball," Roy Campanella said in 1955. "When you're a kid you play it and it starts going down into you when you're a child. Once that feeling leaves you, your will to play is gone. . . . I don't care how old you are, you have to have that spirit. I know I've got it and I don't think I'll ever lose it. Baseball doesn't owe me anything, but I owe it plenty. Everything it's done for me has been good and nothin's been bad. The day they take that uniform off me, they'll have to rip it off. And when they do, they can bury me."[1]

It would have been difficult to find anyone who loved baseball more than Roy Campanella or who was more grateful for the chance to play big league ball. After toiling in the Negro leagues for so many years, he broke in with the Dodgers in 1948 and quickly established himself as a star on one of the game's most successful clubs. He had come a long way since 1939, when he made $1200 for 275 games in the Negro leagues. At the peak of his career in the mid–fifties, his annual baseball salary ($36,000), his liquor store business, his postseason barnstorming tours, and his endorsements and television appearances provided him with an annual income of around $60,000.

After mustering a .318 average, 32 homers, 107 RBIs, and his third MVP Award in 1955, age and nagging injuries brought declines in 1956 (.219 and 20 homers) and 1957 (.242 and 13 homers), but the ever optimistic Campanella was hoping that the move to sunny California would rejuvenate his 36-year-old body and extend his major league career. He had flown out to Los Angeles several times to look at the site of the new stadium and promote ticket sales for the 1958 season. But he would never play there.

Around 3:30 A.M. on January 28, 1958, after working late in his Harlem liquor store, he was making the hour-long drive to his Long Island home when his car skidded on an icy curve, ran off the highway, hit a utility pole, ran part of the way up a small embankment, turned over, and came to rest on its right side, pinning him upside down in the wreckage. The engine kept running, and Campanella, afraid of fire, tried to turn it off, only to discover, he later recalled, "I couldn't move my arm. I couldn't move anything. That's when I knew my whole body was paralyzed."[2] He was trapped in the wreckage for about half an hour before police and emergency personnel could free him and send him by ambulance to Community Hospital in nearby Glen Cove, Long Island.

Hospital x-rays revealed that Campanella had fractured two vertebrae at the base of his neck, leaving him paralyzed from the shoulders down. After enduring a four-hour surgery to repair the vertebrae, he underwent extensive therapy at the New York University Bellevue Institute of Physical Rehabilitation, fighting against great medical odds to regain the normal use of his body. His brave fight received widespread media coverage, and the entire nation was pulling for the "Good Humor Man" to come back from his injury.

Unfortunately, Campanella's great spirit and courage were not enough to overcome his severe injuries. He gradually had to face the reality that he would never be able to walk again, much less play baseball. While in 1958 he had written an article entitled "I'll Walk Again" for the *Saturday Evening Post*, in 1959 he would title his autobiography *It's Good to Be Alive*, showing an acceptance of the permanence of his injury and the need to make the best of his irreversible situation. "I'm a lucky guy," he wrote. "I've got so much to be thankful for." He was lucky that he had not been killed in the wreck and that he "was able to play ball for twenty years, half of them in the big leagues." He related that he could now sit up in a wheelchair, move his head and arms, and eat and drink by himself—little victories beyond his grasp in the first weeks and months after his accident.[3]

The automobile accident brought a great baseball career to an end. No one knows how good he would have been if he had not spent 10 years in the Negro leagues before he got a chance to play in the majors. Like his old teammate, Jackie Robinson, Campanella's career was limited to a decade. He compiled a .276 lifetime batting average, drove in 856 runs, hit 242 homers, won three MVP Awards, led the league in total putouts six times, and in most years was at or near the top in most other defensive categories as well. He also was an inspiring leader and clutch player, and he helped to lead the Dodgers into five World Series. He was the best catcher in Dodger history, one of the best in the postwar period, some say *the* best, though fans of that other catcher in the American League often begged to differ. A great ballplayer, a great man, and a future Hall of Famer, he would be missed on the diamond he loved so much.

Spring, 1958. For the first time since 1882, there would be no opening day for National League clubs in New York. New Yorkers would no longer have to divide their baseball loyalties anymore. Now there was only one team to root for—the Yankees.

Across the continent the Dodgers and Giants were getting used to new balllparks and new fans. Until a new stadium could be constructed, home for the Dodgers would be the Los Angeles Coliseum, built in 1923 and upgraded when the city became the site of the 1932 Olympics. Over the years the Coliseum had been the stage for thousands of events, from football to rodeos to religious gatherings. But it was not built for baseball. Basically a huge football stadium, it was as tall as a six-story building and had 100,000 seats, many of which were so far from the playing field that binoculars became as essential as beer and popcorn. The right field fence was 440 feet from home plate along the foul line, a formidable barrier for left-handed sluggers like Duke Snider who had performed so well in Ebbets Field with its short (296 feet) right field fence. When Willie Mays first saw the right field fence, he said, "They weren't thinking of Duke Snider when they built this ball park. Poor Duke. He ain't gonna reach that fence."[4] Only eight home runs would be hit over the right field fence in 1958.

By contrast, the left field fence was only 251 feet from home plate along the foul line and 320 feet in deep left center, a right-handed hitter's delight. Although a 42-foot high screen would be erected in left field, it still was an inviting target. After hitting three home runs over the screen in three games, Hank Sauer of the new San Francisco Giants claimed that the screen was "an ideal setup. Hell, I could play here till I was 90."[5] Many sports-writers, players, and fans feared that the short left field endangered Ruth's 60 homer mark and would cheapen the record book by promoting so many "Chinese home runs," contemporary jargon for cheap homers. The Coliseum was quickly dubbed "O'Malley's Chinese Theater," "The House that Charlie Chan Built," and other appellations that were not appreciated by California's large Chinese population.

Welcomed to San Francisco by a parade attended by an estimated 200,000, the Giants also had to tolerate temporary quarters while their new park was being constructed. For two years they would play in Seals Stadium, the smallest park (23,900 seating capacity) in the majors. Still, they would draw 1.3 million fans in 1958, almost twice the number that had come through the gate in their last year at the Polo Grounds. In their second year they would do even better, drawing 1.4 million fans.

Tuesday, April 15, was the date of the first regular major league game ever played in California. Appropriately, it was between the Giants and the Dodgers, renewing a rivalry that had been conducted for 67 years some 2500 miles to the east. Over 23,000 fans jammed into Seals Stadium on this warm, spring day, and the home team made it even better for the fans by beating Don Drysdale and the rest of the Dodgers 8–0 behind the six-hit pitching of Ruben Gomez. But the second game, played on Wednesday night, did not go so well for the home team. It was cold, windy, and damp, an ill omen for what lay ahead for night baseball in San Francisco, and the Dodgers pounded the Giants 13–1. The Giants took the third game, 7–4, and the two teams moved to Los Angeles to continue their battles.

On April 18, the first Dodger game in Los Angeles was played before 78,672 fans, a new record for a single game in the major leagues. Among those present were prominent civic leaders and familiar faces from the entertainment world, such as Edward G. Robinson, Danny Kaye, and Dinah Shore. Carl Erskine had the honor of throwing the first major league pitch in Los Angeles. Thanks to the relief work of Johnny Podres in the ninth, Erskine was able to come away with a 6–5 victory. Many fans could barely see what was going on on the field without binoculars, but that did not diminish their joy. One happy fan said, "You can even see the ball once you get acclimated."[6]

In the first two games in the Coliseum, eight home runs were hit over the left field screen, prompting *Sports Illustrated* to report, "Baseball may be good for Los Angeles and Los Angeles may be good for baseball — but both will be better off when they get baseball out of the Coliseum."[7] In spite of all the complaints, the Coliseum did not turn out to be a home run paradise or threat to Ruth's record. By the end of the season, only 193 home runs had been hit, all but 10 to left field. This was far short of the major league record of 219 hit in Cincinnati's Crosley Field in 1957, and only slightly more than the annual average of 190.4 homers hit in Ebbets Field by the Dodgers and their opponents in the five years before the Dodgers left Brooklyn.

The Los Angeles fans loved it. Attendance passed the one million mark on July 23, and two days later eclipsed the total for all 77 home games played at Ebbets Field in 1957. "It's fantastic, simply fantastic," Vice President Buzzie Bavasi said. "And just think what it would be if we were in contention instead of in last place."[8] The Dodgers would wind up the season in seventh place but with a total home attendance of 1.8 million, bringing a $4 million profit and a new record for the Dodger franchise. In the four years the Dodgers played in the Coliseum, they averaged close to 2 million fans each year.

The new California teams were not expected to be pennant winners in 1958. Most experts picked the Braves to repeat as National League champions, and they did, but for over half of the season the outcome was in doubt. On July 4, only seven games separated the league-leading Braves from the cellar-dwelling Dodgers. Gradually the Braves took charge and moved ahead of the pack. By August 17, they had built an eight-game lead. On September 21, after beating back a late surge by the surprising Pirates, who were finally beginning to reap some of the rewards of Branch Rickey's rebuilding efforts, the Braves clinched the pennant when Warren Spahn defeated the Reds by a 6–5 score. The Braves finished the season eight games in front, the same margin they had enjoyed in 1957.

The Braves topped the National League in hitting with a .266 average. Hank Aaron again led the way, hitting .326, with 30 homers and 95 RBIs.

Eddie Mathews's batting average fell off to .251, but he hit 31 homers and drove in 77 runs. Suffering from knee problems, Wes Covington played in only 90 games but still hit .330 with 24 homers and 74 RBIs. Hurricane Hazle could not repeat his 1957 heroics. After managing a puny .179 average in 20 games, he was sold to Detroit where he played only 43 games before bowing out of the majors. Headed by Warren Spahn (22–11) and Lew Burdette (20–10), the Braves' pitching staff led the National League in complete games (72), shutouts (16), and ERA (3.21). Spahn's 22 victories tied him with Pittsburgh's Bob Friend for most wins and gave him his ninth 20-game season.

The most surprising team of 1958 was Danny Murtaugh's Pirates. After eight consecutive years of finishing in seventh or eighth place they provided the biggest challenge to the Braves and wound up in second. Bob Friend's mound work gave them their first 20-game winner since Murry Dickson in 1951, Ron Kline and Vern Law combined for 27 wins, and reliever Roy Face appeared in 57 games and used his forkball to lead the league with 20 saves. Third baseman Frank Thomas led all Pirates with 35 homers and 109 RBIs.

After finishing in sixth place their last two years in New York, the transplanted Giants finished third, 12 games out. Bill Rigney's surprising team featured several top rookies, led by first baseman Orlando Cepeda, who batted .312, hit 25 homers, drove in 96 runs, and captured Rookie of the Year honors. Willie Mays led the league in stolen bases with 31 and pushed batting champion Ritchie Ashburn to the wire before finishing three points behind at .347. Now 27, Mays was a seasoned ballplayer who continued to inspire his teammates with his baseball savvy and dramatic play. Many fans would have agreed with Roger Angell, who early in the spring said that Mays was still "the most exciting player I have ever seen, even when he is only running down to first on a grounder."[9]

After staying close the first half of the season, the other five National League teams faded quickly. Birdie Tebbetts resigned with only 41 games left in the season, and his successor, Jimmy Dykes, could drive the Reds no higher than fourth. The Cubs tied the Cardinals for fifth, the Windy City's best finish in six years, and shortstop Ernie Banks led the league in homers (47) and RBIs (129). Called "Mr. Cub," Banks had become the most popular player in Cub history because of his zest for the game — "It's a great day for baseball, let's play two," he liked to say — and for his performance at bat and in the field. From 1955 to 1960 he hit more homers (248) than any player in the majors. In spite of laboring for a second division club, he won the MVP Award in 1958 and 1959. He finished his 19-year career in 1971 with 512 home runs, but one prize always eluded him — he never got to play in a World Series game.

For the sixth-place Cardinals, Stan Musial got his 3,000th hit in May, becoming only the eighth man in history to reach that mark. Weighing only

182 pounds, just 7 more than in his rookie season, the 37-year-old Musial played like a young man, hitting .337 with 17 homers and 62 RBIs. He was well-compensated for his efforts. His 1958 contract made him the first National League player to reach the $100,000 mark.

Coming in seventh with a 71–83 record were the Dodgers, who were in the throes of rebuilding after a decade of dominance in the National League. Robinson had retired, Campanella had suffered the career-ending injury, Newcombe had been sold to the Reds in June, Reese had become a part-time player who would retire at the end of the season, and Hodges, Furillo, and Snider were in the last years of careers that had seen their best days back in Brooklyn. The Duke of Flatbush, suffering from knee problems and the distant right field fence, hit .312 but managed only 15 homers after five consecutive years of hitting 40 or more.

The Philadelphia Phillies went through two managers (Mayo Smith and Eddie Sawyer) and boasted the league's leading hitter, Ritchie Ashburn (.350), but still took over the cellar from its customary dwellers, the Pirates. Ashburn, who had also won the batting crown in 1955, would have over 200 hits three times in his career, and from 1950 through 1959 would have 1,875 hits, 104 more than the decade's leading hitter, Stan Musial. But playing for the lowly Phillies, he never received the publicity and recognition he deserved.

The American League race was a runaway for the New York Yankees. The Bronx Bombers came out of the gate fast, winning seven of their first eight games while their main rivals, the White Sox, lost seven of their first nine and the Red Sox, who were also expected to be contenders, lost seven of their first eight. The Yankees took first place on the fourth day of the season and never relinquished it. By the time of the All-Star break they boasted a 48–25 record and an 11-game lead over Kansas City and Boston, who were tied for second. This was the largest lead any American League team had ever had at the time of the All-Star break.

Stengel continued his winning ways in the annual All-Star contest, played in Baltimore on July 8. Thanks in part to Gil McDougald, whose pinch-hit single in the sixth inning drove in what turned out to be the winning run, Stengel's squad edged the senior circuit by a 4–3 margin in the first midseason classic played without an extra base hit. The following day, Stengel and some of his players traveled to nearby Washington, where the Old Professor educated the U.S. Senate on the thorny question of baseball monopoly.

In the 1950s, the reserve clause and other monopolistic practices of baseball and other spectator sports had come under increasing scrutiny. The Supreme Court had consistently ruled that the antitrust laws did not apply to baseball, claiming that it was different from other professional sports, that it had always been exempted, and that it was up to the U.S. Congress to change that special status if it needed to be altered. In turn, Congress had offered the same defense of baseball and held that if any changes were needed in baseball's special status it was up to the courts to decide. But in 1957, the Court had removed football's exemption, declaring that "the volume of interstate business involved in organized football places it within the provisions of anti-trust laws." In the process of removing football's exemption, the court also took a swipe at baseball, saying that to continue to grant baseball a special status was "unreasonable, illogical, and inconsistent." But this was as far as the Court was willing to go, again preferring to leave the matter up to Congress.[10]

Soon after the Court's ruling on football, Congress began to attempt to clarify baseball's status. In 1957 the Senate Subcommittee on Antitrust and Monopoly began lengthy hearings on baseball and the antitrust laws. These hearings uncovered little new information about baseball as a business, though some observers were surprised at the committee's findings that seven major league clubs had lost money over the previous five years. The 1957 hearings would be followed by more investigations, more proposals to clarify baseball's status as a business or sport, and more hearings in 1958. Organized baseball was under attack, but it was saved from restrictive legislation by intense lobbying from Ford Frick and other baseball men and by the inability of Congress to agree on what to do about baseball's status.

The dramatic highlight of the 1958 hearings came on July 9, while the Senate Subcommittee on Antitrust and Monopoly was debating a bill to exempt most of the activities of professional sports from the antitrust laws. Organized baseball had been lobbying for such a bill for months, and it had already been passed by the House and had broad support in the Senate. Senator Estes Kefauver of Tennessee, well-known for his televised hearings in 1951 on organized crime and for his unsuccessful quest for the vice-presidency on Stevenson's ticket in 1956, was the chairman of the subcommittee. On July 9, some 300 people crammed into the Senate Caucus Room. Much of the standing-room-only crowd had come to the hearings to see some of baseball's greatest stars, not to listen to dull debates on the antitrust question.

And the stars were there. Mickey Mantle, Ted Williams, Stan Musial, Robin Roberts, and Eddie Yost came and testified that they were satisfied with the way they had been treated and that they saw no need to modify the reserve clause. Williams, refusing to don a tie even for Senate investigations, summed up the opinions of many players and warmed the hearts of the club owners when he said, "Personally, I don't see how baseball could operate without the reserve clause and preserve its dignity."[11]

The star of the show was not a player but the 67-year-old manager of the

Yankees. Shortly after the hearings opened at 10:00 A.M., Kefauver called Stengel to the witness chair. Dressed in a gray suit, white shirt, and blue tie, and wearing glasses, which he rarely did in public, Stengel looked out of place, but after Kefauver asked him, "Will you give us very briefly your background and your views about this legislation?," the Old Professor proceeded to give one of his best performances.[12]

Clearly enjoying taking center stage before the large crowd and television cameras, he rambled on for close to an hour. He kept his audience in stitches as he reminisced about his playing and managing career, working conditions for players in the past and in the present, the pension fund, the business of baseball, and other topics in the stream-of-consciousness manner that had become his trademark. Along the way he told the committee, "I had many years that I was not successful as a ballplayer, as it is a game of skill. And then I was no doubt discharged by baseball, in which I had to go back to the minor leagues as a manager, and after being in the minor leagues as a manager, I became a major league manager in several cities and was discharged. We call it discharged because there is no question that I had to leave." The room broke up in laughter.

Stengel rambled on and on about how he stayed in baseball because it paid better than dentistry, about the costs of club travel, about attendance, and anything else that came to mind. Finally, Kefauver interrupted with "Mr. Stengel, I am not sure I made my question clear." Stengel replied, "Yes, sir. Well, that is all right. I am not sure I am going to answer yours perfectly, either." There was more laughter, more Stengel anecdotes, and his claim that baseball "has been run cleaner than any business that was ever put out in the one hundred years at the present time." He steadfastly refused to directly criticize the legal and economic aspects of the game or to comment on the legislation under consideration. Colorado Senator John A. Carroll tried to steer the discussion back to the main point: "The question Senator Kefauver asked you was what, in your honest opinion, with your forty-eight years of experience, is the need for this legislation in view of the fact that baseball has not been subject to antitrust laws?" Stengel answered, "No." This brought still more laughter.

After several more minutes of humorous but unproductive testimony, Kefauver threw in the towel. "Thank you, very much, Mr. Stengel. We appreciate your presence here." As Stengel got up to return to his seat behind the witness chair, he received a standing ovation.

Mickey Mantle, the crew-cut all-American baseball hero, took the witness chair. Somehow managing to maintain his senatorial dignity after his discussion with Stengel, Kefauver, in a businesslike tone said, "Mr. Mantle, do you have any observations with reference to the application of antitrust laws to baseball?" Mantle grinned and replied, "My views are just about the same as Casey's." This brought down the house.

Recovering, Kefauver smiled and said, "If you would just redefine just what Casey's views were, we would be very happy." Like his manager and most of the other baseball men who testified, Mantle avoided direct criticism of the economic and legal issues of the game and claimed that he agreed with the reserve clause. "I don't have any gripes," he said. "I have been very fortunate." Kefauver gently pressed the Yankee star. "Under the clause . . . they can do anything with you they want to, is that right?" One of the highest-paid players in the game, Mantle provoked still more laughter when he replied, "If they don't do anything different, I don't care what they do." He added, "I don't think about this stuff very much."[13]

The senators were still laughing as the hearings ended and the crowd filed out of the room. Democratic Senator Joseph C. O'Mahoney of Wyoming described the day's hearings as "the best entertainment that we have had around here for a long time." Although no one was quite sure what he had said, Stengel's testimony was the talk of Washington and much of the nation. That night, when NBC's "Huntley-Brinkley Report" showed close to two minutes of clips from Stengel's testimony, the normally reserved David Brinkley laughed so hard on the air that he could hardly speak. The press gave the testimony major coverage. Typical of the reporting was *Sports Illustrated*'s claim that Stengel "delivered a monologue composed of hilarious autobiographical fragments, homemade poetry, pungent *non sequiturs* and guarded revelations of lines of inquiry the subcommittee might profitably follow — an amazingly frank, cheerful, shrewd, patriotic address that left the senators stunned, bewildered and delighted, convulsed his fellow witnesses . . . and set 300 spectators roaring with spontaneous laughter."[14]

The Kefauver hearings heightened Stengel's growing legend as a comic figure and master of confusing and deliberately misleading rhetoric, but they did little to clarify Congress's position on baseball and the antitrust laws. The bill to exempt baseball and other professional sports from the antitrust laws was never reported out of committee. Congress would continue to debate baseball's antitrust exemption, but baseball would manage to escape any restrictive legislation during this decade. It was not until the 1970s that the reserve clause was modified, due to the legal challenges of Curt Flood, Jim "Catfish" Hunter, Andy Messersmith, and Dave McNally. The legal battles mounted by these players would virtually destroy the reserve clause and open the door to free agency and spiraling salaries.

With the All-Star Game and Stengel's congressional testimony behind them, the Yankees continued to roll toward Stengel's ninth pennant in his 10 years at the helm. The Bombers piled up a 15½-game lead by July 26 and increased the bulge to 17 games on August 2. The question now was not who was going to win the pennant, but how early Stengel's team would clinch it and how many games in front they would be at season's end. *Sports Illustrated* even went so far as to claim that the 1958 Bombers "may well be the best Yankee team that ever played ball, better than the best Joe McCarthy ever managed, better even (oh, sacrilege!) than Miller Huggins' heroic buckos of 1927."[15]

But the speculation was premature. After building that huge margin, the Yankees went into a long slump that lasted for the rest of the season and well into the World Series. They dropped 9 of their next 12 games, had a losing record (15–16) in August, and barely broke even (12–12) in September. Injuries, hitting and pitching slumps, and uncharacteristic defense lapses, perhaps induced by overconfidence, turned them from world-beaters into what looked like an ordinary team. Meanwhile the White Sox made a sustained run at the flag, winning 19 of their last 25 games. Still the Yankees coasted in, clinching the pennant in Kansas City on September 14 with a 5–3 victory in the first game of a doubleheader. They finished the season 10 games ahead of the White Sox, Stengel's biggest margin yet, but they did it with six fewer wins than they had in 1957.

In spite of the late season slump, the Yankees led the league in team batting average (.268) and home runs (164). Mantle was again hampered by injuries, but while his batting average fell 61 points to .304, he still drove in 97 runs and led the league in home runs with 42. The only other .300 hitters were Elston Howard (.314) and left fielder Norm Siebern (.300). Berra managed only a .266 average but hit 22 homers and drove in 90 runs.

The Yankees' pitching staff led the league in ERA with 3.22. Bob Turley (21–7) was the league's only 20-game winner, while Whitey Ford won 14 and posted the league's top ERA, 2.01. The top reliever was Ryne Duren, who terrorized hitters with the combination of poor eyesight (caused by a bout with rheumatic fever when he was 20 years old) and a blazing—and sometimes wild—fastball. Called "Rhino" by his teammates, Duren had pitched for Baltimore and Kansas City before the Yankees purchased him in 1957 and sent him to the minors for additional seasoning. He came up to the Yankees in 1958, and for the next two years he was the terror of the American League. Primarily a fastball pitcher, he was so wild that in the minors at San Antonio he once beaned the player waiting in the on-deck circle. When he came into a game he cultivated his reputation for wildness, sometimes deliberately sailing his first warm-up pitch far over the catcher's head. He threw hard and close, sometimes alternating strikes with screaming knock-down pitches. It put fear into the heart of many a hitter who looked out at the mound at a six-foot, 200-pound pitcher with thick eyeglasses, a 100-mile-per-hour fastball, and trouble finding the plate.

"I would not admire hitting against Duren," Stengel once said, "because if he ever hit you in the head you might be in the past tense."[16] One of the many players who dreaded facing Duren was Washington's Rocky Bridges.

Once, as he took his place in the batter's box, he asked Berra, "Are you sure he can see through those things? Can he see home plate? Can he see *me*? Let's go out and check."[17] In 1958 Duren had 6 wins, 20 saves, a 2.02 ERA, and 87 strikeouts in only 76 innings, becoming the first reliever whose strikeouts exceeded the number of innings pitched.

The Yankees would be playing in their ninth World Series in 10 years. In the previous 40 years, they had won 24 pennants, 17 World Series, and finished in the second division only once. No other sports franchise had such a record for greatness and consistency or aroused so much admiration, envy, and hatred. *Life* magazine called them "the organization men" of baseball and claimed that "success had taken the suspense out of the race and made cheering for the Yankees somewhat like cheering for U.S. Steel."[18] More and more, people loved to hate the Yankees.

The second-place "Go-Go" White Sox could not get going soon enough in 1958. Two months into the season they were wallowing in last place, but they managed to recover from their doldrums and take advantage of the Yankee slump to pull to within 10 games by the end of the season. The theft of 101 bases — twice as many as any other club in the league — could not offset their weak bats and generally poor pitching. For Al Lopez, it was bridesmaid time again.

The Red Sox finished third, 13 games off the pace. Ted Williams won his second consecutive batting title, and his sixth overall, with a .328 average, six points higher than teammate Pete Runnels. The two men went into the last game of the season with Williams holding a narrow lead, .326 to .324. Runnels went 0-for-4, while Williams homered and doubled to wind up at .328, six points higher than his teammate. But another teammate, Jackie Jensen, won the league's MVP Award for his .286 average, 35 homers, and league-leading 122 RBIs.

Turning 40 on August 30 did not make Williams any less prone to juvenile temper tantrums. At Fenway Park on September 21, after being called out on strikes, he threw his bat high in the air. It flew 75 feet into a front-row box seat and struck a 60-year-old fan, Gladys Heffernan, the housekeeper for Red Sox General Manager Joe Cronin, slightly above the left eye. Mortified, Williams went over to the stands and, with tears in his eyes, apologized. "I know you didn't mean it," she told him. "Forget about it." But he was deeply upset, and went back to the dugout and sat on the bench embarrassed and in tears. American League President Will Harridge was also upset. He fined Williams $50. Mrs. Heffernan was hospitalized overnight as a precaution, but was released the next day when it was determined that she was not seriously hurt.[19]

Cleveland finished fourth, 14½ games out, and Detroit, Baltimore, Kansas City, and Washington (always Washington, it seemed) rounded out the bottom four.

The fifty-fifth World Series opened in Milwaukee on Wednesday, October 1. Although they had lost to the Braves the previous year, the Yankees were favored. After all, they were the Yankees and they almost always won the fall classic. And history seemed to be against the Braves, as no team had beaten the Yankees two years in a row since John McGraw's Giants did it in 1921 and 1922.

The Yankees' late summer collapse followed them into the Series. Playing before the home fans, the Braves took the first game, 4–3, behind Warren Spahn, and the second, 13–5, behind Lew Burdette, the hero of the 1957 Series. When Burdette gave up a run in the first inning of the second game, it broke his streak of 24⅔ consecutive scoreless innings, knocking him out of contention for the record of 29⅔ innings set by Babe Ruth 40 years earlier. Burdette also hit a homer over the left field fence, the first Series home run by a pitcher since 1940.

After a day off for travel, the two teams resumed their battle in Yankee Stadium. Thanks to Hank Bauer, who drove in four runs with a single and homer, the Yankees took game three by a 4–0 score. In the second inning of the game, while the Braves were at bat, Roy Campanella made his first public appearance since his injury. As he was rolled into the stadium in his wheelchair and carried to his seat by two firemen and a policeman, he received a standing ovation and play on the field stopped. Berra, Campanella's friendly rival for so many years, turned and waved to him, and players on both teams moved to the top of the dugout steps to get a better look at the man who had starred in so many of these postseason contests. He had a front row seat behind home plate, and his wife and two of his children sat with him. When someone asked him how it felt to be back, he said, "It feels great just to be behind the plate, even without a mask and mitt."[20]

The Braves came back and took the fourth game 3–0 as Warren Spahn pitched a two-hitter. Leading three games to one, the Braves had the Yankees on the ropes, but could not deliver the knockout blow. The Bombers took the fifth game 7–0 on a homer by McDougald in the third and a six-run outburst in the seventh to send the Series back to Milwaukee for the last two games. It rained the morning of the sixth game and was still cloudy and dark at game time, so the entire contest was played under the lights — the first time ever in World Series competition. The Yankees normally dependable ace, Whitey Ford, was knocked out of the box in the second, but the Bronx Bombers still won, 4-3, by scoring two runs in the tenth on a homer by McDougald and singles by Howard, Berra, and Skowron. For the fourth year in a row, the Series would go to seven games.

Having once had the Yankees down three games to one, the Braves took the field in Milwaukee County Stadium on Thursday, October 9, with the feeling that the momentum had shifted to the American Leaguers. The lead see-sawed, and going into the eighth the teams were locked in a 2–2 tie. After an obviously tired and struggling Burdette retired McDougald on a fly to right and got Mantle on a called third strike, Berra lashed one of his pitches off the right field wall for a double. Howard followed with a single through the box, scoring Berra from second. Andy Carey then singled, and Skowron followed with a homer deep into the left-center field bleachers to give the Yankees a 6–2 lead. The Braves failed to score in the bottom of the eighth. In the ninth, after reliever Don McMahon held the Yankees scoreless, the Braves managed to get two men on base with a walk and a single. But with two out Red Schoendienst lined out to center to end the game and the Series.

Casey Stengel had his seventh world title, tying him with Joe McCarthy. He had won it after being counted out for losing three of the first four games, making the Yankees the first team since the 1925 Pirates to come back and win a seven-game Series after trailing three games to one. "We showed 'em that we were still the Yankees," Stengel told reporters.[21] The Series win increased the American League's lead over the National to 35–20.

The Braves topped the Yankees in hits (60 to 49), batting average (.250 to .210), and doubles (10 to 5). The Yankees led in homers (10 to 3), RBIs (29 to 24), runs (29 to 25), and ERA (3.39 to 3.71). Bauer wielded the biggest stick, batting .323 and leading all players on both teams in hits (10), home runs (4), RBIs (8), and runs (6). In game three, when his teammates could manage only one hit, he collected three and drove in all four runs to stop the Braves' steamroller. Turley pitched well as a starter and reliever, managing two wins, one save, and a 2.76 ERA. In game five, a game the Yankees had to win, he came up with a five-hit shutout. In game seven he relieved Don Larsen, who had trouble finding the plate, and gave up only two hits for the next 6⅔ innings. Duren was intimidating in relief, striking out 14 Milwaukee batters, garnering a 1.93 ERA, a 1–1 record, and 1 save.

Hank Aaron (.333), Bill Bruton (.412), and Red Schoendienst (.300) provided most of the power for the Braves. For most of the season, Schoendienst had been troubled with colds and respiratory infections that never seemed to clear up completely. His playing time dropped to 106 games, and he became so weak that he began to choke up more and more on the bat, hoping to make better contact with the ball. For the season, he hit only .262 with only one home run. But he played all seven games of the Series, showing superior defense while collecting nine hits, including three doubles and a triple, and scoring five runs. After the Series was over he was diagnosed as having tuberculosis and was treated with rest, drugs, and surgery that excised part of his right lung. He would finally return to the Braves in September of 1959, and by 1960 he had fully recovered.

Spahn and Burdette were the leading Brave pitchers. Spahn won two games, and with his four hits, .333 batting average, and three RBIs he showed that not all pitchers were automatic outs. Burdette picked up one win and slugged a home run, but he was not able to repeat his 1957 mastery of the Yankees. He and Spahn had hoped to combine for four victories, but they, and the Braves, fell one short.

In 1958, the hot stove league had to share the sports pages with an upstart rival for the affection of sports fans. That rival was professional football, which had one of its best seasons ever, capped by what came to be called "the greatest football game ever played."

Although professional football teams and leagues had been around for most of the century, they had never attracted the fans and publicity that major and minor league baseball enjoyed. But in the postwar period, under Bert Bell, who took over as league commissioner in 1946, the National Football League steadily gained popularity and media attention. The adoption of the two-platoon system, the emergence of outstanding passing quarterbacks, running backs, and receivers, the development of a college draft system that kept a steady flow of good players into the professional ranks, and the league's early expansion to the West Coast all helped the professional game to grow rapidly in the fifties. Sellouts of games became more and more common, with one 1957 game in the Los Angeles Coliseum between the Rams and the San Francisco Forty-niners attracting over 102,000 screaming fans. Annual attendance more than doubled during the decade, rising to over 4 million in 1960.

It was television, more than any other factor, that turned professional football into a growth industry that threatened to outstrip the popularity of major league baseball. Played on a rectangular field with the offense and defense moving in predictable directions, football was in many respects more suited to the small screen than baseball was. Bell and the team owners learned quicker than the baseball world that if used correctly, television could create new fans without destroying the financial base of the teams by robbing them of paying customers. In the early fifties, the NFL began blacking out telecasts of home games within a large radius of the site of the game. In 1956 Bell signed a contract with CBS to provide regional telecasts of all games, stipulating a television blackout of the area within a 50-mile radius of the home team, along with nationwide telecasts of postseason contests. This gave professional football critical exposure without emptying the stadiums.

As television brought more and more football games into the nation's homes, the fans were treated to what seemed to be an increasing number of spine-tingling contests played by increasingly talented players. The most dramatic, and certainly the most analyzed and most replayed of these games was the championship game between the Baltimore Colts and the New

York Giants on December 28, 1958. Played on a warm, misty, cloudy day before over 60,000 screaming fans in Yankee Stadium and an estimated 30 million others glued to television sets, the contest was a thriller from beginning to end, marked by exciting touchdown drives, crucial fourth-down situations, blocked field goal attempts, and dramatic goal-line stands. In sudden-death overtime quarterback Johnny Unitas, who was rapidly redefining the notion of what an NFL passing quarterback should be, took over on his own 21-yard line and marched the Colts down to the Giants' one. Alan Ameche plunged over for the touchdown that gave the Colts a 23–17 victory and the NFL championship.

Back in Baltimore, one man listening to the game on his car radio became so excited over Colt Steve Myrha's field goal, which tied the game with only seven seconds to go and sent it into overtime, that he ran off the road and hit a telephone pole. When the Colts returned home they were met at the airport by a swarm of reporters and photographers and an estimated 30,000 delirious fans. Like Don Larsen's perfect World Series game and Bobby Thomson's "shot heard around the world," the game would be quickly immortalized in sports history. The national frenzy surrounding "the greatest football game ever played" showed that outstanding football teams, dramatic games, and television were capable of creating for professional football the same kind of nationwide interest and excitement that baseball had enjoyed for years. It was the first year that the NFL championship game would be more memorable than the World Series, and it created an audience that television and the NFL would steadily build on in the future.[22]

Frank Gifford, who began his professional football career in 1952, once said that when he returned home to California at the end of that year, some of his friends asked, "Where have you been?"[23] By the close of the decade, no one would have to ask where he and other NFL stars had spent the fall and winter months. Gifford, Johnny Unitas, Sam Huff, Jim Brown, and other NFL stars had become almost as famous as Mickey Mantle, Ted Williams, and Willie Mays.

18. Return of the Maverick (1959)

Bill Veeck was back. About a month before the 1959 season began, the American League owners were sorry to hear that the maverick was now the new owner of the Chicago White Sox.

Veeck had not been idle since he left St. Louis. He had tried to buy the Philadelphia Athletics and the Detroit Tigers, attempted to take over the Ringling Brothers Circus, established a public relations firm in Cleveland, worked as a scout for the Indians, and operated the Miami club in the International League. When he learned that Mrs. Dorothy Comiskey Rigney, owner of 54 percent of the stock of the White Sox, was considering selling her shares, he jumped at the chance. On March 10, he paid her $2.7 million for her shares, taking controlling interest in the club from the hands of the Comiskey family for the first time since the team entered the American League in 1901.

The well-traveled Veeck quickly showed that he had not changed his opinions on the running of a baseball franchise. "Most major-league owners are living in the past," he told reporters in the summer of 1959. "In the last 25 years, the biggest change they've made is to require players to take their gloves off the field when they go to bat.... Baseball must change, and in ways we don't think of now."[1]

Veeck was his usual innovative self. He spruced up Comiskey Park, gave away plastic rain capes when it rained during games, and initiated the practice of putting the names of the players on the backs of their uniforms. When he first saw the new uniforms, first baseman Ted Kluszewski joked that "it's a good thing I've got a broad back."[2] Trying to draw more female fans, Veeck redecorated the powder rooms, gave away roses and orchids, and provided free admission for women on Mother's Day. These promotional efforts, plus the team's winning ways on the field, helped push the 1959 attendance to 1.4 million, almost double the draw of previous years and the highest in White Sox history.

One of the gimmicks Veeck did not resurrect at Chicago was the employment of baseball's oldest professional pitcher, Satchel Paige, who lost his major league job when Veeck sold the Browns in 1953. Paige had gone back to barnstorming and then joined the Miami Marlins when Veeck became the vice president of the team in 1956. Although Veeck left the club at the end of that year, Paige stayed on through 1958. Staunchly loyal to his old players, Veeck tried to persuade manager Al Lopez to add Paige to the pitching staff, but Lopez, leery of Paige's age and undisciplined nature, refused. Lopez would later say, "Bill had one thing wrong with him — it was that he fell in love with his players and he hated to get rid of some guys that weren't good ballplayers. But he wanted to keep them around because he loved them."[3]

But then, Paige never seemed to be out of work. He appeared in a Western movie, *The Wonderful Country*, in 1959, picked up extra money barnstorming and playing in the minors, and worked on his autobiography, *Maybe I'll Pitch Forever*, written with David Lipman, which was published in serial form in the *Saturday Evening Post* in 1961 and in book form in 1962. Paige's last major league performance came in 1965, when Charles O. Finley of Kansas City brought him back to pitch one game against the Red Sox as a publicity stunt. At the age of 59 (or so) and 12 years after his last major league appearance, he pitched three innings, allowing only one hit and no runs. In 1968, the Atlanta Braves hired him as a pitching coach so he could complete the five years of major league service he needed to qualify for a pension. The legendary pitcher would be admitted to the Hall of Fame in 1971.

When he took over the White Sox, Veeck already had one of the best managers in the majors, Al Lopez. Joining the White Sox in 1957 after six years with the Indians, Lopez had never finished lower than second in his nine years as a major league manager. When his Indians captured the flag in 1954 he became the only manager to wrest the pennant from the Yankees since Stengel took the helm of the Yankees in 1949. Widely regarded as a managerial genius, Lopez skillfully ran the team on the field, while Veeck and Hank Greenberg, the vice president and treasurer, directed the club behind the scenes.

Lopez's club was a mixture of youth, veterans, has-beens, and castoffs. Catcher Sherman Lollar was 34, but still swung a heavy bat and called a good game behind the plate. The regular first baseman was Earl Torgeson (35 years old), and in the last month of the season he was spelled at the bag by Ted Kluszewski (34), acquired on waivers from Pittsburgh in late August. The former National League slugger suffered from back trouble but still made a key contribution with his bat in the 31 games he appeared in with the club. Second baseman Nellie Fox (31) and shortstop Luis Aparicio (25) formed one of the best double-play combinations in the league, while Billy Goodman (33) and Bubba Phillips (29) alternated duties at third. Center field was held down by Jim Landis (25). Jim McAnany (22), Al Smith (31), and Jim Rivera (36) shared the other outfield positions.

The pitching staff was one of the oldest in the league. It was led by Early Wynn (39), who had been one of the anchors of the Cleveland pitching staff when Lopez managed the Tribe. He had joined his old skipper on the White Sox in 1958. Backing up Wynn in the starting rotation were left-hander Billy Pierce (32) and young right-hander Bob Shaw (26), while right-handers Gerry Staley (38) and Turk Lown (35) helped provide the necessary relief.

For much of the 1959 season, it looked as if the White Sox might be heading toward, at best, a third consecutive second-place finish. The first half of the season belonged to manager Joe Gordon's Cleveland Indians, who won 10 of their first 11 games, 14 of their first 19, and held first place for all but 12 days through July 16. The White Sox stayed close behind but were having a difficult time keeping pace with the streaking Indians.

For many fans the top story in the American League was not the Indians or the White Sox but the miserable showing of the defending champion New York Yankees. Stengel's club got off to a dismal start, winning only 12 of their first 31 games. Then on May 20, after being humiliated 13–6 by the Detroit Tigers, the impossible happened. The New York Yankees, the pride of major league baseball, fell into the cellar for the first time in 19 years, 8½ games out of first. For Yankee fans, it was "Black Wednesday." But for millions of others, it was a day to celebrate.

During the losing streak, the Yankees often beat themselves with mental and physical errors and showed little resemblance to the proud Yankees of old. On the day they hit bottom, they *looked* like a last-place club, playing poorly and walking off the field to the clubhouse with their heads down. But Stengel, who had been a losing manager long before he became a winning one, told reporters, "The world ain't gonna end tomorrow."[4]

After the loss to Detroit, the Yankees traveled to Baltimore to begin a series with the Orioles. Unable to solve Hoyt Wilhelm's knuckler, Stengel's club lost 5–0 for their seventh defeat in the last eight games. When the game was over, Stengel lectured his players behind locked clubhouse doors, then let reporters into his office and fielded their questions. He was patient and friendly, at least until a well-meaning scribe said, "Thanks for your patience, Case. I know these are rough times." Stengel exploded, "Rough times, my bottom. Other clubs are last and nobody gives a damn. We're last and everyone wants to lynch us." With this outburst, the reporters decided it was time to make their exit.[5]

The Yankees stayed in the cellar for eleven humiliating days while Yankee-haters savored the Bombers' misery. Not until May 31, when Bob Turley beat the Senators 3–0, did they begin to rise from the ashes. For a while, they played like the Yankees of old, winning 17 of their next 23 and climbing to fourth place, only 1½ games out, on June 20. But this was as close as they could get. At the break for the first All-Star Game, the Indians still held the top rung, two games in front of the White Sox. In third place were the Baltimore Orioles, 4½ games out, and still in fourth, but now five games behind, were the Yankees.

In 1959 the players and owners decided to play two All-Star games instead of one. The primary reason, of course, was money. With 60 percent of the net gate receipts earmarked for the players' pension fund, the revenues from two games would bolster the fund and allow an increase in payments to needy old-timers who had played before the pension plan was inaugurated 12 years earlier. The first game, played before 35,277 fans at Forbes Field on July 7, was won 5–4 by the National League. The winning run came in the eighth when Willie Mays's long triple brought Hank Aaron home from first. The next day, the *San Francisco Chronicle* reported, "Harvey Kuenn gave it an honest pursuit, but the only center fielder in baseball who could have caught it hit it."[6] In the second game, played August 3 before 55,105 fans in the Los Angeles Coliseum, the American League won a 5–3 slugfest characterized by five home runs, giving the junior circuit a 16–11 edge in the 26-year-old event.

Though many players and fans opposed the two-game format on the grounds that it diluted the significance of the annual gathering of All-Stars, the practice would continue through 1962. In that year it was decided to return to the old one-game format, primarily because of the problems of finding room in the expanded 162-game schedule for two All-Star games and because club owners agreed to donate 95 percent of the net gate receipts, instead of 60, to the players' pension fund.

After the first All-Star Game the Yankees and Orioles dropped out of contention. Cleveland continued to dog the White Sox and was locked in a tie with them for first on July 27, but the next day the Sox took over first place and kept it for the rest of the year. The Indians mounted one last challenge, winning eight in a row and pulling to within one game on August 26. But as they had all year, the White Sox rallied to win the big ones. They came into Cleveland on Friday, August 28, for a four-game set that included a Sunday doubleheader. Before huge crowds, including 70,398 on Friday night and 66,586 on Sunday afternoon, the Sox trounced the Indians in four consecutive games. One of the victories went to Early Wynn, who just a few years earlier had been the darling of the fans who swarmed into Municipal Stadium. By September 4, the White Sox had increased their lead to 6½ games.

Pennant fever had gripped the Windy City all season. Large crowds turned out for nearly every home game to cheer the Sox on. As soon as a runner reached first base, the crowd would chant "Go-Go-Go," and often the runners did. Emphasizing the bunt, the sacrifice, the hit and run, the steal, and other elements of old-fashioned baseball, the team scratched and clawed for every run while the pitchers and fielders were stingy with the runs allowed the opposition. Happy fans were turning out in record numbers and making plans for the World Series. With three weeks to go, a carnival worker named Ralph J. Belcore made his first visit to the ticket office at Comiskey Park to check on World Series tickets. "I'm first in line for World Series tickets," he told a reporter. "I'm going to check in every day until it looks like I better stay. Then, even if I have to park here for two weeks, I'm gonna do it."[7] Mr. Belcore did not have to wait long. On September 22, Early Wynn clinched the pennant with a 4–3 victory over the Indians.

As the White Sox flew back to Chicago after beating the Tribe on their home turf, a happy Al Lopez said, "I can't remember a more exciting night." He gave all the credit to his players. "Hell, what did I do? I didn't win the pennant," he said. "I just had the horses. And boy can they run."[8] Although it was 2:05 A.M. when their plane landed at Midway Airport, a crowd estimated at 100,000 was waiting to welcome the team home. Some delirious fans had climbed telephone poles or were standing on top of buses, cars, or trucks to get a better view of the returning heroes. Mayor Richard Daley was there to greet them, as was Bill Veeck, who had not been able to accompany his team to Cleveland because of a speaking engagement in Bloomington.

White Sox players and fans had good reason to be delirious. They had dethroned the mighty Yankees and won the first pennant since the 1919 club that went down in history as the infamous Black Sox. Not a single player on the 1959 team had even been born when the last pennant had been won. The oldest player on the squad was Wynn, born on January 6, 1920. Lopez had been only 11 years old in 1919.

Playing in an age that emphasized the long ball, the Sox seemed an unlikely candidate for the American League flag. Nellie Fox (.306) was the club's only .300 hitter, and as a team they were sixth in league batting (.250) and last in both leagues in home runs with 97. But their pitching staff led the league in ERA with 3.29. Early Wynn paced the league in wins with 22 and Shaw contributed 18 and Pierce 14. The club led the league in stolen bases (113), almost half of which (56) were swiped by Aparicio, who, along with other speedy Latin and black players like the Giants' Willie Mays and the Dodgers' Maury Wills, were helping to bring the running game back to baseball.

The White Sox also led in defense and hustle. "We connive, scrounge and hustle to get just one measly run," Veeck bragged in September. "We can't afford to give any away, so we don't."[9] The Sox played especially well in the clutch. They won 35 of the 50 one-run games they were involved in and crushed their two major rivals, the Indians and the Yankees, when they had to, compiling a 15–7 record against the Indians and a 13–9 record against the Yankees. Stengel said of the Sox that "those fellers got little bats and big gloves" and admitted that "I'm not so sure we could have beaten them this year if we were at our '58 best."[10]

The second-place finish of the Indians proved that power was not enough to wrest the pennant from a balanced club like the White Sox. The Tribe led the league in batting average (.263), home runs (167), slugging average (.408), and runs (745). Right fielder Rocky Colavito tied Harmon Killebrew of the Senators for the league home run title (42) and drove in 111 runs, just one short of league-leader Jackie Jensen of the Red Sox. On June 10, just a few hours before a night game with the Orioles, Gordon tried to shake Colavito out of a hitting slump by telling him, "Somebody's printed a rumor that you've been traded. It's a phony. I'd never trade you. But if you don't start hitting, I'll send you back to Reading." A few hours later, Colavito helped power Cleveland to an 11–8 victory by hitting four home runs, becoming just the fourth player to hit four in a nine-inning game.[11]

Cleveland's season ended in a bizarre manner. After prolonged conflicts with his manager over strategy, General Manager Frank Lane announced on the day the White Sox clinched that Gordon had been released and that coach Mel Harder would run the club for the rest of the year. But the very next day, after attempts to lure Leo Durocher to the job fell through, Lane reversed himself and brought Gordon back with a new two-year contract and a pay increase. "I made a mistake," Lane said, "and I decided I didn't have to live with it, so I tried to correct it."[12]

The Yankees finished third, only four games over the .500 mark. The defending champions had all kinds of problems. Don Larsen and Tom Sturdivant developed sore arms. Bob Turley, the 1958 Cy Young winner, fell off to 8–11, leaving Whitey Ford with the best mark, 16–10. The pitching staff would have fared even worse had it not been for the relief efforts of Ryne Duren, who followed 1958's performance with an even better one. Over a 2½-month period, he pitched 36 innings in 18 games without giving up a run. On June 26, at the height of his streak, he came in to relieve in the seventh inning against the White Sox and promptly struck out eight of the nine men he faced. In the last part of this pitching streak, he fanned 15 of the last 19 hitters who dared to walk up to the plate. Stengel called him "the most exciting thing in baseball. If the people won't come out to see him, they won't come out to see anybody. When he hops over that bullpen gate, the folks stop eating their peanuts."[13]

But even at the height of his success Duren was an insecure, erratic young man who often turned to alcohol to escape life's problems. The Yankees would trade him to the Los Angeles Angels in 1961, and he played for several other teams before retiring four years later. The troubled young pitcher would regain control of his life only after an attempted suicide and successful treatment for his alcoholism.

Suffering from knee, shoulder, ankle, and finger injuries, Mantle's batting average fell to .285, his lowest since his rookie year, but he led all Yankees with 31 homers and 75 RBIs. Gil McDougald, Moose Skowron, and Andy Carey also suffered from injuries, several players were hit by the Asian flu, and 37-year-old Hank Bauer, long a mainstay in right field, fell off to .238 and 9 homers. The only regular hitting .300 or better was Bobby Richardson (.301).

The press, and even some of his players, blamed the Yankees' 69-year-old manager for the club's poor performance. Several players were tired of Stengel's platooning, the growing impatience he showed in dealing with younger players still learning some of the fundamentals of the game, and his public criticism of players' mistakes. Some of his troops talked behind his back to one another, the press, to players on other teams, and even to people outside of baseball. Jackie Robinson told reporters that several players had complained to him that Stengel was becoming increasing senile and would even doze off in the dugout during games.

The Yankee owners had long felt that the aging Stengel had outlived his usefulness as the Yankee pilot. During the 1958 season Dan Topping and Del Webb had decided that Stengel was getting senile, but they could not very well fire him after he won the pennant and the World Series. In February of 1959, amidst rumors that it would be his last contract, Topping and Webb gave him a two-year pact, calling for $85,000 in 1959 and a raise to $90,000 the following year. They also added Ralph Houk, a former Yankee reserve catcher and minor league manager, to the team as a coach, leading Stengel to believe that the 39-year-old Houk was being groomed to take over his job.

The Detroit Tigers managed to finish in fourth place, thanks in part to the presence of the league's two leading hitters, Harvey Kuenn (.353) and Al Kaline (.327), and three 17-game winners, Don Mossi, Frank Lary, and Jim Bunning. The Tigers were trailed by Boston, Baltimore, Kansas City, and of course, Washington. The Senators attained a new club record of 163 homers, the second best in the league, led by Killebrew (42 homers), Jim Lemon (33), Bob Allison (30), and Roy Sievers (21). But all this power, and the presence of Rookie of the Year outfielder Bob Allison, could not prevent the Senators from their third consecutive last-place finish.

It was not a good year for Ted Williams. Getting off to a bad start because of neck pain and stiffness, his average at the first of the season fell well below .300. At one point the seemingly impossible happened—he was "rested" because of his slump. He played in only 103 games, 24 as a pinch hitter, and finished the year with 10 homers and a .254 average. It was the only time he hit below .300 in his major league career. When Tom Yawkey generously offered him a $125,000 contract for 1960, Williams protested that his 1959 performance did not justify such a salary and that he should take a cut. He did, to $90,000.

His hitting replacement was already being groomed in the minor leagues, where in 1959 the Red Sox had a $100,000 bonus baby playing for Raleigh in the Carolina League. He was Carl Yastrzemski, a 20-year-old infielder who was making life miserable for the young pitchers he faced in Class B ball. Raleigh manager Ken Deal was high on the young prospect. "He can hit, run, field, throw, and bunt," he told reporters. "He has good power, he hits to all fields. What else is there?"[14] In April of 1961, seven months after Ted Williams had his last at bat in the majors, Yastrzemski would open the season as the Red Sox's starting left fielder.

In 1959 the Red Sox marked another milestone in the integration of the majors when they added infielder Elijah "Pumpsie" Green to their roster, giving all 16 clubs at least one black player. But 12 years after Jackie Robinson started the black revolution, Green was still subjected to some of the same old indignities black players before him had endured. During spring training, he was not allowed to stay with the rest of the team in the hotel in Scottsdale, Arizona. Instead, he lodged at the Adams Hotel in Phoenix, 17 miles away. Each morning the Red Sox sent a car to Phoenix to pick him up and take him to the Red Sox training camp.

In the National League the eight teams began the season expecting to spend more time on airplanes than ever before. In late 1958, the major airlines began to offer jet passenger service for both domestic and transatlantic flights, cutting travel time between most cities in half. Coming on the heels of the Dodgers' and Giants' move to the West coast, the introduction of jet service was a boon to major league scheduling and the comfort of team travel.

The two leagues announced in the spring that they had booked 442 charter flights totaling over 292,184 miles, which was over twice the 1958 total and equal to a journey to the moon or to 12 trips around the world. The National League, with two teams on the West Coast, would fly 212,060 miles, while the American League, with Kansas City still the furthermost western franchise, would fly only 80,124 miles. Nine of the clubs planned to travel exclusively by air between cities, while the others still expected to do some or all of their travel by rail.

On June 17, 1959, sportswriter Joe King enlisted the help of American Airlines and a helicopter to illustrate how the airline industry was revolutionizing sports. He attended a Yankee-White Sox game in New York that started at 2:00 P.M., flew to the West Cost (picking up 3 hours in crossing time zones) in time to see a twi-night doubleheader in Los Angeles between the Dodgers and Braves, then jetted back to New York, arriving there at 9:00 A.M. on June 18, 19 hours and 5,244 miles after his odyssey began the day before.

Expansion of major league franchises to Milwaukee, Kansas City, and the West Coast had made flying a virtual necessity for major league teams, but many players and others connected with the game still longed for the days of leisurely train travel. Some questioned whether plane travel was really progress. In late September, after running to catch a bus that was to transport reporters to O'Hare Airport in Chicago, sportswriter Dick Young growled, "I'll be a son of a bitch. There's something wrong when you have to run yourself into a heart attack to catch a jet to save time."[15]

As planes became larger, faster, safer, and more comfortable, travelers were abandoning trains and buses for the airlines. Between 1950 and 1960, the airlines' percentage of combined airline-railroad passenger traffic rose from 24 to 61 percent. The rapid geographical expansion of major league franchises, combined with the shrinking of the railroad and bus schedules, meant that players and others connected with baseball had to adjust to air travel or find some other line of work. The days when players suffering from airplane phobia could travel by rail or automobile while the rest of the team went by air were at an end.

The National League race was the best since the Giant-Dodger battle of 1951. The main obstacles to a third consecutive Milwaukee pennant were expected to be Danny Murtaugh's Pirates and Bill Rigney's Giants, the two clubs that had finished second and third the previous year. Both would be contenders for much of the year, but they would be joined by a team that few people thought had a chance of even rising from the second division, much less making a run for the pennant. That team was the Los Angeles Dodgers, whose first year on the West Coast had been marked by a 71–83 record and a seventh-place finish.

The Dodgers were a team in transition. Pee Wee Reese and Carl Erskine retired in 1958, leaving only Gil Hodges, Carl Furillo, Duke Snider, Johnny Podres, Junior Gilliam, Clem Labine, Don Drysdale, and Sandy Koufax from the glory days in Brooklyn. The club had made a significant trade over the winter, sending Gino Cimoli to St. Louis for outfielder Wally Moon. During the season it called up Roger Craig, Maury Wills, and Larry Sherry from the farm system. In addition to its new faces, the team had a different offensive look. It was not the power club of former years, but instead a balanced club that relied less on the long ball and more on good pitching, defense, and speed on the base paths. It looked more like the 1959 White Sox than the Brooklyn Dodgers of the early and mid–fifties.

The Dodgers were joined in spring training at Vero Beach by the familiar face of Roy Campanella, back as a coach 13 months after his paralyzing injury. His main job was to work with the young catchers, especially his replacement, Johnny Roseboro, and with the pitching staff. When Campanella rolled his wheel chair into the locker room, longtime Dodger clubhouse attendant John "Senator" Griffin greeted him with, "Campy, welcome home." Campanella felt at home, but he had a very difficult moment the first time the players ran out of the locker room to go out onto the field. "It was at that instant that the realization hit me with a finality that jarred me," he wrote in his autobiography, *It's Good to Be Alive*, published later that year. "Because after that first moment when my mind wanted to 'go' but my body couldn't answer the command, I realized as never before that I wasn't ever going to run or even walk with 'em . . . and I wouldn't, ever. . . . It didn't last long—that wave of self-pity or maybe it was frustration. . . . I shook myself back to reality and, right then, I said to myself, 'Campy, you're down here to coach, not play. Now get on with it.'"[16]

Early in the season, the Dodgers held a special night for Campanella with an exhibition game in the Coliseum against the Yankees. It drew a crowd of 93,103, the largest ever to see a baseball game. Another 15,000 were turned away at the gate. When Campanella was first rolled onto the field, the crowd stood and gave him a great ovation. Players and coaches from both teams had lined up along the first and second base lines, and each one was given a silver plaque and a silver baseball on a mahogany stand with the inscription, "Roy Campanella Night May 7, 1959." Tears ran down his face as he spoke to the crowd, telling them, "I thank God I'm living to be here. I thank each and every one of you from the bottom of my heart. It is something I'll never forget."[17] Between the fifth and sixth innings, Reese pushed Campanella out behind second base and the pitcher's mound. The lights were turned out, and Dodger announcer Vin Scully asked everyone in the park to strike a match or lighter. It was a special night, comparable to the special days held for the dying Lou Gehrig and Babe Ruth in Yankee Stadium years before.

The game, which the Yankees won 6–2, was not an official benefit for Campanella, but he did receive an estimated $55,000 to use as he saw fit. He said he would give part of the money to charity. It was a remarkable tribute to the catcher who had never played for the Dodgers in Los Angeles. Looking at the huge turnout, Walter O'Malley's mind drifted to the practical: "This 93,103 is fantastic. . . . No one can now question our moving out here from Brooklyn. We, in baseball, have been a bunch of chumps for not coming out before we did."[18]

Successfully coping with the reality of paralysis, Campanella was involved in many enterprises—a Dodger scout and coach, youth counselor, host of a radio show, owner of a Harlem liquor store, and author. When his autobiography was published later in the year, *Saturday Review* editor Norman Cousins wrote in his review of Campanella's moving life story, "What made him special was that he believed in the game the way a kid does; he carried his enthusiasm with him from the sandlots into professional baseball and kept them pure. He helped fans and players alike to restore some of their lost illusions about the game. Even the cynics took off their hats when Campy passed."[19]

In the 154-game race for the top, the Braves got off to a 6–1 start, built a 4½-game lead by May 19, and managed to hold on to the top spot for all but eight days through the break for the first All-Star Game. At the recess the Braves were in first, followed by the Giants, Dodgers, and Pirates, with only 3½ games separating the first- and fourth-place clubs.

The second half of the season saw the pennant race tighten even more. Two days after the All-Star Game, the Giants took over first place and, except for two days, led the pack for the next two and a half months. Their strengths were the pitching of Johnny Antonelli and "Toothpick Sam" (also called "Sad Sam") Jones and the hitting of Willie Mays, Orlando Cepeda, and Rookie of the Year Willie McCovey. As usual, the 28-year-old Mays was the leader of the team. His annual salary of $75,000 reflected his rise to the star level of Williams, Musial, Mantle, and some of the other highly paid white players. Early in the season when he was asked by one reporter about the often-cited story about how he liked to play ball so much that he never cared about his salary, Mays had replied, "Maybe that makes a good story, but I never said anything like that to Mr. Stoneham."[20]

On September 17, the Giants led both the Dodgers and Braves by two games with just eight games to go. Delirious San Francisco fans were making plans for the first West Coast World Series, and Giants' officials were discussing the feasibility of playing the fall classic in Candlestick Park, which was not scheduled for opening until 1960, rather than in the old and cramped Seals Stadium. But the discussion was premature. The World Series would be played on the West Coast, but not in San Francisco. The Giants collapsed in the last 10 days of the season while the Dodgers came on strong to grab the top prize.

On Friday, September 18, the Dodgers and Giants were scheduled to begin a three-game series at Seals Stadium, but a rainout forced the two teams to play a doubleheader the next day. It seemed like old times when the Bums and Jints used to knock heads in New York for city and league bragging rights. It was the beginning of a disaster for the Giants. Pitching before capacity crowds in Seals Stadium, Roger Craig took the afternoon game from Johnny Antonelli by a 4–1 margin, and that night Don Drysdale outdueled Mike McCormick, 5–3. Meanwhile in Philadelphia, the Braves beat the Phillies in a night game, 9–3. With one week to go, the Dodgers and Giants were tied for first, and the Braves were just a half game back.

The anxiety deepened in San Francisco on Sunday, when the Dodgers took their third straight from the Giants, 8–2, and moved into first place for the first time since April 26. In Philadelphia the Braves downed the Phillies, 8–5, and took over second place, one-half game out. The Giants now suddenly found themselves in third, one game behind. This set the stage for the last incredible week of the season, when the Dodgers and Braves alternated in first place and the Giants desperately tried to stave off mathematical elimination from the race they once thought they had locked up.

While several days of rain played havoc with the schedule, all three clubs stumbled toward the finish line. Going into Sunday, September 27, the last day of the season, the Dodgers and Braves were tied for first and the Giants were 1½ games behind; so as the day began, there was the possibility of a three-way tie if the Dodgers and Braves both lost and the slumping Giants could post a doubleheader win over the Cardinals in St. Louis. Roger Craig beat the Cubs 7–1, guaranteeing the Dodgers at least a tie for first. When the final Dodger-Cub score was posted on the scoreboard in Milwaukee, the Braves were locked in a 1–1 tie with the Phils. The Braves mounted a desperate three-run rally in the seventh to beat the Phils 5–2 and force a pennant playoff, the third in the National League since 1945, all involving the Dodgers. In St. Louis, the dejected Giants dropped a now meaningless doubleheader to the Cardinals, 2–1 and 14–8.

Neither of the front runners had a chance to rest before the playoffs. After defeating the Cubs in Chicago on Sunday, the Dodgers traveled to Milwaukee for Monday's first playoff game. Rain postponed the game for 47 minutes, limiting the crowd to 18,297 and forcing the entire contest to be played under the lights. The Dodgers took a 3–2 victory behind the superb pitching of Larry Sherry, who relieved Danny McDevitt in the second and held the Braves to four hits the rest of the way.

The two teams then flew to Los Angeles for Tuesday's game. Over 36,583 fans came out to the afternoon contest, hoping to see the Dodgers give the city its first pennant. With Lew Burdette baffling the Dodgers on the mound, the Braves led until the bottom of the ninth, when the Dodgers chased him from the mound and rallied from a 5-2 deficit to tie the score and send the game into extra innings. The score remained knotted at 5–5 until the last of the twelfth. Then, with two out, Hodges drew a walk from Bob Rush, the fifth Milwaukee pitcher, and went to second on a single by Joe Pignatano.

This brought up Carl Furillo, now a part-time player with only 93 at bats for the season. Furillo bounced a high hopper which was fielded behind second base by shortstop Felix Mantilla, normally a second baseman who had been switched to short when regular shortstop Johnny Logan was injured in the seventh. With Hodges racing toward third, Mantilla made an off-balance throw to first in an attempt to nip Furillo. His errant throw bounced to the right of first baseman Frank Torre and into the dugout, allowing Hodges to cross the plate with the game-ending, pennant-winning, run. In winning their tenth flag and finally beating the playoff jinx, the Dodgers also made baseball history by becoming the first team to win the pennant after finishing seventh the year before.

The Dodgers were not the powerful hitting club of old. The team batting average was .257, sixth in the league, and they hit only 148 homers, fifth in the league. But they led the league in stolen bases (84), fielding average (.981), saves (26), and strikeouts (1077), and were third in ERA (3.79). The squad was made up of good team players, not stars, and it played consistently, enjoying few long winning streaks or suffering through few losing ones. The longest win streak was seven, compiled in June, and their longest losing streak was five, suffered in May. Aside from that one streak they did not lose more than three consecutive games all year long. In the critical last three weeks of the campaign, they won 13 of 18 and swept the playoffs with the Braves.

Duke Snider led the club with a .308 batting average, 23 homers, and 88 RBIs. Hodges had a good year with a .276 batting average, 25 homers, and 80 RBIs. Newcomer Wally Moon ably filled the gap in left field, hitting .302, driving in 74 runs, and hitting 19 homers, many of them "Moonshots" over the short left-field screen. Called up from Spokane on June 6 after laboring in the Dodger farm system for nearly a decade, Maury Wills took over the shortstop position vacated by Pee Wee Reese and proved that he did, indeed, belong in the big time. Although he hit only .260 in 83 games, he slugged the ball at better than a .400 clip during the crucial final three weeks of the season.

Fireballer Don Drysdale intimidated batters with his speed and size (6 feet 5 inches tall, 190 pounds) and paced all Dodger pitchers with a 17–13 record and a league-leading 242 strikeouts. Podres followed with a 14–9 record. The team was given a big lift by the return of Roger Craig, who had been sent down to the minors in 1958 after developing a sore arm. Recalled in June of 1959, he won 11 games, four of them shutouts, and posted a 2.06 ERA. Another pitcher called up in midseason, 23-year-old right-hander Larry Sherry, was used as both a starter and reliever. After losing his first two games, he was 7–0 for the rest of the year and wound up with a 2.19 ERA. Sandy Koufax (8–6) was still learning his trade and struggling with his control, but on August 31 he electrified a crowd of 82,794 when he not only beat the Giants 5–2 but also struck out 18, tying Bob Feller's 1938 record.

It was a disappointing year for the Braves. Spahn and Burdette each won 21 games, tying Sam Jones of the Giants for most victories, and Bob Buhl contributed 15 wins. The Braves led the league in homers with 177, with Mathews taking the home run crown (46) to go along with his .306 average and 114 RBIs. Henry Aaron flirted with the .400 mark for much of the first half of the season and wound up with a league-leading .355 average, along with 39 homers and 123 RBIs, justifying Haney's claim that "a manager would have to be crazy to want to tell him anything about hitting."[21] Joe Adcock contributed a .292 average, 25 homers, and 76 RBIs.

But the Braves suffered from injuries to several key players and from the failure of their young pitchers to take the load off of Spahn, Burdette, and Buhl. They also missed the leadership of second baseman Red Schoendienst, who was still recovering from tuberculosis and did not join the club until September. The defending league champions were an erratic club, looking like world champions one week and cellar-dwellers the next. Not long after the season's end, Haney left the Braves to take an announcing job with NBC. He was replaced by Los Angeles coach Chuck Dressen.

The Giants played well until near the end. Willie Mays led the team with his .313 average, 34 homers, and 104 RBIs, and paced the league in stolen bases with 27. First baseman Orlando Cepeda hit .317 with 27 homers and 105 RBIs. Willie McCovey came up from Phoenix on July 30 and proceeded to hit .354 and slug 13 homers, 6 of them in his first 14 games. "Toothpick Sam" Jones tied Burdette and Spahn for most victories with 21, and he led the league in ERA with 2.83. The rest of the pitching load was carried by Johnny Antonelli (19–10), Mike McCormick (12–16), Jack Sanford (15–12), and Stu Miller (8–7).

The Pirates finished in fourth place, but the best pitching performance of the year, and one of the best of all time, was turned in early in the season by Pirate left-hander Harvey Haddix. Haddix had broken in with St. Louis in 1952 and had played with the Phillies and Reds before coming to Pittsburgh in 1959. Standing 5 feet 9 inches and weighing 160 pounds but looking even smaller, he had been given the nickname of "the Kitten" by his former Cardinal teammates because of his physical resemblance to former Cardinal pitcher Harry "the Cat" Brecheen.

In a night game in Milwaukee County Stadium on May 29, pitching against Burdette, Haddix was virtually untouchable. Although he had a cold and sore throat and did not feel well warming up before the game, he insisted on starting. Both starters pitched well, but Haddix was as sharp as he had ever been in his baseball life. At the end of nine, neither team had scored. Saliva Lew had given up 8 hits, but Haddix had retired 27 straight hitters, allowed only two balls to be hit out of the infield, and struck out eight. As he walked off the field at the end of the inning with the no-hitter still in progress and the score still tied at 0–0, the 19,194 Milwaukee fans gave him a rousing ovation.

When Haddix took the mound in the tenth, he became the first major league pitcher to carry a perfect game beyond nine innings. When he retired the last Brave in the eleventh, he became the first pitcher to carry a no-hitter more than 10⅔ innings. Still there was no score, and in the twelfth he and Burdette continued to turn frustrated hitters away. At the end of 12, Haddix had retired 36 men in a row, a major league record for one game.

Before Haddix took the field in the thirteenth, manager Danny Murtaugh tried to persuade the obviously tiring pitcher to give way to a reliever and not risk his perfect game. But Haddix refused, and because of it he encountered disaster. The first Brave hitter, Mantilla, hit a ground ball to third baseman Don Hoak, who threw the ball into the dirt and off the knee of first baseman Rocky Nelson. Mantilla had reached base on an error, ending

Haddix's perfect game but not his no-hitter. The next batter, Mathews, sacrificed Mantilla to second. Then, following orders from the dugout, Haddix issued an intentional walk to Aaron, the first walk given up by either pitcher. But percentage baseball failed the Pirates here. Joe Adcock, the next hitter, slammed a high slider over the right center field fence, 375-feet from home, just above the glove of leaping center fielder Bill Virdon. After 12⅓ innings, Haddix had lost his perfect game, his no-hitter, and the game itself, apparently by a score of 3–0.

But then confusion reigned. Aaron thought the ball had fallen on the warning track inside the park, not over the wire fence, so when he saw Mantilla touch home plate he figured the Braves had won 1–0. After touching second base, he cut back through the infield to the Braves dugout on the first base side. Meanwhile, running with his head down, Adcock trotted around the bases. As the players left the field, the umpires did not, and when Fred Haney and his coaches realized what had happened they sent Aaron back onto the field to touch all the bases, as required. Followed by Adcock, Aaron went back and touched third base and home plate. After several minutes of discussion, the umpires called Adcock out for passing Aaron on the bases, and ruled it a 2–0 game. The next day League President Warren Giles ruled that since Adcock had passed Aaron on the bases he was entitled to a double, not a home run, and that the game had officially ended with the score of 1–0 when Mantilla touched home plate. Adcock had lost a home run, but Haddix had lost a no-hitter and the game.

After the game an exhausted and dejected Haddix praised his teammates for the support they had given him and said, "I knew we needed this game to stretch our winning streak and try to catch the Braves and as far as I'm concerned, the records don't mean much if we lose.... It was just another loss, but it hurt a little more."[22] Over in the other locker room, Burdette, happy to get the win but appreciative of a great effort by a fellow pitcher, said that "he deserved to win." Burdette, who had given up 12 hits, would later say, "I'm the guy who won the greatest game ever pitched."[23]

The Pirates also had the best relief pitcher in the league in a season that had so many good ones that it was called "the year of the reliever." Roy Face had made his major league debut with the Pirates in 1953 and spent the next 16 years baffling National League hitters with his famed forkball, a cross between a knuckler and a sinker and a forerunner of the split-fingered fastball. Released from the pitcher's hand like a fastball, the off-speed pitch headed toward the plate with little rotation and then curved down sharply.

Spending most of his career with the Pirates, the little (5 feet 8 inches, 155 pounds) right-hander usually finished near the top of the league in the number of appearances, relief wins, and saves. From May 30, 1958, until he was beaten by the Dodgers on September 11, 1959, he appeared in 97 games, winning 22 and losing *none*. In 1959, he pitched in 57 games and won 18 while losing only one for an incredible winning percentage of .947, a new record for starters or relievers with 15 decisions or more. Teammate Harvey Haddix would later say of Face, "The only word you could use to describe it was amazing. He was always a good pitcher — he was the best relief pitcher of his time, without a question — but that season he was beyond good."[24] In his career, Face would appear in 848 games, winning 92 and saving 193.

It had been a great season, with exciting pennant races in both leagues and total major league attendance topping 19 million, an increase of 9.6 percent over 1958. Late in August *Time* magazine reported, "The game is stronger than it has been in years. . . . This season, in fact, the fans are too busy following the action on the diamond to engage in the old lament of what's-wrong-with-baseball. This summer, nothing is."[25]

The fifty-sixth World Series, and the first played in Comiskey Park since 1919, opened in Chicago on October 1. In the first game, the White Sox showed unaccustomed batting power in banging out 11 hits en route to an 11–0 blowout behind Early Wynn. After the game Bill Veeck told a reporter, "In the third inning, when we scored seven runs, I almost left. I thought I'd gotten into the wrong park."[26] But the Dodgers came back in the second game to take a 4–3 victory behind two homers by second baseman Charlie Neal and a pinch-hit homer by Chuck Essegian.

The two teams flew to Los Angeles for the first World Series ever played west of St. Louis. When the Dodger plane landed at Los Angeles International Airport, a crowd estimated at 5,000 had gathered to welcome the players home with cheers and with placards reading, "WIN OR LOSE, WE LOVE YOU DODGERS" and "LET'S HANG UP THE WHITE SOX TO DRY."[27] All three games in the huge coliseum (capacity close to 92,500 for baseball) were sold out three days before the first one began. The Dodgers took the first two games by scores of 3–1 and 5–4, giving them a 3–1 lead in the series. In the Dodger dressing room, someone wrote "One to Go-Go-Go," on the blackboard, but in the visitors' dressing room no one, least of all Al Lopez, had given up. "We still have a chance," he told reporters.[28] The Sox did stay alive the next day, winning a superb pitching and defensive duel by a 1–0 margin to send the Series back to the Midwest.

But it would not last long. Over 47,000 cheering fans could not spur their favorites past the Dodgers, who took a 2–0 lead in the third and an 8–0 lead in the fourth en route to a 9–3 pounding of the Sox and the clinching of the world championship. In the happy Dodger dressing room after the game, a Dodger player shouted, "The Go-Go Sox is gone."[29]

The Dodgers had played in Brooklyn for 65 years before winning their first Series, but won their first one in Los Angeles in just their second year in the city. To Los Angeles fans, it was a good omen. It was the Dodgers' second world title in 10 attempts, and it gave the National League four of the last six Series. Nonetheless, the American League still had a commanding 35–21 lead.

The two teams had been evenly matched, at least on paper. Both had team batting averages of .261 with 19 RBIs. The Dodgers barely edged the Sox in hits (53 to 52) and fielding average (.983 to .982). The Dodgers had stranded 42 men on base to the Sox's 43 and scored 21 runs to their 23. But the Dodgers had more homers (7–4) and double plays (7–2), and in the area the Sox were supposed to excel in, stolen bases, the Dodgers led 5–2.

The top hitters on both clubs were veterans. Hodges and Kluszewski both had nine hits and a .391 batting average, but Kluszewski, who had hit only four homers during the regular season, hit four homers to Hodges' one and set a record for a six-game series by driving in 10 runs. Neal had a .370 average and led all players with 10 hits, including two homers and two doubles. Suffering from knee problems and reduced to a part-time player in the Series, Snider hit his eleventh homer, tying him with Mickey Mantle for second place on the all-time World Series list. Babe Ruth's 15 were still first.

For the first time in World Series history, no starter finished a game. The pitching star was the Dodgers' regular season phenomenon Larry Sherry, who fed opposing hitters a virtually unhittable mixture of curves, fastballs, and sliders. In the first game of the playoffs with the Braves, he pitched the Dodgers to victory after coming in to relieve in the second inning. During the World Series he set a record by finishing all four winning games. He won two games, saved the other two (won by Drysdale and Podres), and in 12⅔ innings allowed just one run for a 0.71 ERA. When the playoffs and Series had ended, he had compiled an incredible postseason record—in 11 days, he appeared in five games, won three and saved two others, and posted an ERA of 0.44. He would have several more good years before he retired in 1968, but none to match his rookie year.

Thanks to the huge seating capacity of the Coliseum, which attracted a total of 277,750 fans for the three games, the 1959 World Series set a total attendance record of 420,784, some 26,000 more than the seven-game Series between the Braves and Yankees the year before. Gate receipts and radio and television rights added up to a record total of $5.6 million. The players shared in this prosperity, with the winners pocketing $11,238 each and the losers taking home $7,275 each, both new records.

The three consecutive 92,000-plus games in the Coliseum would not be surpassed, since no other park could hold that many fans and the Dodgers had already begun construction on the newer but smaller Dodger Stadium. Continuing litigation over the land at Chavez Ravine, finally resulting in the forceful eviction of 20 families, had delayed work on the new Dodger home. Ground-breaking ceremonies were finally held on

September 17, 1959. When it opened in 1962, Dodger Stadium was the showpiece of the major leagues. Designed especially for major league baseball rather than as an all-purpose arena, the park, along with the area's good weather and the success of the Dodger teams, would draw millions year after year. In 1978 the Dodgers became the first team to draw 3 million fans in one year, vindicating, at least economically, O'Malley's decision to abandon Ebbets Field and the Brooklyn fans.

19. Miracle in Pittsburgh (1960)

It was January 1960, and around both leagues players were mulling over the contract offers they had received from their clubs. For some, the new year brought a pay cut. Thirty-nine-year-old Stan Musial took a $20,000 slice from his 1959 salary ($100,000) without a fuss. "In fact I'm glad to sign this contract," he said. "Because a couple of times in the past the Cards have had me sign for more than we agreed upon orally. This year I thought I'd be kind to them." Whitey Ford, who got the same salary ($35,000) he had made in 1959, when his record fell off to 16–10, told reporters, "The first thing I did was look for a stamp. I wanted to sign that contract and get it back before they changed their minds." Teammate Mickey Mantle was unhappy at suffering a $13,000 cut, even though his $65,000 contract was still one of the highest salaries in the majors. "They cut me more than they shoulda," he said. But out in San Francisco, Willie Mays was elated at being raised to $85,000, making him the highest paid player in either league. "It was a-comin' to me. I deserved a raise," Mays said.[1]

As players gathered in Florida and Arizona for spring training, Brooklynites and baseball fans everywhere marked the passing of a baseball institution. On February 23, a demolition crew began swinging the wrecking ball in Ebbets Field to make way for a housing project. Among the 200 mourners and celebrities gathered there for the special ceremony commemorating the demise of the old field was Lee Allen, a historian for the Hall of Fame, who accepted for the Hall the key used by Charles Ebbets to open the field for play in 1913; Tex Rickards, long-time Dodger public address announcer; Otto Miller, who caught the first game played in Ebbets back in 1913; Roy Campanella, who caught the last game played at Ebbets Field (and also his last, four months before his paralyzing automobile accident) in 1957; and Carl Erskine, who pitched two no-hitters there and also struck out 14 Yankees to set a new World Series record. During the ceremonies, Erskine told another onlooker next to him, "When I look at the field now I see the past. I think of things that happened in this nook and that cranny. I'm remembering bad pitches I made from out there and great days we had. That dugout's empty, but when I look at it I can see all the men that used to be there."[2]

When the ceremonies were over, the two-ton wrecking ball, painted white with red stitches to resemble a baseball, slammed into the visitors dugout. After destroying it, the crane carrying the ball headed to the 376-mark in center field. By the time the ball had finished its work, Ebbets Field itself would exist only as a historical memory. "It's all gone now, never to return," the *Sporting News* mourned. "Things will never be the same in Flatbush."[3]

As one old park died, another one was born. Construction had begun on San Francisco's Candlestick Park in October of 1958, and was completed in time for the opening of the 1960 season. Built by the city for $15 million, it had seating for 43,765, plenty of parking spaces, and a deep outfield — 335 feet to the left and right field fences and 420 feet to deep center. Unfortunately, it would also have strong, gusty winds and cool, damp nights.

Most of the players did not like it. When Willie Mays first practiced there, he hit two long balls that would have been home runs in any other park in the majors. But at Candlestick they were held back by the wind and fell short of the 397-foot fence in left field, causing Mays to complain, "This park is too big. Somebody's gonna get some salary cuts around here." If the park hurt the hitters, it could be a nightmare for fielders trying to guess where the winds might finally allow a fly ball to drop and for offensive and defensive players trying to cope with the dust storms the winds sometimes whipped up. Stan Musial, a gentleman not known for complaining, complained, "You'd think they'd ask a few ballplayers before they built a park."[4]

Conditions at Candlestick got no better as the season progressed. On July 15, the Dodgers and Giants were involved in an unusual contest that rivaled some of the zany events of their battles back in New York. In pregame infield practice — taken in cold, foggy, and windy weather — pop flies hit in the direction of third base blew across the field and landed in foul territory behind *first* base. During the game, the fog became so thick that the scoreboard could not be seen at all. In the third inning the umpires finally halted the game after Willie McCovey hit a fly ball to the outfield that fell in for a triple because Wally Moon and Duke Snider were unable to see the ball after it left McCovey's bat. When the fog lifted after a 24-minute delay, the Dodgers went on to record a 5–3 victory.

Over the years, Candlestick would be called "Baseball's Alcatraz," "The Abomination by the Bay," and similar unflattering names. The winds became legendary, especially the 60-mile-an-hour gust during the 1961 All-Star Game that blew Stu Miller off the mound. In that case, the umpires added insult to injury by charging Miller with a balk. In 1989, the park would also gain notoriety as the site of the first World Series game to be postponed because of an earthquake.

On April 17, one day before the American League season opened, the baseball world was shocked when the Detroit Tigers traded Harvey Kuenn, the 1959 batting champion (.353), to the Cleveland Indians for Rocky Colavito, who in 1959 had shared the home run title (42) with Harmon Killebrew of the Senators. It was a straight player deal, with no cash exchanged, and it shocked and outraged players and fans of both teams.

The Kuenn-Colavito switch was only one of the strange events of the season. Just one day after Philadelphia opened the season with a 9–4 loss to Cincinnati, manager Eddie Sawyer decided not to endure another season mired in last place. He resigned (some rumors claimed that he was fired) and was replaced by Gene Mauch, who led the team to a last-place finish. On May 4, with the Chicago Cubs resting uncomfortably in last place after 17 games, owner Philip K. Wrigley decided on one of the most unusual managerial switches of all time. After negotiating with radio station WGN, which broadcast the Cub games, Wrigley announced that manager Charlie Grimm was going to take over the microphone in the radio booth and that WGN broadcaster and veteran pilot Lou Boudreau would take over the manager's reins. The switch was bad for all parties — Grimm was not particularly effective as an announcer and Boudreau was able to compile only a 54–83 record, leading the Cubs to a seventh-place finish.

Several other bizarre managerial changes were made during the year. In the middle of the season, Boston manager Billy Jurges, who had been hired in the middle of the 1959 season, was fired and replaced by Mike "Pinky" Higgins, the man he had replaced. The middle of the season also saw the Tigers and Indians, the two teams that engineered the Kuenn-Colavito trade, trade managers. On August 3, with the Indians in fourth place and the Tigers in sixth, General Manager Frank Lane of the Indians and President Bill DeWitt of the Tigers struck a deal. Cleveland manager Joe Gordon, who had been fired and then quickly rehired by Lane at the end of the 1959 season, was sent to Detroit for Jimmy Dykes. Both teams played below .500 ball for the rest of the season and finished in the same place in the standings they had been at the time of the trade.

There were still other strange events. In the middle of the season, Don Newcombe of the Cincinnati Reds was thrown out of a game before play even began. On July 17, when Big Newk came out to the mound to begin the second game of a doubleheader with the Pirates, the Pirates protested that his sweatshirt's left sleeve was longer than the right one. Umpire Dusty Boggess ordered Newcombe to change shirts. Newcombe went to the dugout, changed shirts, then returned to the mound, where he made the mistake of asking Boggess, "Supposing Pete Gray came out on the mound? What would you do then?" The two men exchanged words, and Boggess tossed Newcombe out of the game. He had not even thrown his warm-up pitches before he headed for the showers.[5]

The season had a number of fights between players, the most publicized one involving Billy Martin, who brought his brawling ways to the Cincinnati Reds of the National League after playing in New York, Kansas City, Detroit, and Cleveland. Martin was involved in a highly publicized incident on August 4 at Wrigley Field with Jim Brewer of the Cubs. In the second inning, after being brushed back by a pitch from the 22-year-old rookie, Martin went out to the mound and punched him in the face. The blow damaged Brewer's cheekbone and eyesocket so severely that he had to be hospitalized for two months and undergo two reconstructive surgeries to the cheekbone and eyesocket.

For this latest outrageous act in his stormy career, Martin was handed a slap on the wrist—ejection from the game, a $500 fine, and a five-day suspension. A $1 million lawsuit filed against Martin by the Cubs was later dropped, but a private suit initiated by Brewer dragged through the courts for nine years and wound up with Martin being ordered to pay $22,000 in damages to the injured pitcher. Brewer recovered from the injury, and went on to become one of the most successful relievers in the National League during a 17-year career spent mostly with the Cubs and Dodgers. Martin's playing career would end at the close of the 1961 season, when he appeared in 108 games for the Braves and the Twins.

In 1952, when the Pittsburgh Pirates landed in the cellar again with 112 losses, manager Billy Meyer told his players, "You clowns could go on 'What's My Line' in full uniform and stump the panel."[6]

The Pirates had not won a pennant in 33 years, the longest dry spell in major league history. In the postwar era they were the perennial doormat of the National League. From 1945 through 1957, they had finished last seven times, sixth once, fourth three times. In 1958, with Danny Murtaugh in his first full season at the helm, the team finished in second place, its first .500 season in 10 years. After the Pirates had fallen into the cellar again in 1957 for the sixth time since 1950, Branch Rickey quipped that "the team was last on merit,"[7] but the second-place finish in 1958 led many Pirate fans to hope that Rickey's rebuilding efforts were finally going to pay off. However in 1959 the team dropped to 78–76 and a fourth-place finish.

At the beginning of the 1960 season, it looked like it might be another long year for the Pirates and their fans. On opening day, the Giants, Braves, and Dodgers, who had been picked to finish one-two-three by most experts, all seemed to serve notice that they were indeed the class of the league. The Giants inaugurated Candlestick Park with a 3–1 victory over the Cardinals, the defending champion Dodgers continued to find gold in Los Angeles as 67,550 fans turned out to watch them defeat the Cubs in a 3–2, 11-inning thriller, and in Milwaukee the Braves defeated the Pirates 4–3. But the 1960 flag would not go to any of the three franchises that had dominated the league in the 1950s. Instead, it would go to the Pirates.

The 1960 Pirates were one of those miracle teams that appear occasionally, out of nowhere, to grab the attention of the press and the fans. Early in the season, the Pirates and their fans sensed that this would be a different year. In the first week of the season the team could do no better than a 3–3 mark, but then it launched a nine-game winning streak, the club's longest since 1944, and rode into first place. In May the Pirates yielded the top rung to the Giants on two occasions, once for 12 days and then again for five. But on May 30 they regained the lead, and except for yielding it to the Braves for one day near the end of July, they kept it for the rest of the year.

From late May through the rest of the season, Pittsburgh was swept by pennant fever, an affliction that seems to hit hardest the teams and fans who have not had it for decades. All over Pittsburgh, and in much of Pennsylvania as well, "Beat 'em Bucs" pennants and signs were proudly displayed. Success on the field was also paying off at the gate. In their first 24 home games, the team drew 480,648 fans, a gain of almost 100,000 over the same period in 1959. For the year, they drew 1,705,828, a new club record.

The Pirates gradually built their lead. In the first part of June they were 1½ games ahead of San Francisco and 5½ ahead of Milwaukee. By the time of the All-Star break (July 11-13), they had increased their lead to 5½ over the second-place Braves.

The two players receiving the loudest applause at the beginning of the two All-Star games were Ted Williams and Stan Musial, both chosen mostly on sentiment. The two had begun the season as the best hitters of the decade. They were the only two active players who had hit over 400 home runs (Williams had 493, Musial 412 on opening day), and it was the second straight decade in which they had stood at the top of major league hitters in batting average. In the forties, Williams had hit .356 and Musial .346, and in the fifties, based on the records of players who had been active during at least 7 of the last 10 years (1950–1959), Williams had a .336 average, while Musial was not far behind with a .330 average. Musial had won the batting crown seven times, and Williams six.

Other players, writers, and fans were all wondering just how much longer the two stars could play. Williams, who began his major league career in 1939, was 41, and Musial, who began in 1941, was 39. Both were in the twilight of their careers, and had dropped below .300 for the first time in 1959. Williams had already said that this would be his last season, and this time he really seemed to mean it. Although Musial had made no predictions about retirement, he had been having his problems with injuries.

Musial hit a home run in each game, setting a new record of six career All-Star homers, while Williams recorded a pinch single in the second game. In the dressing room after the second contest, Williams, who had begun the year with back pain and a pinched nerve in his neck, told reporters, "I'm not going to hit .340 this year. I just want to hit .300. I'm tired. I need a rest. This has got to be my last year." In the National League clubhouse, Musial said, "I can hit. I can still hit."[8]

After the National League took both games, a 5–3 affair in Kansas City and a 6–0 embarrassment of the junior circuit in New York, giving the National League 9 of the last 13 and narrowing the gap to 16–13, the Pirates continued their quest for the flag. In the second half they had to fight off serious challenges not only from the Braves but also from an unexpected quarter. The St. Louis Cardinals pulled to within 5½ games at the end of August. But the Pirates rallied, won 17 of their next 23 games, and clinched the pennant on September 25. At season's end they led the Braves by 7, the Cardinals by 9, and the Dodgers by 13. The Giants, Reds, Cubs, and Phillies brought up the rear.

The Pirates had been dubbed the "team of destiny" early in the season, and their play showed that they deserved it. Although they never broke the race wide open and did not clinch the pennant until the last week of the season, they led for most of the year. A balanced and consistent team that played like they expected to win and took temporary setbacks in stride, their longest losing streak was four games. They had six winning streaks of five or more games, usually when they needed to beat back challenges by the Cardinals and the Braves. They seemed to play best when they had their backs to the wall. On 23 occasions they scored the winning run in their last turn at bat, and in 12 of these victories they pulled it off after two were out. Gone were the days when fans streamed out of Forbes Field after Ralph Kiner had taken his last turn at bat.

Pittsburgh was a young team that had been in the rebuilding process for much of the decade. Most of the players were in their mid– to late–twenties. Veteran left-handed slugger Smoky Burgess shared the catching duties with right-handed hitter Hal Smith. Burgess hit .294 with 9 homers and 39 RBIs, while Smith hit .295 with 11 homers and 45 RBIs. First baseman Dick Stuart hit only .260, but he was the team's leading home run hitter (23) and drove in 83 runs. Second baseman Bill Mazeroski hit a respectable .273 with 11 homers and 64 RBIs and sparkled in the field. One of the best second baseman to ever play the game, "Dazzling Maz" or "the Boy Bandit," as he was often called, led the league in putouts, assists, fielding average, and double plays.

His double-play partner at shortstop was another defensive standout, Dick Groat, the team captain and the league's Most Valuable Player. At the plate, Groat led the league in batting with a .325 average despite missing three weeks of action in September with a fractured wrist. While he was sidelined his spot on the field was ably filled by 25-year-old switch-hitter Dick Schofield, who hit .403 in 21 games as the Pirates closed in on the pennant. Third base was held down by Don Hoak, who had played with the

Dodgers, Cubs, and Reds before coming to Pittsburgh in 1959. In 1960 the veteran had one of his best seasons, hitting .282 with 16 homers and 79 RBIs.

The left field duties were handled by Bob Skinner, a mediocre fielder who hit .273 with 15 homers and 86 RBIs. Bill Virdon, a light hitter (.264 average, 8 homers, 40 RBIs) but outstanding defensive player, played center field. In right was Roberto Clemente, the young Latin player who was often compared with Willie Mays because of his all-around ability and exciting brand of play. Clemente contributed a .314 average, 16 homers, and 94 RBIs.

The Pirates' pitching staff was anchored by veteran right-hander Vernon Law, whose 20–9 record brought him the Cy Young Award. Right-hander Bob Friend was 18–12, left-hander Harvey Haddix had a 11–10 record, and another lefty, Wilmer "Vinegar Bend" Mizell, acquired from St. Louis in May, compiled a 13–5 mark. The top reliever was Roy Face, the forkball specialist who could not duplicate his 18–1 record of 1959 but still won 10 and lost 8, led the league in appearances with 68, and saved 24, second only to Lindy McDaniel of St. Louis, who had 26.

The Pirates lacked home run punch, hitting only 120, sixth best in the league, but they led the league in team batting with a .276 average and in runs scored with 734. A good fielding team, they had a fielding average of .979 and led the league in double plays with 163.

The second-place Braves played well at home (51–26), but they lost the pennant on the road, where they dropped over half of their games, including 8 of 11 at Pittsburgh's Forbes Field. As usual, the Braves got outstanding mound work from Warren Spahn (21–10) and Lew Burdette (19–13). Although no regular hit over .300, the Braves led the league in home runs (170), with Hank Aaron (40 homers and a league-leading 126 RBIs) and Eddie Mathews (39 homers and 124 RBIs) providing a formidable one-two punch in the middle of the lineup. But Ernie Banks of the Cubs won the home run crown with 41.

The Cardinals were the surprise of the league, rising from seventh to third. Ernest Broglio (21–9) tied Spahn for the league lead in wins, while reliever Lindy McDaniel appeared in 65 games, fashioning a 12–4 record and leading the league in saves with 26. Third baseman Ken Boyer was the hitting star with a .304 average, 32 homers, and 97 RBIs. Musial gave the club a lift when it needed it the most. After being benched early in the year, he got hot in midseason and won several key games with his bat during the stretch when the Cardinals were seriously challenging the Pirates. He finished with a .275 batting average, 17 homers, and 63 RBIs.

Musial was obviously nearing the end of his career, but what a career it had been. Each year he had been at or near the top in almost every offensive category. He won seven batting championships, the last in 1957 at the age of 37, and his average never dipped below .300 until 1959, when age and injuries began to catch up with him and helped lower it to .255. His career batting average was .331, and he struck out only 696 times, once in every 15 at bats, a remarkable record for someone who also hit 475 home runs. Ironically, he never won a home run title. By the time he hung up his spikes in 1963, he had collected three MVP awards and set 51 records, including the National League record for games (3,026), at bats (10,972), hits (3,630), runs (1,949), and RBIs (1,951). He was remarkably consistent, getting 1,815 hits at home and the exact same number on the road and hitting .310 or better for 16 consecutive seasons. Teammate Vinegar Bend Mizell once quipped, "Stan hasn't done so much. He's just been on a 20-year hitting streak."[9] Many of his records would later be broken by Hank Aaron and Pete Rose, two men who, like Musial, would be consistent hitters over a long career.

Musial played in four World Series, all in the first four years of his major league career. In 86 at bats, he had 22 hits, one homer, and a .256 average. He always seemed to play well during All-Star games, hitting .317 and a record 6 home runs in 24 midseason contests.

The Los Angeles Dodgers, the miracle team of 1959, fell to fourth place. Walt Alston held several stormy clubhouse meetings trying to light a fire under a club that just never got going. The club's only .300 hitter was first baseman Norm Larker, who finished at .323 and lost the batting title to Dick Groat in the last three days of the season. The team's top home run hitter was Frank Howard, who hit 23 and drove in 77 runs after being called up from Spokane in May. The big right fielder was named Rookie of the Year, the fifth Dodger to capture the honor since the award began in 1947.

Over in the American League, most experts expected the White Sox to repeat, but Stengel did not. On January 20, speaking at a charity dinner in Manchester, New Hampshire, he said, "I would have to say that the Yankees will bounce back bigger than ever and will win the pennant this coming season." He continued, "Not until Christmas did most of my players realize that the Yankees did not win the pennant. They realized it at that time because they were reminded by their wives that there would not be any Cadillacs, fur coats, deep freezers, et cetera, at Christmas."[10]

Expecting his twelfth year at the helm of the Bronx Bombers to be his last, Stengel wanted to make up for the third-place finish of 1959 and prove that he was not too old to manage. All season he drove his players hard, often criticizing them in public, while they became more disgruntled and bolder, talking back to him and behind his back. All year there was talk around the league and in the press that this would be his last year. And he was getting old—he turned 70 in July, a milestone he marked with the observation that "most people my age are dead at the present time."[11]

For the first part of the season the American League race was a three-way battle between the defending champion White Sox, the Baltimore Orioles, and the Cleveland Indians. All three were in first place at some point during April and May, while the Yankees struggled to play .500 ball and seemed destined to repeat their third-place finish. But in June they began to play like Yankees. Holding a 20–20 record on June 4, they won 20 of their next 28, took over first place in the middle of June after taking four straight from the White Sox, and were still sitting atop the standings at the All-Star break. The Old Professor's club slumped briefly after the first All-Star Game, but managed to stay in first place through most of the rest of the season. Still, the race remained close. As late as September 16, with only 16 days remaining in the season, the Yankees led Baltimore by only two percentage points and the pesky White Sox by only two games.

But then the Bronx Bombers launched a four-game sweep of the Orioles and never looked back, finishing the season with 15 consecutive victories and clinching the pennant on September 25. Winding up with a 97–57 record, Stengel's club finished 8 games in front of Baltimore, 10 in front of Chicago, and 21 in front of Cleveland. Washington, Detroit, Boston, and Kansas City made up the second division. Boston's Pete Runnels won the batting title with a .320 average, the lowest winning average since Snuffy Stirnweiss's .309 back in 1945.

The Yankees won the pennant because Stengel turned in one of his best jobs of managing and because of Yankee batting power. The club had made a shrewd trade with Kansas City in December of 1959, sending Don Larsen, Hank Bauer, Norm Siebern, and Marv Throneberry to the Athletics for Roger Maris, Joe DeMaestri, and Kent Hadley. With the addition of Maris, the Yankees set a new league record with 193 homers, 35 more than the 1927 team with its famous "murderers' row." Mantle and Maris teamed up to provide back-to-back home run punch matched only by Aaron and Mathews of Milwaukee. Although his average dropped to .275, Mantle led the league with 40 homers, while right fielder Maris, a young left-handed slugger who found the right field fence just 301 feet away to be an inviting target, hit 39 and led the league in RBIs with 112. Bill Skowron hit .309, the only Yankee regular to reach the .300 mark, and contributed 26 homers and 91 RBIs. The hitting helped to make up for a mediocre pitching staff. Art Ditmar led all starters with 15 wins, followed by Jim Coates (13), Whitey Ford (12), and Ralph Terry (10).

The surprising Orioles finished with an 89–65 record, their first .500 season since leaving St. Louis at the end of the 1953 season. They did it with a young club that provided plenty of playing time for rookies and saw short-stop Ron Hansen take Rookie of the Year honors.

For Al Lopez, it was a disappointing year. His White Sox won fewer games than they had in 1959 and dropped into third place, the first time in his managerial career he had not finished in first or second. Although the Sox led the league in team batting (.270), their pitching collapsed and their 112 home runs placed them seventh in the league in the department that helped the Yankees regain the top rung.

But Veeck continued to provide White Sox fans with the circuses he was famous for. In 1960 he came up with a new attraction—an exploding scoreboard, installed at Comiskey Park in 1960 at a cost of over $300,000. A dazzling display of modern technology rising 130 feet into the air, the scoreboard was designed to display a variety of messages and advertisements and to celebrate the home run. When a White Sox player hit a home run, a White Sox official, usually Veeck himself, pushed a button to unleash the scoreboard's bedlam. From its powerful loudspeakers came sounds of rushing trains, foghorns, military battles, the "Lone Ranger" theme from the William Tell Overture, the "Hallelujah Chorus" from Handel's Messiah, and other sounds. Strobe lights flashed on and off and fireworks were shot high in the air by workers behind the scoreboard out of sight of the crowd. The show lasted for 32 seconds, perhaps not long enough, since the White Sox hit the fewest homers in the league. Each time the scoreboard went off it cost the White Sox $104.98, but it helped to draw the fans.

The scoreboard made some opposing pitchers nervous and angry. It was bad enough to give up a home run without having to stand on the mound while Veeck's newest electronic device rubbed salt in the wound. Some managers and players did not like it, and neither did some reporters. When Dan Daniel saw it for the first time he wrote, "It was colorful and loud and apparently pleasing to the fans. But to me, it was bush."[12]

One player who especially disliked it was Cleveland center fielder Jim Piersall. On Memorial Day, after catching a long fly ball to end the second game of a doubleheader, Piersall turned around and fired the ball at the scoreboard. It fell short, but Veeck was outraged. He phoned Piersall in the clubhouse and told him that he could have damaged the scoreboard and that he better not try it again. But Piersall showed no remorse. "It's damn nerve-wracking," he told reporters. "All those lights flashing and those bombs bursting all over the place. I thought it was funny the first time it went off—but once was enough." And he refused to promise that he would not do it again. "What if I do throw at it again—what's Veeck going to do? Fine me?"[13]

Meanwhile, Yankee public relations director Bob Fishel, Casey Stengel, and the Yankee players had been making plans to mock Veeck's new mechanical marvel. On June 17, when Clete Boyer hit a homer in the second inning, the secret Yankee plan was put into action. Stengel and several of his players lit sparklers in the dugout and strutted around holding the fireworks high over their heads for the White Sox players and fans to see.

When Mantle homered in the fifth, the Yankees again brought out the sparklers. This time the Yankee bullpen got into the act, lighting sparklers and setting them on the bullpen fence. Even the home crowd roared its approval at this joke at Veeck's expense, while Veeck claimed it was a good show and praised the Yankees for being so economical.

Veeck would remain with the White Sox until 1961, when ill health (the seventh surgery on his right leg was done in 1960) forced him to sell the club and retire. His colorful autobiography, *Veeck—As in Wreck,* appeared in 1962. As might be expected, it was a candid, irreverent look at the baseball establishment and the national pastime. The restless maverick would buy the club again in 1976 and run it until 1980, when failing health again forced him into retirement.

After finishing second in 1959, the Cleveland Indians finished in fourth place with a 76–78 record. The Tribe was a contender for the first half of the season, and in fact was only 1½ games off the pace in the middle of July. But injuries and subpar hitting and pitching caused the team's fortunes to plunge in the second half. The team—and the fans—seemed to miss the home run bat of Rocky Colavito, who hit 35 homers for Detroit. Harvey Kuenn, the man he was traded for, hit .308, but his 9 homers and 54 RBIs could not supply the extra hitting punch the club needed. In December of 1960, Kuenn would be traded to San Francisco for pitcher Johnny Antonelli and outfielder Willie Kirkland.

The 1960 season brought the end of the career of Ted Williams. As his nineteenth season began, Williams was 41 years old and no longer the Splendid Splinter, but he was determined to avenge the terrible season he had in 1959, when he fell below .300 for the only time in his career. He began the 1960 campaign with 492 home runs, trailing Ruth (714), Foxx (534), Ott (511), and Gehrig (493). He was hoping to at least pass Gehrig and Ott on the all-time list.

Williams started the year like he was a 21-year-old slugger rather than an old veteran. On opening day in Griffith Stadium, he hit a booming home run over the wall in dead center field off Camilo Pascual, who grudgingly remarked afterward, "Ted's like old wine. He gets better with age."[14] The next day he hit another homer, to move past Gehrig into undisputed possession of fourth place. But injuries and a viral infection caused him to miss several weeks and limited him to 310 at bats in 113 games. Still, he passed Ott on the home run list, and on September 2, he hit his 25th homer of the year and the 517th of his career. It came off Washington's Don Lee, the son of Thornton Lee, a left-handed pitcher for the Indians and White Sox in the thirties and forties who had given up a homer to Williams in 1940. Williams was the only major league player to ever hit home runs off a father and son pitching combination.

On Wednesday, September 28, the Red Sox entertained the Orioles for the last home game of the season. The Yankees had clinched the pennant, the Orioles were clinging to second, and the hapless Red Sox were in seventh. Only 10,454 fans showed up on this cool, foggy, rainy day, drawn there mainly by the knowledge that this would be Ted Williams's last game in Fenway Park. In the pregame ceremonies at home plate, Red Sox announcer Curt Gowdy introduced Williams as "the greatest hitter who ever lived." After further accolades Williams was presented with a $4,000 check for his favorite charity, the Jimmy Fund, an organization devoted to raising money for the Children's Cancer Hospital in Boston. He also received several personal gifts, including a plaque "on behalf of visits to kids' and veterans' hospitals." It was announced that his number "9" would be retired after the game, the first time the club had ever retired a uniform number.[15]

When Williams stepped to the microphone, he thanked the mayor for the gift to the Jimmy Fund, then told the crowd, "Despite the fact of the disagreeable things that have been said of me—and I can't help thinking about it—by the knights of the keyboard out there [he jerked his head toward the press box], baseball has been the most wonderful thing in my life. If I were starting over again and someone asked me where is the one place I would like to play, I would want it to be in Boston, with the greatest owner in baseball and the greatest fans in America. Thank you." He then strode over to the dugout, where his teammates had joined the rest of the fans in standing and applauding.[16]

Williams wanted to make a dramatic exit, but he drew a walk in his first at bat. In his next two turns at the plate, hitting against right-handed pitcher Jack Fisher, born in 1939, Williams's rookie year with the Red Sox, he flied out to the outfield. In the eighth, when he came up for his last at bat, the crowd gave him a two-minute, standing ovation. The cheering continued as Fisher threw his first pitch, a ball. The crowd quieted, although it was still standing, waiting to see what Fisher and Williams would do. Fisher threw his second pitch, a high slider. Williams swung from his heels, but missed. With the count 1–1, Fisher tried a low fastball, but it got away from him and came in belt high on the outside corner. Williams swung, and the ball headed like a shot toward center field, cleared the fence, and landed in the bullpen.

In spite of the tremendous ovation he received, he did not tip his cap as he rounded the bases and crossed home plate. Years later, in his autobiography, *My Turn at Bat,* he wrote, "I thought about tipping my hat . . . but by the time I got to second base I knew I couldn't do it. . . . It just wouldn't have been me."[17] Red Sox catcher Jim Pagliaroni said, "That was the most magnificent farewell speech I ever saw."[18] It was home run number 521, leaving him 13 behind Jimmie Foxx. It gave the Red Sox a 4–3 lead, and they went on to win 5–4. For young Jack Fisher, it was a home run that would keep his name alive in the baseball memory book far more than his lifetime record of 86-139. Almost a year later, he would get into the record books again, this time when he served up home run number 60 to Roger Maris, who was chasing Ruth's record.

Williams entered the dugout and sat down. The crowd continued to stand and cheer for about five minutes, at one point chanting over and over again, "We want Ted. We want Ted." The first base umpire, Williams's teammates, and manager Pinky Higgins all urged him to go out on the field and acknowledge the applause. But he would not. Perhaps, as one of his teammates later said, "He got just as much a kick out of refusing to go out and tip his hat to the crowd as he did out of the homer."[19] But novelist John Updike, covering the game for *The New Yorker,* had a different explanation for Williams's behavior. "Gods do not answer letters," he wrote.[20]

Williams did not travel with the team to New York for the final three-game set with the Yankees. He could not improve on the dramatic departure from Fenway Park, and he would let it stand as his departure from baseball. He ended the season with 29 homers, 72 RBIs, and a .316 batting average.

Thus ended a career that had begun on April 20, 1939, when Williams made his debut as a 20-year-old right fielder when the Red Sox opened the season in Yankee Stadium against their perennial rivals. Williams had a double in four trips to the plate. From the beginning of his career he had often said that his main goal in life was to be able to walk down the street and have people say, "There goes Ted Williams, the greatest hitter who ever lived."[21] Military service had cost him close to 700 games and 2,000 at bats, and over his long career he missed the equivalent of another season because of numerous injuries and painful marital difficulties culminating in a divorce.

Yet, at his retirement he had established himself as the greatest hitter of his generation, second only to Babe Ruth in his ability to hit for average and power. Playing in 2,292 games, he compiled a lifetime average of .344 (still the sixth best in baseball history), hit 521 homers (eighth), won six batting crowns, four home run and RBI titles, and two Triple Crowns (1942 and 1947). His 17 grand slam homers tied him with Foxx for second place behind Lou Gehrig's 23. His slugging percentage was .634, second only to Ruth's .690. As evidence of the fear he put into the hearts of opposing pitchers, he led in bases on balls eight times, winding up his career with 2,019, second only to Ruth's 2,056 and equal to four full seasons of at bats. And he struck out only 709 times, a remarkably low figure for a power hitter who played until he was 41 years old. No wonder that *The Sporting News,* in naming Williams the "Player of the Decade" in 1960, concluded that "truly, here is a player not only 'of the decade' but of our generation."[22]

Still, many Boston fans and sportswriters felt that he had failed them. When Williams arrived in Boston in 1939, fans and teammates raved about his rookie performance and saw him as the man who could turn the club into perennial pennant winners and end the Yankee domination of the American League that began when the Red Sox were foolish enough to trade Ruth to the Bombers in 1920. Unfortunately, it did not turn out that way. During the Williams era the Red Sox won only one pennant, in 1946, and failed to end the long World Series drought dating back to 1918. The Sox finished second to the Yankees in 1939, 1941, and 1942, third in 1947, lost a postseason playoff with the Indians in 1948, then lost to the Yankees on the last day of the 1949 season. In the 1950s they never finished better than third and dropped to a dismal seventh in 1960.

Boston's pennant frustrations, Williams's volatile temperament, and sniping from some of the Boston press corps helped fill the Williams years with controversy. Fans and writers often accused him of loafing in the field, and the Boston fans sometimes booed when he misplayed a ball in the outfield or did not seem to be hustling. Center fielder Jimmy Piersall once claimed, "I ought to get two salaries. I'm covering both fields."[23] The press often accused him of being arrogant, sullen, childish, throwing temper tantrums, having rabbit ears, and of caring nothing about the team but only for his individual hitting statistics. In *My Turn at Bat*, written almost a decade after he retired, Williams was still seething about the bad publicity he received during his playing years. "I hated that Boston press," he said. "I've outlived the ones who were really vicious, who wrote some of the meanest, most slanderous things.... I can still remember the many things they wrote, and they still make me mad."[24]

Yet this volatile player rarely argued with umpires or other players. Off the field he led a quiet life, seeking the company of working-class men like firemen, policemen, and cab drivers rather than the rich and famous, and preferring hunting and fishing to the night life many other players thrived on. Behind the scenes, he often visited children in hospitals and gave time and money to charities, especially to his favorite, the Jimmy Fund. He contributed thousands of dollars to the fund himself, and helped raise close to $4 million for it.

He was a complex, controversial man, and one of the best hitters in the history of the game. No one was surprised when he was inducted into the Hall of Fame in 1966, just six years after his retirement.

On October 5, the New York Yankees and Pittsburgh Pirates squared off at Forbes Field in the fifty-seventh World Series. For Stengel and most of his players, it was not a novelty; in fact, it had become the norm. It was his tenth managerial appearance in the series, one better than John McGraw of the Giants. He had won seven times, losing only to the Dodgers in 1955 and the Braves in 1957. Stengel's seven world titles tied him with former great Yankee manager Joe McCarthy, and he was out to break the record and establish a new one all his own. For the Yankee franchise, it was the twenty-fifth trip to the World Series, and so far it boasted an 18–6 record.

It was different for the Pirates. After losing to the Braves in the first World Series in 1903, they had returned to the fall classic to defeat Detroit in 1909 and Washington in 1925. In their fourth trip they had run up against one of baseball's greatest teams, the 1927 Yankees, managed by Miller Huggins and led by Babe Ruth and Lou Gehrig. The Yankees humiliated the Pirates, sweeping them in four games. This was the last time the Pirates had gone to the October classic. Memories of this embarrassment were rekindled in the press in 1960, with frequent references to Mantle and Maris as the heirs to the Ruth and Gehrig slugging duo of 1927.

The chances of a Yankee sweep vanished when the Pirates won the first game 6–4 off the hitting of Mazeroski and Virdon. But the Yankees came back with a vengeance the next day, slamming six Pirate pitchers for 19 hits, two of them tremendous home runs by Mickey Mantle, for a 16–3 massacre.

One of the observers at the World Series was Ted Williams, who was covering the classic for *Life* magazine. In the second game he was sitting in his box seat at Forbes Field when a woman approached him and said, "Ted, I'm Stan Musial's mother. You have always been my hero. Would you mind if I had my picture taken with you?" Ted obliged, and posed with her while Ed Musial, Stan's brother, took the photograph. Williams also signed her program. Williams would later say, "I told her she ought to be signing my program."[25]

The Pirates' humiliation continued two days later when the Series resumed in Yankee Stadium. The Yankees bombarded six pitchers en route to a 16-hit, 10–0 victory behind Whitey Ford's four-hitter. The Pirates evened the score the next day with a 3–2 victory, then took game five by a 5–2 margin to put them to within one victory of a world championship. But when the Series moved back to Forbes Field for game six, the Yankees unloaded against six Pirate pitchers for 17 hits and 12 runs as Ford gained his second shutout of the Series. As they had in games two and three, the Yankees feasted off the Pirate pitchers. For the fifth time in the last seven years, the Series had gone to seven games.

On Thursday, October 13, nearly 37,000 fans jammed into Forbes Field for the finale matching Bob Turley against Vernon Law. The Pirates drew first blood. First baseman Rocky Nelson hit a two-run homer in the first inning. The Pirates added two more runs in the second, driving Turley from the mound and giving Law a 4–0 lead, which he carried into the fifth. But the Yankees got on the scoreboard in the fifth with a solo homer by Bill Skowron, and erupted for four more runs in the sixth when Mantle singled a run home and Yogi Berra blasted a three-run homer into the upper right field seats off reliever Roy Face. The Yankees had a 5–4 lead. They padded it to 7–4 in the eighth when Johnny Blanchard's single brought Berra home from second and Clete Boyer's double into the left field corner allowed Skowron to score easily from third.

The Pirates came to bat in the eighth down by three runs. But all year they had managed to rally in the late innings, and this game would be no exception. Gino Cimoli, pinch hitting for Face, singled to right field off Bobby Shantz, bringing up Virdon and setting the stage for the turning point of the game and one of the most famous plays in World Series history. Virdon hit what should have been an easy double-play ground ball to short-stop Tony Kubek, but the ball took a bad hop and hit Kubek in the neck, knocking him to the ground and allowing Cimoli to reach second and Vir-don to take first. Stunned and in great pain, Kubek was taken out of the game and replaced by Joe DeMaestri.

As they had all year, the Pirates capitalized on their opponent's misfor-tunes. The next hitter, Dick Groat, singled past third base, driving Cimoli home and sending Virdon to second. Jim Coates came in to relieve Shantz. It seemed that he might get the Yankees out of the inning without any fur-ther damage, as he retired Skinner on a sacrifice and Nelson on a fly ball to right. But Clemente singled to bring Virdon home and advance Groat to third. Then Hal Smith, who had replaced Burgess in the top of the eight, hit a three-run homer over the left field wall. Ralph Terry came in to end the inning by getting Hoak on a fly ball to left, but the damage had been done. The Pirates had scored five runs to take a 9–7 lead with the Yankees having only one more at bat.

The Bombers were not through yet. Bob Friend, the third Pirate pitcher, came in to relieve Face but left the game after yielding singles to Bobby Richardson and pinch hitter Dale Long, a former Pirate best remembered for hitting homers in eight consecutive games in 1956. Harvey Haddix came in to try to put out the fire, but the Yankees tallied two runs when Richard-son came home on a single by Mantle, and McDougald, who had come in to run for Long, scored when Berra grounded out to first. The Yankees had tied the score at 9–9 with the Pirates coming to bat in the last of the ninth.

The first hitter Ralph Terry had to face was Mazeroski, the defensive whiz who had also been swinging a hot bat during the Series. He had helped the Pirates win the first game with a two-run homer, and contributed a two-run double to the Pirate victory in the fifth game. "When we trotted off the field for our turn at bat in the ninth," Mazeroski later recalled, "I was think-ing, 'I'd like to hit a home run and win it all.' "[26] He took Terry's first pitch, a high slider, for a ball. The second pitch was a high, inside fastball. Mazeroski swung, and the ball headed like a rocket toward left field. Berra moved back a step or two to the warning track and then stood helplessly as the ball soared over the wall at the 402-foot mark, almost the same spot as Smith's homer the inning before.

Mazeroski raced toward first base, rounded the bag, and then as he saw the ball disappear and the umpire waving his arm in a circle, he broke into a happy gallop, swinging his batting helmet in the air as he circled the bases to the deafening roar of the crowd. As he approached third he was met by the third base coach and a legion of fans who swarmed onto the field and ran with him the last 90 feet. As he carefully touched home plate, he was pounded by teammates and fans, and then he and the jubilant Pirates ran off the field and into the clubhouse. Stunned, the Yankees trudged off the field in shock and disbelief. Bobby Shantz would later recall, "As soon as I saw Mazeroski hit that ball I knew it was going to be a long winter."[27]

It was one of the greatest moments in baseball, certainly the most dramatic home run since Bobby Thomson's "shot heard around the world" in 1951. Mazeroski's homer was all the more dramatic in that it was the last play of the game, a sudden, stunning ending, like Thomson's homer. It was the first time a World Series had ended with a home run, and only the third time that the world title had been clinched on the last turn at bat. Commissioner Ford Frick, who had been around baseball for a long time, said, "I never saw a finish like this one."[28]

One of the most exciting games in World Series history, the seventh game gave the National League its fifth World Series victory in the last seven years, to go along with its nine victories in the last 13 All-Star games. Many thought the failure of the American League to aggressively sign black players was the main reason for its decline in World Series and All-Star competition.

The Pirates held a two-hour party in the clubhouse after the game. After all, it had been 35 years between celebrations. Reporters crowded around Mazeroski, who told them, "I came to bat intending to go for the long ball.... I caught it on the fat of my bat. I knew immediately it was a good hit ball. I watched it sail over the fence as I rounded the bases.... What did I think? I was too excited to think. It was the greatest moment of my life."[29] Hal Smith, who had hit a big home run himself in the eighth, said it was a "wonderful, wonderful day. We came back like we always did." Manager Danny Murtaugh was not surprised at the come-from-behind victory. "We've been winning them like this all year," he told reporters. "The fans keep looking forward to a finish like this."[30]

The Yankee clubhouse was gloomy. Kubek lay on a table with a blood-stained towel wrapped around his neck. He would be taken to a Pittsburgh hospital after the game but released the next day. He had suffered a severely bruised vocal cord but made a full recovery. Some Yankee players walked around shaking their heads in disgust and disbelief, while others sat in silence or in tears. As arrogant in defeat as they were in victory, many still could not believe that they had lost to the upstart Pirates, the traditional whipping boys of the National League. "The Pirates should never beat our club," Maris said. "I think if we played them all season, we'd beat them real bad. They were real lucky. I think it's impossible for them to get any more breaks than they had in this series."[31] Two decades later Mickey Mantle would look back on it as the worst moment of his career. "That one hurt all winter. In fact, it still hurts. Twenty years later I still can't believe they beat us in that Series," he said.[32]

By all odds, the Yankees should have won the Series. They led the Pirates in virtually every department and set new records for hits, team batting average, extra base hits, and runs. Their batting average was .338, well above the previous high of .316 set by the Philadelphia Athletics in 1910. The Pirates, by contrast, had a team average of only .256. In the three games they won, the Yankees bombed the Pirates by scores of 16–3, 10–0, and 12–0.

The Yankees had individual stars, too. Bobby Richardson hit a grand slam and set new records of 6 RBIs in one game and a total of 12 for the Series. Mantle hit .400 with 11 RBIs, 3 home runs, and 8 runs scored. Elston Howard hit .462, Bill Skowron .375, Richardson .367, and Berra .318, including a homer and 8 RBIs.

But these statistics, impressive as they were, were misleading. Many of the Yankee hits and runs came when the game had long been decided. Maris got eight hits in the series, but six of these were in the first two games and he drove in only two runs. Mantle's homers were not decisive ones — he hit two in the second game when the Yankees won by 16–3 and one in the third game when they won by 10–0. Likewise, Richardson's grand slam was hit in the lopsided third game.

Dan Topping and other Yankee officials believed that Casey Stengel was partly to blame. They questioned several of his managerial moves, especially his decision to start Art Ditmar in game one and to save ace Whitey Ford for the third game, thereby limiting Ford to two starts instead of three. But Stengel was not willing to be the scapegoat. He started Ditmar in the first game, he said, because "he throws grounders" and claimed that "we got beat on the damndest, craziest bouncer I've seen in my long career in baseball. Maybe God can do something about such a play; man cannot."[33]

The Pirates could not match the team or individual statistics of their opponents, but instead of being crushed by the lopsided defeats, they kept bouncing back, refusing to be intimidated by what the Yankees did or what the press wrote. They took advantage of little opportunities, such as a pitcher not covering the bag when he should or a ball hitting the shortstop in the throat. In the close games they got the hits they needed, while the Yankees did not. They wasted few runs, winning by scores of 6–4, 3–2, 5–2, and 10–9. As Murtaugh said after the Series, "The Yankees set all the records, but they will pay off on most games won."[34]

Mazeroski was clearly the hero of the Series, with his superb defensive work, .320 batting average, five RBIs, four runs, and two homers, especially his dramatic Series-ending one. The highlight of his career had come early, when he was only 24. He would play for the Pirates for 12 more years, bringing his 17-year career—all spent with Pittsburgh—to a close in 1972. When he retired, he was the proud possessor of seven Golden Glove awards. As a hitter he had achieved a respectable career batting average of .260 with 138 homers and 853 RBIs. He would not make the Hall of Fame, but his home run on October 13, 1960, would ensure him a permanent high place in the list of baseball's most dramatic moments.

Clemente, Burgess, Nelson, and Smith all hit over .300, while Virdon made several excellent catches in the outfield and drove in five runs. Law and reliever Harvey Haddix each picked up two victories, while Face tallied three saves. As it had been all year, the victory was a team effort.

The Pirate victory improved their Series record to 3–2, but the 1960 team was not the dynasty its fans had hoped for. The club plummeted to sixth place in 1961, rose to fourth in 1962, then fell to eighth in 1963. Not until 1971 would they make it back to the fall classic, where they defeated the Baltimore Orioles in seven games. Mazeroski would make one appearance, pinch hitting in the seventh inning of the first game and flying out to left.

After being denied a victory party for so many years, the city of Pittsburgh erupted in a 12-hour celebration after the last game. Fans threw confetti from office windows, snake-danced through the streets, blew automobile horns and whistles, made noise with anything they could find to make noise with, and rode in cars with streamers through the crowded streets. So many automobiles and people jammed the downtown area that the harassed police finally had to close off the bridges and tunnels leading into the city to keep any more fans from crowding into the already impossibly crowded city. One police lieutenant wired headquarters that "this is preposterous."[35] The municipal party lasted far into the night. When it was over, it cost the city around $50,000 to clean up the bottles, streamers, confetti and other trash left behind by the revelers. Most Pirate fans, who had not had an excuse for a victory party in 35 years, felt that it was money well spent.

20. End of an Era

For the country, 1960 was a landmark year in many ways. The thaw in the Cold War was coming to an end, as the Russian capture in May of downed U-2 pilot Francis Gary Powers brought the collapse of the Paris Summit and a rapid deterioration in Russian-American relations. In this threatening atmosphere the United States test-fired an ICBM in May, then followed this feat in July with the first successful trial of a Polaris missile fired from an underwater nuclear submarine, the U.S.S. *George Washington.* Meanwhile, Cuban dictator Fidel Castro was moving his little country into the Soviet orbit, and by September he and Soviet Premier Nikita Khrushchev were at the United Nations denouncing the United States. In November, as Dwight Eisenhower played out his lame duck presidency and the political and military situation in the American-backed nation of South Vietnam deteriorated, young John F. Kennedy, preaching the need for a "new generation of leadership," narrowly defeated Richard Nixon for the U.S. presidency.

The year also saw the introduction of the first birth control pill (Enovid), the tranquilizer Librium, and the Xerox 914 copier, along with the launching of the world's first communications satellite (Echo I) and weather satellite (Tiros). Civil rights sit-ins occurred at lunch counters in cities all across the South, student protests broke out at several universities, and respected Harvard psychologist Timothy Leary established the Center for Research in Personality and began a crusade to legalize mind-altering drugs. The nation of nearly 180 million people was about to enter the turbulent 1960s.

For baseball, too, 1960 was a year of important milestones. Besides marking the close of Ted Williams's career and the celebration of the first Pittsburgh Pirate world title in 35 years, it brought the firing of Casey Stengel, the death of Negro league baseball, the closing of the Cuban player pipeline, and the end of the familiar lineup of 16 major league teams playing 154-game schedules. It was also the year when relief pitcher Jim Brosnan shocked the baseball establishment with an insider book revealing what major league baseball was really like.

Five days after Mazeroski's dramatic blast brought the last golden age to a close, the New York Yankees held a noon press conference at New

York's Savoy Hilton Hotel on Fifth Avenue. The room was jammed with reporters, photographers, and newsreel and television cameramen. All year long, rumors had circulated that Casey Stengel would be let go when his contract expired at the end of the season. It was no secret that the Yankee owners had been wanting to get rid of him for the past two years, and now they had the perfect opportunity. He was 70 years old, Ralph Houk was ready to take over the reins, and the humiliation at the hands of the Pirates seemed to show that the Old Professor was indeed too old and had lost his touch. When he had been asked shortly before the Series if he would retire if he lost, Stengel had replied, "Well, I made up my mind, but I made it up both ways."[1]

Yankee owner Dan Topping began the press conference by reading a carefully worded statement that heaped praise upon Stengel, referring to his departure in words that suggested that he was retiring of his own volition rather than being forced out.[2] "Casey Stengel has been—and deservedly—the highest paid manager in baseball history," Topping said. "He has been—and is—a great manager. Two years ago Casey quite reluctantly signed a two-year contract . . . with the understanding that after the first year he could retire if he desired to do so." Continuing, Topping revealed that Stengel would receive $160,000 in profit sharing and expressed his hope that the Hall of Fame could waive its five-year waiting period and induct him as soon as possible. Impatient with the circumlocutions, an exasperated reporter shouted, "Do you mean he's through? Has he resigned?"

The Yankee owner ignored the question, and handed the microphone over to Stengel. Unfortunately for Topping, he also turned control of the conference over to the wizened old manager. "Mr. Webb and Mr. Topping have started a program for the Yankees," Stengel said, looking nervous and uncomfortable in his dark blue suit and striped tie. "They want to put in a youth program as an advanced way of keeping the club going. They needed a solution as to when to discharge a man on account of age. They have paid me off in full and told me my services are not desired any longer by this club. I told them if this was their idea not to worry about Mr. Stengel, he can take care of himself." As he rambled on, a reporter finally interrupted by shouting, "Casey, were you fired?" Stengel shot back, "No, I wasn't fired. I was paid up in full." Clearly irritated at the whole situation, Stengel snapped, "Write anything you want. Quit, fired, whatever you please. I don't care."

This was not the scene the Yankee owners had wanted, but it was too late to regain control of the conference. Reporters gathered around Stengel at the microphone and later at the bar, anxious to get down in their notebooks the other nuggets he might drop that day. He speculated that he might manage somewhere else, and his bitterness showing, he said, "I'll never make the mistake of being seventy again."[3] After spinning story after story about his baseball career to reporters at the bar, he went into the dining room for a dinner with Yankee officials, where he told Topping, "I'm taking a jet home, and I'm charging it to the club. A man gets his transportation home even if they don't want him anymore."[4] After the dinner he hung around the bar for a little while longer, drinking and reminiscing, and then, over three hours after the press conference began, he shook hands all around and left the hotel. As he did, one photographer lamented, "I'm gonna miss that old bastard."[5]

In the days after Stengel's departure, the Yankee office was flooded with telegrams, letters, and phone calls condemning the way he had been treated. Many senior citizens were angered that age, not performance, could be used as grounds for not renewing his contract. Most of the press, too, was critical of the firing of one of baseball's most popular figures and source of so much good copy for the readers. An outraged Arthur Daley fumed in the *New York Times,* "It's a shabby way to treat the man who has not only brought them glory but also given their dynasty firmer footing than it had ever had. So long, Case. You gave us twelve unforgettable years."[6]

He certainly had. Generally branded a failure in his first nine years as a major league manager, Stengel rose to greatness after he came to the Yankees in 1949. He won five straight pennants between 1949 and 1953, four more between 1955 and 1958, and his tenth and last in 1960, tying him with John McGraw for the most pennants won by a manager. In World Series competition he was unsurpassed, tying his illustrious predecessor, Joe McCarthy, for the most World Series titles (7), and leading all pilots in games managed (63) and won (37). By contrast, Connie Mack had managed in the American League for 50 years and succeeded in winning only nine pennants and five World Series. Stengel always bristled at those who hated the Yankees because they won so frequently. "Why is everyone so mad at us?" he once asked. "What do they expect us to do, roll over and play dead? Draw up a chair and sit by the roadside until the rest catch up?"[7]

Stengel would resurface in 1962 to manage the hapless expansion club, the New York Mets, making him the only man to be associated with all four New York teams — the Dodgers, Giants, Yankees, and Mets — as a player or manager. With the Mets, he would continue to draw fans into the ballpark and to delight players, reporters, and fans with his "Stengelese," but his glory days had been left behind in Yankee Stadium. When he retired from the Mets two-thirds of the way into the 1965 season, the club was headed towards its fourth consecutive last-place finish. He was inducted into the Hall of Fame in 1966, nine years before his death.

There were so many momentous events in baseball in 1960 that few fans paid much attention to the news that the black major leagues would not open the 1961 season. The integration of the white majors had been a landmark victory for black players and civil rights in general but a disaster for the Negro leagues. From 1947 on, their attendance had dwindled as their best talent defected to the majors and black fans shifted their interest to the major league clubs. They were also being damaged by the televising of major league games, the appeal of other television programs, and the attraction of other sports and amusements to the growing black middle class.

By 1957, there was only one Negro league, the Negro American League. All six of its clubs were losing money, and its All-Star Game, which had often attracted close to 50,000 fans back in the pre–Robinson days, drew only 7,516 fans. Three years later, at the end of the 1960 season, the league folded, ironically a victim of black progress. Acknowledgment of the Negro leagues' rich baseball history would be slow in coming, but finally in 1969, the Hall of Fame began to recognize some of their players, with Satchel Paige being the first to be inducted.

The steady deterioration in American-Cuban relations in 1960 brought an end to the connection between Cubans and American baseball that dated back to the days of the Spanish-American War in 1898, when young Cubans learned the game from American soldiers at Camp Columbia just outside Havana. Over the years, many Cubans played in the majors. In 1960 the number included Minnie Minoso of the White Sox; Pedro Ramos, Camilo Pascual, Julio Becquer, Jose Valdivelso, and Zoilo Versalles of the Senators; Mike Fornieles of Boston; Chico Fernandez and Sandy Amoros of Detroit; and Mike de la Hoz of Cleveland. But when the outgoing Eisenhower administration severed diplomatic relations with Castro's regime in January of 1961, this fertile ground of major league talent was cut off. Baseball would remain the national pastime in Cuba, but Cuban players could no longer aspire to play for American minor and major league teams.

Another sign of the passing of the old era was the announcement that major league baseball was going to begin a significant new age of expansion. The major league lineup had already changed dramatically since 1945, when major league ball was still played by 16 teams, most of them in the Northeast, and when four cities had two teams—Boston, Chicago, Philadelphia, and St. Louis—and New York had three. By 1960, only Chicago could boast of two teams, big league ball had moved into Milwaukee, Baltimore, Kansas City, and all the way to San Francisco and Los Angeles. In 1960 the game was on the verge of adding new teams.

The Dodgers and Giants moves to the West Coast had whetted the appetites of other cities for a major league franchise. The old cartel that had monopolized major league baseball for half a century had been crumbling ever since the Braves left Boston for Milwaukee. In the late fifties several forces were at work to hasten the spread of the national game. Jets were making travel easy and convenient, Congress was raising the threat of antitrust action if competition were not opened up, the population was exploding in the West and the South, television was holding out the lure of big contracts, and investors with big bankrolls were looking for major league franchises for their cities. Sixteen major league teams might have served the nation well at the turn of the century, when the population stood at 76 million and the railroad provided the fastest transportation possible, but there were not enough teams to go around in a nation of nearly 180 million in the jet age of the late 1950s.

As the decade closed and major league owners discussed moving franchises but not expanding the total number of teams, plans for a third major league emerged from the minds and pocketbooks of New York lawyer William A. Shea and other promoters in cities across the country. Shea had been one of many fans who had been outraged by the flight of the Giants and Dodgers, and he felt that New York deserved a National League team and that several other cities in the nation deserved a major league franchise. The efforts of Shea and others finally bore fruit in August of 1959 with the founding—on paper at least—of the Continental League, with Branch Rickey as president. Now 77 years old, Rickey had suffered a heart attack the year before, but he was as indomitable as ever, full of energy and ideas. As early as 1945, he had predicted that population shifts and improvements in air travel would bring "not only a revision of the present map, but a third major league."[8] He had long been an advocate of the geographical and numerical expansion of major league teams and was anxious to play a role in it.

In August of 1959, the Continental League had plans for teams in New York, Houston, Denver, Toronto, and Minneapolis-St. Paul, and was hoping to begin play in 1961 with from 8 to 12 teams. By the spring of 1960, three more cities—Atlanta, Ft. Worth-Dallas, and Buffalo—were added. New York City had authorized the construction of a new 55,000 seat stadium in Flushing Meadow in Queens, and in August of 1960 officials in Harris County, Texas, announced plans for a radically new multi-purpose, dome-covered stadium to serve as the home of Houston's entry into the league. But four of the eight cities had no adequate ballparks nor serious plans to build one, the National and American Leagues controlled the minor leagues and most of the 4,000 players in organized baseball, large indemnities would have to be paid to minor league teams if a major league team were established in their market, and there was no certainty the fans would support a third league, especially if it did not seem to be of true major league caliber. Still, Rickey and other Continental League supporters were optimistic. The Continental League, Rickey was fond of saying, was "as inevitable as tomorrow, but not as imminent."[9]

In spite of its problems, the Continental League had its supporters. Besides the fans and financial backers in the eight proposed cities, it was championed by much of the nation's press, and it had friends in high places—the U.S. Congress, especially Representative Emanuel Celler, a

New York Democrat who headed a committee investigating baseball. Shortly after the establishment of the new league, Celler said that "our investigation showed that baseball was big business, virtually 'frozen' in ownership and location. We recommended broadening it, bringing big league ball to the entire country. . . . Now we have a third league. And the present owners of the big league teams will have to support it. If they don't, they'll show they are monopolists. That could cost them the immunity from antitrust suits they've enjoyed so far."[10]

These and similar threats from Congress weighed heavily on the minds of the owners of the 16 major league clubs. Ever since the end of the war, the "Lords of Baseball," as Harold Parrott called them,[11] had been jealously guarding their territorial rights, the reserve clause, and other privileges they had held for so long. Only when pushed by legal or economic threats had they given in and provided pension plans, more player participation in decision-making, and the movement of franchises to more profitable locations. Each of the two leagues had been studying the possibility of expanding to 10 or 12 teams since the middle of the decade, but had avoided taking any action. Faced with the prospect of Congressional action and competition from a new league that might bring an expensive war for players and television revenues, the owners moved to abort the new circuit by absorbing some of its members into the existing structure. No one wanted to repeat the nightmare of the bloody baseball wars of the Federal League era during World War I. As Ford Frick would later write, "Baseball was scared. . . . A baseball war would be a calamity beyond comprehension. Compromise was in order, and it came quickly."[12]

The National League made the first move. On October 17, 1960, four days after the end of the World Series, league owners met in the Sheraton Blackstone Hotel in Chicago and agreed by unanimous vote to expand to 10 teams by opening day of 1962. The two Continental League teams brought in were New York and Houston. They would enter the league as the New York Mets and the Houston Colt 45s. Nine days later the American League owners also voted to add two teams, but got a jump on the senior circuit by agreeing to begin play under the new structure in 1961, rather than 1962. Calvin Griffith was given permission to move his Washington Senators to Minneapolis-St. Paul, where they would be known as the Minnesota Twins, and to avoid the Congressional uproar that would undoubtedly ensue if the nation's capital were left without a team, Washington was promised a new club. Los Angeles would also be granted a second franchise, the Angels. To stock the new clubs, an expansion draft would be instituted, allowing the new teams to buy players at a cost of $75,000 each from a pool of minor and major league players provided by the 16 existing major league clubs.

In announcing these changes, American League President Joe Cronin, who had taken over when Will Harridge retired in 1958, called the move to 10 teams "only the first step." The American League, he said, was "considering other fine baseball cities for a possible future expansion to twelve clubs."[13] To accommodate the two new teams, the league would go to a 162-game schedule and the National League would follow suit when it expanded in 1962.

Once again, in this era of change and transition, an old baseball tradition was crumbling. The expansion to 20 teams and a 162-game schedule upset the old yardsticks that had been used in measuring performance since the early 1900s — the 100-RBI season, the 20-game winner, Ruth's season record of 60 home runs and Ty Cobb's season record of 96 stolen bases. Problems arose as early as 1961, when Mickey Mantle and Roger Maris chased Ruth's single season record in homers. Ford Frick ruled that if it were broken after the 154th game, Ruth's record would remain in the record book along with the new mark. Not only was that record shattered when Maris hit 61 homers in 1961, but just one year later, another old record fell when the Dodgers' Maury Wills stole 104 bases.

As professional baseball planned for expansion it was operating in a more competitive sports market than ever before. Throughout the fifties, collegiate basketball and football grew steadily, attracting more and more fans and media coverage. So did professional basketball, football, ice hockey, and tennis. Professional football grew the fastest, and emerged as professional baseball's biggest rival. While major league baseball attendance languished in the fifties, professional football attendance more than doubled, from a little less than 2 million in 1950 to over 4 million in 1960. In that same period, major league baseball, playing far more games than the NFL, suffered heavy losses before bouncing back with modest gains, beginning the decade with 17.5 million fans in 1950 and closing with 19.9 million in 1960. The NFL began to get more space in newspapers and magazines, even in publications like *The Sporting News,* which had once been devoted almost exclusively to baseball. Some baseball fans accused the Baseball Bible of heresy, but its growing coverage of the gridiron was just a reflection of the fact that the diamond no longer held the prominence it once did.

In 1959, the year following "the greatest football game ever played," professional football was shaken by the establishment of a rival league, the American Football League, which began play in 1960 with teams in eight cities and a television contract with ABC. This would bring another war over players and fans, but professional football would soar to new heights of popularity. By the mid–1960s, watching professional football on television on Sunday afternoons had become a firmly established tradition and sports commentators were claiming that football was a faster, more exciting game than baseball and had replaced it as the national pastime.

By 1960, television and sports were inextricably linked, to the mutual benefit of both, and in the future the link would only strengthen. Down the road lay more televised games in all sports and a growing dependence on television revenues for the financial health and very existence of sports franchises. In fact, the explosion in the number of leagues and franchises would not have been possible without television money.

As the fifties progressed, television had altered the nation's perception of baseball players as heroic and mythological figures. It had been easier for the fans to idolize baseball players in the past because they were rarely seen in person. Their very distance added to the reverence with which they were held. But as fans saw more and more games on television, some of the awe, excitement, and wonder that had surrounded individual games, plays, and heroes naturally disappeared. Since so many games were shown, with so many dramatic events, the great moments and heroes came quicker and in greater number than ever before, and they often did not last as long, for soon in some other game another great moment and hero would arise to displace the older ones. Players were also becoming more familiar, not just as baseball players, but as hawkers of shaving cream and a wide variety of other consumer produces on the television screen.

The decline of the heroic image and mythological nature of baseball was also promoted by newspaper, magazine and television accounts of contract disputes, Supreme Court and Congressional investigations into baseball's business practices, Duke Snider's and Jackie Jensen's admissions that they played baseball for money and not for fun, and the movement of franchises to other cities. All these events increased the growing realization among fans that baseball was a business. More and more, young people were choosing their heroes from the world of television, rock music, and teenage movies churned out by Hollywood, with Elvis Presley and other teen-age idols rivaling and probably exceeding Mickey Mantle's popularity with the young.

Another blow to the mythological status of major leaguers came in 1960 from inside the baseball establishment. It was the publication of a diary of the 1959 season kept by Cincinnati relief pitcher Jim Brosnan, who had played for both the Cubs and the Cardinals before being traded to the Reds early in 1959. The 6-feet 4-inch, 210-pound right-hander fashioned an 8–3 record with them in 1959, and followed this in 1960 with 57 appearances, a 7–2 record, 12 saves, and a 2.36 ERA.

Brosnan was not the typical ballplayer. He smoked a pipe, wore horn-rimmed glasses and a beret, kept books in his locker and suitcase, and read Stendhal, Dostoyevsky, philosophy, and murder mysteries. He loved jazz and classical music, and could play the music of his favorite composer, Béla Bartók, on the piano. When the team was on the road and the other players were spending their afternoons playing cards, watching television, sleeping, or at the movies, Brosnan was likely to be found at the local public library or museum. Not surprisingly, this intellectual, loner, and maverick had been tagged with the nickname "professor" by his teammates on the Cubs. He was of course a far cry from that other professor who managed the New York Yankees.

Brosnan was also a published writer. That was not at all that unusual for baseball players—Joe DiMaggio, Babe Ruth, Bob Feller, Mickey Mantle, and dozens of others had written books, magazine articles, and newspaper columns. But the great majority of these literary efforts had been ghostwritten, and sometimes players barely knew what went out to the public under their byline. Babe Ruth was fond of greeting his ghostwriter with the phrase, "Hi! What did I say today?"[14] Most players who "wrote" articles and books romanticized the game and its players, touting them as larger-than-life heroes worthy of the adulation heaped upon them by most sportswriters and fans and as proper role models for the children of America. A good example was Joe DiMaggio's life story, which summed up his attitude toward the game in its title, *Lucky to Be a Yankee* (1946), which contained no disparaging words about the great game of baseball and the heroic men who played it.

But Brosnan and his book were different. He actually wrote his own material, and far more than Duke Snider and Jackie Jensen, who had earlier published articles undermining the mythical nature of major league baseball, he wrote about the game as it really was. Excerpts from *The Long Season* appeared in *Sports Illustrated* in the Spring of 1960 and it was published in book form in July. It became a best-seller, and the royalties provided a welcome supplement to the $20,000 the Reds were paying him for throwing baseballs that year.

Written in diary form in a conversational, witty, engaging style, *The Long Season* was a personal view of baseball from the day in January of 1959 when Brosnan received his contract until the season ended in late September. A candid insider's view of what baseball teams and players, managers, and coaches were really like during the long grind of a 154-game season, it was articulate, cynical, humorous, sarcastic, and realistic.

Brosnan portrayed players as ordinary young men doing a job that for most was far from glamorous. Instead, it was often routine, boring, tiresome, and stressful. Most players tired of the travel, missed their families, suffered from the pressures of trying to perform at a high level every day, and were sensitive to the verbal abuse from the stands. They were also bullied by their managers and coaches, who treated their charges like children and ordered them around like army recruits. Brosnan's former manager, Solly Hemus of the Cardinals, was depicted as one of the worst of the lot—a bombastic bully, a racist, and a semi-intelligent and incompetent pilot. Brosnan did not spare other members of the baseball establishment from his criticism, including popular Cardinal broadcaster Harry Caray, whom he called "old blabbermouth."

Brosnan depicted the culture that baseball players lived in as a young male culture characterized by macho posturing and by almost continuous profanity and obsession with sex. "Bullpen conversations," he wrote, "cover the gambit of male bull sessions. Sex, religion, politics, sex. Full circle. Occasionally the game — or business — of baseball intrudes."[15] It was a racist culture in which blacks were still resented and treated like outsiders, and in which Latin American players were derisively referred to as "Bean Bandits." It was a dog-eat-dog business in which a small number of owners, managers, coaches, players, and sportscasters were trying to make a living at a boy's game. It was a competitive, insecure world where players had little if any bargaining power at contract time and could be bought and sold almost like slaves, shipped halfway across the country or back to the minor leagues, or released with little warning. Naturally, they would do almost anything to win and keep their jobs. Brosnan wrote, "The spitball is illegal, of course, although it's quite popular in the National League," and admitted that he and other pitchers sometimes threw at hitters.[16]

The Long Season sold 20,000 copies in its first year and found a welcome reception among many fans and writers who were fascinated by its insider look at behind-the-scenes baseball. Jimmy Cannon called it "the greatest baseball book ever written,"[17] and Mark Harris saw it as "a fine, frank volume infinitely more valuable than the several tons of articles 'as told to' with which we are annually forced to contend."[18] William German in the *San Francisco Chronicle* correctly saw that one of the great merits of the book was that it "puts the reader right down there with the teams on the field. So at long last the underprivileged fan is able to eavesdrop, like God or a uniformed player, on the very conversations and mental processes of the dugout, bullpen or even the pitcher's mound."[19] Some players liked it, too. Pirate pitcher Harvey Haddix told some of his teammates that they should read the book "during the wintertime when you want to get back into the mood and the atmosphere of the game."[20]

But much of the baseball world was outraged. Brosnan had violated the precept that had been a part of major league baseball for decades and was expressed in a sign that was displayed prominently in many clubhouses in both leagues: "What you see here, what you say here, let it stay here when you leave here."[21] Many baseball people felt that his candid observations betrayed the baseball fraternity and tended to undermine players' stature as larger-than-life heroes to be idolized by the public. It was as if the secrets about the game and its players had been finally hung out on the line for all the public to see.

Cardinal manager Solly Hemus claimed, "Brosnan's way out of bounds" and snapped, "if you think Brosnan's funny in that book, you oughta see him on the mound." Former Cardinal teammate and pitcher Larry Jackson wondered "why a guy should rap his profession. But Brosnan never did seem to have the right attitude."[22] Cardinal announcer Joe Garagiola, the former major league catcher whose witty stories about baseball had made him a popular banquet speaker, characterized Brosnan as a "kookie beatnik" and a "mediocre pitcher," and claimed that "a guy who wouldn't be anything if it weren't for baseball has no business rapping it that way."[23] Even Bill Veeck, breaker of so many traditions, did not think much of this iconoclast. While admitting that the book contained "undeniably colorful material," he saw it mostly as a vehicle for Brosnan's "satisfaction of his personal vendettas."[24]

The Long Season had an impact that went far beyond the praise and condemnation heaped on Brosnan in 1960. Although Reds manager Fred Hutchinson, whom Brosnan admired and called a "Freudian father," said that "I don't care what he writes or says, just so long as he pitches,"[25] officials on the Reds and other clubs began to try to crack down on what their players could write for publication. Cleveland general manager Frank Lane rejected Johnny Temple's request for permission to have a weekly column in a Cleveland newspaper. The Cardinals, who had been burned the most by their former employee's book, told infielder Daryl Spencer, a former Giant who now played with the Cardinals, not to write an exposé of why the Giants folded in the 1959 pennant race. In New York, the Yankees put strict regulations on their players' public appearances, television and radio appearances, commercials, and writings.

Brosnan had a running battle with the Reds and later the White Sox over his right to publish books and articles on his profession. These conflicts eventually helped to end his playing career. In 1961, he played a key role in the Reds' drive to the National League pennant, appearing in 53 games and fashioning a 10–4 record with 16 saves and a 3.04 ERA. He also kept a diary of the season, published in 1962 as *The Pennant Race*. It, too, was a best-seller. After compiling a 4–4 record in 1962 and an 0–1 record in the early part of 1963, Brosnan was traded to the White Sox after refusing to give in to the Reds' demand that he submit his writings to owner Bill DeWitt for "review" before publication. For the season, he compiled a 3–9 record and a 3.13 ERA.

Brosnan and the White Sox had a protracted debate over his literary activities. As one club official put it, "We believe such writing . . . can undermine team spirit."[26] In January of 1964, Brosnan was sent a contract calling for a salary of $24,000, a cut of $1,000 over 1963, plus a clause barring him from publishing during the regular season. Unable to live with these restrictions, he rejected the contract and the White Sox put him on waivers. When no team offered the $1 necessary to pick him up, the club released him in late February. He and many others felt that the major league owners were guilty of collusion, refusing to employ what they regarded as a troublemaker and detriment to the game. Brosnan then began a successful career as a writer and television sports commentator. He never played major league ball again.

Written before the famous "insider" books of Jim Bouton (*Ball Four*) and other players (and their ghostwriters) of a later age, *The Long Season* remains the first, and many still think the best, of the "insider" books on baseball. After reading it, no baseball fan could ever look at his diamond heroes in quite the same uncritical way again.

In 1969, nine years after his retirement, Ted Williams said in his autobiography, *My Turn at Bat: The Story of My Life*, "I should have had more fun than any player who ever lived. I played in what I think was baseball's best-played era, the years just before World War II, and then the really booming years, 1946 through the early 50s."[27] In that same year, Stan Musial, speaking at his induction into the Hall of Fame, agreed with his old rival. "I believe I played in the most exciting era of big league baseball," he said. "I saw the game change from day to night, from regional to national, from long train rides to short plane flights, from cabbage leaves under the cap in hot weather to air-conditioned dugouts."[28] And several years after his retirement, Ralph Kiner, another Hall of Famer, claimed, "The postwar years up until expansion in 1961 were the golden years of major league baseball. You had more outstanding athletes in the game than any time before or since."[29]

These three stars of the postwar period could be expected to choose their time as the greatest age of baseball, just as Ty Cobb and other players before and after them looked upon their era as the golden age and claimed that "they don't play baseball like they used to." Comparing different eras in a changing game is difficult, and as baseball historian Lawrence Ritter has said, "From an emotional standpoint . . . each individual fan has his own 'Golden Age.' It's the period when that fan was between 8 and 16 years old. That's when baseball first captured the imagination; when players had appeal beyond human bounds."[30]

For many fans, that period was the 15 years following the close of World War II. It was not the only golden age, but it certainly was the time of some of baseball's best players, most dramatic games, most exciting pennant races and World Series, and most profound changes. It was also the last time baseball ruled as the king of spectator sports.

Major league baseball had undergone many transformations during the last golden age — integration, the steady rise in night games, the television revolution, the transfer of franchises, expansion to the West Coast, the emergence of the relief pitcher and other strategy changes. It had also suffered a tarnishing of the heroic image of the players and a steady erosion in its claim to be the national pastime. As Roger Kahn wrote in the *New York Times Magazine* near the end of the decade, "Baseball is losing some of its magic. The old gods are disappearing, or, perhaps worse, they are simply proving to be mortal. The game is not in danger of extinction, but neither is it likely ever again to dominate a great portion of our national scene."[31]

Even more changes in the game and its place in American society lay ahead. Professional baseball would continue to lose status and fans to college and professional football and basketball as well as other sports. Down the road lay expansion to 28 teams, making baseball truly a national game serving an increasing number of fans in all regions of the country. Eventually expansion would lead to another dramatic change in the structure of the game, when in 1969 each league would split into two divisions and playoffs would be instituted to decide the pennant winners. In 1973, amidst much controversy, the designated hitter would be adopted by the American League.

Equipment would also change. Fielder's gloves would become larger and better, batting gloves would become standard for many hitters, and the old baggy, flannel uniform would give way to tighter, more comfortable and more colorful ones, along with more colorful footwear and shoes made especially for play on fields with artificial surfaces. Stadiums would become more uniform, as the old ones were gradually razed and replaced by new ones built to the specifications outlined in the new rule of 1959 requiring that all fields constructed after June 1 of that year have a minimum distance of 325 feet down the foul lines to the left and right field fences and 400 feet to the center field fence. In 1965, baseball would become impervious to the weather in the new Houston Astrodome, the first of several domed stadiums to be built and the first to introduce an artificial playing surface.

The players would become better educated, more individualistic, more vocal, and more inclined to hire agents to represent them in contract negotiations with management. Long after Danny Gardella's challenge to the reserve clause, the efforts of players and their agents would lead to bitter salary disputes, lawsuits, salary arbitration, free agency, the virtual end to the reserve clause, and astronomical salaries. There would be threats of strikes and actual strikes by players and umpires. To help meet the growing cost of owning and operating a major league ball club, the owners would raise ticket prices, obtain lucrative television packages, and, to draw fans through the turnstiles, resort to gimmicks that would have made Bill Veeck proud.

Former umpire Ron Luciano once summed up these changes in his humorous way when he said, "When I started, baseball was played by nine tough competitors on grass in graceful ballparks. By the time I finished, the game was played indoors on plastic, and I spent half my time watching out for a man dressed in a chicken suit who was trying to kiss me."[32]

In the decades after 1960 major league baseball would still feature good teams, outstanding players, dramatic games, great moments, and warm memories for old and new fans alike. It would, after a time, attract more fans and dollars than ever before. But it would never again command the attention and affection it had in the decade and a half after World War II, when it still occupied center stage and the other sports were played in its shadow.

Notes

Preface

1. Angell, "Baseball: The Perfect Game," 81.
2. Ritter, in Foreword to Connor, *Baseball for the Love of It*, x.

Chapter 1: War's End

1. Honig, *Power Hitters*, 75.
2. *New York Times*, 17 June 1945.
3. Schlossberg, *Baseball Catalog*, 98.
4. Panaccio, "How It Was During the War Years," 70.
5. *New York Times*, 24 February 1943.
6. Goldstein, *Spartan Seasons*, 214.
7. "Pete Gray, Symbol," 75.
8. Panaccio, "How It War During the War Years," 69.
9. Mead, *Even the Browns*, 15.
10. Graham, "When Baseball Went to War," 78.
11. *Sporting News*, 18 January 1945.
12. Honig, *Baseball America*, 247.
13. Schlossberg, *Baseball Catalog*, 285.
14. Goldstein, *Spartan Seasons*, 201.
15. *Sporting News*, 22 January 1942.
16. *Sporting News*, 19 April 1945.
17. *New York Times*, 25 April 1945.
18. Mead, *Even the Browns*, 227.
19. Meany, "World Series Laughs," 33.
20. Dickey, *History of American League Baseball*, 168.
21. Goldstein, *Spartan Seasons*, xii.
22. *Sporting News*, 16 August 1945.

Chapter 2: The National Pastime

1. Daley, "Why We Worship the Babe Ruths," 64.
2. Young, "Jackie Robinson Era," 153.
3. Peterson, *Only the Ball Was White*, 175.
4. *Sporting News*, 3 March 1948.
5. Rust, *"Get That Nigger Off the Field,"* 127.
6. Peterson, *Only the Ball Was White*, 158.

7. "Home Run Josh," 74.
8. Ibid.
9. David, *Insider's Baseball*, 110.
10. "World War II's Impact on Mankind," 68.
11. Frommer, *Rickey and Robinson*, 104.
12. Rice, "Thoughts on Baseball," pt. I, 32.
13. Rickey and Riger, *American Diamond*, 46.
14. For Robinson's court-martial, see Jules Tygiel, "The Court-Martial of Jackie Robinson," 34–39.
15. Frommer, *Rickey and Robinson*, 6; Mann, "Truth About the Jackie Robinson Case," pt. I, 21.
16. Mann, "Truth About the Jackie Robinson Case," pt. I, 21.
17. Rowan and Robinson, *Wait Till Next Year*, 117.
18. Polner, *Branch Rickey*, 67.
19. Honig, *Baseball America*, 259.
20. Ibid.
21. Barber, *1947—When All Hell Broke Loose in Baseball*, 60–61.
22. *Sporting News*, 1 November 1945.
23. Reaction to Robinson's signing: *Sporting News*, 1 November 1945; Tygiel, *Baseball's Great Experiment*, 72–80.
24. *Sporting News*, 1 November 1945.
25. Ibid.
26. Ibid.
27. Rogosin, *Invisible Men*, 203.
28. Rust, *"Get That Nigger Off the Field,"* 112.
29. Paige and Lipman, *Maybe I'll Pitch Forever*, 172–73.
30. *New York Herald Tribune*, 25 October 1945.

Chapter 3: The Return of the Major Leagues (1946)

1. Goldstein, *Spartan Seasons*, 280.
2. *Sporting News*, 28 March 1946.
3. Halberstam, *Summer of '49*, 19.
4. *Sporting News*, 25 April 1946.
5. "Southpaw Truman," 43.
6. Dworkin, *Owners Versus Players*, 55.
7. *Sporting News*, 11 April 1946.
8. *New York Times*, 17 April 1946.
9. Durso, *Baseball and the American Dream*, 235.
10. Lowenfish and Lupien, *Imperfect Diamond*, 159.
11. "Trial for Life," 82.
12. Broeg and Miller, *Baseball from a Different Angle*, 238.
13. Lowenfish and Lupien, *Imperfect Diamond*, 151.
14. "Play Ball," 67.
15. *Sporting News*, 23 May 1946.
16. Chamberlain, "Ted Williams: Baseball's Foremost Problem Child," 112.
17. "Hit Kid," 86.
18. Chamberlain, "Ted Williams: Baseball's Foremost Problem Child," 112.
19. "Lopsided Stars," 28.
20. "Photo Finish," 62.
21. Allen and Fitzgerald, *You Can't Beat the Hours*, 188.

22. Chieger, *Voices of Baseball,* 139.
23. Allen, *Baseball's 100,* 17.
24. Reddy, "Stan, the Incredibly Durable Man," 180.
25. Reichler, *Game and the Glory,* 183.
26. Shutt, "When Baseball Came Home from the War," 32.
27. Reidenbaugh, *Baseball's 50 Greatest Games,* 72.
28. Shutt, "When Baseball Came Home from the War," 33.
29. Shaughnessy, *Curse of the Bambino,* 63.
30. Gross, "Emancipation of Jackie Robinson," 14.
31. Mann, "Truth About the Jackie Robinson Case," pt. II, 150.

Chapter 4: Ty Cobb in Technicolor (1947)

1. Holway, "Jose Gibson," 69.
2. Parrott, *Lords of Baseball,* 208–09.
3. *Sporting News,* 16 April 1947.
4. Allen, *Giants and the Dodgers,* 193.
5. Gutman, *It Ain't Cheating if You Don't Get Caught,* 139.
6. "Buttoned Lip," 87.
7. *New York Times,* 16 April 1947.
8. *Sporting News,* 23 April 1947.
9. *"Rookie of the Year,"* 72–73.
10. Phillies' heckling of Robinson: Frommer, *Rickey and Robinson,* 136–37; Robinson and Duckett, *I Never Had It Made,* 71.
11. Robinson and Duckett, *I Never Had It Made,* 71.
12. Ibid., 73.
13. Parrott, *Lords of Baseball,* 218.
14. Woodward's column: *New York Herald-Tribune,* 9 May 1947; Tygiel, *Great Experiment,* 185–89.
15. Veeck and Linn, *Veeck — As in Wreck,* 170.
16. Eskenazi, *Veeck,* 41.
17. Honig, *Baseball America,* 258.
18. Frommer, *Rickey and Robinson,* 135.
19. *Sporting News,* 17 September 1947.
20. Frommer, *Rickey and Robinson,* 147.
21. Zoss and Bowman, *Diamonds in the Rough,* 164.
22. Honig, *Mays, Mantle, Snider,* 26.
23. Zoss and Bowman, *Diamonds in the Rough,* 354.
24. Nelson, *Greatest Stories Ever Told (About Baseball),* 94.
25. *Sporting News,* 24 September 1947.
26. *Sporting News,* 8 October 1947.
27. Barber, *1947 — When All Hell Broke Loose in Baseball,* 329.
28. Jennison, *Wait 'Til Next Year,* 26.
29. *New York Times,* 6 October 1947.
30. Jennison, *Wait 'Til Next Year,* 28.
31. *New York Times,* 14 July 1985.

Chapter 5: The King, the Hustler, and the Satchel Man (1948)

1. Dickson, *Dickson Baseball Dictionary,* 203.
2. Salisbury, *Answer Is Baseball,* 32.

3. Nelson, *Baseball's Greatest Quotes*, 42.
4. Shaughnessy, *Curse of the Bambino*, 2.
5. *New York Times*, 17 August 1948.
6. *New York Times*, 14 June 1948.
7. *Sporting News*, 23 June 1948.
8. Creamer, *Babe: The Legend Comes to Life*, 423.
9. *Sporting News*, 4 August 1948.
10. Lardner, "Ruth," 69.
11. *New York Times*, 17 August 1948.
12. *Sporting News*, 1 September 1948.
13. "The Babe Ruth Story," 46.
14. Mourners at Ruth's funeral: *Sporting News*, 1 September 1948; "Thousands Stand in Rain for Babe Ruth's Funeral," 20–21.
15. Nelson, *Baseball's Greatest Quotes*, 44.
16. Eskenazi, *Veeck*, 28.
17. Axthelm, "The Outsider Who Was King," 62.
18. Veeck and Linn, *Veeck—As in Wreck*, 112–13.
19. Ibid., 116–17.
20. *Sporting News*, 14 July 1948.
21. The National Baseball Hall of Fame and Museum, Inc; the National Baseball Library; Gerald Astor, *The Baseball Hall of Fame 50th Anniversary Book*, 209.
22. Thorn and Holway, *The Pitcher*, 67.
23. Paige and Lipman, *Maybe I'll Pitch Forever*, 227.
24. *Sporting News*, 21 July 1948.
25. "Satchel the Great," 58.
26. Paige and Lipman, *Maybe I'll Pitch Forever*, 12.
27. "Big Guy," 72.
28. *New York Times*, 5 October 1948.
29. Parrott, *Lords of Baseball*, 218.
30. "Black Friday," 32.
31. *The Rivals*, 58.
32. "Big Leagues Head for Photo Finish," 17.
33. "Video Sports: To Be or Not to Be," 80.
34. Ibid.

Chapter 6: Mighty Casey Establishes a Dynasty (1949)

1. Parker, "Baseball's Bombshell," 80.
2. Ibid., 12, 83.
3. "Baseball at the Bar," 63.
4. Lowenfish and Lupien, *Imperfect Diamond*, 165.
5. *New York Times*, 6 June 1949.
6. Robinson, *Home Run Heard 'Round the World*, 4.
7. Creamer, *Stengel*, 212.
8. Ibid., 262.
9. Nelson, *Baseball's Greatest Quotes*, 93.
10. Chieger, *Voices of Baseball*, 49.
11. Frommer, *Baseball's Greatest Managers*, 224.
12. Creamer, *Stengel*, 223.

13. Sugar, *Baseball's 50 Greatest Games*, 92.
14. Okrent and Lewine, *Ultimate Baseball Book*, 254.
15. DiMaggio, "It's Great to Be Back," 66.
16. *Sporting News*, 12 October 1949; De Gregorio, *Joe DiMaggio*, 204.
17. "Fantastic Finish," 42.
18. Veeck's mock funeral: *Sporting News*, 5 October 1949; Veeck and Linn, *Veeck—As in Wreck*, 113–14.
19. Eskenazi, *Veeck*, 83.
20. Robinson and Dexter, *Baseball Has Done It*, 9.
21. Zoss and Bowman, *Diamonds in the Rough*, 164–65.
22. Robinson and Duckett, *I Never Had It Made*, 94.
23. "Fantastic Finish," 42.
24. *Chicago Daily Tribune*, 15 June 1949; *Sporting News*, 22 June 1949.
25. Waitkus's shooting: *Chicago Daily Tribune*, 15 June 1949; *Sporting News*, 22 June 1949; "Silly Honey," 20; "Silly Honey with a Gun," 36; "Fanatic Fan," 49–50.
26. *Chicago Daily Tribune*, 16 June 1949.
27. Haines and Esser, "Case History of Ruth Steinhagen," 741.
28. De Gregorio, *Joe DiMaggio*, 200–201.

Chapter 7: Heroes, Bonus Babies, and Whiz Kids (1950)

1. Daley, "Why We Worship the Babe Ruths," 19.
2. Gregory, *Baseball Player*, 121–22.
3. Salary figures: Voigt, *American Baseball*, pt. III, 221–23; "Why Baseball Is in Trouble," 102; Schlossberg, *Baseball Catalog*, 304.
4. Paxton, "Have the Bonus Boys Paid Off for Baseball?," 103.
5. *Sporting News*, 3 May 1950.
6. *San Francisco Chronicle*, 2 October 1950.
7. Jennison, *Wait 'Til Next Year*, 62.
8. "One More Rescue": 74.
9. *Sporting News*, 21 June 1950.
10. *Sporting News*, 3 January 1951.
11. "Psychiatrist's Delight," 82.
12. *New York Times*, 19 October 1950.
13. *New York Herald Tribune*, 19 October 1950.
14. Donovan, *Tumultuous Years*, 319.
15. *Sporting News*, 6 December 1950.
16. *Sporting News*, 13 December 1950.
17. *Sporting News*, 3 January 1951.

Chapter 8: The New York Game

1. Murray, "I Hate the Yankees," 28.
2. Frommer, *New York City Baseball*, 148.
3. Barber and Creamer, *Rhubarb in the Catbird Seat*, 290.
4. Shannon and Kalinsky, *The Ballparks*, vii.
5. Schlossberg, *Baseball Catalog*, 184.
6. Smith, *Voices of the Game*, 4.
7. Ibid.

8. Silverman, "Take Me Out to the Binder," 51.
9. *Sporting News,* 12 April 1950.
10. "Swing, Swanged, Swunged," 60.
11. Chieger, *Voices of Baseball,* 164.
12. Tolbert, "Dizzy Dean: He's Not So Dumb," 104.
13. Smith, *Voices of the Game,* 151.
14. Allen and Graham, *It Takes Heart,* 37.
15. Halberstam, *Summer of '49,* 14.
16. Cannon and Cannon, *Nobody Asked Me, But...,* 36.
17. Allen, *Where Have You Gone, Joe DiMaggio?,* 117.
18. *Sporting News,* 14 February and 14 March 1951.
19. Kerrane, *Dollar Sign on the Muscle,* 16.
20. *Sporting News,* 4 April 1951.
21. Murray, "Mickey Mantle," 92.
22. Allen, *You Can't Beat the Hours,* 112.
23. Ibid., 113.
24. "Now Look, Son," 78.
25. Durocher and Linn, *Nice Guys Finish Last,* 309–10.
26. Frommer, *Baseball's Greatest Records, Streaks, and Feats,* 130.
27. Sugar, *Baseball's 50 Greatest Games,* 10.
28. For Berraisms, see Pepe, *Wit and Wisdom of Yogi Berra;* Nelson, *Greatest Stories Ever Told (About Baseball),* 180–82: Dickson, *Baseball's Greatest Quotations,* 41–45; Fusselle, *Baseball ... A Laughing Matter,* 31–36; *Sporting News,* 17 March 1986.
29. Allen and Graham, *It Takes Heart,* 240–41.
30. Frank, "Nobody Loves Baseball More Than Campy," 114.
31. "Big Man from Nicetown: Roy Campanella," 55.
32. Rust, *"Get That Nigger Off the Field,"* 129.

Chapter 9: The Year of the Midget and the Giants (1951)

1. *Sporting News,* 14 February 1951.
2. Richman, "War, Weather Cloud 1951 Outlook," 24.
3. MacArthur, *Reminiscences,* 400–404.
4. *Sporting News,* 2 May 1945.
5. Sugar, *Baseball's 50 Greatest Games,* 191.
6. "Master of the Joyful Illusion," 55.
7. Thorn, *Relief Pitcher,* 104.
8. Eskenazi, *Veeck,* 90.
9. Ibid., 93.
10. Rosenthal, *The 10 Best Years of Baseball,* 85.
11. *Sporting News,* 29 August 1951.
12. Kiernan, *Miracle at Coogan's Bluff,* 57.
13. *Sporting News,* 9 May 1951.
14. Ibid.
15. Ibid.
16. Reidenbaugh, *Baseball's 25 Greatest Pennant Races,* 9.
17. *Sporting News,* 15 August 1951.
18. *Sporting News,* 10 October 1951.
19. *Sporting News,* 9 May 1951.

20. *Sporting News*, 5 September 1951.
21. "Willie the Whoop," 64.
22. Fitzgerald, "The 'Barber' of the Giants," 76.
23. *Sporting News*, 5 September 1951.
24. Allen and Graham, *It Takes Heart*, 251.
25. Kaese, "Baseball's Most Dramatic Moment—When Thomson's Homer Vanquished the Dodgers," 24.
26. Robinson, *Shot Heard 'Round the World*, 226.
27. Branca and Ross, "They'll Never Forget," 72.
28. "Big Man from Nicetown: Roy Campanella," 54.
29. Hodges and Hirshberg, *My Giants*, 113–14; *Sporting News*, 2 January 1952.
30. Frommer, *New York City Baseball*, 167.
31. Mays and Sahadi, *Say Hey*, 15.
32. Flaherty, "Love Song to Willie Mays," 15.
33. Durso, *Baseball and the American Dream*, 240.
34. Angell, "Farewell My Giants," 164.
35. Cited in Kiernan, *Miracle at Coogan's Bluff*, 19.
36. *New York Herald-Tribune*, 4 October 1951; Smith, *Views of Sport*, 33.
37. Kaese, "Baseball's Most Dramatic Moment," 72.
38. Ibid.
39. Reidenbaugh, *Baseball's 50 Greatest Games*, 15.
40. *New York Times*, 7 February 1987.
41. "Baseball: A Great Year," 18.
42. Honig, *October Heroes*, 81.
43. Connor, *Baseball for the Love of It*, 230.
44. "Never Saw a Report Like It," 133.
45. De Gregorio, *Joe DiMaggio*, 236.
46. DiMaggio's press conference: *New York Times*, 12 December 1951; *Sporting News*, 19 December 1951.
47. Allen, *Baseball's 100*, 21.

Chapter 10: Old Timers, Women, and the Russians (1952)

1. Parker, "Why Happy Was Sent to the Showers," 19–20; Danzig and Reichler, *History of Baseball*, 116–17.
2. Lowenfish and Lupien, *Imperfect Diamond*, 173.
3. Cobb, "They Don't Play Baseball Any More," pt. I, 137, 150.
4. Ibid., 147.
5. Ibid., 137, 141.
6. "Letters to the Editor," *Life* 32 (7 April 1952): 17.
7. *Sporting News*, 26 March 1952.
8. *Sporting News*, 9 April 1952.
9. *Sporting News*, 16 April 1952.
10. *Sporting News*, 26 March 1952.
11. Ibid.
12. Will, *Men at Work*, 293.
13. *Sporting News*, 23 April 1952.
14. *Sporting News*, 20 February 1952.
15. Rutledge Books, *Baseball Century*, 84.
16. Robinson and Salzberg, *On a Clear Day They Could See Seventh Place*, 182.

17. Sugar, *Rain Delays*, 131.
18. Robinson and Salzberg, *On a Clear Day They Could See Seventh Place*, 185.
19. *Sporting News*, 6 August 1952.
20. For Piersall's antics and breakdown, see Piersall and Hirshberg, *Fear Strikes Out*.
21. Okrent and Wulf, *Baseball Anecdotes*, 218.
22. Dickey, *History of the World Series*, 169.
23. *Sporting News*, 2 July 1952.
24. Ibid.
25. Ibid.
26. For the AAGPBL, see "Women Players in Organized Baseball," 157–61; Nicholson, "Women's Pro Baseball Packed the Stands," 22–24; "Babette Ruths," 68–69; Biemiller, "World's Prettiest Ballplayers," 50–51, 75–85; Zoss and Bowman, *Diamonds in the Rough*, 208–13.
27. Biemiller, "World's Prettiest Ballplayers," 77.
28. *Smena* article is summarized in *New York Times*, 16 September 1952, and "Truth About Beizbol," 77.
29. Stanky, "All Out for 'Beizbol,'" 24–25.
30. *Sporting News*, 10 December 1952.
31. Ibid.

Chapter 11: Same Old Story (1953)

1. *Washington Post*, 3 April 1953.
2. Ibid.
3. New York Times, 5 April 1953.
4. *Sporting News*, 25 March 1953.
5. *New York Times*, 19 March 1953.
6. Dickey, *History of National League Baseball*, 18.
7. "Musical Chairs," 66.
8. *Sporting News*, 3 June 1953.
9. Jennison, *Wait 'Til Next Year*, 93.
10. Honig, *Baseball's Ten Greatest Teams*, 110.
11. Connor, *Baseball for the Love of It*, 143.
12. *Sporting News*, 16 September 1953.
13. *Sporting News*, 11 March 1953.
14. "Historic Homer: Mickey Mantle," 76.
15. Golenbock, *Dynasty*, 76.
16. *Sporting News*, 15 July 1953.
17. Daley, "Philosophy of Casey Stengel," 14.
18. *Sporting News*, 5 August 1953.
19. *Sporting News*, 19 August 1953.
20. Okrent and Wulf, *Baseball Anecdotes*, 249.
21. Piersall and Hirshberg, *Fear Strikes Out*, 205.
22. Piersall and Whittingham, *The Truth Hurts*, 29–30.
23. *New York Times*, 14 June 1982; Nash and Zullo, *Hall of Shame #2*, 85–86.
24. Miller, *Baseball Business*, 26.
25. *New York Times*, 30 September 1953.
26. Donovan, "The Fabulous Satchel Paige," pt. III, 54.
27. Thorn, *Relief Pitcher*, 105.

28. "Baseball's Curve Balls: Are They Optical Illusions?" 83–89.

29. *Sporting News*, 19 August 1953.

30. "Camera and Science Settle the Old Rhubarb About Baseball's Curve Ball," 105–107.

31. *Sporting News*, 19 August 1953.

32. Drury, "Hell It Don't Curve," 102.

33. "Does a Curve Curve?," 100.

34. Spink, *Sporting News Guide and Record Book*, 120; Allen, *Giants and the Dodgers*, 215.

35. *Sporting News*, 14 October 1953.

Chapter 12: A Changing, Troubled Pastime

1. "Negro Comes of Age in Baseball," 41.

2. Zoss and Bowman, *Diamonds in the Rough*, 174.

3. Meany, "Where Are Baseball's .300 Hitters?," 17.

4. Kahn, *Boys of Summer*, 141.

5. *Sporting News*, 24 September 1952.

6. Quigley, *Crooked Pitch*, 101.

7. *Sporting News*, 22 February 1956.

8. Frisch and Meany, "Let's Legalize the Spitball," 90.

9. Young, "Outlawed Spitter Was My Money Pitch," 61.

10. Quigley, *Crooked Pitch*, 162.

11. Ibid.

12. Chieger, *Voices of Baseball*, 190.

13. Soule, "How They're Using Mathematics to Win Ball Games," 224.

14. *Sporting News*, 22 January 1958.

15. *Sporting News*, 30 July 1952.

16. For decline of minor leagues, see Sullivan, *The Minors*, 235–55.

17. *New York Times*, 22 May 1939.

18. "First U.S. Sports Is Televised by NBC," 70.

19. Frank, "Main Event: TV vs. SRO," 48.

20. DeOrsey, "Big Leagues Are Killing Baseball," 19.

21. Radar, *In Its Own Image*, 52–53.

22. Schacht, "Who's Killing Minor League Baseball?," 15.

23. Maney, "Shades of Abner Doubleday," 20.

24. *Sporting News*, 2 May 1956.

25. Daley, "Sports Explains the Nations," 75.

26. Gipe, *Great American Sports Book*, 151.

27. Kelso, "They're Mercenary Today," 77.

28. Angell, "Baseball: The Perfect Game," 88.

29. Talese, "Gray-Flannel-Suit Men at Bat," 15, 19.

30. Snider and Kahn, "I Play Baseball for Money—Not Fun," 42–46.

31. Ibid., 42.

32. Ibid.

33. *Sporting News*, 23 May 1956.

34. Jensen and Hirshberg, "My Ambition Is to Quit," 31, 142–44.

35. Coughlan, "Baseball: Nine Men, a Diamond, and $10 Million," 21.

36. "Shape of Things; Controversial Reserve Clause," 100.

37. Lowenfish and Lupien, *Imperfect Diamond*, 179–180.

38. *Sporting News*, 28 May 1952.
39. *Sporting News*, 18 November 1953.
40. Ibid.
41. Gregory, *Baseball Player*, 200.
42. Ibid., 201.
43. Dworkin, *Owners Versus Players*, 28.

Chapter 13: The Year the Yankees Lost the Pennant (1954)

1. Lardner, "Mutiny in the Tropics," 79; Lardner, "Cloud Passes," 64.
2. *Sporting News*, 29 August 1956.
3. *Sporting News*, 17 March 1954.
4. *Sporting News*, 22 September 1954.
5. Reidenbaugh, *Baseball's 25 Greatest Teams*, 86.
6. Nash and Zullo, *Baseball's Hall of Shame #2*, 123.
7. Chieger, *Voices of Baseball*, 177.
8. Creamer, *Stengel*, 256.
9. *Sporting News*, 10 March 1954.
10. "Say, Hey," 85.
11. Kahn, *How the Weather Was*, 62.
12. *New York Times*, 25 November 1953.
13. "He Came to Win," 46.
14. "Willie Mays: The Hottest Thing Since Babe Ruth," 74.
15. Ibid.
16. Ibid.
17. Honig, *Power Hitters*, 157.
18. For Bauman, see Walton, *The Rookies*, 109; James, *The Bill James Historical Baseball Abstract*, 217; and Ripp, "When Joe Bauman Hit 72 Home Runs," 26–29.
19. *Winston-Salem Journal*, 29 April 1990.
20. Okrent and Lewine, *Ultimate Baseball Book*, 244.
21. Smith, *Voices of the Game*, 268.
22. Thorn and Palmer, *Total Baseball*, 534.
23. Dickey, *History of the World Series*, 174.
24. *Sporting News*, 13 October 1954.
25. Ibid.
26. Hynd, *Giants of the Polo Grounds*, 371.
27. Ibid.
28. Durocher and Linn, *Nice Guys Finish Last*, 317–18.
29. Smith, "One for the Rhodes," 57.
30. Honig, *Mays, Mantle, Snider*, 130.
31. *Sporting News*, 13 October 1954.
32. Dickey, *History of the World Series*, 178.
33. *Sporting News*, 13 October 1954.
34. Cannon and Cannon, *Nobody Asked Me, But . . .*, 34.
35. "Out at Home," 47.
36. Nelson, *Baseball's Greatest Quotes*, 83.
37. Voigt, *American Baseball, III*, 288.
38. Kahn, *Joe and Marilyn*, 269.

Chapter 14: Next Year (1955)

1. "Helmets In, Buttons Out?" 22.
2. Creamer, "Brooklyn's Happy Streak," 34–35.
3. *Sporting News*, 20 July 1955.
4. Thorn, *Century of Baseball Lore*, 176.
5. "Money Pitcher," 88.
6. "Duke or Willie? A Vote for Snider," 17.
7. Flaherty, "Love Song to Willie Mays," 15.
8. Meany, "Tom Meany's 1955 Baseball Preview," 28.
9. Ibid.
10. Snider and Gilbert, *Duke of Flatbush*, 145.
11. Gipe, *Great American Sports Book*, 91.
12. "Westward the A's," 64.
13. "It's Great to Be a Yankee," 50.
14. Allen, *You Could Look It Up*, 172.
15. Allen, *Baseball's 100*, 97.
16. Shaughnessy, *Curse of the Bambino*, 94.
17. "The Dodgers, Etc.," 9.
18. Reese and Meany, "Baseball Is a Different Game Now," 43.
19. *Washington Post*, 5 October 1955.
20. Reidenbaugh, *Baseball's 50 Greatest Games*, 99.
21. Marsh and Ehre, *Best Sports Stories: A Panorama of the 1955 Sports Year*, 58.
22. *Washington Post*, 5 October 1955.
23. *Sporting News*, 12 October 1955.
24. Creamer, "The Year, the Moment, and Johnny Podres," 20.
25. *New York Times*, 5 October 1955; *Sporting News*, 12 October, 1955.
26. Golenbock, *Bums*, 408; Frommer, *New York City Baseball*, 192.
27. *Sporting News*, 7 December 1955.

Chapter 15: The Mick, the Barber, and the Night Rider (1956)

1. Creamer, "Not Rain, Nor Snow Nor Sleet," 23.
2. *Sporting News*, 9 May 1956.
3. *Sporting News*, 2 May 1956.
4. Kahn, "Oklahoma's Mickey Mantle: Can the Young Yankee Beat the Babe?," 64.
5. Frommer, *Baseball's Greatest Records, Streaks, and Feats*, 56.
6. *Sporting News*, 21 March 1956.
7. Cramer, "What Do You Think of Ted Williams Now?," 89.
8. *New York Times*, 8 August 1956.
9. Ibid.
10. *Sporting News*, 23 May 1956.
11. *Sporting News*, 26 September 1956.
12. "Site of Distraction," 30.
13. Ibid., 31.
14. "Time for the Elders," 75.
15. Ibid.
16. Dickey, *History of American League Baseball*, 193, 195; Marazzi and Fiorito, *Aaron to Zuverink*, 249.

17. Allen and Fitzgerald, *You Can't Beat the Hours*, 173.
18. *Washington Post*, 9 October 1956.
19. *Sporting News*, 17 October 1956.
20. Okrent and Lewine, *Ultimate Baseball Book*, 261.
21. Creamer, "Curtain Rises," 29.
22. Dickey, *Great No-Hitters*, 19.
23. *Washington Post*, 9 October 1956.
24. *Sporting News*, 17 October 1956.
25. *Sporting News*, 24 October 1956.
26. Golenbock, *Dynasty*, 191.
27. Nelson, *Baseball's Greatest Quotes*, 67.
28. *Sporting News*, 19 December 1956.
29. "After Ten Years," 49.
30. Robinson, "Why I'm Quitting Baseball," 91–92.
31. *Sporting news*, 16 January 1957.
32. Ibid.
33. "If You Can't Beat Him," 43.
34. Frommer, *Rickey and Robinson*, 204.
35. Snider and Gilbert, *Duke of Flatbush*, 22.
36. Kahn, *Boys of Summer*, 393.
37. "A Hard Out," 91.
38. Tygiel, *Baseball's Great Experiment*, 343.

Chapter 16: Three-Time Loser (1957)

1. Meany, "Tom Meany's 1957 Baseball Preview," 105.
2. Voigt, *American Baseball, III*, 128.
3. Jennison, *Wait 'Til Next Year*, 150.
4. *Sporting News*, 28 August 1957; *New York Times*, 20 August 1957.
5. Angell, "Farewell My Giants," 8.
6. Creamer, "Twilight of the Bums," 8.
7. "That Big League Yearning," 16.
8. *New York Times*, 29 June 1957.
9. Schlossberg, *Baseball Catalog*, 129.
10. "Great Rhubarb," 68.
11. Honig, *Baseball Between the Lines*, 218.
12. *Sporting News*, 15 May 1957.
13. Ibid.
14. "U.S. Winced," 27.
15. Giants' last home game: *Sporting News*, 9 October 1957.
16. Dodgers' last home game: *Sporting News*, 2 and 9 October 1957.
17. *New York Times*, 14 October 1957.
18. *New York Times*, 9 October 1957.
19. Barber and Creamer, *Rhubarb in the Catbird Seat*, 290.
20. Schlossberg, *Baseball Catalog*, 186.
21. Reichler, *Game and the Glory*, 115.
22. Frommer, *New York City Baseball*, 26.

Chapter 17: On to California (1958)

1. "Big Man from Nicetown: Roy Campanella," 55.
2. Campanella, "I'll Walk Again," pt. I, 14.
3. Campanella, *It's Good to Be Alive*, 6–7.
4. *New York Times*, 19 April 1958.
5. "Everyone a Babe Ruth?," 81.
6. "California Goes Big League in a Big Way," 31.
7. "Then, Farce in the Coliseum," 21.
8. *Sporting News*, 16 July 1958.
9. Angell, "Farewell My Giants," 164.
10. Danzig and Reichler, *History of Baseball*, 119; Lowenfish and Lupien, *Imperfect Diamond*, 187.
11. *Sporting News*, 16 July 1958.
12. Stengel's testimony: *New York Times*, 10 July 1958; *Washington Post*, 10 July 1958; *Sporting News*, 16 July 1958; Allen, *You Could Look It Up*, 193–95.
13. Mantle's testimony: *New York Times*, 10 July 1958; *Washington Post*, 10 July 1958; *Sporting News*, 16 July 1958.
14. "Casey Stengel Gives the Senate a Lecture on the Spirit of '76," 24.
15. Creamer, "Greatest Yankee Team Ever," 11.
16. Golenbock, *Dynasty*, 240.
17. Paxton, "Is Baseball Comedy Dead?," 49.
18. "Organization Men of Baseball," 95.
19. *Sporting News*, 10 October 1958.
20. *Sporting News*, 15 October 1958.
21. "He Just Keeps Rolling," 102.
22. For account of this game, see Maule, "Best Football Game Ever Played"; *Sporting News*, 7 January 1959; and Klein, *Game of Their Lives*.
23. "Golden Age of Sport," 18.

Chapter 18: Return of the Maverick (1959)

1. Zimmerman, "Veeck—A New Bill for the White Sox," 95.
2. Eskenazi, *Veeck*, 132.
3. Ibid.
4. "Day the Yankees Fell Into the Cellar," 98.
5. "They Want to Lynch Us," 63.
6. Cited in Einstein, *Willie's Time*, 114.
7. "It's Mad, It's Chicago," 77.
8. *Sporting News*, 30 September 1959.
9. "Going, Going, Gone?," 56.
10. "Season in the Sun," 54; *Sporting News*, 23 September 1959.
11. "They Said It," 26.
12. *Sporting News Guide and Record Book, 1960*, 114.
13. Golenbock, *Dynasty*, 239.
14. *Sporting News*, 5 August 1959.
15. Koppett, *All About Baseball*, 224.
16. Campanella, *It's Good to Be Alive*, 272–74.
17. *Sporting News*, 20 May 1959.
18. Ibid.

19. Cousins, "His Life Is the Greatest Game: Roy Campanella," 46.
20. Brown, "Onliest Way I Know," 135.
21. "It Comes Naturally: Hank Aaron," 97.
22. *Sporting News*, 3 June 1959.
23. "Sweet Smell of Failure," 34; Thorn and Holway, *The Pitcher*, 228.
24. *Greensboro Daily News*, 5 August 1989.
25. "Season in the Sun," 55.
26. "A Series of Strange Events," 17.
27. "Daffy Dodgertown," 77.
28. "Series of Strange Events," 21.
29. "New Dynasty?," 66.

Chapter 19: Miracle in Pittsburgh (1960)

1. "Totem Pole," 29.
2. Rice, *Seasons Past*, 434.
3. *Sporting News*, 9 March 1960.
4. "Lighting the Candlestick," 47.
5. *Sporting News*, 27 July 1960.
6. Sugar, *Baseball's 50 Greatest Games*, 19.
7. "Winner in Pittsburgh," 59.
8. "Old Stars Never Die," 99–100.
9. Reddy, "Stan the Incredibly Durable Man," 177.
10. *Sporting News*, 3 February 1960.
11. Creamer, *Stengel*, 286.
12. *Sporting News*, 1 June 1960.
13. *Sporting News*, 8 June 1960.
14. Seidel, *Ted Williams*, 320.
15. Linn, "The Kid's Last Game," 59.
16. Ibid., 60.
17. Williams, *My Turn at Bat*, 240.
18. *Boston Globe*, 29 September 1960.
19. Linn, "The Kid's Last Game," 61.
20. Updike, "Hub Fans Bid Kid Adieu," 131.
21. Williams, *My Turn at Bat*, 7.
22. *Sporting News*, 28 December 1960.
23. *Washington Post*, 9 August 1956.
24. Williams, *My Turn at Bat*, 9.
25. *Sporting News*, 19 October 1960; Williams, *My Turn at Bat*, 244.
26. Kuenster, "What They Thought When the Pressure Was the Greatest," 8.
27. Honig, *Baseball Between the Lines*, 153.
28. *Sporting News*, 19 October 1960.
29. *Washington Post*, 14 October 1960.
30. *Sporting News*, 19 October 1960.
31. Ibid.
32. Connor, *Baseball for the Love of It*, 161.
33. Vecsey, "Terry and the Pirates," 66; Lieb, *Baseball As I Have Known It*, 240.
34. Reichler, *World Series*, 94.
35. "Bucs Heist Series and the Lid Blows Off," 32.

Chapter 20: End of an Era

1. Creamer, *Stengel*, 287.

2. For Yankees' press conference, see *Sporting News*, 26 October 1960; Creamer, *Stengel*, 290; Williams, "Goodby, Casey, Goodby," 63–65.

3. Allen, *You Could Look It Up*, 207.

4. Creamer, *Stengel*, 291; Williams, "Goodby, Casey, Goodby," 65.

5. Williams, "Goodby, Casey, Goodby," 65.

6. *New York Times*, 19 October 1960.

7. Frommer, *Baseball's Greatest Managers*, 222.

8. *Sporting News*, 23 August 1945.

9. "Third Major League — When, If Ever?," 80.

10. "Can Another Big League Club Pay Its Way?" 50.

11. Parrott, *Lords of Baseball*.

12. Frick, *Games, Asterisks, and People*, 128–29.

13. *New York Times*, 27 October 1960.

14. Einstein, "Covering the World Series," 34.

15. Brosnan, *Long Season*, 255.

16. Ibid., 84.

17. Silverman, "Major League Intellectual," 24.

18. *New York Times Book Review*, 10 July 1960.

19. *San Francisco Chronicle*, 3 July 1960.

20. Brosnan, "I Broke Baseball's Rules," 90.

21. Johnson, "Interview with Jim Brosnan," 40.

22. Brosnan, "I Broke Baseball's Rules," 39, 89.

23. *Newsday*, 15 March 1960.

24. *Chicago Tribune*, 10 July 1960.

25. *Sporting News*, 23 March 1960.

26. Andreano, *No Joy in Mudville*, 22.

27. Williams, *My Turn at Bat*, 8.

28. Reichler, *Game and the Glory*, 183.

29. Connor, *Baseball for the Love of It*, 298.

30. Dickson, *Dickson Baseball Dictionary*, 182.

31. Kahn, "Something's Changing About Baseball," 49.

32. Nelson, *Baseball's Greatest Insults*, 9.

Bibliography

Books

Alexander, Charles C. *Our Game: An American Baseball History.* New York: Henry Holt, 1991.

Allen, Lee. *The Giants and the Dodgers: The Fabulous Story of Baseball's Fiercest Feud.* New York: G.P. Putnam's, 1964.

Allen, Maury. *Baseball's 100: A Personal Ranking of the Best Players in Baseball History.* New York: A & W Visual Library, 1981.

_____. *Where Have You Gone, Joe DiMaggio? The Story of America's Last Hero.* New York: E.P. Dutton, 1975.

_____. *You Could Look It Up: The Life of Casey Stengel.* New York: Times Books, 1979.

Allen, Mel, and Ed Fitzgerald. *You Can't Beat the Hours: A Long, Loving Look at Big League Baseball — Including Some Yankees I Have Known.* New York: Harper & Row, 1964.

_____, and Frank Graham. *It Takes Heart.* New York: Harper & Brothers, 1959.

Andreano, Ralph. *No Joy in Mudville: The Dilemma of Major League Baseball.* Cambridge, Massachusetts: Schenkman, 1965.

Barber, Red. *1947 — When All Hell Broke Loose in Baseball.* Garden City, New York: Doubleday, 1982.

_____, and Robert Creamer. *Rhubarb in the Catbird Seat.* Garden City, N.Y.: Doubleday, 1968.

Benson, Michael. *Ballparks of North America: A Comprehensive Historical Reference to Baseball Grounds, Yards, and Stadiums, 1845 to the Present.* Jefferson, N.C.: McFarland, 1989.

Broeg, Bob, and William J. Miller, Jr. *Baseball from a Different Angle.* South Bend, Indiana: Diamond Communications, 1988.

Brosnan, Jim. *The Long Season.* New York: Grosset & Dunlap, 1960.

Campanella, Roy. *It's Good to Be Alive.* Boston: Little, Brown, 1959.

Cannon, Jack, and Tom Cannon, eds. *Nobody Asked Me, But . . . The World of Jimmy Cannon.* New York: Penguin Books, 1983.

Carter, Craig, ed. *The Complete Baseball Record Book.* St. Louis: Sporting News, 1986.

_____. *Take Me Out to the Ball Park.* 2d ed. St. Louis: Sporting News, 1987.

Charlton, James, ed. *The Baseball Chronology: The Complete History of the Most Important Events in the Game of Baseball.* New York: Macmillan, 1991.

Chieger, Bob. *Voices of Baseball: Quotations on the Summer Game.* New York: New American Library, 1983.

Coffin, Tristram Potter. *The Old Ball Game: Baseball in Folklore and Fiction.* New York: Herder & Herder, 1971.

Connor, Anthony J. *Baseball for the Love of It: Hall of Famers Tell It Like It Was.* New York: Macmillan, 1982.

Creamer, Robert W. *Babe: The Legend Comes to Life.* New York: Simon & Schuster, 1974.

_____. *Stengel: His Life and Times.* New York: Simon & Schuster, 1984.

Danzig, Allison, and Joe Reichler. *The History of Baseball: Its Great Players, Teams, and Managers.* Englewood Cliffs, N.J.: Prentice-Hall, 1959.

David, L. Robert, ed. *Insider's Baseball: The Finer Points of the Game, As Examined by the Society for American Baseball Research.* New York: Charles Scribner's, 1983.

De Gregorio, George. *Joe DiMaggio: An Informal Biography.* New York: Stein & Day, 1981.

Dickey, Glenn. *The Great No-Hitters.* Radnor, Pa.: Chilton, 1976.

_____. *The History of American League Baseball Since 1901.* New York: Stein & Day, 1980.

_____. *The History of National League Baseball Since 1876.* New York: Stein & Day, 1979.

_____. *The History of the World Series Since 1903.* New York: Stein & Day, 1984.

Dickson, Paul, ed. *Baseball's Greatest Quotations.* New York: HarperCollins, 1991.

_____. *The Dickson Baseball Dictionary.* New York: Facts on File, 1989.

Donovan, Robert J. *Tumultuous Years: The Presidency of Harry S. Truman.* New York: Harper, 1956.

Durocher, Leo, with Ed Linn. *Nice Guys Finish Last.* New York: Simon & Schuster, 1975.

Durso, Joseph. *Baseball and the American Dream.* St. Louis: Sporting News, 1986.

Dworkin, James B. *Owners Versus Players: Baseball and Collective Bargaining.* Boston: Auburn House, 1981.

Einstein, Charles. *Willie's Time: A Memoir.* Philadelphia: J.B. Lippincott, 1979.

Eskenazi, Gerald. *Veeck: A Baseball Legend.* New York: McGraw-Hill, 1988.

Frick, Ford. *Games, Asterisks, and People: Memoirs of a Lucky Fan.* New York: Crown, 1973.

Frommer, Harvey. *Baseball's Greatest Managers.* New York: Franklin Watts, 1985.

_____. *Baseball's Greatest Records, Streaks, and Feats.* New York: Atheneum, 1983.

_____ *New York City Baseball: The Last Golden Age, 1947–1957.* New York, Macmillan, 1980.

_____. *Rickey and Robinson: The Men Who Broke Baseball's Color Barrier.* New York: Macmillan, 1982.

_____. *Sports Roots: How Nicknames, Namesakes, Trophies, Competitions and Expressions Came to Be in the World of Sports.* New York: Atheneum, 1979.

Fusselle, Warner, with Rick Wolff and Brian Zevnick. *Baseball: A Laughing Matter.* St. Louis: Sporting News, 1987.

Gipe, George. *The Great American Sports Book.* Garden City, N.Y.: Doubleday, 1978.

Goldstein, Richard. *Spartan Seasons: How Baseball Survived the Second World War.* New York: Macmillan, 1980.

Golenbock, Peter. *Bums: An Oral History of the Brooklyn Dodgers.* New York: G.P. Putnam's, 1984.

_____. *Dynasty: The New York Yankees, 1949–1964.* Englewood Cliffs, N.J.: Prentice-Hall, 1975.

Gregory, Paul Michael. *The Baseball Player: An Economic Study*. Washington: Public Affairs Press, 1956.

Gutman, Dan. *It Ain't Cheating If You Don't Get Caught: Scuffing, Corking, Spitting, Gunking, Razzing, and Other Fundamentals of Our National Pastime*. New York: Penguin, 1990.

Halberstam, David. *Summer of '49*. New York: William Morrow, 1989.

Hodges, Russ, and Al Hirshberg. *My Giants*. Garden City, N.Y.: Doubleday, 1963.

Honig, Donald. *Baseball America: The Heroes of the Game and the Times of Their Glory*. New York: Macmillan, 1985.

_____. *Baseball Between the Lines: Baseball in the '40s and '50s as Told by the Men Who Played It*. New York: Coward, McCann, and Geoghegan, 1976.

_____. *Baseball's Ten Greatest Teams*. New York: Macmillan, 1982.

_____. *Mays, Mantle, Snider: A Celebration*. New York: Macmillan, 1988.

_____. *The October Heroes: Great World Series Games by the Men Who Played Them*. New York: Simon & Schuster, 1979.

_____. *The Power Hitters*. St. Louis: Sporting News, 1989.

Hynd, Noel. *The Giants of the Polo Grounds: The Glorious Times of Baseball's New York Giants*. New York: Doubleday, 1988.

Izenberg, Jerry. *The Rivals*. New York: Holt, Rinehart & Winston, 1968.

James, Bill. *The Bill James Historical Baseball Abstract*. New York: Villard, 1986.

Jennison, Christopher. *Wait 'Til Next Year*. New York: W.W. Norton, 1974.

Kahn, Roger. *The Boys of Summer*. New York: Harper & Row, 1971.

_____. *How the Weather Was*. New York: Harper & Row, 1973.

_____. *Joe and Marilyn: A Memory of Love*. New York: William Morrow, 1986.

Kerrane, Kevin. *Dollar Sign on the Muscle: The World of Baseball Scouting*. New York: Beaufort, 1984.

Kiernan, Thomas. *The Miracle at Coogan's Bluff*. New York: Thomas Y. Crowell, 1975.

Klein, Dave. *The Game of Their Lives*. New York: Random House, 1976.

Koppett, Leonard. *All About Baseball*. New York: Quadrangle, 1974.

Lieb, Frederick G. *Baseball As I Have Known It*. New York: Coward, McCann & Geoghegan, 1977.

Lowenfish, Lee, and Tony Lupien. *The Imperfect Diamond: The Story of Baseball's Reserve System and the Men Who Fought to Change It*. New York: Stein & Day, 1980.

MacArthur, Douglas. *Reminiscences*. New York: McGraw-Hill, 1964.

Marazzi, Rich, and Len Fiorito. *Aaron to Zuverink*. New York: Avon, 1982.

Marsh, Irving T., and Edward Ehre, eds. *Best Sports Stories: A Panorama of the 1955 Sports Year*. New York: E.P. Dutton, 1956.

Mays, Willie, with Lou Sahadi. *Say Hey: The Autobiography of Willie Mays*. New York: Simon & Schuster, 1988.

Mead, William B. *Even the Browns*. Chicago: Contemporary Books, 1978.

Miller, James Edward. *The Baseball Business: Pursuing Pennants and Profits in Baltimore*. Chapel Hill, N.C.: University of North Carolina Press, 1990.

Nash, Bruce, and Allan Zullo. *The Baseball Hall of Shame #2*. New York: Pocket Books, 1986.

The National Baseball Hall of Fame and Museum, Inc., the National Baseball Library, and Gerald Astor. *The Baseball Hall of Fame 50th Anniversary Book*. New York: Prentice-Hall Press, 1988.

Neft, David S., and Richard M. Cohen. *The World Series: Complete Play-By-Play of Every Game, 1903–1989.* New York: St. Martin's Press, 1990.

————, Roland T. Johnson, Richard M. Cohen, and Jordan A. Deutsch. *The Sports Encyclopedia: Baseball.* 1993 ed. New York: St. Martin's Press, 1993.

Nelson, Kevin, comp. *Baseball's Greatest Quotes: The Wit, Wisdom, and Wisecracks of America's National Pastime.* New York: Simon & Schuster, 1982.

————. *The Greatest Stories Ever Told (About Baseball).* New York: Perigee, 1986.

Okrent, Daniel, and Harris Lewine, eds. *The Ultimate Baseball Book.* Boston: Houghton Mifflin, 1988.

————, and Steve Wulf. *Baseball Anecdotes.* New York: Oxford University Press, 1989.

Paige, Leroy (Satchel), and David Lipman. *Maybe I'll Pitch Forever.* Garden City, N.Y.: Doubleday, 1962.

Parrott, Harold. *The Lords of Baseball.* New York: Praeger, 1976.

Pepe, Phil. *The Wit and Wisdom of Yogi Berra.* New York: Hawthorn, 1974.

Peterson, Robert. *Only the Ball Was White.* Englewood Cliffs, N.J.: Prentice-Hall, 1970.

Piersall, Jim, and Al Hirshberg. *Fear Strikes Out: The Jim Piersall Story.* Boston: Little, Brown, 1955.

————, with Richard Whittingham. *The Truth Hurts.* Chicago: Contemporary Books, 1985.

Polner, Murray. *Branch Rickey: A Biography.* New York: Atheneum, 1982.

Porter, David L., ed. *Biographical Dictionary of American Sports: Baseball.* Westport, Conn.: Greenwood Press, 1987.

Quigley, Martin. *The Crooked Pitch: The Curveball in American Baseball History.* Chapel Hill, N.C.: Algonquin, 1984.

Radar, Benjamin G. *In Its Own Image: How Television Has Transformed Sports.* New York: Free Press, 1984.

Reichler, Joseph L., ed. *The Baseball Encyclopedia: The Complete and Official Record of Major League Baseball.* 9th ed. New York: Macmillan, 1993.

————. *The Game and the Glory.* Englewood Cliffs, N.J.: Prentice-Hall, 1976.

————. *The World Series: A 75th Anniversary.* New York: Simon & Schuster, 1978.

Reidenbaugh, Lowell. *Baseball's 50 Greatest Games.* St. Louis: Sporting News, 1986.

————. *Baseball's 25 Greatest Pennant Races.* St. Louis: Sporting News, 1987.

————. *Baseball's 25 Greatest Teams.* St. Louis: Sporting News, 1986.

Rice, Damon. *Seasons Past.* New York: Praeger, 1976.

Rickey, Branch, and Robert Riger. *The American Diamond: A Documentary of the Game of Baseball.* New York: Simon & Schuster, 1965.

Robinson, George, and Charles Salzberg. *On A Clear Day They Could See Seventh Place: Baseball's Worst Teams.* New York: Dell, 1991.

Robinson, Jackie, edited by Charles Dexter. *Baseball Has Done It.* Philadelphia: J.B. Lippincott, 1964.

————, as told to Alfred Duckett. *I Never Had It Made.* New York: G.P. Putnam's, 1972.

Robinson, Ray. *The Home Run Heard 'Round the World: The Dramatic Story of the 1951 Giants-Dodgers Pennant Race.* New York: HarperCollins, 1991.

Rogosin, Donn. *Invisible Men: Life in Baseball's Negro Leagues.* New York: Atheneum, 1983.

Rosenthal, Harold. *The 10 Best Years of Baseball: An Informal History of the Fifties.* Chicago: Contemporary Books, 1979.

Rowan, Carl T., with Jackie Robinson. *Wait Till Next Year: The Life Story of Jackie Robinson.* New York: Random House, 1960.

Rust, Art, Jr. *"Get That Nigger Off the Field."* New York: Delacorte, 1976.

Rutledge Books. *A Baseball Century: The First 100 Years of the National League.* New York: Rutledge, 1976.

Salisbury, Luke. *The Answer Is Baseball.* New York: Times Books, 1989.

Schlossberg, Dan. *The Baseball Catalog.* Updated edition. Middle Village, N.Y.: Jonathan David, 1989.

Seidel, Michael. *Ted Williams: A Baseball Life.* Chicago: Contemporary Books, 1991.

Shannon, Bill, and George Kalinsky. *The Ballparks.* New York: Hawthorn Books, 1975.

Shatzin, Mike, ed. *The Ballplayers: Baseball's Ultimate Biographical Reference.* New York: William Morrow, 1990.

Shaughnessy, Dan. *The Curse of the Bambino.* New York: Penguin, 1991.

Slaughter, Enos, with Kevin Reid. *Country Hardball: The Autobiography of Enos "Country" Slaughter.* Greensboro, N.C.: Tudor, 1991.

Smith, Curt. *Voices of the Game: The First Full-Scale Overview of Baseball Broadcasting, 1921-Present.* South Bend, Ind.: Diamond Communications, 1987.

Smith, Myron J., Jr. *Baseball: A Comprehensive Bibliography.* Jefferson, N.C.: McFarland, 1986.

Smith, Red. *Views of Sport.* New York: Alfred A. Knopf, 1954.

Snider, Duke, with Bill Gilbert. *The Duke of Flatbush.* New York: Zebra, 1988.

Spink, J.G. Taylor. *Baseball Guide and Record Book.* St. Louis: Sporting News, 1945–1960.

Sugar, Bert Randolph. *Baseball's 50 Greatest Games.* New York: Exeter Books, 1986.

————. *Rain Delays: An Anecdotal History of Baseball Under One Umbrella.* New York: St. Martin's Press, 1990.

Sullivan, Neil J. *The Dodgers Move West.* New York: Oxford University Press, 1987.

————. *The Minors: The Struggles and Traditions of Baseball's Poor Relations from 1876 to the Present.* New York: St. Martin's, 1990.

Thorn, John. *A Century of Baseball Lore.* New York: Galahad Books, 1976.

————. *The Relief Pitcher: Baseball's New Hero.* New York: E.P. Dutton, 1979.

————, and John B. Holway. *The Pitcher.* New York: Prentice-Hall Press, 1987.

————, and Pete Palmer, eds. *Total Baseball.* 2d ed. New York: Warner Books, 1991.

Tygiel, Jules. *Baseball's Great Experiment: Jackie Robinson and His Legacy.* New York: Oxford University Press, 1983.

Veeck, Bill, with Ed Linn. *Veeck—As in Wreck.* New York: G.P. Putnam's, 1962.

Voigt, David Quentin. *American Baseball: Vol. 3, From Postwar Expansion to the Electronic Age.* University Park., Pa. and London: Pennsylvania State University Press, 1983.

Walton, Ed. *The Rookies.* New York: Stein & Day, 1982.

Will, George. *Men at Work: The Craft of Baseball.* New York: Macmillan, 1990.

Williams, Ted, with John Underwood. *My Turn at Bat: The Story of My Life.* New York: Simon & Schuster, 1969.

Zoss, Joel, and John Bowman. *Diamonds in the Rough: The Untold History of Baseball.* New York: Macmillan, 1989.

Articles

"After Ten Years." *Newsweek* 48 (24 December 1956): 49.

Angell, Roger. "Baseball: The Perfect Game." *Holiday* 15 (May 1954): 80–94.

————. "Farewell My Giants." *Holiday* 23 (May 1958): 82–85, 159–65.

Axthelm, Pete. "The Outsider Who Was King." *Newsweek* 107 (13 January 1986): 62.

"The Babe Ruth Story." *Time* 52 (30 August 1948): 46–48.

"Babette Ruths." *Newsweek* 28 (29 July 1946): 68–69.

"Baseball: A Great Year." *Life* 31 (8 October 1951): 48.

"Baseball at the Bar." *Time* 53 (21 February 1949): 63.

"Baseball's Curve Balls: Are They Optical Illusions?" *Life* 11 (15 September 1941): 83–89.

Biemiller, Carl L. "World's Prettiest Ballplayers." *Holiday* 11 (June 1952): 50–51, 75–85.

"Big Guy." *Time* 52 (4 October 1948): 66–68.

"Big Leagues Head for Photo Finish." *Life* 25 (6 September 1948): 17–23.

"Big Man from Nicetown: Roy Campanella." *Time* 66 (8 August 1955): 50–55.

"Black Friday." *Time* 52 (26 July 1948): 32–33.

Borden, Paul. "Baseball's Best Years: The 1950s?" *Baseball Digest* 34 (January 1975): 80–87.

Branca, Ralph, as told to John M. Ross. "They'll Never Forget." *Sport* 12 (May 1952): 10–11, 72–74.

"Brooklyn Rolls, the U.S. Rocks: Dodgers Champions." *Life* 39 (17 October 1955): 38–43.

Brosnan, Jim. "I Broke Baseball's Rules." *Sport* 31 (May 1961): 38–39, 89–90.

Brown, Joe David. "The Onliest Way I Know: Willie Mays." *Sports Illustrated* 10 (13 April 1959): 130–38.

"Bucs Heist Series and the Lid Blows Off." *Life* 49 (24 October 1960): 32–35.

"Buttoned Lip." *Newsweek* 29 (21 April 1947): 87–88.

"California Goes Big League in a Big Way." *Life* 44 (28 April 1958): 129–36.

"Camera and Science Settle the Old Rhubard About Baseball's Curve Ball." *Life* 35 (27 July 1953): 104–07.

Campanella, Roy. "I'll Walk Again." *Saturday Evening Post* 231 (26 July 1958): 13–15, 79–80; (2 August 1958): 26, 52–53.

"Can Another Big League Pay Its Way?" *U.S. News and World Report* 47 (7 September 1959): 50–52.

"Casey Stengel Gives the Senate a Lecture on the Spirit of '76." *Sports Illustrated* 9 (21 July 1958): 24–25.

Chamberlain, John. "Ted Williams: Baseball's Foremost Problem Child." *Life* 21 (23 September 1946): 108.

Cobb, Ty. "They Don't Play Baseball Any More." *Life* 32 (17 March 1952: 136–53; (24 March 1952): 63–68, 73–80; Discussion in "Letters to the Editor" in *Life* 32 (7 April 1952): 12–17.

Cole, Robert. "Al Helfer and the Game of the Day." *Baseball Research Journal* 10 (1981): 93–100.

Coughlan, Robert. "Baseball: Nine Men, a Diamond and $10 Million." *Sports Illustrated* 4 (27 February 1956): 21–23, 55–58.

Cousins, Norman. "His Life Is the Greatest Game: Roy Campanella." *Saturday Review* 42 (21 November 1959): 46–47.

————. "We're on Dizzy's Side." *Saturday Review* 29 (3 August 1946): 16–17.

Cramer, Richard Ben. "What Do You Think of Ted Williams Now?" *Esquire* 105 (June 1986): 74–92.

Creamer, Robert. "Brooklyn's Happy Streak." *Sports Illustrated* 2 (2 May 1955): 34–38.

_____. "The Curtain Rises." *Sports Illustrated* 5 (15 October 1956): 18–29.

_____. "The Greatest Yankee Team Ever." *Sports Illustrated* 9 (25 August 1958): 14–17.

_____. "Not Rain, Nor Snow Nor Sleet." *Sports Illustrated* 4 (30 April 1956): 22–25.

_____. "Twilight of the Bums." *Sports Illustrated* 6 (1 April 1957): 8–13.

_____. "The Year, the Moment and Johnny Podres." *Sports Illustrated* 4 (2 January 1956): 19–22.

"Daffy Dodgertown." *Newsweek* 54 (12 October 1959): 77.

Daley, Arthur. "The Philosophy of Casey Stengel." *New York Times Magazine* (26 July 1953): 14.

_____. "Why We Worship the Babe Ruths." *New York Times Magazine* (16 April 1950): 19, 60–64.

Daley, Robert. "Sports Explains the Nations." *New York Times Magazine* (23 August 1959): 66–75.

"The Day the Yankees Fell into the Cellar." *Life* 46 (1 June 1959): 95–98.

DeOrsey, C.D. Leo. "Big Leagues Are Killing Baseball." *Look* 22 (15 April 1958): 17–20.

DiMaggio, Joe. "It's Great to Be Back." *Life* 27 (1 August 1949): 66–72.

"The Dodgers, Etc." *Sports Illustrated* 3 (19 September 1955): 9.

"Does a Curve Curve?" *Newsweek* 53 (6 April 1959): 100.

Donovan, Richard. "The Fabulous Satchel Paige." *Collier's* 131 (30 May 1953): 62–69; (6 June 1953): 20–24; (13 June 1953): 54–59.

Drury, Joseph F., Jr. "The Hell It Don't Curve." *American Mercury* 76 (May 1953): 100–06.

"Duke or Willie? A Vote for Snider." *Sports Illustrated* 2 (27 June 1955): 17, 48.

Einstein, Charles. "Covering the World Series." *Harper's* 209 (September 1954): 33–37.

"Everyone a Babe Ruth?" *Newsweek* 51 (5 May 1958): 81.

"Exit Casey." *Time* 49 (21 April 1947): 55–56.

"Fanatic Fan." *Newsweek* 35 (24 April 1950): 49–50.

"Fantastic Finish." *Time* 54 (10 October 1949): 42.

"First U.S. Sports Is Televised by NBC." *Life* 6 (5 June 1939): 70–71.

Fitzgerald, Ed. "The 'Barber' of the Giants." *Sport* 13 (September 1952): 35–37, 72–76.

Flaherty, Joe. "Love Song to Willie Mays." *Saturday Review* 55 (26 August 1972): 15–16.

Frank, Stanley. "Main Event: TV vs. SRO." *Nation's Business* 37 (March 1949): 46–48, 84.

_____. "Nobody Loves Baseball More Than Campy." *Saturday Evening Post* 226 (5 June 1954): 25, 114–16.

Frisch, Frank, as told to Tom Meany. "Let's Legalize the Spitball." *Saturday Evening Post* 230 (10 August 1957): 25, 89–90.

Furlong, William Barry. "Master of the Joyful Illusion." *Sports Illustrated* 13 (4 July 1960): 55–60.

_____. "That Big League Yearning." *New York Times Magazine* (16 June 1957): 14–16.

"Girls' Baseball." *Life* 18 (4 June 1945): 63–66.
"Going, Going, Gone?" *Time* 74 (14 September 1959): 56.
"The Golden Age of Sport." *Time* 89 (2 June 1967): 18–19.
Graham, Frank, Jr. "When Baseball Went to War: World War II." *Sports Illustrated* 26 (17 April 1967): 78–86.
"Great Rhubarb." *Newsweek* 49 (24 June 1957): 68.
Gross, Milton. "The Emancipation of Jackie Robinson." *Sport* 11 (October 1951): 12–15, 80–85.
Haines, William H., and Robert A. Esser. "Case History of Ruth Steinhagen." *American Journal of Psychiatry* 106 (April 1950): 737–43.
Hano, Arnold. "A Family Affair at the Polo Grounds." *Sports Illustrated* 7 (7 October 1957): 62–67.
"A Hard Out." *Time* 100 (6 November 1972): 90–91.
"He Came to Win." *Time* 64 (26 July 1954): 46–51.
"He Just Keeps Rolling." *Newsweek* 52 (20 October 1958): 102.
"Helmets In, Buttons Out." *Sports Illustrated* 4 (18 June 1956): 22.
"Historic Homer: Mickey Mantle." *Time* 61 (27 April 1953): 76.
"The Hit Kid." *Newsweek* 27 (22 April 1946): 85–86.
Holway, John. "Josh Gibson: Greatest Slugger of Them All." *Baseball Digest* 30 (March 1971): 62–69.
"Home Run Josh." *Newsweek* 26 (27 August 1945): 72–73.
"If You Can't Beat Him." *Time* 68 (24 December 1956): 43.
"It Comes Naturally: Hank Aaron." *Newsweek* 53 (15 June 1959): 94, 97.
"It's Great to Be a Yankee." *Ebony* 10 (September 1955): 50–54.
"It's Mad, It's Chicago." *Newsweek* 54 (14 September 1959): 77.
Jensen, Jackie, as told to Al Hirshberg. "My Ambition Is to Quit." *Saturday Evening Post* 231 (4 April 1959): 31, 142–44.
Johnson, Dick. "Interview with Jim Brosnan." *The SABR Review of Books* 5 (1990): 35–42.
"Joy in Brooklyn." *Time* 66 (17 October 1955): 64–65.
Kaese, Harold. "Baseball's Most Dramatic Moment—When Thomson's Homer Vanquished the Dodgers." *Baseball Digest* 29 (September 1970): 68–72.
Kahn, Roger. "Oklahoma's Mickey Mantle: Can the Young Yankee Beat the Babe?" *Newsweek* 47 (25 June 1956): 63–67.
Kelso, John. "They're Mercenary Today." *Baseball Digest* 9 (November 1950): 77–79.
Kuenster, John. "What They Thought When the Pressure Was the Greatest." *Baseball Digest* 20 (June 1961): 5–8.
Lardner, John. "Cloud Passes." *Newsweek* 44 (27 September 1954): 64.
————. "Mutiny in the Tropics." *Newsweek* 43 (29 March 1954): 79.
————. "Ruth." *Newsweek* 32 (30 August 1948): 69.
"Lighting the Candlestick." *Time* 75 (25 April 1960): 47.
Linn, Ed. "The Kid's Last Game." *Sport* 31 (February 1961): 52–63.
"Lopsided Stars." *Newsweek* 28 (22 July 1946): 81.
Maney, Richard. "Shades of Abner Doubleday!" *New York Times Magazine* (10 September 1950): 20, 54–56.
Mann, Arthur. "The Truth About the Jackie Robinson Case." *Saturday Evening Post* 222 (13 May 1950): 19–21, 118–25; (20 May 1950): 36, 149–54.
Maule, Tex. "The Best Football Game Ever Played." *Sports Illustrated* 10 (5 January 1959): 8–11, 60.
Meany, Tom. "Tom Meany's 1955 Baseball Preview." *Collier's* 135 (4 March 1955): 28–31.

_____. "Tom Meany's 1957 Baseball Preview." *Look* 21 (19 March 1957): 105–11.
_____. "Where Are Baseball's .300 Hitters?" *Collier's* 131 (7 February 1953): 16–19.
_____. "World Series Laughs." *Collier's* 136 (30 September 1955): 32–33.
"Money Pitcher." *Newsweek* 45 (20 June 1955): 86–88.
Murray, Arch. "Mickey Mantle: Gold-Plated Rookie." *Sport* 10 (June 1951): 70–71. 91–92.
Murray, James. "I Hate the Yankees." *Life* 28 (17 April 1950): 25–36.
"Musical Chairs." *Newsweek* 41 (23 March 1953): 66.
"The Negro Comes of Age in Baseball." *Ebony* 14 (14 June 1959): 41–46.
"Never Saw a Report Like It." *Life* 31 (22 October 1951): 133–38.
"A New Dynasty?" *Newsweek* 54 (19 October 1959): 66–67.
Nicholson, William G. "1945 — Baseball's Most Chaotic Year." *Baseball Digest* 30 (August 1971): 70–78.
_____. "Women's Pro Baseball Packed the Stands." *Womensports* 3 (April 1976): 22–24.
"Now Look, Son . . ." *Newsweek* 41 (6 April 1953): 77.
"Old Stars Never Die." *Newsweek* 56 (25 July 1960): 99–100.
"One More Rescue." *Newsweek* 35 (6 March 1950): 74.
"The Organization Men of Baseball." *Life* 45 (29 September 1958): 94–101.
"Out at Home." *Time* 64 (18 October 1954): 47.
Panaccio, Tim. "How It Was During the War Years." *Baseball Digest* 36 (January 1977): 68–70.
Parker, Dan. "Baseball's Bombshell: The Reserve Clause." *Sport* 6 (April 1949): 12–13, 80–83.
_____. "Why Happy Was Sent to the Showers." *Baseball Digest* 10 (February 1951): 19–20.
Paxton, Harry T. "Have the Bonus Boys Paid Off for Baseball?" *Saturday Evening Post* 224 (21 June 1952): 28–29, 100–103.
_____. "Is Baseball Comedy Dead?" *Saturday Evening Post* 232 (11 June 1960): 48–49, 85–90.
"Pete Gray, Symbol." *Newsweek* 26 (27 August 1945): 74–75.
"Photo Finish." *Time* 48 (7 October 1946): 61–62.
"Play Ball." *Time* 47 (29 April 1946): 67.
"Psychiatrist's Delight." *Newsweek* 36 (16 October 1950): 82.
Reddy, John. "Stan, the Incredibly Durable Man." *Reader's Digest* 82 (April 1963): 175–80.
Reese, Pee Wee, with Tom Meany. "Baseball Is a Different Game Now." *Collier's* 136 (19 August 1955): 38–43.
Rice, Robert. "Thoughts on Baseball." *New Yorker* 26 (27 May 1950): 32–46; (13 June 1950): 30–47.
Richman, Milton. "War, Weather Cloud 1951 Outlook." *Baseball Digest* 10 (February 1951): 24–28.
Ripp, Bart. "When Joe Bauman Hit 72 Home Runs." *Baseball Research Journal* 9 (1980): 26–29.
Robinson, Jackie. "Why I'm Quitting Baseball." *Look* 21 (22 January 1957): 90–92.
"Rookie of the Year." *Time* 50 (22 September 1947): 70–76.
"Satchel the Great." *Time* 52 (19 July 1948): 56–58.
"Say, Hey." *Newsweek* 43 (5 April 1954): 83–85.
Schacht, Al. "Who's Killing Minor League Baseball?" *American Mercury* 79 (September 1954): 15–18.

"Season in the Sun." *Time* 74 (24 August 1959): 50–55.

"A Series of Strange Events." *Sports Illustrated* 11 (12 October 1959): 15–21.

"Shape of Things: Controversial Reserve Clause." *Nation* 173 (11 August 1951): 103.

Shutt, Timothy Baker. "When Baseball Came Home from the War." *Sports History* 1 (July 1987): 26–33.

"Silly Honey." *Time* 53 (27 June 1949): 20.

"Silly Honey with a Gun." *Life* 26 (27 June 1949): 36.

Silverman, Al. "Major League Intellectual." *Saturday Evening Post* 234 (13 May 1961): 24, 97–99.

_____. "Take Me Out to the Binder." *Saturday Review* 38 (23 April 1955): 21, 51.

"Site of Distraction." *Sports Illustrated* 5 (15 October 1956): 30–31.

Smith, Red. "One for the Rhodes." *Sports Illustrated* 1 (11 October 1954): 57.

Snider, Edwin (Duke), with Roger Kahn. "I Play Baseball for Money—Not Fun." *Collier's* 137 (25 May 1956): 42–46.

Soule, Gardner. "How They're Using Mathematics to Win Ball Games." *Popular Science* 171 (July 1957): 64–66.

"Southpaw Truman." *Life* 20 (29 April 1946): 43–46.

Stanky, Eddie. "All Out for 'Beizbol.'" *Saturday Review* 34 (4 October 1952): 24–25.

"Sweet Smell of Failure." *Sports Illustrated* 10 (8 June 1959): 34–35.

"Swing, Swanged, Swunged." *Time* 55 (24 April 1950): 59–60.

Talese, Gay. "Gray-Flannel Suit Men at Bat." *New York Times Magazine* (30 March 1958): 15–21.

"Then . . . Farce in the Coliseum." *Sports Illustrated* 8 (28 April 1958): 21–22.

"They Said It." *Sports Illustrated* 9 (21 July 1958): 22.

"They Said It." *Sports Illustrated* 10 (22 June 1959): 26.

"They Want to Lynch Us: Yankees." *Newsweek* 53 (1 June 1959): 63–64.

"Third Major League: When, If Ever?" *Newsweek* 55 (16 May 1960): 80–81.

"Thousands Stand in Rain for Babe Ruth's Funeral." *Life* 25 (30 August 1948): 20–21.

"Time for the Elders." *Newsweek* 48 (15 October 1956): 75.

Tolbert, Frank X. "Dizzy Dean, He's Not So Dumb." *Saturday Evening Post* 224 (14 July 1951): 25, 102–04.

"The Totem Pole." *Sports Illustrated* 12 (8 February 1960): 29.

"Trial for Life." *Newsweek* 27 (27 May 1946): 82–83.

"The Truth About Beizbol." *Time* 60 (29 September 1952): 77.

Tygiel, Jules. "The Court-Martial of Jackie Robinson." *American Heritage* 35 (August-September 1984): 34–39.

Updike, John. "Hub Fans Bid Kid Adieu." *New Yorker* 36 (22 October 1960): 109–31.

"The U.S. Winced." *Sports Illustrated* 6 (20 May 1957): 26–27.

Vecsey, George. "Terry and the Pirates." *New York Times Magazine* (29 September 1985): 57, 66–68.

"Video Sports: To Be or Not to Be," *Newsweek* 32 (13 December 1948): 80.

"Westward the A's." *Time* 64 (22 November 1954): 64–66.

"Where Are the Bonus Babies?" *Life* 31 (16 July 1951): 95–100.

Williams, Roger. "Goodby, Casey, Goodby." *Sports Illustrated* 13 (31 October 1960): 63–65.

"Willie Mays: The Hottest Thing Since Babe Ruth." *Newsweek* 44 (19 July 1954): 74–76.

"Willie the Whoop." *Newsweek* 38 (10 September 1951): 63–64.

"A Winner in Pittsburgh." *Newsweek* 55 (13 June 1960): 59.

"Women Players in Organized Baseball." *Baseball Research Journal* 12 (1983): 157–61.

"World War II's Impact on Mankind." *U.S. News and World Report* 87 (10 September 1979): 65–71.

Young, A.S. "Doc." "The Jackie Robinson Era." *Ebony* 11 (November 1955): 152–56.

Young, Dick. "The Outlawed Spitball Was My Money Pitch." *Sports Illustrated* 3 (4 July 1955): 18–21, 60–61.

Zimmerman, Gereon. "Veeck . . . A New Bill for the White Sox." *Look* 23 (4 August 1959): 92–96.

Newspapers

Atlanta Constitution
Boston Globe
Chicago Daily Tribune
Greensboro Daily News
Los Angeles Times
Newsday

New York Herald Tribune
New York Times
San Francisco Chronicle
Sporting News
Washington Post
Winston-Salem Journal

Index